WESTMAR COLLEGE LIBRARY

W9-BRK-865

JOACHIM JEREMIAS

NEW TESTAMENT THEOLOGY

Advisory Editors

ALAN RICHARDSON Dean of York

C. F. D. MOULE Lady Margaret's Professor of Divinity in the
University of Cambridge

C. F. EVANS Professor of New Testament Studies, King's College, London

FLOYD V. FILSON formerly Professor of New Testament Literature and History
at the McCormick Theological Seminary, Chicago

JOACHIM JEREMIAS

NEW TESTAMENT THEOLOGY

The Proclamation of Jesus

CHARLES SCRIBNER'S SONS
NEW YORK

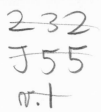

2 3 2
J 5 5
v. 1

BT
202
·J 3913

English language edition translated by John Bowden

Copyright © 1971 Joachim Jeremias

German language edition published 1971 by Gütersloher Verlagshaus Gerd Mohn under the title Neutestamentliche Theologie I. Teil: Die Verkündigung Jesu.

All rights reserved. No part of this book may be reproduced in any form without the permission of Charles Scribner's Sons.

B-10.72 (H)

Printed in the United States of America
Library of Congress Catalog Card Number 70-143936
SBN684-12363-0

86884

CONTENTS

ABBREVIATIONS
Journals and Series

AGSU	Arbeiten zur Geschichte des Spätjudentums und Urchristentums
AKG	Arbeiten zur Kirchengeschichte
ASNU	Acta Seminarii Neotestamentici Upsaliensis
ASTI	*Annual of the Swedish Theological Institute*
ATANT	Abhandlungen zur Theologie des Alten und Neuen Testaments
BEvTh	Beiträge zur evangelischen Theologie
BFCT	Beiträge zur Förderung christlicher Theologie
BHTh	Beiträge zur historischen Theologie
BJRL	*Bulletin of the John Rylands Library*
BWANT	Beihefte zur Wissenschaft vom Alten und Neuen Testament
BZ	*Biblische Zeitschrift*
BZAW	Beihefte zur Zeitschrift für die alttestamentliche Wissenschaft
BZNW	Beiträge zur Zeitschrift für die neutestamentliche Wissenschaft
CBQ	*Catholic Biblical Quarterly*
EvTh	*Evangelische Theologie*
ExpT	*Expository Times*
FRLANT	Forschungen zur Religion und Literatur des Alten und Neuen Testaments
GCS	Die griechischen christlichen Schriftsteller
HNT	Handbuch zum Neuen Testament
IES	*Indian Ecclesiastical Studies*
JBL	*Journal of Biblical Literature*
JEH	*Journal of Ecclesiastical History*
JTS	*Journal of Theological Studies*

KlT	Kleine Texte für theologische und philosophische Vorlesungen
LThK	*Lexikon für Theologie und Kirche*
MeyerK	Kritisch-Exegetischer Kommentar über das Neue Testament, begründet von Heinrich August Wilhelm Meyer
NovTest	*Novum Testamentum*
NovTestSuppl	Supplements to *Novum Testamentum*
NTA	Neutestamentliche Abhandlungen
NTD	Das Neue Testament Deutsch
NTS	*New Testament Studies*
RB	*Revue Biblique*
RGG	*Die Religion in Geschichte und Gegenwart*
RHPR	*Revue d'Histoire et de Philosophie religieuses*
SBT	Studies in Biblical Theology
StTh	*Studia Theologica*
SUNT	Studien zur Umwelt des Neuen Testaments
TDNT	*Theological Dictionary of the New Testament* (English translation of *TWNT*)
ThBl	*Theologische Blätter*
ThStKr	Theologische Studien und Kritiken
TLZ	*Theologische Literaturzeitung*
TQS	*Theologische Quartalschrift*
TTZ	*Trierer Theologische Zeitschrift*
TU	Texte und Untersuchungen
TWNT	Kittel, *Theologisches Wörterbuch zum Neuen Testament*
WMANT	Wissenschaftliche Monographien zum Alten und Neuen Testament
WUNT	Wissenschaftliche Untersuchungen zum Neuen Testament
ZDPV	*Zeitschrift des deutschen Palästina-Vereins*
ZNW	*Zeitschrift für die neutestamentliche Wissenschaft*
ZsystT	*Zeitschrift für systematische Theologie*
ZThK	*Zeitschrift für Theologie und Kirche*

ABBREVIATIONS
Books cited frequently in the text

This sign ‡ refers to a work listed at the beginning of a particular section

BAUER–ARNDT–GINGRICH
W. F. Arndt and F. W. Gingrich, *A Greek-English Lexicon of the New Testament and Other Early Christian Literature*, a translation of Walter Bauer's *Wörterbuch*, Chicago and Cambridge 1957.

BILLERBECK
H. L. Strack – P. Billerbeck, *Kommentar zum Neuen Testament aus Talmud und Midrasch*, München, I 1922, II 1924, III 1926, IV 1928, V (edited by J. Jeremias, compiled by K. Adolph) 1956, VI (edited by J. Jeremias in collaboration with K. Adolph) 1961 (=^{3}I – IV 1961, ^{2}V/VI 1963).

BULTMANN, *Synoptic Tradition*
R. Bultmann, *The History of the Synoptic Tradition*, Oxford ^{2}1968.

Theology
R. Bultmann, *Theology of the New Testament*, New York and London 1952, 1955 (two vols.).

BLASS–DEBRUNNER–FUNK
F. W. Blass and A. Debrunner, *A Greek Grammar of the New Testament and Other Early Christian Literature*, translated by R. W. Funk, Chicago and Cambridge 1961.

DALMAN, *Grammatik*[2]
G. Dalman, *Grammatik des jüdisch-palästinischen Aramäisch*, Leipzig 1894, ^{2}1905=Darmstadt 1960.

Jesus-Jeschua
G. Dalman, *Jesus-Jeschua*, Leipzig 1922, Supplement 1929= Darmstadt 1967: ET *Jesus-Jeshua*, London 1929 (of the German first edition, with additional notes).

Words of Jesus
G. Dalman, *Die Worte Jesu* I, Leipzig 1898, ²1930=Darmstadt 1960; ET *The Words of Jesus*, Edinburgh 1902 (the revisions made by the author for the ET make it almost a second edition, but it lacks the appendices contained on pp. 283–402 of the second German edition).

DODD, *Parables*
C. H. Dodd, *The Parables of the Kingdom*, London 1935 (reprinted many times).

DIBELIUS, *Tradition*
M. Dibelius, *From Tradition to Gospel*, London 1934 (ET of *Die Formgeschichte des Evangeliums*, Tübingen 1919, ²1933=⁵1966).

FLUSSER, *Jesus*
D. Flusser, *Jesus in Selbstzeugnissen und Bilddokumenten*, Rowohlts Monographien 140, Reinbeck bei Hamburg 1968.

HENNECKE–SCHNEEMELCHER–WILSON
E. Hennecke – W. Schneemelcher – R. McL. Wilson, *New Testament Apocrypha* I (London and Philadelphia 1963); II (London and Philadelphia 1966).

G. JEREMIAS, *Lehrer der Gerechtigkeit*
G. Jeremias, *Der Lehrer der Gerechtigkeit*, SUNT 2, Göttingen 1963.

JEREMIAS, *Abba*
J. Jeremias, *Abba. Studien zur neutestamentlichen Theologie und Zeitgeschichte*, Göttingen 1966.

Eucharistic Words²
J. Jeremias, *The Eucharistic Words of Jesus*, Oxford 1955, second completely revised edition London and New York 1966.

Jerusalem
J. Jeremias, *Jerusalem in the Time of Jesus*, London and Philadelphia 1969 (ET of the third German edition).

Parables²
J. Jeremias, *The Parables of Jesus*, London and New York 1954, ²1963.

MANSON, *Teaching*[2]
> T. W. Manson, *The Teaching of Jesus*, Cambridge 1931, [2]1935
> (reprinted many times).

> *Sayings*[2]
> T. W. Manson, *The Sayings of Jesus*, London 1937, [2]1949
> (reprinted many times).

PERRIN, *Rediscovering*
> N. Perrin, *Rediscovering the Teaching of Jesus*, London and New
> York 1967.

THE PROCLAMATION OF JESUS

(Full details of the titles shown in abbreviated form are to be found on pp. xiii–xv.)
Dalman, *Words of Jesus*; id., *Jesus-Jeshua*; A. Schlatter, *Die Geschichte des Christus*,
Stuttgart 1909, ²1923; A. Schweitzer, *The Quest of the Historical Jesus*, London 1910,
³1954; H. L. Strack, *Jesus, die Häretiker und die Christen nach den ältesten jüdischen
Angaben*, Schriften des Institutum Judaicum 37, Leipzig 1910; J. Klausner, *Jesus of
Nazareth*, London 1929; H. Windisch, 'Das Problem der Geschichtlichkeit Jesu. Die
ausserchristlichen Zeugnisse', *ThR* 1, 1929, 266–88; Manson, *Teaching*²; R. Meyer,
Der Prophet aus Galiläa, Leipzig 1940; M. Black, *An Aramaic Approach to the Gospels
and Acts*, Oxford 1946, ³1967; E. Percy, *Die Botschaft Jesu*, Lund 1953; D. Daube,
The New Testament and Rabbinic Judaism, London 1956; Bultmann, *Synoptic Tradition*;
id., *Theology*; Jeremias, *Parables*²; id., *Eucharistic Words*²; id., *Unknown Sayings of
Jesus*, London 1957, ²1964; W. Grundmann, *Die Geschichte Jesu Christi*, Berlin
1957=³1960; H. Conzelmann, 'Jesus Christus', *RGG*³ III, 1959, cols 619–53;
H. Ristow – K. Matthiae (eds.), *Der historische Jesus und der kerygmatische Christus*,
Berlin 1960; E. Stauffer, *Jesus and his Story*, London 1960; A. Vögtle, 'Jesus
Christus', *LThK* V, 1960, cols. 922–32; G. Gloege, *The Day of his Coming*, London
1962; M. Dibelius, *Jesus*, with additional material by W. G. Kümmel, London
1963; G. Jeremias, *Lehrer der Gerechtigkeit*; C. Burchard, 'Jesus', *Der kleine Pauly.
Lexikon der Antike* II, Stuttgart 1967, cols. 1344–54; Perrin, *Rediscovering*; R.
Slenczka, *Geschichtlichkeit und Personsein Jesu Christi*, Göttingen 1967; O. Betz,
What do we know about Jesus?, London 1968; Flusser, *Jesus*; H. Conzelmann, *An
Outline of the Theology of the New Testament*, London 1969.

I

HOW RELIABLE IS THE TRADITION OF
THE SAYINGS OF JESUS?

THIS FIRST chapter is concerned with the *problem of the historical Jesus*.[1] I shall concentrate on what for present purposes is the decisive question, that is, whether our sources are sufficient to enable us to bring out the basic ideas of the preaching of Jesus with some degree of probability, or whether this hope is over-optimistic from the start.

There are two considerable difficulties. First, whereas we possess documents originally written by Paul, not a single line has come down to us from Jesus' own hand. It was more than thirty years after his death before anyone began to write down what he said in an ordered sequence, and by that time his sayings had long been translated into Greek. It was inevitable that during this long period of oral transmission alterations took place in the tradition. A comparison of the two versions, say, of the Lord's Prayer or the Beatitudes in Matthew and Luke give some indication of this process, though at the same time they are also a warning that we should not exaggerate it. A second development makes it even more urgent for us to discover how reliably the message of Jesus has been handed down: not only have we to reckon with the fact that sayings of Jesus were altered in the

---

[1] The name was pronounced *Yēšūaʿ* (with an ʿ*ayin*) in Judaea, as we know through ossuary inscriptions from the neighbourhood of Jerusalem (instances in W. Foerster, Ἰησοῦς, *TDNT* III, 1965, 284–93: 285; a graffito which I found in the south wall of the southern pool at Bethesda, now covered in, also read [*y*]*šwʿ*, see my: *The Rediscovery of Bethesda*, New Testament Archaeology Monograph No I, Louisville, Ky., 1966, 31 n.107; illus. p. 32). The form *Yēšū* (without an ʿ*ayin*), which is that used predominantly in the Talmud (instances in H. L. Strack, *Jesus, die Häretiker und die Christen nach den ältesten jüdischen Angaben*, Leipzig 1910, *passim*) is hardly a deliberate truncation made for anti-Christian motives; rather, it is 'almost certainly' (Flusser, *Jesus*, 13) the Galilean pronunciation of the name; the swallowing of the ʿ*ayin* was typical of the Galilean dialect (Billerbeck I 156f.).

period before they were written down, but in addition we have to consider the possibility that new sayings came into being. The seven letters of Christ to the seven churches in Asia Minor (Rev. 2–3) and other sayings of the exalted Lord handed down in the first person (e.g. Rev. 1.17–20; 16.15; 22.12ff.) allow the conclusion that early Christian prophets addressed congregations in words of encouragement, admonition, censure and promise, using the name of Christ in the first person. Prophetic sayings of this kind found their way into the tradition about Jesus and became fused with the words that he had spoken during his lifetime. The discourses of Jesus in the Gospel of John provide an example of this development; to a considerable degree they are homilies on sayings of Jesus composed in the first person.

In view of these uncertainties, the course that has long – and quite rightly – been adopted towards answering the question of authenticity is the comparative method. Its chief instrument is the 'criterion of dissimilarity';[1] it finds the earliest tradition where a saying or a theme cannot be derived either from Judaism or from the early church. One example of the difference between Jesus and the Judaism of his time would be his message of God's love for sinners; this was so offensive to the majority of his contemporaries that it cannot be derived from the thinking current in his environment. On the other hand, sayings of Jesus cannot be said to come from the early church, say, where they express an expectation which was not fulfilled;[2] in such instances it may be taken as proven that the sayings come from the period before Easter. This criterion may be said to have gained general acceptance, and we shall keep it in mind. But it has one weakness: its comparison of the sayings of Jesus with the religious ideas of Palestinian Judaism and of the early church is one-sidedly based on the principle of originality; as a result, it only covers *some* of the sayings of Jesus that are to be taken as early. All the cases in which Jesus takes up already available material, whether apocalyptic ideas or Jewish proverbs or language current in his environment, slip through the net, as do the cases in which the early church handed down words of Jesus unaltered, as e.g. *'Abbā* as a mode of addressing God. Indeed, it has to be said that the way in which the 'criterion of dissimilarity' is often used today as a password is a serious source of error. It foreshortens and distorts the historical situation, because it overlooks the continuity between Jesus and Judaism.

---

[1] Perrin, *Rediscovering*, 39–43.   [2] See below, pp. 139f.

It is therefore all the more important that we have a further aid in investigating the pre-Easter tradition in addition to the comparative method: an examination of *language and style*. The three sections of Chapter I will be devoted to a discussion of this largely neglected expedient.

§ 1 · THE ARAMAIC BASIS OF THE *LOGIA* OF JESUS IN THE SYNOPTIC GOSPELS

(The literature mentioned at the head of each section is referred to in the notes with this sign ‡.)
Dalman, *Grammatik*[2]; id., *Words of Jesus*; J. Wellhausen, *Einleitung in die drei ersten Evangelien*, Berlin 1905, [2]1911, 7–32; Dalman, *Jesus-Jeshua*; C. F. Burney, *The Poetry of Our Lord*, Oxford 1925; P. Joüon, *L'Évangile de Notre-Seigneur Jésus-Christ*, Verbum Salutis 5, Paris 1930; C. C. Torrey, *The Four Gospels*, London 1933; M. Black, *An Aramaic Approach to the Gospels and Acts*, Oxford 1946, [3]1967.

The sayings of Jesus handed down by the synoptic gospels are clad in the garb of a *koine* Greek with a number of Semitic characteristics. Although in a Hellenistic setting this Semitic colouring must have been felt to be unattractive and in need of improvement, by and large the tradition has been very restrained in giving the sayings of Jesus a more pronounced Greek style. This reserve, which stems from reverence towards the *Kyrios*, comes out particularly strongly in the case of Luke, in whose writing the more Semitic-type *logia* stand out strikingly from the smooth Greek of the framework in which they are set.

The idiom underlying the sayings of Jesus is to be defined as part of the western branch of the Aramaic family of languages.[1] Since G. Dalman produced the pioneering demonstration of this in 1898[2] and with his Grammar of Palestinian Jewish Aramaic[3] and his Lexicon[4] created a basis for study which has yet to be surpassed, J.

[1] At the time of Jesus, western Aramaic consisted essentially of the Aramaic dialects spoken and written in Palestine.

[2] *Die Worte Jesu mit Berücksichtigung des nachkanonischen jüdischen Schrifttums und der aramäischen Sprache erörtert* I, Leipzig 1898, [2]1930=Darmstadt 1960 (ET of the first edition: *The Words of Jesus*, Edinburgh 1902).

[3] *Grammatik des jüdisch-palästinischen Aramäisch*, Leipzig 1894, [2]1905=Darmstadt 1960.

[4] *Aramäisch-neuhebräisches Handwörterbuch zu Targum, Talmud und Midrasch*, Leipzig 1897–1901, [3]Göttingen 1938=Hildesheim 1967.

Wellhausen,[1] P. Joüon[2] and M. Black[3] in particular have, in their syntactical observations, produced such rich confirmatory material that there can no longer be any doubt about the rightness of this recognition.

More precisely, it should be said that the mother-tongue of Jesus was *a Galilean version of western Aramaic*. We find the nearest linguistic analogies to the sayings of Jesus in the popular Aramaic passages of the Palestinian Talmud and Midrashim which have their home in Galilee.[4] That these passages were only given fixed written form in the period from the fourth to the sixth centuries AD does not diminish their value. It is highly probable that even in the time of Jesus, the Aramaic used in everyday conversation in Galilee differed from that of southern Palestine (Judaic Aramaic) in pronunciation,[5] different forms and uses of particular words[6] and lapses of grammar.[7] Another reason for this difference was that it was not influenced to such a degree by the language of the Bible and of the Rabbinic schools.[8] Matthew presupposes that a Galilean could be recognized in Jerusalem by his dialect (26.73).

The original Aramaic has been preserved in the *logia* of Jesus in the following instances: the word of command ταλιθὰ κοῦμ (Mark 5.41);[9]

---

[1] ‡Wellhausen.

[2] In addition to a series of articles see especially the translation of the gospels with commentary in ‡Joüon.

[3] ‡Black.

[4] Critical editions of texts were made by G. Dalman, *Aramäische Dialektproben*, Leipzig 1896, [2]1927=Darmstadt 1960, as an appendix to the reprint of *Grammatik*[2]; H. Odeberg, *The Aramaic Portions of Bereshit Rabba with Grammar of Galilaean Aramaic*, Lunds Universitets Årsskrift N. F. Avd. 1, 36, 4, Lund-Leipzig 1939.

[5] Namely, but not only, by undifferentiated pronunciation of gutturals (b. Er. 53b Bar.); cf. Dalman, *Grammatik*[2], 52–106 and *passim*. There is an example at p. 1, n.1.

[6] See the lists in Dalman, *Grammatik*[2], 44–51.

[7] See note 9.

[8] Dalman, *Worte Jesu*[2], 371.

[9] As a girl is being addressed, one would expect the feminine form of the imperative κοῦμι ending in -*i* (thus A D Θ ς). The absence of the ending is usually explained as being the result of Syriac influence. But that is impossible, because there is no evidence of such influence of Syriac on the feminine form of the imperative in Galilean Aramaic; rather, the feminine form of the imperative in -*ī* or -*īn* was a fixed usage in Galilean Aramaic. In fact, the form κοῦμ in Mark 5.41 is a case of the use of the masculine form with a feminine meaning; the popular preference for the masculine as *genus potius* was idiomatic in Galilean usage; cf. especially for the case of the feminine singular imperative: *sīb*, Midr. Lam. on 1.16 instead of the

Matt. 5.17b in rabbinic tradition;[1] and the cry from the cross ἠλὶ ἠλὶ λεμὰ σαβαχθάνι (Matt. 27.46 par. Mark 15.34).[2] There are also a number of individual words used by Jesus.[3] No complete list of this vocabulary has yet been made, so it has been set out below (Aramaic place-names,[4] personal names,[5] designations of descent[6] or of groups[7] which occur in the *logia* of Jesus have been disregarded, as no clear conclusions about Jesus' own language can be drawn from them). The following Aramaic words occur on the lips of Jesus:

'abbā[8]	'anā[9]	'atā[10]
bar[11]	be'ēl[12]	de[13]
'ellā[14]	gēhinnām[15]	yesap[16]
kēpā[17]	lā[18]	lemā[19]

---

sībī that might be expected (Targ. II Kings 4.36 *sabī*); there are two further instances in Dalman, *Grammatik²*, 275 §62.2.

[1] b. Shab. 116b (see below, p. 83).

[2] Matthew (ἠλὶ ἠλὶ λεμὰ σαβαχθάνι) apparently offers a composite text: the address is Hebrew and the question Aramaic; in Mark (ἐλωΐ ἐλωΐ λαμὰ σαβαχθάνι), on the other hand, the whole sentence is Aramaic. The misunderstanding about Elijah (Mark 15.35 par. Matt. 27.47), which presupposes an *'ēlī*, suggests that Matthew's is the earlier tradition. However, it is misleading to describe Matthew as a composite text, because the Hebrew *'ēl* had been taken over into Aramaic, as is shown by the text of the Targum on Ps. 22.1: *'ēlī 'ēlī metūl mā šebaqtanī* (ed. *princeps*, Venice 1517). Thus the cry from the cross in Matt. 27.46 has been transmitted *in toto* in Aramaic.

[3] For ἐφφαθά (Mark 7.34) see p. 7, n.4.

[4] Βηθσαϊδά Matt. 11.21 par. Luke 10.13; Καφαρναούμ Matt. 11.23 par. Luke 10.15.

[5] Ζακχαῖος Luke 19.5; Μάρθα 10.41.

[6] Γαλιλαῖος Luke 13.2; Ἰουδαῖος John 4.22; 18.36; Σαμαρίτης Matt. 10.5.

[7] Σαδδουκαῖος Matt. 16.6, 11f.; Φαρισαῖος Mark 8.15 etc.

[8] Mark 14.36; see below pp. 61ff.

[9] b. Shab. 116b.

[10] b. Shab. 116b.

[11] Matt. 16.17; the plural *benē* Mark 3.17 (see p. 6, n.8).

[12] Matt. 10.25; 12.27 par. Luke 11.19.

[13] b. Shab. 116b.

[14] b. Shab. 116b. For a variant reading see p. 83, n.7.

[15] Mark 9.43, 45, 47; Matt. 5.22, 29f.; 10.28; 18.9; 23.15, 33; Luke 12.5. That γέεννα is Aramaic follows from the ending -a, which points to the Aramaic pronunciation *gēhinnām*; the suppression of the ending -m in Greek has a parallel in *Maryām*/Μαρία (cf. Dalman, *Grammatik²*, 183f.).

[16] b. Shab. 116b.

[17] John 1.43.

[18] b. Shab. 116b.

[19] Matt. 27.46.

$m^a\dot{h}ar^1$ $m\bar{a}m\bar{o}n\bar{a}^2$ $'\bar{o}r\bar{a}y^et\bar{a}^3$
$pash\bar{a}^4$ $p^e\dot{h}at^5$ $q\bar{a}m^6$
$rabb\bar{\imath}^7$ $r^egi\check{s}^8$ $r\bar{e}q\bar{a}^9$
$\check{s}abb^et\bar{a}^{10}$ $s\bar{a}t\bar{a}^{11}$ $s\bar{a}t\bar{a}n\bar{a}^{12}$
$\check{s}^ebaq^{13}$ $tal\bar{\imath}t\bar{a}^{14}$

In addition to the sentences and words preserved in the original Aramaic, there are many passages in which an underlying Aramaic wording can be disclosed. This includes expressions which are idiomatic in Aramaic but alien to both Hebrew and Greek (Aramaisms),[15]

[1] In the fourth petition of the Lord's Prayer, according to Jerome, *Commentary on Matthew*, on Matt. 6.11 (see below, p. 199).

[2] Matt. 6.24; Luke 16.9, 11, 13. μαμωνᾶς is a Greek form of the Aramaic emphatic state ending in -*a*.

[3] b. Shab. 116b.

[4] Mark 14.14 par.; Matt. 26.2; Luke 22.8, 15. πάσχα is a transcription of the Aramaic *pashā*; the Hebrew *pesaḥ*, on the other hand, is without exception transcribed as φάσεκ/φάσεχ/φέσε/φέσα (Jeremias, *Eucharistic Words*[2], p. 15, n.1).

[5] b. Shab. 116b.

[6] Mark 5.41.

[7] Matt. 23.7f., cf. Dalman, *Grammatik*[2], 147 n.4; id., *Words of Jesus*, 337; J. Jeremias, *The Prayers of Jesus*, SBT II 6, 42.

[8] Mark 3.17. Βοανηργές is probably a rendering of *b^enē r^egiš*, 'sons of uproar', with *'aleph prostheticum*, obscuration of the *š^ewā* mobile in the first syllable and a metathesis of liquids to avoid the hiatus *ē-a*.

[9] Matt. 5.22; cf. J. Jeremias, ῥακά, *TDNT* VI, 1968, 973–76.

[10] Mark 3.4; Matt. 12.5, 11f. The remarkable use of the plural τὰ σάββατα in these passages to denote a single sabbath has nothing to do with the Greek plural in the case of names of festivals (thus Blass-Debrunner §141.3), but can be explained from the Aramaic: the emphatic state sing. *šabb^eta* was wrongly taken to be a plural form.

[11] Matt. 13.33 par. Luke 13.21 (cf. Dalman, *Grammatik*[2], 201 n.1).

[12] Mark 3.23, 26; 8.33; Matt. 12.26; 16.23; Luke 10.18; 11.18; 13.16; 22.31. For the ending -âs see note 2 above.

[13] Mark 15.34 par. Matt. 27.46.

[14] Mark 5.41.

[15] Instances: the use, alien to both Greek and Hebrew, of the word ὀφείλημα which denotes a money debt for 'guilt', 'sin', in the Lord's Prayer (Matt. 6.12) indicates an underlying Aramaic *ḥōbā*, which is very often used in a religious sense (e.g. j. Hag. 77d 40ff., *ed. princeps*, Venice 1523; frequently in the Targum). The use of εἰς/ἐν as a multiplicative form before cardinal numbers (Mark 4.8 εἰς τριάκοντα καὶ ἐν ἑξήκοντα καὶ ἐν ἑκατόν, cf. v.20) can be explained by the corresponding function of the Aramaic *ḥad* (cf. Dan. 3.19). On the other hand, the assertion, constantly repeated since E. Nestle, 'Zum neutestamentlichen Griechisch', *ZNW* 7, 1906, 279f.; cf. 8, 1907, 241; 9, 1908, 253, that the construction of ὁμολογεῖν with ἐν (*b^e*) is Aramaic and alien to Hebrew, is false; cf. the Aramaic *'ōdī b^e*, b. Shab. 39b; Hebrew *hōdā b^e*, b.B.M. 3a.

translation mistakes which show up when recourse is had to Aramaic,[1] and finally variants of tradition which arose in an Aramaic-speaking milieu.[2]

An investigation in a different direction, to examine the *Hebrew* words handed down on the lips of Jesus, produces minimal results. We cannot include ἀμήν and ἠλί, as both words had been taken over into Aramaic;[3] there is dispute as to whether ἐφφαθά (Mark 7.34) is Aramaic or Hebrew;[4] κορβᾶν (Mark 7.11, as opposed to κορβανᾶς in Matt. 27.6) is indeed Hebrew, but not everyday language: it is a formula of refusal.[5] As far as I can see, that leaves $z^eb\bar{u}l$, 'dwelling', as the only Hebrew word on the lips of Jesus. Even here, however, we do not have simple, everyday language, but a word-play which comes from the context of theological discussion. Jesus interprets βεελζεβούλ as οἰκοδεσπότης, 'master of the house' (Matt. 10.25), by splitting the word into the Aramaic $b^e{}^c\bar{e}l$ and the Hebrew $z^eb\bar{u}l$ ('house').

This evidence shows yet again how untenable is the theory that Hebrew was used as an everyday language in Palestine, and especially in Judaea, in the time of Jesus.[6] That is not to deny that Jesus

[1] E.g. Luke 7.45, where εἰσῆλθον '(since) *I* entered the house' makes no sense, and εἰσῆλθεν '(since) *she* entered the house' might be expected. There is obviously a translation error here; in Galilaean Aramaic *'atayit* has both meanings, 'I came' and 'she came' (cf. Dalman, *Grammatik*[2], 338, 342f., 406). On μωρανθῇ as a translation error in Matt. 5.13 par. Luke 14.34 see p. 28 below.

[2] E.g. Mark 8.38 par. Luke 9.26 ὃς γὰρ ἐὰν ἐπαισχυνθῇ με ($=h^apar$, 'be ashamed of'), contrast Matt. 10.33 par. Luke 12.9 ὅστις δ' ἂν ἀρνήσηταί με ($=k^epar=$'deny'). The bifurcation of the tradition ('be ashamed'/'deny') must have taken place during the course of oral tradition in an Aramaic-speaking milieu. Similarly, Matt. 5.13b and Luke 14.34f. indicate how, by translating back into Aramaic, we can still see (see below, p. 29) a different paronomasia (Matthew *mišt^edē/'itt^edāšā*; Luke *tāpēl/yittabbēl/zabbālā*); again, the bifurcation must have taken place in an Aramaic milieu.

[3] For ἀμήν see below, pp. 35f.; for ἠλί, see above, p. 5, n.2.

[4] The thesis of I. Rabinowitz, supported by much learning, that ἐφφαθά is Hebrew, because Palestinian Aramaic would not have assimilated the *t* to *p* ('"Be opened"='Εφφαθά (Mk. 7, 34): Did Jesus Speak Hebrew?', *ZNW* 53, 1962, 229–38), is expressly rejected by M. Black. He calls attention to examples of this assimilation in the Targum, e.g. Cod. Neofiti I Gen. 3.7 marg. (letter of 28.12.1967). The judgment of J. A. Emerton is rather more restrained, 'MARANATHA and EPHPHATHA', *JTS* 18, 1967, 427–31. He concedes that ἐφφαθά could be Hebrew, but leaves open the possibility that Galilean Aramaic made the assimilation in everyday speech.

[5] Billerbeck I 711–17; see below, p. 210.

[6] Against H. Birkeland, *The Language of Jesus* (Avhandlinger utgitt av Det

knew Hebrew. The report in Luke 4.16–19 that he read the Hebrew lection from the prophets (*haptārā*) in the synagogue service presupposes this. But there are only quite isolated indications that an original Hebrew text underlay the version of the sayings of Jesus that we now possess, and they are mostly to be found in particularly solemn discourse. For example, in view of a number of Hebraisms,[1] we must reckon with the possibility that Jesus spoke the words of institution in the sacred language.[2]

The discovery that the sayings of Jesus are to be set against an Aramaic background[3] is of great significance for the question of the reliability of the gospel tradition. This linguistic evidence takes us back into the realm of Aramaic oral tradition. It also confronts us with the task of comparing not only the content of the sayings of Jesus (as has so often been done), but also their language and style with the characteristics of Semitic language current in contemporary Judaism.

§ 2 · WAYS OF SPEAKING PREFERRED BY JESUS

Dalman, *Words of Jesus*; C. F. Burney, *The Poetry of Our Lord*, Oxford 1925; M. Black, *An Aramaic Approach to the Gospels and Acts*, Oxford 1946, ³1967; E. Pax, 'Beobachtungen zum biblischen Sprachtabu', *Studii Biblici Franciscani* 1961/2, Jerusalem 1962, 66–112.

If we compare the language and style of the sayings of Jesus handed down in the first three gospels with the manner of speaking characteristic of his environment, it is striking how a number of expressions occur unusually often on Jesus' lips.

Norske Videnskaps-Akademi i Oslo, Hist. -Filos. Klasse 1954, 1), Oslo 1954; J. M. Grintz, 'Hebrew as Spoken and Written Language in the Last Days of the Second Temple', *JBL* 79, 1960, 32–47. That there is Hebrew literature at Qumran does not mean more than that Hebrew was also a living language for literature and law as well as cult and theology.

[1] The term 'Hebraism' denotes specifically Hebrew constructions, phrases and expressions which underlay our Greek texts (whereas in the preceding sections we spoke of Hebrew words preserved as foreign words in the Greek text).

[2] ‡Black, 238f. ('The Original Language of the Last Supper'); Jeremias, *Eucharistic Words*², 196–98.

[3] Most recently J. A. Emerton (see p. 7, n. 4), 431: 'Aramaic was the language normally used by him'.

(i) The 'divine passive'

Even in the pre-Christian period[1] there was a prohibition against uttering the tetragrammaton,[2] to ensure that the second commandment (Ex. 20.7; Deut. 5.11) was followed as scrupulously as possible and to exclude any misuse of the divine name. Later on, but still in the pre-Christian period, there arose the custom of speaking of God's actions and feelings in *periphrases*.[3] Jesus certainly had no hesitation in using the word 'God' (see below, p. 97), but to a large extent he followed the custom of the time and spoke of the action of God by means of circumlocutions.

The following circumlocutions are to be found in the sayings of Jesus:

1. The use of the passive in place of the divine name, which occurs frequently throughout the sayings (see pp. 10ff.);

2. οἱ οὐρανοί, which also occurs in the singular (which reflects Greek influence). It occurs thirty-one times in Matthew in the phrase ἡ βασιλεία τῶν οὐρανῶν; elsewhere ἐν (τῷ) οὐρανῷ/ἐν (τοῖς) οὐρανοῖς = 'with God',[4] εἰς τὸν οὐρανόν = 'to God'[5] and ἐξ οὐρανοῦ = 'from God';[6]

3. ὁ πατήρ (μου, σου, ἡμῶν, ὑμῶν): there is an increasing number of instances in the later strata of the tradition;[7]

4. The third person plural: only in the Lucan special material: Luke 6.38; 12.20, 48c (twice); 16.9; 23.31;[8]

5. (ὁ) κύριος: apart from Mark 5.19; 13.20 this is only used as a periphrasis for the tetragrammaton in quotations from scripture, sometimes with the article (Mark 5.19; 12.36 par., quot.; Matt. 5.33, quot.), sometimes without (Mark 12.11 par., quot.; 13.20; Matt. 23.39 par., quot.; Luke 4,18, quot., 19, quot.);[9]

[1] Dalman, *Words of Jesus*, 182.

[2] For the few, strictly paraphrased exceptions, see Billerbeck II 311–13. The scribes handed down the pronunciation of the divine name to their pupils as secret learning (b. Kidd. 71a; j. Yom. 40d 57ff.).

[3] Dalman, *Words of Jesus*, 179–233; Billerbeck I 862–65 ('heaven'); II 308–11.

[4] Mark 10.21 par.; 12.25 par.; 13.32; Matt. 5.12 par. Luke 6.23; Matt. 6.20 par. Luke 12.33; Matt. 16.19bc; 18.18ab; Luke 10.20; 15.7.

[5] Luke 15.18, 21.

[6] Mark 11.30 par.

[7] Mark 4 times; *logia* common to Matthew and Luke 7 times; Luke alone 6 times; Matthew alone 32 times; John 109 times. Instances in J. Jeremias, *The Prayers of Jesus*, SBT II 6, in the lists on p. 36 ('Father' as title for God) and p. 54 ('Father' as address to God).

[8] The usual periphrasis in Rabbinic literature; cf. Billerbeck I 443; II 221.

[9] Unfortunately the Greek (ὁ) κύριος does not tell us what Hebrew or Aramaic

6. ὁ κύριος τοῦ οὐρανοῦ καὶ τῆς γῆς: Matt. 11.25 par. Luke 10.21;

7. ἡ δύναμις: Mark 14.62 par. Matt. 26.64 (with the secondary addition of τοῦ θεοῦ Luke 22.69); perhaps also Mark 12.24 par. Matt. 22.29;

8. ἡ σοφία: Matt. 11.19 par. Luke 7.35; with the secondary addition of τοῦ θεοῦ Luke 11.49;

9. τὸ ὄνομα: Matt. 6.9 par. Luke 11.2;[1]

10. ἡ βασιλεία: see below §11, p. 102;

11. οἱ ἄγγελοι: only in Luke: Luke 12.8f.; 15.10 (τοῦ θεοῦ will be a secondary addition in all three passages);

12. ἐνώπιον (Luke 12.6; 16.15; cf. 15.10), ἔμπροσθεν (Matt. 11.26 par.; 18.14) τοῦ θεοῦ: the angels standing 'before God' are introduced as agents in place of God, to dissociate feelings and decisions from God;

13. ὁ μέγας βασιλεύς: only in Matt. 5.35 (=Ps. 48.3);

14. ὁ ὕψιστος: on Jesus' lips only in Luke 6.35;

15. ἅγιος (adjective): Mark 3.29; 8.38 par.; 12.36; 13.11; Matt. 12.32 par.; Luke 11.13; 12.12;

16. ἄνωθεν: only in John: 3.3,7; 19.11; cf. ἐκ τῶν ἄνω 8.23;

17. Participial phrases: e.g. Mark 9.37 τὸν ἀποστείλαντά με; Matt. 10.28 τὸν δυνάμενον; 23.21 ἐν τῷ κατοικοῦντι αὐτόν [τὸν ναόν], 22: ἐν τῷ καθημένῳ ἐπάνω αὐτοῦ [τοῦ θρόνου].

18. Periphrases using a verb: γίνεσθαι: Mark 2.27 (ἐγένετο, 'God created'); 4.11; 6.2; Matt. 11.21 (twice), 23 (twice); Luke 4.25; 11.30; 19.9; 23.31; λαμβάνειν: Mark 10.30 (λάβῃ, 'God gives him') par.; 11.24 par.; 12.40 par.; Matt. 7.8 par.; 10.41 (twice) etc.; ἀνιστάναι: Mark 9.31 (ἀναστήσεται, 'God will raise him up'), etc.

The great number and variety of circumlocutions for God which occur in the sayings of Jesus is striking, even when we note that some of them occur only once or twice (nos 6–9, 13, 14) and the appearance of others is limited to one of the strata of the tradition (nos 4,11,16). Even more notable than the number and variety of these circumlocutions is the strong preference for one of them, the 'divine passive'. A great many of the sayings of Jesus only make their full impression when we realize that the passive is a veiled hint at an action on the part of God. Thus e.g. Matt. 5.4 might appropriately be rendered:

equivalent Jesus used as a substitute for the tetragrammaton outside worship. Within the context of worship the regular usage was to substitute *ᵃdōnāy.

[1] Even today, šēma (with the accent on the first syllable) replaces the tetragrammaton among the Samaritans; cf. J. Jeremias, *Die Passahfeier der Samaritaner*, BZAW 59, Giessen 1932, 19.

'Blessed are those who mourn, for there is one who will comfort them';
Matt. 10.30 par. Luke 12.7: 'There is one who has numbered all the
hairs of your head'; Mark 2.5: 'My son, there is one who forgives you
your sins'. The 'divine passive' occurs round about a hundred times in
the sayings of Jesus, though it should be stressed that there are a
number of borderline cases in which it is not certain whether the
passive is intended as a circumlocution for an action on the part of
God or whether it is used without this consideration.[1] In the first
three gospels, the 'divine passive' is distributed among the sayings of
Jesus in the following way (here and elsewhere the instances are
classified so that parallels are only counted once):

Mark	21 times[2]
Logia common to Matthew and Luke	23 times[3]
Matthew only	27 times[4]
Luke only	25 times[5]

[1] The following are ignored in this survey, as not being relevant: (a) intransitive
passives; (b) instances in which God is mentioned directly or indirectly as the
logical subject, because by definition they are not 'divine passives' in the strict
sense; (c) the formal introduction of scriptural quotations with γέγραπται and ἐρρέθη,
because with γέγραπται the logical subject is the particular biblical author (cf.
Mark 10.5; 12.19; John 1.45; 5.46), whereas the subject of ἐρρέθη is obscure
(God?, the Torah?, the men of old?).

[2] Mark: αἴρω 4.25; ἀλίζω 9.49; ἀπαίρω 2.20; ἀφίημι 2.5, 9; 3.28; 4.12; βάλλω
9.45, 47; γίνομαι 12.10; δίδωμι 4.11, 25; 8.12; 13.11; ἑτοιμάζω 10.40; μετρέω 4.24;
παραδίδωμι 9.31; 14.41; προστίθημι 4.24; πωρόω 8.17; σώζω 13.13.

[3] *Logia* common to Matthew and Luke: ἁγιάζω Matt. 6.9 (Luke 11.2); ἀνοίγω
Matt. 7.7 (Luke 11.9); Matt. 7.8 (Luke 11.10); ἀποκαλύπτω Matt. 10.26 (Luke
12.2); ἀποστέλλω Matt. 23.37 (Luke 13.34); ἀριθμέω Matt. 10.30 (Luke 12.7);
ἀφίημι Matt. 12.32a (Luke 12.10a); Matt. 12.32b (Luke 12.10b); Matt. 23.38
(Luke 13.35); Matt. 24.40 (Luke 17.34); Matt. 24.41 (Luke 17.35); γινώσκω Matt.
10.26 (Luke 12.2); δίδωμι Matt. 7.7 (Luke 11.9); ἐκβάλλω Matt. 8.12 (Luke 13.28);
κρίνω Matt. 7.1 (Luke 6.37); μετρέω Matt. 7.2 (Luke 6.38 [ἀντιμετρέω]); παραλαμβάνω
Matt. 24.40 (Luke 17.34); Matt. 24.41 (Luke 17.35); προστίθημι Matt. 6.33 (Luke
12.31); ταπεινόω Matt. 23.12 (Luke 14.11; 18.14); χορτάζω Matt. 5.6 (Luke 6.21a);
ὑψόω Matt. 11.23 (Luke 10.15); Matt. 23.12 (Luke 14.11; 18.14). In one case the
'divine passive' occurs only in Matthew and not in Luke: παρακαλέω Matt. 5.4
(Luke 6.21 γελάω); in two instances which belong together it occurs only in Luke
and not in Matthew: ἐκζητέω Luke 11.50 (Matt. 23.35 ἔρχομαι); Luke 11.51 (Matt.
23.36 ἥκω). These three instances are included in notes 4 and 5 respectively.

[4] Matthew: αἴρω 21.43; ἀποστέλλω 15.24; βάλλω 5.29; 7.19; γίνομαι 6.10; 9.29;
26.42; δέω 16.19; 18.18; δίδωμι 19.11; 21.43; δικαιόω 12.37; εἰσακούω 6.7; ἐκκόπτω
7.19; ἐκριζόω 15.13; ἐλεέω 5.7; ἑτοιμάζω 25.34, 41; καλέω 5.9, 19 (twice); καταδικάζω
12.37; καταράομαι 25.41; κρίνω 7.2; λύω 16.19; 18.18; παρακαλέω 5.4.

[5] Luke: ἀνταποδίδωμι 14.14; ἀποκαλύπτω 17.30; ἀπολύω 6.37; ἀφίημι 7.47 (twice),

The astonishing thing is that this phenomenon is almost completely absent from Talmudic literature. The dozen or so examples collected by Dalman, Billerbeck and myself[1] can now be multiplied, but even so, the evidence, in comparison with the extent of the Talmudic literature, is infinitesimally small. In the schools, the usual form of the verb for circumlocutions expressing the action of God was the third person plural (cf. p. 9, no.4). Dalman was therefore rash enough to suggest that the 'divine passives' in the synoptic gospels derive from such active forms without a subject.[2] This, however, was a makeshift solution for which there was no support at all in the texts. As a result, our first discovery is a negative one: public teaching in the Palestinian schools was certainly not the *Sitz im Leben* for the 'divine passive'. But in that case, where does it come from?

The 'divine passive' is more prominent in the literature of the Diaspora, as can be inferred, for example, from the letters of Paul. The Septuagint may be partly responsible for this state of affairs, as occasionally it uses the passive where the Hebrew text has the active (e.g. Gen. 15.6: ἐλογίσθη). In such cases it was presumably influenced less by theological motives than by Greek linguistic sensibility – the general restraint in the use of the passive which is characteristic of Aramaic is alien to Greek. We can see that Paul is influenced by the Septuagint in his use of the passive, for example, by the way in which he quotes ἐλογίσθη (Gen. 15.6 LXX, mentioned above) four times in Rom. 4 (vv. 3, 9, 22f.) and in connection with these quotations himself uses the passive λογίζεσθαι three times in the same chapter (vv. 5, 11, 24) as a 'divine passive'. This raises the question whether the 'divine passives' in the sayings of Jesus contained in the gospels are to be explained on the basis of Greek-Jewish linguistic usage, i.e. whether they may not have found their way into the tradition only at a secondary stage. By and large, this suggestion may be rejected: where we can trace the process of redaction, i.e. in the treatment of Mark by Matthew and Luke, no particular predilection for

---

48; διατάσσω 17.10; δίδωμι 6.38; 12.48; δικαιόω 18.14; ἐγγράφω 10.20; ἐκζητέω 11.50, 51; ζητέω 12.48; καταδικάζω 6.37; κλείω 4.25; κρύπτω 19.42; ὁρίζω 22.22; παραδίδωμι 24.7; παρακαλέω 16.25; πέμπω 4.26; πληρόω 4.21; 22.16; στηρίζω 16.26; τελειόω 13.32.

[1] Dalman, *Words of Jesus*, 225; *Worte Jesu*[2], 383; Billerbeck I 443; Jeremias, *Eucharistic Words*[2], 202.

[2] Dalman, *Words of Jesus*, 224.

the 'divine passive' can be discovered.¹ Furthermore, the way in which the instances are fairly evenly distributed over the strata of the synoptic tradition (as shown by the table on p. 11) hardly indicates that the phenomenon is to be attributed to secondary editorial activity.

The solution to the riddle lies in the discovery that there is a limited section of the literature of Palestinian Judaism of the time of Jesus in which the 'divine passive' is firmly established: apocalyptic literature. It occurs frequently for the first time in the book of the prophet Daniel. Although there is still a complete lack of collections of material, much less special investigations, it can be said that during the following period in Palestine the 'divine passive' remains one of the characteristics of apocalyptic, even if that is not exclusively its domain.² It was not only used out of reverence, to avoid uttering the name of God, but served above all as a way of describing in veiled terms God's mysterious activity in the end-time.³ Thus the 'divine passive' has its *Sitz im Leben* in the esoteric instruction of the scribes.⁴

There can be no doubt that in his frequent use of the passive as a circumlocution for the divine activity, Jesus followed the *style of apocalyptic*. We may not, however, put the connection between the two in any stronger terms. For Jesus accords to the 'divine passive' an

¹ True, Matthew has introduced a number of passives into the Marcan material, but hardly with the intention of avoiding God's name. Rather, in 12.32b; 18.8 he is providing a parallelism in contrast to Mark, and the way in which he often replaces ἀνιστάναι by ἐγείρεσθαι (16.21; 17.9, 23; 20.19) is an introduction of the language of the church. Only in Matt. 24.22 (ἐκολοβώθησαν/κολοβωθήσονται contrast Mark 13.20 ἐκολόβωσεν/ἐκολόβωσεν) has Matthew inserted a genuine 'divine passive' into the Marcan material, but he has altered the 'divine passive' in Mark 10.40 (ἡτοίμασται) by the addition of ὑπὸ τοῦ πατρός μου. Luke has eliminated it three times in the Marcan material (8.17; 21.15, 19); we must therefore ask whether there are not merely stylistic grounds for replacing ἐξῆλθεν (Mark 1.38) with ἀπεστάλην (Luke 4.43), as for the replacing of ἀναστῆναι (Mark 8.31) with ἐγερθῆναι (Luke 9.22). It remains questionable how far Luke felt the three passives which he has added to the Marcan material (8.12 σωθῶσιν; 18.31 τελεσθήσεται; 20.35 καταξιωθέντες) to be periphrases.
² A typical example is Matt. 3.10 par. Luke 3.9.
³ It is significant that the Revelation of John always has God acting through messengers or uses the 'divine passive'. Only in Rev. 21.5–8, which speaks of the final consummation, is there a direct mention of God's speaking and acting (cf. K.-P. Jörns, *Das hymnische Evangelium*, Diss. theol. Göttingen 1966, typescript, 20–22).
⁴ For apocalyptic as an ingredient of the esoteric instruction of the Rabbinate, see Jeremias, *Eucharistic Words*², 127f.; *Jerusalem*, 237ff.

incomparably greater place than it is given in apocalyptic. He uses it not only in apocalyptic sayings in the strict sense (e.g. about the last judgment and the eschatological division), but also – enlarging its scope – to describe God's gracious action in the present: even now God forgives, even now he unveils the mystery of his reign, even now he fulfils his promise, even now he hears prayers, even now he gives the spirit, even now he sends messengers and protects them, whereas he delivers up the one who has been sent. All these 'divine passives' announce the presence of the time of salvation, albeit in a veiled way, for the consummation of the world has dawned only in a veiled form. The extension of the 'divine passive' beyond purely future apocalyptic sayings, which has been carried out so widely, is connected with the central part of Jesus' preaching and is one of the clearest characteristics of his way of speaking.

(ii) Antithetic parallelism

It was the judgment of E. Norden[1] that, after the putting of the verb in first place, parallelism of clauses was the most certain Semitism to be found in the New Testament. As far as the sayings of Jesus in particular are concerned, C. F. Burney went further, and came to the conclusion that of the different kinds of Semitic parallelism (synonymous, antithetic, synthetic and climactic), antithetic parallelism 'characterizes our Lord's teaching in all the Gospel-sources'.[2] Indeed, he goes so far as to say that we are nearer to the *ipsissima verba* of Jesus in cases of marked antithetic parallelism 'than in any sentence otherwise expressed'.[3]

In fact, antithetic parallelism occupies a considerable space in the sayings of Jesus. Even if we leave aside antitheses (e.g. Mark 2.17a, 17b; 10.45) and restrict ourselves to cases of antithetic parallelism (though in some cases the differentiation of these two categories could be a matter of dispute), we are led to the conclusion that in the synoptic gospels,[4] antithetic parallelism occurs well over a hundred times in the sayings of Jesus. According to my counting it occurs as follows:

[1] *Agnostos Theos*, Leipzig-Berlin 1913=Darmstadt[4] 1956, 365.
[2] ‡Burney, 83.
[3] *Op. cit.*, 84.
[4] In the Fourth Gospel, antithetic parallelism occurs more than thirty times in the sayings of Jesus. This number does not, however, lend itself to a comparison, as it is affected by Johannine dualism.

Mark   30 times[1]
Logia common to Matthew and Luke   34 times[2]
Additional instances in Matthew only   44 times[3]

[1] Mark 2.19b//20, 22a//c, 27a//b; 3.28//29, 33//34 (the question in v. 33 is not neutral, but has a negative sense); 4.4–7//8, 11b//c, 21a//b, 25a//b, 31//32; 6.10//11; 7.6b//c (quot.), 8a//b, 10a//b (quot.), 10//11f. (v. 10 is the first clause of the antithetic parallelism in vv. 10–12 and is at the same time itself constructed antithetically), 15a//b; 8.12b//c, 35a//b; 10.18a//b, 27b//c, 31a/b, 42//43f.; 11.17b//c; 12.44a//b; 13.11a//b, 20a//b, 31a//b; 14.7a//b, 38bα//β, 58b//c.

[2] Antithetic parallelism occurs in both Matthew and Luke in thirty-four instances: Matt. 6.22b//23a (Luke 11.34b//c); Matt. 6.24b//c (Luke 16.13b//c); Matt. 6.31//33 (Luke 12.29//31); Matt. 7.3a//b (Luke 6.41a//b); Matt. 7.4a//b (Luke 6.42a α//β); Matt. 7.3f.//5 (Luke 6.41, 42a//b) (the two verses Matt. 7.3, 4 are the first clause of the antithetic parallelism in vv. 3–5 and are at the same time themselves constructed antithetically; similarly Luke); Matt. 7.18a//b (Luke 6.43a//b); Matt. 7.24, 25//26, 27 (Luke 6.47f.//49); Matt. 8.20b//c (Luke 9.58b//c); Matt. 9.37b//c (Luke 10.2a β//γ); Matt. 10.13a//b (Luke 10.6a//b); Matt. 10.28a//b (Luke 12.4//5); Matt. 10.32//33 (Luke 12.8//9); Matt. 10.34a//b (Luke 12.51a//b); Matt. 10.39a//b (Luke 17.33a//b); Matt. 11.7f.//9 (Luke 7.24f.//26) (the positive statement follows two negative ones); Matt. 11.11a//b (Luke 7.28a//b); Matt. 11.18//19 (Luke 7.33//34); Matt. 11.23a//b, quot. (Luke 10.15a//b, quot.); Matt. 11.25b α//β (Luke 10.21b α//β); Matt. 12.27//28 (Luke 11.19//20,); Matt. 12.32a//b (Luke 12.10a//b); Matt. 12.35a//b (Luke 6.45a//b); Matt. 12.39a//b (Luke 11.29b//c); Matt. 13.16//17 (Luke 10.23//24); Matt. 20.16a//b (Luke 13.30a//b); Matt. 23.4a//b (Luke 11.46a//b); Matt. 23.12a//b (Luke 14.11a//b; 18.14b//c); Matt. 23.23a//b (Luke 11.42a//b); Matt. 23.25a//b (Luke 11.39a//b); Matt. 24.40b//c (Luke 17.34b//c); Matt. 24.41b//c (Luke 17.35b//c); Matt. 24.45–47//48–51 (Luke 12.42–44//45–46); Matt. 25.29a//b (Luke 19.26a//b). To these thirty-four instances the following ten should be added: in eight cases the antithetic parallelism occurs only in Matthew, and not in Luke: Matt. 4.4a//b (quot.) (contrast Luke 4.4); Matt. 6.13a//b (contrast Luke 11.4); Matt. 6.19//20 (contrast Luke 12.33); Matt. 7.13//14 (contrast Luke 13.24); Matt. 7.21a//b (contrast Luke 6.46); Matt. 8.11//12 (contrast Luke 13.28); Matt. 23.27b//c (contrast Luke 11.44); Matt. 23.28a//b (contrast Luke 11.44). In two instances the antithetic parallelism occurs only in Luke, and not in Matthew: Luke 11.47a//b (contrast Matt. 23.29f.); Luke 11.48b//c (contrast Matt. 23.31). These ten instances are counted in n.3 and p. 16, n.1.

[3] Matt. 5.17a//b, 19a//b, 21b//c (quot.), 21//22 (v. 21 is the first clause of the antithetic parallelism in vv. 21–22 and is at the same time itself constructed antithetically), 27//28, 31//32, 33//34–37, 38//39–42, 43b//c (quot.), 43//44–48 (another case where the first clause of the antithetic parallelism is itself constructed antithetically); 6.2//3f., 5//6, 14//15, 16//17f., 34a//b; 7.15b//c, 17a//b; 10.5a//b, 24//25a; 12.33a//b, 37a//b; 13.30c//d, 48bα//β; 16.19b//c; 18.18a//b; 21.28f.//30, 32a//b (par. Luke 7.29f., not as a saying of Jesus); 22.8b//c, 14a//b; 23.3a//b, 16b//c, 18a//b, 24a//b; 25.3//4, 34–40//41–45, 46a//b (quot.). To these thirty-six instances are to be added eight cases mentioned in note 2 (end).

Additional instances in Luke only   30 times[1]

Numerous technical devices are used. The parallelism is achieved by the use of nouns, adjectives or verbs as opposites (usually pairs of opposites), by negation (usually of the second member), by the contrast of question and statement,[2] by inversion,[3] by polarization,[4] by complementary expressions[5] (including periphrases for totalities),[6] and very often by the combination of an opposition with a negation.[7]

Unfortunately, any verdict on the use of antithetic parallelism in the sayings of Jesus is made more difficult by the lack of any comprehensive investigation of Semitic antithetic parallelism. In particular, we are still completely in the dark about the extent to which it was used in the environment of Jesus. Still, despite the

---

[1] Luke 6.20–23//24–26 (these two antithetic strophes are made up of the following four antithetic parallelisms: 20b//24, 21a//25a, 21b//25b, 22f.//26); 7.44b//c, 45a//b, 46a//b, 47a//b; 10.16a//bc (the second half-verse v. 16bc is twice as long as the first and is in itself a climactic parallelism), 20a//b; 11.27//28 (where only the second half-verse comes from Jesus); 12.47//48a, 56a//b; 14.8f.//10, 12//13f.; 15.17b//c, 29//30; 16.10a//b, 15a//b, c//d, 25a//b, c//d; 17.20b, 21a//b (here the first half of the verse, which rejects any statement of the time or place of the coming of the reign of God, is twice as long as the second), 23//24 (see below, p. 101); 22.31//32, 35//36; 23.28b//c. To these twenty-eight instances are to be added two cases (11.47a//b, 48b//c) mentioned on p. 15, n. 2. Cf. also Luke 6.5D.

[2] Mark 3.33f. par.; 8.12; 10.18 par.; 11.17; Matt. 7.3–5 par.; 10.23 par.; 12.27f. par.; Luke 12.51; 22.35. The second member is in the form of a question in Luke 12.56; both members are in Mark 4.21.

[3] Inversion is to be found in Mark 2.27; 8.35 par. (cf. Matt. 10.39 par. Luke 17.33); 10.31 par. (cf. Matt. 20.16 par. Luke 13.30); Matt. 6.24 (par. Luke 16.13); Matt. 7.18 (par. Luke 6.43); Matt. 23.12 (par Luke 14.11; 18.14).

[4] Two extremes are contrasted so sharply that no room is left for any intermediaries: Mark 4.25 par.; 10.31 par.; Matt. 6.24 par.; Luke 14.8–10.

[5] The second line enlarges on what the first line says, but we cannot speak of synthetic parallelism, because the antithetical element is in the foreground: Mark 2.19b f. par. – Matt. 11.11 par.; 23.23 par., 25 par. – Matt. 5.21f., 27f., 43f.; 6.13; 16.19; 18.18 – Luke 10.20.

[6] Two extremes stand for the whole thing, including intermediaries: Matt. 5.21f. (total prohibition), 27f. (id.); 16.19 (total authority); 18.18 (id.).

[7] Mark 2.19b f.; 3.28f.; 4.21, 25; 6.10f.; 7.15; 10.27; 13.11, 31; 14.7; – Matt. 4.4 (quot.); 6.13, 19f., 31/ 33 par.; 7.21, 24–27 par.; 10.11–14 par., 13 par., 28 par., 34 par.; 11.11 par., 18f. par., 23 par.; 12.32 par.; 13.16f. par.; 23.4 par.; 25.29 par.; – Matt. 5.17, 33–36; 6.2–4, 5f., 14f., 16–18; 10.5f., 24–25a; 21.32; 23.3; 25.3f., 34–40/ 41–45; – Luke 6.5D; 7.44, 45, 46; 10.20; 12.47f., 56; 14.8–10, 12–14; 15.29f.; 17.20f.; 23f., 22.35f.; 23.28.

reservations that this makes necessary, it is possible to venture a few remarks.

(*a*) It is noteworthy that the table above shows that all four strata of the synoptic tradition are unamimous in attesting that Jesus frequently used antithetic parallelism. It is still more important that this parallelism is distributed approximately equally among the sayings of Jesus in the four strata. The reason why the number of instances per page adds up to 0·6/0·75 in Mark and in the Lucan special material and to 2·2 in the *logia* common to Matthew and Luke and the Matthaean special material respectively is that in the former, narrative material takes up much more space.

(*b*) The following may be said about the relative share of tradition and redaction in the origination of antithetic parallelism:

Matthew has taken over only 25 of the 30 antithetic parallelisms offered to him by Mark;[1] in several cases he has abbreviated them and tautened them to bring out the parallelism more sharply,[2] but he has not constructed any new antithetic parallelisms within the framework of the Marcan material. *Luke* found 17 antithetic parallelisms in the Marcan material that he took over in blocks, of which he used only 11.[3] The numerous instances in which he has weakened antithetic parallelisms show that he felt this Semitic mode of speech to be unattractive.[4]

As for the *tradition* preceding the gospels, in one case the secondary construction of an antithetic parallelism can be attributed to it with a high degree of probability: the concluding petition of the Lord's Prayer has one member in Luke (11.4) and

---

[1] Mark's five antithetical parallelisms which do not appear in Matthew are: Mark 2.27; 4.21, 25; 7.8; 12.44. In three cases, however (4.21, 25; 12.44), the whole section is missing from Matthew.

[2] Matt. 12.31 is considerably abbreviated in comparison with Mark 3.28f. Compare also Matt. 15.11 with Mark 7.15. Matt. 13.11 is tauter than Mark 4.11; compare Matt. 16.24 with Mark 8.35; Matt. 19.26 with Mark 10.27; Matt. 26.11 with Mark 14.7. This shows that it is wrong to assume that the pure form is always to be found at the beginning of the tradition.

[3] The following are not taken over by Luke: Mark 2.27; 3.33f.; 10.27, 31; 13.20; 14.7.

[4] Luke may have constructed an antithetic parallelism in 20.34f. to clarify Mark 12.25 and have made the *logion* Luke 9.24 (contrast Mark 8.35) tauter by abbreviation (so also Matt. 16.25), but otherwise in 8.21 (contrast Mark 3.33f.); 18.27 (contrast Mark 10.27) he destroys the antithetic parallelism, and in 8.10 (contrast Mark 4.11) relaxes it by abbreviation. By noting the language used, it can be shown in the *logia* material that Luke has weakened the antithetic parallelism by additions in 12.4f. (contrast Matt. 10.28), by abbreviations in 6.47–49 (contrast Matt. 7.24–27); 10.6 (contrast Matt. 10.13) and 11.34 (contrast Matt. 6.22f.), and by both additions and abbreviations in Luke 6.45 (contrast Matt. 12.35) and 17.33 (contrast Matt. 10.39).

two in Matthew (6.13). Liturgical usage has been at work here. The antithetic parallelism in Matt. 7.13f. may also be secondary in comparison with Luke 13.24.[1]

The evidence shows that the large number of cases of antithetic parallelism in the sayings of Jesus cannot be attributed to the process of redaction, and only in isolated examples is it to be seen as the work of the tradition. It is probable, therefore, that we have to derive the frequency of this usage from Jesus himself.

(c) Whereas in cases of antithetic parallelism in the Old Testament the second member serves, on the whole, to illuminate and to deepen the first by an opposed statement (e.g. Prov. 10.1: 'A wise son makes a glad father, but a foolish son is a sorrow to his mother.'),[2] in the sayings of Jesus exactly the opposite is the case: there the stress is almost always on the second half. In the extensive material collected in p. 15, n. 1 – p. 16, n. 1 there is no instance where the accent is the same in each half, and there are very few passages where the stress is clearly on the first half: Mark 2.19f., 27; Matt. 5.43; 6.34; Luke 12.47–48a. It is hardly a coincidence that Mark 2.27 has also been handed down in the Talmud ('The sabbath is delivered to you, and you are not delivered to the sabbath'),[3] that in Matt. 5.43 ('You shall love your fellow countryman, but you need not love your enemy')[4] Jesus is not using his own words but is quoting a popular maxim, and that there is a Talmudic parallel at least to the first line of Matt. 6.34 ('Do not be troubled about tomorrow's troubles');[5] Luke 12.47–48a may also be taking up proverbial wisdom. As these instances can be left on one side, it emerges that the use of antithetic parallelism in the sayings of Jesus is uniformly characterized by the way in which the stress lies on the second line.

This observation is of direct significance for exegesis. We have a whole series of sayings of Jesus in antithetic parallelism where it is not immediately clear what accentuation was originally intended – whether on the first half or on the second.

---

[1] The eschatological note recedes in the Matthaean version, and the *logion* is developed along the lines of the pattern of the two ways (cf. J. Jeremias, πύλη, πυλών, *TDNT* VI, 1968, 921–28: 922f.).

[2] See O. Eissfeldt, *The Old Testament: An Introduction*, Oxford 1965, 57ff.; K. Koch, *The Growth of the Biblical Tradition: The Form-Critical Method*, London 1969, 103f.; G. Fohrer, *Introduction to the Old Testament*, London 1970, 45f.

[3] Mek. Ex. on 31.13, 14 (Simeon b. Menasya, *c.* 180; b. Yom. 85b gives R. Jonathan b. Joseph, *c.* 140, as the author); Billerbeck II 5.

[4] For a justification of this translation see below, p. 213, n.3.

[5] b. Sanh. 100b (Billerbeck I 441).

Often each alternative gives quite a different sense (e.g. with the accent on the first half Matt. 23.12 is a threat, but with the accent on the second half it is a word of encouragement).[1] The evidence as a whole shows that in all these instances the stress should be taken to be on the second half.

(*d*) Like the Old Testament, the Judaism of Jesus' day used antithetic parallelism predominantly to formulate proverbial wisdom, maxims, legal axioms, truths of life and rules for wise conduct; it also occurred in apocalyptic sayings. Devotional literature, on the other hand, preferred synonymous parallelism. In fact, the cases of antithetic parallelism in the sayings of Jesus for which we have fairly exact parallels in Jewish literature belong in the context of teaching. Besides Mark 2.27 (see page 18 above), the relevant passages are Matt. 7.3–5;[2] 6.14f.;[3] 23.12;[4] Mark 8.35.[5] The number of parallels is relatively small because antithetic parallelism is used in the sayings of Jesus in far more than the context that has been described. In addition, it is used as a vehicle for attack,[6] reprimand,[7] accusation,[8] warning,[9] threat,[10] the proclamation of judgment,[11] defence,[12] rebuff,[13] repudiation,[14] intimidation,[15] the instruction of disciples,[16] words of commissioning,[17] promise,[18] strengthening,[19] acknowledgment,[20] self-descriptive statements.[21] It is worth noting how often antithetic parallelism occurs in metaphors and parables.[22] This versatility might

---

[1] From the Marcan material I would regard the following antithetic parallelisms as ambiguous, depending on where the stress is laid: Mark 6.10f.; 10.31 (cf. Matt. 20.16; Luke 13.30). From the *logia* material: Matt. 7.18 par.; 7.24–27 par.; 10.13 par.; 10.32f. par.; 23.12 par.; Luke 10.8–12 par. From Matthew: 7.17 (cf. 12.33); 16.19; 18.18. From Luke: 6.20–26; 16.10.

[2] b. Arak. 16b Bar. (Billerbeck I 446). The author is R. Tarphon (*c.* 110). It is not impossible that Tarphon may be dependent on Jesus.

[3] j.B.K. 6c 20f. (R. Gamaliel II, *c.* 90; Billerbeck I 425).

[4] b. Er. 13b (Billerbeck I 921 and the parallels there).

[5] b. Tam. 66a (=32a).   [6] E.g. Mark 7.8.   [7] E.g. Matt. 11.18f.

[8] E.g. Matt. 23.23.   [9] E.g. Matt. 7.24ff.   [10] E.g. Mark 10.25.

[11] E.g. Matt. 11.23.   [12] E.g. Matt. 12.27f.   [13] E.g. Mark 10.18.

[14] E.g. Mark 8.12.   [15] E.g. Matt. 10.34.   [16] E.g. Matt. 6.2–4.

[17] E.g. Mark 6.10f.   [18] E.g. Matt. 25.46.   [19] E.g. Mark 13.20.

[20] E.g. Mark 12.44.   [21] E.g. Matt. 5.17.

[22] E.g. in the reflex parables Matt. 7.24–27 par. Luke 6.47–49 (building a house on rock and sand); Matt. 21.28–30 (two sons); Matt. 24.45–51 par. Luke 12.42–46 (faithfulness and unfaithfulness in servants); cf. Matt. 7.13f. (broad and narrow ways); 25.34–45 (the blessed and the cursed). The expression 'reflex parable' was coined by E. Biser, *Die Gleichnisse Jesu. Versuch einer Deutung*, Munich 1965, 71. In double parables the same idea is illustrated by means of *different* imagery; in reflex parables the *same* picture is repeated antithetically.

be compared, say, with the monotonous and wearisome confrontation of the fool and the wise man, the wicked and the righteous, in Prov. 10.1–15.33.

On the basis of the relatively large number of instances and their fairly even distribution among the *logia* of the different strata of the synoptic tradition (see p. 17, section a) together with the peculiar use of the device in both form (see p. 18, section c) and content (see p. 19, section d), we may speak of a preference for antithetic parallelism on the part of Jesus. One reason for this is certainly the urgency of this way of speaking, and the ease with which it can be remembered. This can be inferred, among other things, from the large number of doublets.[1] The numerous antithetic parallelisms in the *logia* of Jesus express the way in which he constantly confronted men with the dawn of the reign of God and with God's promise and claim; his incessant warnings against spiritual self-assurance and self-righteousness; his steadfast summons to be in earnest about God and his promise.

(iii) Rhythm

When C. F. Burney translated the sayings of Jesus back into Aramaic, he was struck by the degree to which they had a rhythmic shape, like so many of the prophetic sayings in the Old Testament. He found three rhythms (four-beat, three-beat, and the *kīnā* metre); I should like to add a fourth, two-beat rhythm. Each of these four rhythms expresses to a special degree, if not exclusively, a different mood, and therefore finds its place in a particular area of thought. As in the Old Testament, it should be noted that the rhythms are not used with slavish strictness; considerable freedom prevails.[2]

(a) Two-beat

I begin with examples of two-beat rhythm in the synoptic sayings

---

[1] Matt. 10.39/16.25; 12.39/16.4; 13.12/25.29; 19.30/20.16; Luke 8.16/11.33; 8.18/19.26; 9.4f./10.8–11; 9.24/17.33; 12.11f./21.14f.

[2] The Palestinian Syriac lectionary (sy^pal) has proved considerably more usable as an aid towards translating back into Aramaic than the two old Syriac versions (sy^sin cur). Among modern renderings, chief use has been made here of conjectures by G. Dalman and secondarily of those by C. F. Burney. It is not meant to be a slight on the latter's remarkable pioneer work if one points out that in some cases his accentuation does not stand up to close examination. On the rules for accentuation see ‡Burney, 43–62: 'The Principles of Stress-accentuation in Hebrew Poetry'.

of Jesus, because in this case the rhythn can be clearly detected even in the Greek text.

τυφλοὶ ἀναβλέπουσιν,
χωλοὶ περιπατοῦσιν,
λεπροὶ καθαρίζονται·
καὶ κωφοὶ ἀκούουσιν,
νεκροὶ ἐγείρονται,
πτωχοὶ εὐαγγελίζονται·
καὶ μακάριός ἐστιν ὃς ἐὰν μὴ σκανδαλισθῇ ἐν ἐμοί

(Luke 7.22f. par. Matt. 11.5f.)

Six two-beat lines are followed at the end by a three-beat line.[1]

The commission with which the disciples are sent out is terse and decisive; it rhymes, both in Aramaic (in -*ūn*) and in Greek, and consists of four lines in asyndeton:

ἀσθενοῦντας θεραπεύετε,
νεκροὺς ἐγείρετε,
λεπροὺς καθαρίζετε,
δαιμόνια ἐκβάλλετε

(Matt. 10.8)

The instruction to the messengers is equally terse and sharp:

| δωρεὰν ἐλάβετε | ʿal maggán qabbeltŭn |
| δωρεὰν δότε | ʿal maggán hᵃbŭn |

(*ibid.*, end)

The command to love one's enemies (Luke 6.27f.) and the injunction to forgive (vv. 37–38a) are made more pointed by two double two-beat lines; in the latter case, the closing line with its description of the overflowing divine gift (v. 38b) breaks the bounds of any metre. Matt. 25.35f. enumerates six works of love in a sequence of two-beat lines. The first half of the Lord's Prayer, which takes up the Kaddish, is also expressed in two-beat lines. This is true of the address in the earlier[2] Lucan version (πάτερ = ʾ*Abbā*), too, for here the law of the

---

[1] Thus Luke's division (three lines + three lines + closing line); Matthew has καί before each line, but remarkably not before the third (thus two lines + two lines, continued as polysyndeton + closing line). But the different division has no influence on the rhythm.

[2] See below pp. 193ff.

pause[1] is applied, in accordance with which the second beat is omitted and replaced by a pause:

πάτερ
ἁγιασθήτω τὸ ὄνομά σου
ἐλθάτω ἡ βασιλεία σου[2]

Only with the petitions in the first person plural does the Lord's Prayer go over to four-beat rhythm, to return abruptly to a two-beat line in the closing petition.

Because of its brevity, the two-beat line necessitates terse and abrupt formulations, whose sparseness and monotony lends them the utmost urgency. A further look at the themes of the examples given above will immediately show that Jesus used the two-beat line above all to impress upon his hearers *central ideas* of his message.

(b) Four-beat

The context in the sayings of Jesus reserved for the four-beat line is different, as the following examples indicate:

'īn milḥá tāpél
bᵉmá tᵉtabbᵉlún

(Mark 9.50)[3]

'ᵃná sātár hēkᵉlá hādén
ūbitᵉlátá yōmín nibné ḥōránd

(Mark 14.58)[4]

šᵉbóq mītayyá qābᵉrín mītēhón

(Matt. 8.22 sy^pal par. Luke 9.60 sy^pal)

min mōtᵉréh dᵉlibbá pummá mᵉmallél

(Matt. 12.34 sy^pal par. Luke 6.45)

'īhab lák maptᵉḥayyá dᵉmalkūtá dišᵉmayyá
ūmá dᵉtēsór bᵉ'arʿá yittᵉsár bišᵉmayyá
ūmá dᵉtišré bᵉ'arʿá yištᵉré bišᵉmayyá

(Matt. 16.19)[5]

---

[1] K. G. Kuhn, *Achtzehngebet und Vaterunser und der Reim*, WUNT 1, Tübingen 1950, 39. Further examples of the law of pause after the address are Matt. 11.26 (see below, p. 24); 25.37.

[2] For a translation into Aramaic see p. 196.

[3] For word-play see below, pp. 28f; M. Black, *An Aramaic Approach to the Gospels and Acts*³, Oxford 1967, 166f.

[4] See G. Dalman, *Orte und Wege Jesu*³, Gütersloh 1924, 324. The pair of opposites χειροποίητος/ἀχειροποίητος has not been translated because it does not appear in par. Matt. 26.61; Mark 15.29 par. Matt. 27.40; John 2.19; Acts 6.14; in Mark 14.58 it may be an addition.

[5] ‡Burney, 117.

The pattern 4+4+2 occurs again and again in sayings of Jesus: in the petitions in the first person plural in the Lord's Prayer (see the translation back into Aramaic on p. 196), and as follows:

kol mán de'īt léh yíty^ehēb léh
w^ekol mán d^elēt léh 'úp má de'īt léh
yitn^eśéb minnéh

(Mark 4.25; Luke 19.26)

kol mán d^ebā'é m^ehallāká bāt^eráy
yikpór b^egarméh w^eyiṭ'án ṣ^elībéh
w^eyēté bāt^eráy

(Mark 8.34 par. Matt. 16.24; Luke 9.23)[1]

lét talmīdá   le'él min rabbéh
w^elét 'abdá   le'él min māréh
missát l^etalmīdá dīhé k^erabbéh
w^e'abdá k^emāréh

(Matt. 10.24)[2]

The repose which characterizes the four-beat as opposed to the two-beat line, and the matter-of-factness which distinguishes it from the *kīnā* metre, make it especially appropriate for conveying didactic themes. It is hardly a concidence that many sayings with four-beat lines are addressed to the inner circle of followers and the messengers, for the most part giving instructions but also bringing consolation. The four-beat line is pre-eminently the rhythm for the *instruction of disciples*.[3]

(c) Three-beat

When we turn to the synoptic sayings of Jesus clad in the garb of the three-beat line, we are confronted with another area of subject-matter.

l^eta'^alayyá ———— 'īt l^ehón hőrín
ūl^e'ōpá diś^emayyá ———— qinnín
ūl^ebár 'e^enāśá lēt léh
hán d^eyarkén réśéh

(Matt. 8.20 par. Luke 9.58)[4]

[1] Cf. Dalman, *Jesus-Jeshua*, 191. See also p. 242 below.
[2] *Ibid.* 229. – Burney includes the following among the *logia* in four-beat rhythm: Mark 6.8–11 (p.122, but vv. 8f. in Mark are not words of Jesus); 13.9–13 (118); Matt. 6.9–13 (112, 161); 6.24 (116); 10.16 (122); 10.24–27 (122f.); 11.4–6 (117f.); 13.52 (116); 16.17–19 (117); Luke 6.27–29 (113f., 169); 6.36–38 (114); 10.16 (124); 11.9f. (114f.); 12.32–37 (115, 170f.); 12.42f. (116).
[3] ‡Burney, 124.
[4] *Ibid.*, 169. In the first line Burney reads *bōrīn* (holes), but the Greek φωλεός matches *hōrīn* (caves) better, thus sy^{pal}.

Note the double rhyme and the application of the law of compensation in the second line: the verb of the first line is not repeated in the second, but a disruption of the rhythmic balance is avoided by compensating for the missing stress with the genitive *diš^emayyā*.[1]

*mōdénā lák 'abbá
māré diš^emayyá ūd^e'ar'á
diṭ^emárt hallén min ḥakkīmín w^esukl^etānín
w^egallít 'innún l^eṭalyín
'ín 'abbá ———
dikdén ra'^awá q^odāmák*

(Matt. 11.25f. par. Luke 10.21f.)[2]

*ṭūbēkón mísk^enayyá
d^edīl^ekón malkūtá dēlāhá*

(Luke 6.20, following sy^{pal})

*ṭūbēhón d^eraḥ^amánayyá
d^ehinnón yítraḥ^amún
ṭūbēhón did^eké libbá
d^ehinnón yaḥmūnéh lēlāhá
ṭūbēhón d^e'āb^edín š^elāmá
d^eyitq^erón b^enóy dēlāhá*

(Matt. 5.7, 8, 9)

*lá yāk^elá m^edīná d^etiṭṭ^emár
dil^e'él min ṭúr mitt^esāmá*

(Matt. 5.14)[3]

*kol mán d^ekā'és 'al 'aḥúh
y^ehé mitḥayyáb bēt dīná
ūmán d^e'āmár l^e'aḥúh rēqá
y^ehé mitḥayyáb sanhedrīná
ūmán d^e'āmár šaṭyá
y^ehé mitḥayyáb nūr gēhinnám*

(Matt. 5.22)[4]

*lēt k^esí d^elá yitg^elé
ūṭ^emír d^elá yity^edá'*

(Matt. 10.26 par. Luke 12.2)

*hēk^edēn yanhár n^ehōr^ekón q^odām b^enē 'enāšá
d^eyiḥmón 'ōbādēkón ṭābayyá
wišabb^eḥún la'^abūkón d^ebiš^emayyá*

(Matt. 5.16 sy^{pal})[5]

[1] *Op. cit.*, 106. Further examples of the use of the law of compensation in the three-beat line: Ps. 24.5; 15.1; Amos 5.24; Mark 13.25 (‡Burney, 105f.).

[2] *Op. cit.*, 171f. Burney deletes the fourth beat in the third line, but this correction is not necessary, as such licence is allowed; nor does the fifth line need to be filled out, as the law of the pause, mentioned on pp. 21f. above, is applied here.

[3] *Op. cit.*, 130f.

[4] Dalman, *Jesus-Jeshua*, 73.

[5] At the beginning of the second line, sy^{pal} also has *liglēl* = ὅπως; in Palestinian Aramaic, simple *d^e* corresponds to this.

lā tihᵃbún qaddīšá lᵉkalbayyá,
wᵉlā tirmón margᵉliyyātᵉkón bᵉʾáppē hᵃzirayyá

(Matt.7.6)[1]

hᵃwōn ʿarīmín kᵉgón hiwwāwátá
ūtᵉmīmín kᵉgón yōnayyá

(Matt. 10.16)[2]

saggīʾín dᵉʾinnún zᵉmīnín
wᵉṣibhád dᵉʾinnún bᵉhīrín

(Matt. 22.14)[3]

A combination of three-beat and two-beat lines:

šaʾᵃlún ūmityᵉhéb lᵉkón
bᵉʿún wᵉʾattún maškᵉhín
ʾartᵉqún ūmitpᵉtáh lᵉkón
dᵉkol man dᵉšāʾél nᵉsáb
udᵉbāʿé maškáh
ūdᵉmartíq mitpᵉtah léh

(Matt. 7.7f. syᵖᵃˡ par.)[4]

Rhyme is to be found particularly often with three-beat lines; the very first example (Matt. 8.20 par. Luke 9.58) provided an instance. It is difficult to say whether the rhyme was deliberate and conscious in every case.

Even in the wisdom literature of the Old Testament, the three-beat line is used by preference for conveying meditative thoughts, aphorisms, proverbs and experiential wisdom; it is also used very often in the psalms. It is the most frequent rhythm to be used in the sayings of Jesus; it serves *to drive home important sayings and maxims.*[5]

(d) The kīnā *metre*

The *kīnā* metre has the most individual rhythm:[6] 3+2 with occasional variations of 2+2 and 4+2. It derives from the lament for the

[1] J. Jeremias, 'Matthäus 7, 6a', in: *Abraham unser Vater*, Festschrift *für O. Michel*, Leiden-Köln 1963, 271–75 = in: *Abba*, 83–87. For the placing of the accent ‡Burney, 169.

[2] Dalman, *Jesus-Jeshua*, 227.

[3] *Op. ci.t*, 228.

[4] Burney includes the following among the *logia* in three-beat rhythm: Mark 7.8 (p. 104); 13.25 (106); Matt. 5.3–10 (166); 5.14–16 (130, 170); 6.14f. (107); 6.22f. (131); 7.6 (131, 169); 7.17 (104); 8.20 (106, 132, 169); 11.25–27 (133, 171f.); 12.30 (132); 15.14 (133); 23.12 (104); 23.29 (103); 25.31ff. (142f., 172–74, alternating with the *kīnā*; connecting clauses bracketed out); Luke 9.62 (132, 170); 12.48 (107); 16.10 (104).

[5] Burney, 130: 'pithy sayings of a gnomic character'.

[6] *Op. cit.*, 34–43, 137–46.

dead (*kīnā*), in which the singer who leads the lament utters a longer cry (three-beat) to which the lamenting women make answer with a shorter echo (two-beat). In one passage in the gospels, we find Jesus taking up a real *kīnā*.

εἰ ἐν ὑγρῷ ξύλῳ ταῦτα ποιοῦσιν,
ἐν τῷ ξηρῷ τί γένηται;
ʾīn beqēsắ raṭṭībắ ʿābedīn hēk
beyabbīšắ mā nihwé

(Luke 23.21)[1]

The children's sing-song

zemárnan lekốn welā[2] raqqēdtún
ʿalénan welā ʾarqēdtún

(Matt. 11.17 par. Luke 7.32)

is an imitation *kīnā* with word-play (*raqqēdtūn*/*ʾarqēdtūn*) and rhyme (–*nan*, –*tūn*).

Further examples of the *kīnā* metre are:

bimekīletắ deʾattún mekīlīn báh
mittekál lekốn

(Mark 4.24; Matt. 7.2 par. Luke 6.38)[3]

man dibeʿ ắ[4] leḥayyāʾ ắ[5] napšéh
mōbéd yātáh
ūman demōbéd napšéh beginnī[6]
meḥayyé yātáh

(Mark 8.35 par. Luke 9.24; 17.33)

habún dilqēsár leqēsár
wedilēlāhắ lēlāhắ

(Mark 12.17 par. Matt. 22.21; Luke 20.25)

lā tihwốn sebīrín da ʾaṭáyit
lemipḥát min ʾōrāyetắ [ʾo nebīʾayyā][7]

[1] Cf. Dalman, *Jesus-Jeshua*, 232.
[2] ‡Burney, 57: 'The negative *lō* is normally unstressed'; similarly Aram. *lā*.
[3] Dalman, *op. cit.*, 225, but he misses the divine passive.
[4] θέλῃ Mark 8.35 par. and ζητήσῃ Luke 17.33 are variant translations of *beʿā*; of. M. Black, *An Aramaic Approach to the Gospels and Acts*[3], Oxford 1967, 244.
[5] σῶσαι Mark 8.35 par. and περιποιήσασθαι/ζῳογονήσει Luke 17.33 are variant translations of *ḥayyāʾā* (*ibid.*, 188).
[6] καὶ τοῦ εὐαγγελίου is missing from all the parallels: Matt. 16.25 par. Luke 9.24; Matt. 10.39 par. Luke 17.33; John 12.25.
[7] Is absent from b. Shab. 116b.

lá lᵉmip̱ḥát ʾᵃtáyit
ʾellá lᵉʾōsopé

(Matt. 5.17)[1]

man dᵉlētéh mᵉkanné̆š ʿimmí
hú mᵉbaddár

(Matt. 12.30 = Luke 11.23)[2]

yᵉhón ʾaḥrāyé̆ qadmaín
wᵉqadmayé̆ ʾaḥraín[3]

(Matt. 20.16) Note the rhyme.

hán dihwé̆ pugrá
mitkannᵉšín nišrayyá

(Matt. 24.48 par. Luke 17.37 sy^pal) Rhyme![4]

The *kīnā* metre serves above all to express *strong inner emotion*. It covers a wide span, including laments, warnings, threats, admonitions and summons as well as beatitudes and messages of salvation.

To sum it up: it may be affirmed that the accumulation of rhythms in the sayings of Jesus allow us to draw the conclusion that we have to do with a distinct characteristic of his. In addition, they indicate a Semitic background and provide an important pointer towards the antiquity of the tradition. A comparison of the parallel traditions shows that much of this rhythmic language was lost when the sayings were translated into Greek, and while they were being handed on in a Greek milieu.

(iv) Alliteration, assonance and paronomasia

Matthew Black deserves credit for being the first to have noticed that when the sayings of Jesus are translated back into his mother-tongue they display to an unusual degree the phenomena which give

---

[1] See below, p. 83.

[2] Cf. Dalman, *Jesus-Jeshua*, 229; see also the *Ergänzungsheft* to the German edition, Leipzig 1929, 16.

[3] Cf. Dalman, *Jesus-Jeshua*, 228.

[4] ‡Burney finds the *kīnā* metre in the following *logia*: Mark 2.19–22 (p. 140, but this only works out if one follows Matthew); 8.34–38 (141f., but v. 34 is four-beat, see p. 23 above; Burney disguises this by taking καθ᾽ ἡμέραν from Luke 9.23 for reasons of metre; v. 35, see p. 26; Matthew is again preferred in vv. 37f., but in v.38 τῶν ἁγίων is taken over from Mark); Matt. 11.28–30 (144f.); 13.16f. (145); 23.37–39 (146, problematic); 25.31ff. (142f., 172f., alternating with three-beat lines; the connecting clauses are left out of account); Luke 10.41f. (145, problematical); 13.23–27 (138–40, connecting clauses in vv. 24, 25, 26, 27 again bracketed out).

this section its title. The reader's attention is called to his collection of material (pp. 160–85), from which Luke 15.7 might be mentioned as an example: οὕτως χαρὰ ἐν τῷ οὐρανῷ ἔσται ἐπὶ ἑνὶ ἁμαρτωλῷ μετανοοῦντι. The conclusion of this parable is given a particularly impressive character by the alliteration with the guttural ḥ:

joy = ḥedwā   one = ḥᵃdā   sinner = ḥāṭᵉyā[1]

The saying about salt (Mark 9.50 par. Matt. 5.13; Luke 14. 34f.) may serve as a second example:

Mark: ἐὰν δὲ τὸ ἅλας   ἄναλον γένηται,   ἐν τίνι αὐτὸ ἀρτύσετε;
Matthew: ἐὰν δὲ τὸ ἅλας   μωρανθῇ,   ἐν τίνι   ἁλισθήσεται;
Luke: ἐὰν δὲ καὶ τὸ ἅλας μωρανθῇ,   ἐν τίνι   ἀρτυθήσεται;
Matthew: εἰς οὐδὲν ἰσχύει ἔτι
Luke: οὔτε εἰς γῆν οὔτε εἰς κοπρίαν εὔθετόν ἐστιν".

Matthew: εἰ μὴ βληθὲν ἔξω καταπατεῖσθαι ὑπὸ τῶν ἀνθρώπων.
Luke: ἔξω βάλλουσιν αὐτό.

We must start from the remarkable fluctuation of the tradition in the ἐάν clause between 'if the salt becomes saltless' (ἄναλον) (Mark 9.50) and 'if the salt becomes foolish' (μωρανθῇ) (Matt. 5.13; Luke 14.34). The Marcan wording (salt becoming unserviceable for seasoning) makes sense,[2] whereas the wording of Matthew and Luke (salt acting or speaking in a silly way) is extremely hard, even if we assume that the evangelists had in mind the foolish disciples[3] or unrepentant Israel.[4] J. Lightfoot (1602–1675)[5] was the first to recognize that the solution lies in the ambiguity of the root *tpl* = 1. 'Be saltless', 2. 'Drivel'. That means that the Marcan tradition (ἄναλον γένηται) offers the correct translation, whereas μωρανθῇ (Matthew/ Luke) is a translation error.

In the apodosis, the three verbal forms ἀρτύσετε (Mark)/ἁλισθήσεται (Matt.)/ ἀρτυθήσεται (Luke) are different translations of the verb *tabbēl* ('season', 'salt'). Thus if we translate the clause back into Aramaic we get a word play *tāpēl/tabbēl*:[6]

'*in milḥā tāpēl*
bᵉmā tᵉtabbelūn   (Mark 9.50)[7]

These observations can be taken still further. It can be shown that the onomatopeia continues in the second clause, which occurs only in Matthew and Luke, who diverge considerably here in their wording. The two evangelists go different ways.[8]

---

[1] ‡Black, 184.
[2] I.e. the salt could contain impurities which would remain as useless refuse when the salt was dissolved by moisture, cf. Jeremias, *Parables*[2], 168f.
[3] ‡Black, 166.
[4] Jeremias, *ibid.*, 169.
[5] *Opera omnia* II, Rotterdam 1686, 540b on Luke 14.34.
[6] ‡Black, 166f.
[7] See above, p. 22: four-beat.
[8] ‡Black, 167, harmonizes both traditions by addition and renders καταπατεῖσθαι by *rā'a'*, but this means 'dash to pieces', 'shatter'.

In Luke (οὔτε εἰς γῆν οὔτε εἰς κοπρίαν εὔθετόν ἐστιν) either the noun *ziblā* or the verb *zabbālā* (pa'el infinitive) lies behind κοπρία; thus here we have the word-play, using the labials *b* and *p*, *tāpēl* (μωρανθῇ)/*yittabbēl* (ἀρτυθήσεται)/*zabbālā* (κοπρίαν). A translation of Matthew's βληθὲν ἔξω καταπατεῖσθαι back into Aramaic produces onomatopoeia with the dentals *t*, *d* and the sibilant *s*: *miš'dē* (βληθὲν)[1]/*'itt'dāšā* (καταπατεῖσθαι).[2]

The proverb quoted by Jesus in Luke 4.23 is also characterized by onomatopoeia (three-beat):

'asyā 'assî garmāk.

§3 · CHARACTERISTICS OF THE *IPSISSIMA VOX*

Dalman, *Words of Jesus*; Jeremias, *Parables*[2]; id., 'Characteristics of the *ipsissima vox Jesu*', in: *The Prayers of Jesus*, SBT II 6, London 1967, 108–15.

So far we have been discussing linguistic and stylistic phenomena which did not represent a completely new development, but appeared in the sayings of Jesus with unusual frequency. Now we turn to characteristics of Jesus' speech to which there is no analogy in contemporary literature and which may therefore be designated as characteristics of the *ipsissima vox Jesu.*

(i) *The parables of Jesus*

We find nothing to be compared with the parables of Jesus, whether in the entire intertestamental literature of Judaism, the Essene writings, in Paul, or in Rabbinic literature. One immediate difference is that some of the types of parabolic speech are not to be found in the sayings of Jesus at all. Thus, for example, we read in the Essene *Genesis Apocryphon* a fable which depicts how the palm tree (Sarai) pleads for the cedar tree (Abram) to be spared (1QGenAp ar 19.14–17). This fable continues the series of Old Testament plant-fables in which cedar, olive, fig tree, vine, bramble bush and thistle behave like human beings.[3] We find no fables on the lips of Jesus; fig tree and vine do not speak in his sayings.[4] Also, in Ethiopian Enoch

---

[1] Ithpe'el participle of *š'dā* ('throw').

[2] Ithpe'el infinitive of *dūš* ('tread').

[3] Judg. 9.8–15; II Kings 14.9; Ezek. 17.3–8; 31.3–14. Cf. also IV Ezra 4.13–21: the trees and the waves hold councils of war because they want to fight each other.

[4] M. D. Goulder, 'Characteristics of the Parables in the Several Gospels', *JTS* 19, 1968, 51–69: 51.

(chs. 85–90) we read an outline of the history of Israel in the form of a long-winded allegory involving various animals. Jesus indeed regularly uses the familiar metaphors, mostly drawn from the Old Testament and familiar to everyone at that time, but he does not construct allegories.[1] His parables take us, rather, into the midst of throbbing, everyday life. Their nearness to life, their simplicity and clarity, the masterly brevity with which they are told, the seriousness of their appeal to the conscience, their loving understanding of the outcasts of religion – all this is without analogy. If we want to find anything comparable we have to go back a long way, to the high-points of prophetic proclamation: the parable of Nathan (II Sam. 12.1–7), the song of the vineyard (Isa. 5.1–7) and perhaps the comparison with father and son in Hos. 11 (though that is hardly a parable, i.e. a 'short story').[2] Even in these cases we have only a few, scattered examples, whereas the first three gospels give us no fewer than forty-one parables of Jesus. It is generally recognized today – despite the need for a critical analysis of every single parable and the history of its tradition – that the parables belong to the bedrock of the tradition about him.

(ii) The riddles

Among the sayings of Jesus there are a considerable number which are riddles. Not only are they riddles for us today; they were even felt to be riddles, at least by outsiders, at the time when Jesus uttered them. One might mention the following: sayings about John the Baptist like Matt. 11.11 par., where John is described paradoxically as the greatest among those born of woman and less than the least in the reign of God, or the strange saying about the forcing of the basileia (Matt. 11.12 par.);[3] sayings about the mission of Jesus like 11.5f. par. with the juxtaposition of salvation and scandal; pictorial sayings about the old and the new like Mark 2.21f. par. and about the coming time of distress like Mark 14.58; Luke 11.49; Matt. 10.34; Luke 22.36; sayings about the fate of Jesus like the word-play in Mark 9.31 (cf. p. 282), that God will deliver up the man (sing.) to men (plur.); the saying about Elijah in Mark 9.11; sayings about the three days like

[1] Jeremias, Parables[2], 88f.
[2] The expression was used by G. Eichholz, Einführung in die Gleichnisse (Biblische Studien 37), Neukirchen-Vluyn 1963, 18.
[3] For a suggestion about the meaning, see below pp. 111f.

Luke 13.32f.; riddles like that of the three kinds of eunuch in Matt. 19.12. Indeed, Mark 4.11, detached from its present secondary context,[1] says of the whole preaching of Jesus that it must be in riddles to those ἔξω. All this is quite unusual. Teachers of the time did not teach in this way, and the early church did not invent riddles (*me̊šālîm*) for Jesus; on the contrary, it clarified them, a tendency that can be studied, for example, in the prophecies of the passion.[2]

(iii) The reign of God

As a designation of God's reign, the term βασιλεία (τοῦ θεοῦ/τῶν οὐρανῶν)[3] occurs on the lips of Jesus in the following way:

Mark	13 times[4]
Logia common to Matthew and Luke	9 times[5]
Additional instances in Matthew only	27 times[6]
Additional instances in Luke only	12 times[7]
John	2 times[8]

The explanation for the disproportionately high number in Matthew is that a group of his examples represents redactional activity: in five instances he has inserted the term in the Marcan text (Matt. 13.19; 18.1; 20.21; 21.43; 24.14); two examples occur in the interpretation of the parable of the wheat and the tares (13.38,[43), where his editorial work is considerable,[9] and in eight further instances we have an introduction to parables ὁμοία ἐστὶν [or ὡμοιώθη, ὁμοιωθήσεται] ἡ βασιλεία τῶν οὐρανῶν preferred by Matthew or his source (13.24, 44, 45, 47; 18.23; 20.1; 22.2; 25.1).[10] Luke has added the term to the Marcan text three times (Luke 4.43; 18.29; 21.31).

[1] Jeremias, *Parables*[2], 13–18.

[2] Cf. below, pp. 277ff. The misunderstandings of ambiguous words or phrases in the Fourth Gospel are not comparable with the synoptic *me̊šālîm*. Some of them are extremely crude (cf. John 2.20; 3.4; 4.15; 7.35; 8.22, 57) and are no more than a stylistic means used e.g. to give a decisive turn to the dialogue.

[3] On the question which of the two forms is the original, see p. 97, below.

[4] Mark 1.15 par.; 4.11 par., 26, 30 par.; 9.1 par., 47; 10.14 par., 15 par., 23 par., 24, 25 par.; 12.34; 14.25 par.

[5] Matt. 5.3 (par. Luke 6.20); 6.10 (par. Luke 11.2), 33 (par. Luke 12.31); 8.11 (par. Luke 13.29); 10.7 (par. Luke 10.9); 11.11 (par. Luke 7.28), 12 (par. Luke 16.16); 12.28 (par. Luke 11.20); 13.33 (par. Luke 13.20).

[6] Matt. 5.10, 19a, b, 20; 7.21; 8.12; 13.19, 24, 38, 43, 44, 45, 47, 52; 16.19; 18.1, 3, 4, 23; 19.12; 20.1; 21.31, 43; 22.2; 23.13; 24.14; 25.1.

[7] Luke 4.43; 9.60, 62; 10.11; 12.32; 13.28; 17.20a, b, 21; 18.29; 21.31; 22.16, 18.

[8] John 3.3, 5.

[9] Jeremias, *Parables*[2], 82–84.

[10] *Ibid.*, 101f.

An investigation of Jewish literature produces a completely different picture.[1] The term reign (of God) occurs only rarely in the Apocrypha and Pseudepigrapha of the Old Testament,[2] in the Targums[3] and in Philo;[4] otherwise it occurs in pre-Christian times only in the Kaddish (see below, p. 198) and a few prayers related to it;[5] Josephus mentions βασιλεία on only one occasion[6] in connection with God (he does not have the term 'reign of God' itself). Instances begin to increase somewhat only when we come to the Rabbinic literature, but as a rule they are limited to stereotyped phrases like 'take the reign of heaven upon oneself', i.e. 'subject oneself to God', 'repeat the *Sh*e*ma*c', 'become a proselyte'.[7] This general picture has been amply confirmed by the Dead Sea scrolls: the phrase 'reign (of God)' occurs only three times in the whole of the Essene literature so far as it is at present known to us.[8] If we compare the figures in the tables above with this sparse collection, we have to admit that the accumulation of instances in the synoptic gospels is unusual (even taking into account the part played by redaction, which is particularly evident in the Gospel of Matthew).

Still more remarkable than this purely numerical differentiation is the fact that in the sayings of Jesus which deal with the βασιλεία, a great many phrases appear which have *no parallels* (not even secular ones) in the language of Jesus' contemporaries. Even if we apply the strictest standards, the following phrases must be noted as new instances:

ἁρπάζειν τὴν βασιλείαν τῶν οὐρανῶν	(Matt. 11.12)
βιάζεται ἡ β. τ. οὐ.	(*ibid.*)
ἤγγικεν ἡ βασιλεία τοῦ θεοῦ	(Mark 1.15 par.; Matt. 10.7 par.; Luke 10.11, cf. 21.31 ἐγγύς ἐστιν ἡ β.τ.θ.)

---

[1] Dalman, *Words of Jesus*, 91–147; see also *Worte Jesu*², 310–14, 361–63, 375–78; Billerbeck I, 172–84, 418f.

[2] Dan. 3.54 LXX; 4.34Θ; Tobit 13.2; Ps. Sol. 5.18; 17.3; Eth. En. 84.2; Ass. Mos. 10.1; Wisdom 6.4; 10.10; Or. Sib. 3.47, 766.

[3] Examples in Dalman, *Words of Jesus*, 101; *Worte Jesu*², 312, 361. See below, p. 102, n.4.

[4] Instances in K. L. Schmidt, βασιλεία κτλ, *TDNT* I, 1964, 571–93: 574f.

[5] Dalman, *Words of Jesus*, 99f., 109; *Worte Jesu*², 311 361f. See below, p. 267, n. 5.

[6] *Antt.* 6.60: τὸν μὲν θεὸν ἀποχειροτονοῦσι τῆς βασιλείας.

[7] Dalman, *Words of Jesus*, 98; Billerbeck I, 174ff.

[8] *m*e*lūkā* (of God): 1 QM 6.6: 'And the reign shall be to the God of Israel' (a free quotation of Obadiah 21). – *malkūt* (of God) 1 QM 12.7: 'terrible in the glory of thy reign' (cf. Ps. 144.11ff.); 1 QSb 4.25f. 'in the temple of the reign'.

εἰσέρχεσθαι εἰς τὴν β.τ.ϑ. (Mark 9.47; 10.15 par.; 10.23 par., 24, 25 par.; Matt. 5.20; 7.21; 18.3; 23.13; John 3.5; there is a New Testament echo in Acts 14.22)

ἐλάχιστος ἐν τῇ β.τ.οὐ. (Matt. 5.19)

ἡ β.τ.ϑ.ἐντός τινός ἐστιν (Luke 17.21)

ἔρχεται ἡ β.τ.ϑ. (Mark 9.1; Matt. 6.10 par. Luke 11.2; Luke 17.20; 22.18)[1]

ἡ ἡτοιμασμένη βασιλεία (Matt. 25.34)

εὐνούχισαν ἑαυτοὺς διὰ τὴν β.τ.οὐ. (Matt. 19.12)

ζητεῖν τὴν β. αὐτοῦ (God's: Matt. 6.33 par. Luke 12.31)

αἱ κλεῖδες τῆς β.τ.οὐ. (Matt. 16.19)

κλείειν τὴν β.τ.οὐ. (Matt. 23.13)

οὐ μακρὰν εἶναι ἀπὸ τῆς β.τ.ϑ. (Mark 12.34)

μέγας (Matt. 5.19), μείζων (18.1, 4), μικρότερος (11.11) ἐν τῇ β.τ.οὐ.

τὸ μυστήριον τῆς β.τ.ϑ. (Mark 4.11 par.)

ὁμοιοῦν τὴν β.τ.ϑ., ὁμοία ἐστιν ἡ β.τ.ϑ. (Mark 4.26, 30 par.; Matt. 13.33 par. Luke 13.20 and eight special instances in Matthew: see p. 31)

[1] The phrase has no analogy in the Old Testament nor in Jewish literature, cf. M. Burrows, 'Thy Kingdom Come', *JBL* 74, 1955, 1–8. For the only comparable passage, Micah 4.8 ('. . . the former dominion shall come, the kingdom to the daughter of Jerusalem'), together with the paraphrase in the Targum ('. . . to you [the Messiah] will the kingdom come') does not speak of the reign of God, but of the reign of Jerusalem, or the Messiah. Furthermore, it should be noted that both in the original text and in the Targum the 'coming' is bound up with the preposition *lᵉ*; i.e. it is said that the reign will 'be granted to' Jerusalem or the Messiah, whereas when Jesus speaks of the 'coming' of the reign of God, he says that it will be revealed. (The difference can be made clear by a comparison between Rev. 11.15 ἐγένετο ἡ βασιλεία . . . τοῦ κυρίου ἡμῶν and Luke 19.11 μέλλει ἡ βασιλεία ἀποφαίνεσθαι.) The fact that in Luke 17.20a the Pharisees ask πότε ἔρχεται ἡ βασιλεία τοῦ θεοῦ; might be claimed as better evidence that Judaism spoke of the coming of the reign of God, but in view of v. 20b we have to ask whether in this case a formula from Jesus has not been placed on their lips. Mark 11.10 (εὐλογημένη ἡ ἐρχομένη βασιλεία τοῦ πατρὸς ἡμῶν Δαυίδ) is a secondary explanation of the preceding quotation from the psalms (118.25f.); moreover, it speaks of the reign of David, not that of God. In the absence of any other evidence, it is of decisive importance to note that, as shown by the Kaddish (*yamlēk* [*v.l. yimlōk*] *malkūtēh*; text in Dalman, *Worte Jesu*[1], 305, n.3, unfortunately not repeated in the second edition), Palestinian Judaism did not speak of the 'coming' but of the 'reigning' of the reign of God.

προάγειν εἰς τὴν β.τ.ϑ.   (Matt. 21.31)
ἔφϑασεν ἐφ᾿ ὑμᾶς ἡ β.τ.ϑ.   (Matt. 12.28 par. Luke 11.20)

consequi regna caelestia (agraphon in Tertullian, De baptismo 20.2).[1]

Despite the lack of exact Jewish parallels, the following instances have not been included in the list given above:

(a) all phrases for which there are secular parallels (e.g. οἱ υἱοὶ τῆς β. Matt. 8.12; 13.38; cf. bᵉnē malkūtā Targ. Qoh. 5.8; εὔϑετος εἶναι τῇ β.τ.ϑ. Luke 9.62, cf. kāšer lᵉmalkūt Mek. Ex. on 12.1, Venice 1545, 2b 5);

(b) ἀνακλίνεσϑαι ἐν τῇ β.τ.οὐ. (Matt. 8.11 par.) and πίνειν ἐν τῇ β.τ.ϑ. (Mark 14.25 par.), because in Luke 14.15 the related phrase φάγεται ἄρτον ἐν τῇ β.τ.ϑ. appears on the lips of a table-companion of Jesus;

(c) phrases added by Matthew and Luke to the sayings of Jesus in their version of Mark, which are therefore redactional: e.g. ὁ λόγος τῆς β. (Matt. 13.19 contrast Mark 4.15); τὸ εὐαγγέλιον τῆς β. (Matt. 24.14 contrast Mark 13.10); εὐαγγελίζεσϑαι τὴν β. (Luke 4.43 contrast Mark 1.38); to these should be added on grounds of language[2] and content the passive εὐαγγελίζεται ἡ β.τ.ϑ. (Luke 16.16 contrast Matt. 11.12); διαγγέλειν τὴν β.τ.ϑ. (Luke 9.60 contrast Matt. 8.22) and μαϑητεύεσϑαι τῇ β.τ.οὐ. (Matt. 13.52).

The early church hardly had a share in the proceeʃ of the creation of the new language which is reflected in this list. The phrases about the βασιλεία which it coined are of a different kind; they represent a secondary transformation of eschatological terminology into missionary language;[3] furthermore, the term 'reign of God' becomes less frequent outside the synoptic tradition of the sayings of Jesus. It is already rare in Paul, and it occurs only twice in the Gospel of John (3.3, 5).[4] This power to create new eschatological language, which shows its effect in the numerous new phrases of our list, thus comes from Jesus himself. It is, of course, no coincidence that this process of new creation is concentrated on the βασιλεία; we shall see later that

---

[1] See Jeremias, Unknown Sayings of Jesus, London ²1964, 73–75.

[2] Cf. Dalman, Words of Jesus, 104f., 140.

[3] διαγγέλειν τὴν β.τ.ϑ. (Luke 9.60); διαμαρτύρεσϑαι τὴν β.τ.ϑ. (Acts 28.23); εὐαγγελίζεσϑαι τὴν β.τ.ϑ. (Luke 4.43; 8.1) or περὶ τῆς β.τ.ϑ. (Acts 8.12); εὐαγγελίζεται ἡ β.τ.ϑ. (Luke 16.16); τὸ εὐαγγέλιον τῆς β. (Matt. 4.23; 9.35; 24.14); κηρύσσειν τὴν β. (Acts 20.25); τοῦ ϑεοῦ Luke 9.2; Acts 28.31); λαλεῖν περὶ τῆς β.τ.ϑ. (Luke 9.11); λέγειν τὰ περὶ τῆς β.τ.ϑ. (Acts 1.3); ὁ λόγος τῆς β. (Matt. 13.19); μαϑητεύεσϑαι τῇ β.τ.οὐ. (Matt. 13.52); πείϑειν περὶ τῆς β.τ.ϑ. (Acts 19.8); συνεργοὶ εἰς τὴν β.τ.ϑ. (Col. 4.11); οἱ υἱοὶ τῆς β. (Matt. 13.38, given a Christian form in comparison with 8.12).

[4] Outside the gospels there are only ten instances in the whole of the Pauline corpus of letters, eight in Acts, one each in Hebrews and James and two in Revelation.

Jesus not only made the term the central theme of his proclamation, but in addition filled it with a new content which is without analogy (see below, pp. 103ff).

(iv) Amen

A new use of the word '*āmēn* emerges in the sayings of Jesus in the four gospels, which is without any parallel in the whole of Jewish literature and the rest of the New Testament.[1] The Hebrew word '*āmēn*, taken over by Aramaic, means 'certainly'.[2] It is a solemn formula with which already the Israelite of Old Testament times took up a doxology, an oath, a blessing, a curse or an execration.[3] Without exception it is used in answers assenting to the words of another, as also in I Cor. 14.16; II Cor. 1.20; Rev. 5.14; 7.12; 19.4; 22.20. In the gospels, on the other hand, '*āmēn* is used, also without exception, to introduce and to strengthen a person's own words; in this unprecedented usage it is strictly confined to the words of Jesus. This introductory '*āmēn* occurs there as follows:

Mark	13 times[4]
Logia common to Matthew and Luke	9 times[5]
Matthew only	9 times[6]
Luke only	3 times[7]
John (here always in the form '*āmēn*, '*āmēn*)	25 times[8]

[1] Jeremias, 'Characteristics', 112–115 = *Abba* 148–51.

[2] W. Baumgartner, *Hebräisches und aramäisches Lexikon zum Alten Testament*[3], Lieferung I, Leiden 1967, 62b.

[3] Dalman, *Words of Jesus*, 226–29; Billerbeck I 242–44; III 456–61.

[4] Mark 3.28; 8.12; 9.1, 41; 10.15, 29; 11.23; 12.43; 13.30; 14.9, 18, 25, 30.

[5] Matt. 5.18, 26; 8.10; 10.15; 11.11; 13.17; 18.13; 23.36; 24.47. ἀμήν does not occur in any of the nine passages in the Lucan version; in the Lucan version its place is taken by δέ (Luke 10.12, contrast Matt. 10.15), γάρ (Luke 10.24, contrast Matt. 13.17), ναί (Luke 11.51, contrast Matt. 23.36), ἀληθῶς (Luke 12.44, contrast Matt. 24.47); in the remaining five cases the ἀμήν is omitted in Luke without any replacement.

[6] Matt. 6.2, 5, 16; 10.23; 18.18; 21.31; 25.12, 40, 45; (also 18.19, as a variant).

[7] Luke 4.24; 12.37; 23.43.

[8] John 1.51; 3.3, 5, 11; 5.19, 24, 25; 6.26, 32, 47, 53; 8.34, 51, 58; 10.1, 7; 12.24; 13.16, 20, 21, 38; 14.12; 16.20, 23; 21.18. The duplication derives from Jewish liturgical usage; it is attested (only with '*āmēn* as a response!) in the Old Testament, in Qumran, in Pseudo-Philo, in the Talmud, in prayers, on inscriptions and in magical texts (cf. the instances in *TLZ* 83, 1958, col. 504).

The retention of this alien word shows how strongly the tradition felt that the way of speaking was new and unusual. An explanation of its meaning must start from the fact that in the words of Jesus 'āmēn is always followed by λέγω ὑμῖν (σοι). The only substantial analogy to ἀμὴν λέγω ὑμῖν that can be produced is the messenger-formula 'Thus says the Lord',[1] which is used by the prophets to show that their words are not their own wisdom, but a divine message. In a similar way, the ἀμὴν λέγω ὑμῖν that introduces the sayings of Jesus expresses his authority. The novelty of the usage, the way in which it is strictly confined to the sayings of Jesus, and the unanimous testimony by all the strata of tradition in the gospels show that here we have the creation of a new expression by Jesus.[2]

(v) 'Abbā

The use of the everyday word 'abbā as a form of address to God is the most important linguistic innovation on the part of Jesus. It will be discussed at length in §7.

Not every single occurrence of the characteristic expressions mentioned in §2 and 3 is in itself a proof of authenticity. We must

[1] Manson, Teaching[2], 207.

[2] V. Hasler, Amen. Redaktionsgeschichtliche Untersuchung zur Einführungsformel der Herrenworte 'Wahrlich, ich sage euch', Zürich-Stuttgart 1969, puts forward the hypothesis that the formula 'Truly, I say to you' arose in the liturgy of the Hellenistic communities and was only secondarily placed on the lips of Jesus. He justifies his view with the assertion that even in Judaism 'āmēn had lost the character of a response and was used to strengthen a man's subsequent statement (p. 173). He attempts to demonstrate this from four Rabbinic texts and from Rev. 7.12; 22.20. The four Rabbinic texts are, however, really a single text with parallels (the second reference of which has been wrongly copied from Billerbeck I 243, while the two most important versions, of which Billerbeck gives the wording, are not mentioned), and this text says exactly the opposite to what Hasler reads out of it: it attests that 'āmēn has the character of a response. In Rev. 7.12 the 'āmēn is a response to the benediction in v. 10, and in Rev. 22.20b to the promise of Jesus' imminent return in v. 20a. That means that in the sphere of Judaism and the primitive Christian liturgy 'āmēn always and without exception has the character of a response; the new terminology of the gospels is without analogy. (In other respects, too, the work lacks the necessary care. On p. 173 the following should be noted: Neh. 5.13 is not a doxological conclusion; anyone who lists Tobit 14.15 as an instance of 'āmēn despite its doubtful authenticity ought also to include Judith 16.25; for Rev. 7.11 read Rev. 7.12; the reference Deut. 27.33 is wrong, as the chapter has only 26 verses; in n.148 all the Hexaplaric material is ignored – all this on one page!)

distinguish between *ipsissima vox* and *ipsissma verba*. The presence of a way of speaking preferred by Jesus (*ipsissima vox Jesu*) does not relieve us of the necessity of examining each individual instance to see whether we have a genuine *logion* (*ipsissimum verbum*). For example, to claim that the use of ἀμήν to introduce his own words is the *ipsissima vox Jesu* does not of itself imply that all twenty-five instances in John (see p. 35, n. 8 above) are *ipsissima verba*. The question of authenticity cannot, therefore, be settled in a purely schematic way on the basis of the linguistic and stylistic evidence. We must also consider the content of the sayings. Nevertheless, we can say in conclusion that the linguistic and stylistic evidence presented in §2–3 shows so much faithfulness and such respect towards the tradition of the sayings of Jesus that we are justified in drawing up the following principle of method: In the synoptic tradition it is the inauthenticity, and not the authenticity, of the sayings of Jesus that must be demonstrated.[1]

Appendix to I: THE SYNOPTIC PROBLEM

I do not intend to provide a full discussion of the synoptic problem here, but to show the reader quite briefly the view of synoptic literary criticism that has been presupposed in this work.

1. *Mark* writes the most primitive Greek. As far as content is concerned, too (e.g. in respect of christology, the censuring of the disciples, etc.), he is the least sophisticated of the evangelists. That indicates that his gospel is the earliest of the four canonical gospels. In addition, the observation of C. Lachmann (1835),[2] that Matthew and Luke go together in sequence only so far as they correspond with Mark and that on the other hand they diverge where they deviate from Mark, shows that Mark formed the basis of the other two synoptic gospels. The gospel did not arise from an arrangement of individual stories and individual *logia*, but from *complexes of tradition* which had developed out of teaching discourses (διδασκαλίαι).[3] It is immediately obvious that in Mark 4.1–34 we have a complex of tradition on the theme of 'parables', held together by the pre-Marcan connecting formula καὶ ἔλεγεν (vv. 9, 26, 30) and worked over by Mark;[4]

---

[1] Cf. C. Colpe, ὁ υἱὸς τοῦ ἀνθρώπου, *TWNT* VIII, 1965ff., 403–81: 437.13f.
[2] *De ordine narrationum in evangeliis synopticis*, ThStKr 8, 1835, 570ff.
[3] Papias in Eusebius, *HE* III 39.15.
[4] Jeremias, *Parables*[2], 13f.

similarly, 4.35–5.43 is characterized by the theme of 'miracle stories'. It can, however, also be shown, as I believe, that the *whole* of the Gospel of Mark consists of complexes of tradition, namely: 1.1–15; 1.16–39; 1.40–3.7a; 3.7b–19; 3.20–35; 4.1–34; 4.35–5.43; 6.1–32; 6.33–7.37; 8.1–26; 8.27–9.1; 9.2–29; 9.30–50; 10.1–31; 10.32–45; the passion narrative begins with 10.46 or 11.1 and the complexes of tradition in 12.1–44; 13.1–37 have been worked into it.[1] In these circumstances, the search for a systematic structure of the gospel is a lost labour of love.

2. The *Gospel of Matthew* is a version of Mark, revised in style and expanded by more than a half through the addition of new material. A majority today supports the two-source theory, according to which the first and third evangelists used a second source, the *Logia-source Q*, alongside the Gospel of Mark. In this form, however, the theory is an over-simplification, as can be seen simply from the fact that Luke did not come across the *logia* material in an independent setting; it had already been fused with the special Lucan material (see below, pp. 40f). In addition, there is doubt whether the *Logia-source Q* ever existed. Four considerations may be mentioned.

(i) What was once the main support of the Q hypothesis, the witness of Papias (Ματθαῖος μὲν οὖν 'Εβραΐδι διαλέκτῳ τὰ λόγια συνετάξατο)[2] can no longer bear the burden; it may be taken as proved that by τὰ λόγια Papias did not mean a collection of sayings of Jesus, but a gospel.[3]

(ii) The *logia* in Matthew and Luke differ quite considerably from each other; where we have translation variants or the probability of a bifurcation of the tradition in an Aramaic-speaking milieu (see p.7, n.2), a source common to Matthew and the Lucan material is excluded. It is true that about a fifth of the *logia* in Matthew and Luke show a word-for-word or almost word-for-word correspondence; but as H.-T. Wrege has shown,[4] in most cases this happens with particularly memorable material (metaphors, short parables, antithetic parallelisms), which could have found a fixed form even in oral tradition.

---

[1] For the demarcation of the passages, over which different views can be held in particular cases, see Jeremias, *Eucharistic Words*², 92 n.1.

[2] In Eusebius, *HE* III 39.16.

[3] This is already the way in which Irenaeus, *Adv.Haer.* III 1.1, understood Papias' note. Cf. J. Kürzinger, 'Das Papiaszeugnis und die Erstgestalt des Matthäusevangeliums', *BZ* 4, 1960, 19–38.

[4] H.-T. Wrege, *Die Überlieferungsgeschichte der Bergpredigt*, WUNT 9, Tübingen 1968.

(iii) The sequence of the *logia* diverges extremely widely, with the exception of one or two patterns which, however, need not point to a written source, but could equally well have developed in oral tradition (e.g. baptism – temptation; discourse of Jesus – centurion of Capernaum).[1]

(iv) It is most important to note that in numerous instances one and the same *logion* in Matthew and Luke can be found connected to its setting by a different linking word. Three examples may serve as an illustration of many: Matt. 5.15 is linked with its context backwards through the association of κρυβῆναι v.14/ὑπὸ τὸν μόδιον v.15, and forwards by the word λάμπει v.15/λαμψάτω v.16. On the other hand, the parallel Luke 11.33 is linked with v.34 by the word λύχνος. In Matt. 10.19f. the linking term is παραδῶσιν/v.17 παραδώσουσιν/v.21 παραδώσει, but in the parallel, Luke 12.11f., it is ἅγιον πνεῦμα v.12/v.10. In Matt. 7.22f. the linking term is κύριε, κύριε, v.21; in the parallel, Luke 13.26f., it is οὐκ οἶδα ὑμᾶς πόθεν ἐστέ v.25.[2] As the association by linking-word as a mnemonic aid points to oral tradition, we can see that already at that stage at least two branches had developed in the *logia* material, one of which was used by Matthew and the other by the Lucan source. This conclusion is important, because it does not allow the ascription of the differences in the versions of the *logia* in Matthew and Luke to the redactional work of the two evangelists without linguistic proof. Most of the differences developed much earlier in the course of the history of the tradition.[3]

3. A recognition of *Luke's* technique of working in blocks is basic to any understanding of the composition of his gospel: Marcan material (283 verses = $\frac{1}{4}$) and new material (553 verses = $\frac{2}{3}$)[4] alternate in blocks. The *Marcan material taken over by Luke* begins at Luke 4.31;[5] the first Marcan block consists of the section Luke 4.31–44.

---

[1] Cf. the survey of the sequence of Q passages in Matt. and Luke in H. Appel, *Einleitung in das Neue Testament*, Leipzig-Erlangen 1922, 251f., who is followed in technique and method in the list in Kümmel, *Introduction to the New Testament*, London and New York 1966, 51f. The differences between the two lists show that the evidence is often ambiguous.

[2] I have given further examples, which can be multiplied quite considerably, in 'Zur Hypothese einer schriftlichen Logienquelle Q', *ZNW* 29, 1930, 147–49 = *Abba*, 90–92.

[3] For Matthew's redaction see p. 307, n. 1.

[4] In this reckoning the passion narrative is included in the new material; the reason is given on p. 40.

[5] This important demonstration was made by B. H. Streeter, *The Four Gospels*[5], London 1936, 205ff. He showed that there is no case of dependence upon Mark in

Here Luke follows the second evangelist verse for verse. This fact is so important, that the reader is expressly requested to assure himself, by comparing Luke 4.31–44 with Mark 1.21–39, how the two texts run side by side almost like railway lines. This picture is repeated in the remaining five blocks of Marcan material: Luke 5.12–6.19; 8.4–9.50; 18.15–43; 19.29–38; 19.45–22.13. Luke has thoroughly worked over the Marcan material for style, he has omitted doublets and occasionally shifted a few words or a clause – but he has kept almost pedantically to the sequence of the Marcan pericopes. Only in two places does he diverge from the Marcan sequence: first, the two sections Mark 3.7–12 (the multitude coming to Jesus) and 13–19 (the call of the twelve) have changed places (compare Luke 6.12–16: the call of the twelve; 17–19: the coming of the multitude), because the sermon on the plain (6.20–49) follows better after the account of the concourse of the multitude. One cannot even speak of a transposition in the second deviation (Luke 8.19–21 = Mark 3.31–35), for here Luke merely adds a pericope which stood in Mark 3.20–35, a section omitted by him. That Luke resolutely follows the Marcan sequence must also determine our judgment on the passion narrative, Luke 22.14–24.53. Its sequence of pericopes diverges so widely from that in Mark that it must be included among the new material.[1]

Luke has also taken over the *new material*, in which the *logia*-matter (Q) and the special Lucan material had been fused together, in blocks: Luke 1.5–4.30; 5.1–11; 6.20–8.3; 9.51–18.14; 19.1–28, 39–44; 22.14–24.53. The most important literary characteristic of the new material can best be seen from the great block 9.51–18.14; it is completely free from Marcan influence. This is also true of the other blocks of new material. Only in the last block, the passion narrative (22.14–24.53), can it be asked in one or two places whether we have a common primitive Christian tradition or the influence of Mark.

This results in the following picture:

A. *New material*	B. *Marcan material*	
1. Luke 1.1–4.30	—	
2. —	Luke 4.31–44 =	Mark 1.21–39

Luke 1.5–4.30; the few verses in which Luke touches on Marcan material (Luke 3.3f., 16, 21f.; 4.1–2a) are cases either of a *logia* tradition or of common primitive Christian material.

[1] See J. Jeremias, 'Perikopen-Umstellungen bei Lukas?', *NTS* 4, 1957/58, 115–19 = *Abba*, 93–97.

3. Luke 5.1–11	—	
4. —	Luke 5.12–6.19 =	Mark 1.40–3.19
5. Luke 6.20–8.3	—	
6. —	Luke 8.4–9.50 =	Mark 4.1–25; 3.31–35; 4.35–6.44; 8.27–9.40
7. Luke 9.51–18.14	—	
8. —	Luke 18.15–43 =	Mark 10.13–52
9. Luke 19.1–28	—	
10. —	Luke 19.29–38 =	Mark 11.1–10
11. Luke 19.39–44	—	
12. —	Luke 19.45–22.13 =	Mark 11.15–14.16
13. Luke 22.14–24.53	—	

As we know the linguistic and stylistic characteristics of the evangelist Luke both from his revision of Mark and from the second part of the two-volume work, the Acts of the Apostles, we are in a position to distinguish redaction from tradition in the new material, too. The most important result of these investigations (only made possible by the recognition of Luke's technique of working in blocks and still not published) is that whereas Luke has made considerable stylistic changes in all the material that belongs to the framework, especially the introductions and endings to pericopes, he treats the words of Jesus with the greatest reverence and refrains from making greater alterations to them.

II

THE MISSION OF JESUS

THE PLACE at which one starts is of the utmost importance for any account of the proclamation of Jesus.

Until quite recently, Matt. 4.17 (ἀπὸ τότε ἤρξατο ὁ Ἰησοῦς κηρύσσειν καὶ λέγειν · μετανοεῖτε· ἤγγικεν γὰρ ἡ βασιλεία τῶν οὐρανῶν) has continually misled scholars into thinking that Jesus made his appearance with a call to repentance. But if it is a mistake to build an account of the proclamation of Jesus on a summary, it is even more so in the case of Matt. 4.17, as Matthew (and only Matthew!) also sums up the preaching of John the Baptist in exactly the same words (3.2). Moreover, it is questionable whether it is really the intention of Matt. 4.17 to put the preaching of repentance in first place, rather than the announcement of the nearness of the reign of God – note the γάρ! At any rate, that is what is clearly said in Mark 1.15, which underlies Matt. 4.17, and the Jesus-tradition as a whole bears witness to it. Fortunately, today this recognition has won almost universal acceptance.

But have we found the right starting-point if we begin with Jesus' announcement of the reign of God? Does that really take us to the beginning? Does this starting-point not forget something, the question how Jesus came to make an appearance and to proclaim the good news? There can be no doubt that something preceded the proclamation of the gospel by Jesus. The only question is whether we can come to any historical understanding of this first and most profound stage. Are we not up against that which cannot be described? At least, we can put our questions here only with the utmost caution and the utmost restraint. Nevertheless, we can make some very definite and clear statements which give us a clue to what comes *before* Jesus' appearance, to his mission.

§ 4 · JESUS AND JOHN THE BAPTIST

M. Dibelius, *Die urchristliche Überlieferung von Johannes dem Täufer*, Göttingen 1911; J. Jeremias, 'Der Ursprung der Johannestaufe', *ZNW* 28, 1929, 312–20; E. Lohmeyer, *Das Urchristentum*. 1. *Buch: Johannes der Täufer*, Göttingen 1932; W. H. Brownlee, 'John the Baptist in the New Light of Ancient Scrolls', *Interpretation* 9, 1955, 71–90 = in K. Stendahl (ed.), *The Scrolls and the New Testament*, New York 1957 = London 1958, 33–53, 252–256; C. H. H. Scobie, *John the Baptist*, London 1964; B. F. Meyer, 'Jesus and the Remnant of Israel', *JBL* 84, 1965, 123–30; H. Braun, *Qumran und das Neue Testament* II, Tübingen 1966, 1–29; W. Wink, *John the Baptist in the Gospel Tradition*, Society for New Testament Studies Monograph Series 7, Cambridge 1968.

(i) Jesus' relationship to John the Baptist

The appearance of Jesus was immediately preceded by the activity of John the Baptist. John was conscious of a mission to call men to repentance (Matt. 3.8 par.) in the last hour before the imminent divine judgment (3.10 par.) and to baptize those who did repent. Conjectures of a most varied kind have been made about the nature of John's baptism, but a satisfactory religious setting has yet to be found. It seems most probable that we should think of Essene influences. The very nearness of the place of baptism to Qumran makes the assumption of relationships between the two a likely one. As the rapid flow of the Jordan permits baptism to be carried out only at one of the few fords, and as Mark 1.5 ('Ιουδαία, 'Ιεροσολυμῖται) indicates a ford on the lower course of the Jordan, it is worth trusting a tradition which begins as early as Origen,[1] that Bethabara in Peraea (John 1.28) was situated at the ford of *hadšla*, south-east of Jericho, where the place of John's baptizing is still pointed out today.[2] From here to Qumran is less than eight miles as the crow flies.

To this close geographical proximity must be added the fact that, like John the Baptist, the Essenes issued a summons to repentance and that for their departure 'into the wilderness' they appealed to the very passage of scripture on which John based his activity on the Judaean steppes: Isa. 40.3.[3] However, the facts that the baptism of John

[1] *Commentary on John* 1.28 (GCS 10.149).

[2] G. Dalman, *Orte und Wege*[3], Gütersloh 1924, 97; see also the good maps in C. Kopp, *Die heiligen Stätten der Evangelien*, Regensburg 1959, 141.

[3] 1 QS 8.12–16; 9.19f.; Mark 1.3 par. It does not make any great difference that the Essenes take the words 'in the wilderness' with what follows ('in the wilder-

was only given once and was administered widely together rule out
the possibility of deriving it from the constantly repeated lustrations
of the people of Qumran. To answer the question what led John to
administer his baptism, we shall rather have to begin from the Jewish
doctrinal statement (which can be traced back to the beginning of the
first century AD) that on Sinai Israel was prepared for receiving
salvation by means of a bath of immersion (cf. I Cor. 10.1f.).[1]
According to a stereotyped apocalyptic pattern of thought, the
Israelites in the wilderness were regarded as a type of the eschatological community of salvation;[2] thus the tenet of their bath of immersion
included the expectation that in the end-time Israel would again be
prepared for salvation by a bath of immersion. John the Baptist may
have felt this purification of the people of God at the eschatological
hour to be his task. If so, he will have been guided by the prophecy of
Ezekiel that God would purify his people by water in the last days:

For I will take you from the nations, and gather you from all the countries, and
bring you into your own land. *I will sprinkle clean water upon you*, and you shall be
clean from all your uncleannesses, and from your idols I will cleanse you . . . . And
you . . . shall be my people, and I will be your God. And I will deliver you from
all your uncleannesses (36.24f., 28f.).

It is questionable whether the more immediate purpose of the
baptism of John can be read out of Mark 1.4 par. (εἰς ἄφεσιν ἁμαρτιῶν),
because this formulation could have been influenced by Christian
terminology (cf. especially Acts 2.38). In any case, Josephus expressly
disputes that the baptism of John had anything to do with the forgiveness of sins (*Antt.* 18.117), and perhaps this note should not be
put on one side as lightly as usually happens. At any rate, it is as well
to look for an answer to the question of the purpose of John's baptism
on the basis of another passage: Matt. 3.7 par. Luke 3.7. This provides information about the baptism which is quite unconsidered and
has to be read from between the lines. According to this passage,
John used baptism to gather those who were prepared to repent into

---

ness make ready the way') and the gospels take them with what precedes them
('one calls in the wilderness').

[1] Cf. ‡Jeremias, 'Johannestaufe', 314f.; *Infant Baptism in the First Four Centuries*,
London 1960, 31f.
[2] Billerbeck I 85. There are countless instances in the New Testament; cf. W.
Wiebe, *Die Wüstenzeit als Typus der messianischen Heilszeit*, Diss. theol. Göttingen
1939.

the eschatological people of God, to save them from condemnation at the last judgment.

John the Baptist's summons to repent, be baptized and be saved led to a great movement of repentance and revival. Crowds streamed from all sides to the place in the deserted Jordan valley where he baptized. The four gospels and Acts (1.22) agree in reporting that Jesus, too, undertook to be baptized (together with his mother and brothers, according to the Gospel of the Nazareans).[1] The fact that, as the sources show, this report was offensive to the early church on two grounds, suggests that it may well be trustworthy. First, Jesus' subordination of himself to John by allowing himself to be baptized by John was hard to accept (Matt. 3.14f.). Second, it was felt to be difficult that Jesus underwent a baptism 'for the forgiveness of sins'.[2] Such a scandalizing piece of information cannot have been invented. But after that, the sources go in different directions. From the synoptic gospels it seems as if the contact between Jesus and John was limited to the moment of his baptism. According to the Johannine account it was otherwise. John 1.26, 31 depicts Jesus as the unknown figure in a great crowd of John's followers, and then goes on to report that Jesus himself administered baptism alongside John (3.22–4.3).

This report cannot simply be pushed on one side with the observation that the synoptic gospels are silent about any administration of baptism by Jesus. On the contrary, a number of considerations suggest that it is trustworthy. First, we need only point out how offensive would have been the idea that Jesus worked as a 'Baptist' alongside John, thus putting himself on a level on which he would be regarded as John's rival (3.26); the qualification καίτοι γε Ἰησοῦς αὐτὸς οὐκ ἐβάπτιζεν ἀλλ' οἱ μαθηταὶ αὐτοῦ (John 4.2) is meant to free Jesus from this odium, but its language,[3] style,[4] and content show that it is an addition.[5] Second, the account in John 3.22–4.3 contains a number of features of some antiquity, e.g. the note in John 3.23, that John baptized ἐν Αἰνὼν ἐγγὺς τοῦ Σαλίμ (a place which can no longer be located), and the erratic block formed by the mysterious v. 25, which mentions a dispute between a Ἰουδαῖος and some of John's disciples over Jesus' activity in

[1] In Jerome, Contra Pelagium 3.2 (E. Klostermann, Apocrypha II³, KlT 8, Berlin 1929, 6).

[2] Gospel of the Nazareans, in Jerome, ibid.: Quid peccavi ut vadam et baptizer ab eo? For the subject at issue, cf. what is said on p. 44 above on Mark 1.4, on the one hand, and Matt. 3.7 par., on the other: Jesus has himself baptized in order to attach himself to the eschatological people of God.

[3] καίτοι and γέ (only here in the Fourth Gospel); absence of the article before Ἰησοῦς.

[4] Parenthesis.

[5] Presumably from the editor of the gospel, who in 21.24 distinguishes himself from its author (ὁ γράψας).

46   THE MISSION OF JESUS

baptizing, where the issue was purification. These individual details do not look as if they have been invented. Finally, it is easier to understand the quite remarkable fact that the primitive community began to baptize after Easter[1] if Jesus himself had already been active in administering baptism. However, at some point he must have given it up (this is the only explanation of the fact that none of the four gospels says anything about Jesus having baptized at a later stage of his ministry), and it is again remarkable that no reason is given us for the cessation.[2]

Be this as it may, we cannot by any means view the connection between Jesus and John the Baptist as only a fleeting one. It is easy to understand why the synoptic gospels compress the encounter of the two men into the moment of Jesus' baptism. The tradition avoided, as far as possible, anything that might look like an equation of Jesus with the Baptist or even a subordination of Jesus to him. Any reports of this kind were passed over or toned down.

(ii) Jesus' recognition of John the Baptist

Jesus acknowledged John the Baptist's mission with almost extravagant words. His baptism was 'from God' (Mark 11.30 par.). Ἦλθεν . . . ἐν ὁδῷ δικαιοσύνης (Matt. 21.32), a biblicism which means 'he brought the right way'.[3] He was 'more than a prophet', a super-prophet (Matt. 11.9 par. Luke 7.26), indeed he was 'the greatest of all men' (Matt. 11.11 par. Luke 7.28). This is also the place where the *logion* Matt. 11.12f. par. Luke 16.16 belongs; a word needs to be said about it.

Matt. 11.12f.

ἀπὸ δὲ τῶν ἡμερῶν Ἰωάννου
τοῦ βαπτιστοῦ ἕως ἄρτι ἡ βασιλεία
τῶν οὐρανῶν βιάζεται,
καὶ βιασταὶ ἁρπάζουσιν αὐτήν.
(13) πάντες γὰρ οἱ προφῆται
καὶ ὁ νόμος ἕως Ἰωάννου
ἐπροφήτευσαν.

Luke 16.16

ὁ νόμος καὶ οἱ προφῆται
μέχρι Ἰωάννου.
ἀπὸ τότε ἡ βασιλεία τοῦ θεοῦ
εὐαγγελίζεται καὶ πᾶς εἰς αὐτὴν
βιάζεται.

The phrase 'until John', which has been underlined in the Greek text, can be understood either inclusively or exclusively. If ἕως/μέχρι[4] is meant to be inclusive (i.e. 'The

---

[1] That Paul was baptized is clear from the basis of his own testimony (I Cor. 12.13; Rom. 6.3).
[2] Presumably occasioned by the arrest of John the Baptist.
[3] *bō' bᵉ* 'come with', i.e. 'bring'.
[4] Translation variants.

prophets and the law prophesied up to and including John'), then the Baptist still belongs to the time of the old aeon. This was Luke's understanding. For he keeps stressing in Acts that the time of salvation began after the death of John the Baptist (1.5; 10.37; 13.24f.; 19.4). On the other hand, the Matthaean tradition understood the ἕως/μέχρι exclusively, as the phrase ἀπὸ δὲ τῶν ἡμερῶν Ἰωάννου τοῦ βαπτιστοῦ (11.12) shows. This phrase, which is not a usual Greek way of speaking, is a Semitism, which came about because Semitic languages have no regular word for 'time' in a durative sense, and use the phrase 'the days of x' as an expedient for describing a lifetime, reign or period of activity. Ἀπὸ δὲ τῶν ἡμερῶν Ἰωάννου thus means 'from the time of the activity of John the Baptist'. That is to say that what is new has been at work from the time of John's ministry. We have a different evaluation of John, and indeed a different view of the history of salvation, depending on whether ἕως/μέχρι are understood inclusively or exclusively. According to Luke, who understands μέχρι inclusively, the Baptist still belongs to the period of the law and the prophets, and the period of salvation only begins with Jesus. According to Matthew, who understands ἕως exclusively, John the Baptist is already part of the new aeon, or introduces an intermediary period which forms the prelude to the new aeon.

The more difficult statement is without question that which sees the Baptist as the inaugurator of the new aeon. The early church had an understandable tendency to subordinate the Baptist to Jesus. Where he is set alongside Jesus, we always have a sign of ancient tradition. Matthew, whose text shows itself to be the earlier also on other grounds,[1] thus gives the right view; the time of prophecy reached only up to the appearance of John the Baptist. Fulfilment began already with him. This exegesis is also supported by Mark 11.9 par. Luke 7.26, where Jesus designates the Baptist a prophet; we shall see later[2] that the possession of the spirit which characterizes the prophet signalizes the dawn of the time of salvation.

This is the most astonishing remark that Jesus made about John the Baptist: he introduced the time of salvation. All the sayings that betray such a high estimate of the Baptist are certainly authentic. The early church, which had to compete with communities of followers of John the Baptist, did not invent anything of this kind.

(iii) The influence of John the Baptist on Jesus

Jesus followed the Baptist in many ways. According to John 1.35–39 he took over his first disciples from John. The Johannine description of the call of the first disciples diverges completely from that in the synoptics (Mark 1.16–20), but the report that Jesus' first disciples were adherents of John the Baptist has considerable intrinsic

---

[1] Luke (16.16) has removed the synonymous parallelism βιάζεται/βιασταί (Matt. 11.12) with the help of his favourite phrase ἡ βασιλεία τοῦ θεοῦ εὐαγγελίζεται, and produced the correct sequence νόμος-προφῆται.

[2] See below, pp. 82ff.

probability, especially as something similar is presupposed by Acts in the account of the restoration of the group of twelve (1.21f.).

Jesus also followed John in the way in which he made his appearance. Like John, Jesus also preached out of doors, unlike the scribes of his time; like John, he gave his disciples a prayer to characterize them as a group and to keep them together (Luke 11.1–4).[1] Above all, however, Jesus' proclamation followed that of the Baptist. Like John, Jesus issued a summons to repentance (Matt. 3.8 par./Luke 13.1–9, etc.). Like John, he gave this call to repentance an urgent and inexorable character by destroying any trust in the prerogative of Israel and announcing the imminent divine judgment as a judgment not on the Gentiles, but on Israel (Matt. 3.7 par./12.41f. par.). Like John, he went so far in rejecting any national or political expectation that he threatened that God would give Israel's place to the Gentiles, who would stream in, if Israel refused to repent (Matt. 3.9 par./8.11f. par.). It is of particular importance that we are told that John himself rejected the self-righteous (Matt. 3.7–10 par./Matt. 23 par.) and accepted notorious sinners (Luke 3.12/Mark 2.16). He gathered together the holy remnant, but not, like the Pharisees and Essenes, as a separatist remnant. His was an 'open remnant',[2] which he opened – according to reports which sound trustworthy – even to publicans, police agents[3] and prostitutes who were willing to repent (Luke 3.12–14; 7.29; Matt. 21.32); that is, to people who had been written off by the synagogue, the Pharisaic conventicles and Qumran.[4]

Does all this perhaps give us the decisive stimulus towards the appearance of Jesus – that Jesus continued the work of the murdered messenger of God? The answer must be no. For much as Jesus has in common with John, and though he certainly saw in the Baptist the

[1] J. Jeremias, 'The Lord's Prayer in the Light of Recent Research', in: *The Prayers of Jesus*, SBT II 6, London 1967, 82–107.

[2] ‡Meyer, 123–30.

[3] P. Joüon, *L'Évangile de Notre-Seigneur Jésus-Christ*, Verbum Salutis 5, Paris 1930, 310f., has rightly concluded from the admonitions in v.14b that στρατευόμενοι in Luke 3.14 (in contrast to στρατιῶται) refers to the police who accompanied the tax-collectors. They would therefore have been Jews.

[4] For the question of authenticity see H. Sahlin, 'Die Früchte der Umkehr', *Studia Theologica* I, 1947, 54–68. Note, too, the quite different orientation of the two mentions of publicans in Luke 3.12f. and 19.1–10: in the pericope about John the Baptist the publicans are confronted with God's demand; the Zacchaeus pericope depicts the reaction of the publican to the experience of the goodness of Jesus that overwhelms him.

intermediary between the old aeon and the new, there is a fundamental difference between John and Jesus (which according to Matt. 11.18f. par. Luke 7.33f. was felt very clearly by people of the time who maintained that John was an *ascetic*, while Jesus was *open to the world*). John proclaimed, '*Judgment* is at hand, repent!'. Jesus proclaimed, 'The *kingly reign of God* is dawning; come, you who are troubled and overburdened!'.[1] John the Baptist remains within the framework of *expectation*; Jesus claims to bring *fulfilment*. John still belongs in the realm of the *law*; with Jesus, the *gospel* begins.[2] Therefore the smallest in the *basileia* is greater than John (Matt. 11.11b par. Luke 7.28b).

Here is the gulf which separates the two men, despite all the affinities between them. The consequence of it was that the movements begun by Jesus and John ran side by side as rivals. This gulf rules out the possibility of seeing the activity of John as the decisive stimulus towards the appearance of Jesus.

§ 5 · THE CALL OF JESUS

A. von Harnack, 'Zur Textkritik und Christologie der Schriften des Johannes. Zugleich ein Beitrag zur Würdigung der ältesten lateinischen Überlieferung und der Vulgata', *Sitzungsberichte der Preussischen Akademie* 1915, 534–573 = A. von Harnack, *Studien zur Geschichte des Neuen Testaments und der Alten Kirche I*, AKG 19, Berlin-Leipzig 1931, 105–152; H. Sahlin, *Studien zum dritten Kapitel des Lukasevangeliums*, Uppsala Universitets Aarsskrift 1949, 2, Uppsala-Leipzig 1949; A. Vögtle, 'Exegetische Erwägungen über das Wissen und Selbstbewusstsein Jesu', *Gott in Welt. Festgabe für Karl Rahner*, Bd. I, Freiburg-Basel-Wien 1964, 608–667.

Jesus experienced his call when he underwent John's baptism, in order to take his place among the eschatological people of God that the Baptist was assembling.[3]

(i) *The Sources*

A five fold tradition records Jesus' baptism: first, Mark 1.9–11 and Matt. 3.13–17, which is dependent on it; second, a related tradition

[1] Rightly recognized in the tradition reproduced by Justin, *Dial.* 51.2f.: Ἰωάννης . . . βοῶν τοῖς ἀνθρώποις μετανοεῖν, καὶ Χριστὸς . . . ἔπαυσέ τε αὐτὸν . . . λέγων ὅτι ἐγγύς ἐστιν ἡ βασιλεία τῶν οὐρανῶν.
[2] Cf. further p. 177.
[3] See above, pp. 44f.

in Luke 3.21f. which is, however, in all probability an independent literary form;[1] third, John the Baptist's account in John 1.32–34; fourth, the secondary, but independent account in 'the gospel composed in the Hebrew tongue which the Nazaraeans read'.[2] Fifth, two passages from the Testaments of the Twelve Patriarchs, which in all probability make use of ancient Jewish-Christian tradition about the baptism of Jesus, have points of contact with these accounts. The first occurs in the Testament of Levi 18.6f., where the call of the messianic high priest of the end-time is depicted in the following words:

The heavens shall be opened,
And from the temple of glory shall come upon him sanctification,
With the Father's voice as from Abraham to Isaac.
And the glory of the Most High shall be uttered over him,
And the spirit of understanding and sanctification shall rest upon him in the water.

The Testament of Judah 24.2f. speaks of the Messiah in similar terms:

And the heavens shall be opened unto him,
To pour out the spirit, the blessing of the Holy Father;
And He shall pour out the spirit of grace upon you;
And ye shall be unto Him sons in truth.[3]

---

[1] As we have seen, in the Gospel of Luke, the special source and the Marcan material alternate in blocks. The account of the baptism of Jesus belongs to the block 1.1–4.30, which is independent of Mark, see above, p. 39, n.4.

[2] In Jerome, *Comm. in Isa.* 11.2 (E. Klostermann, *Apocrypha* II[3], KlT 8, Berlin 1929, 6): *Factum est autem, cum ascendisset dominus de aqua, descendit fons omnis spiritus sancti et requievit super eum et dixit illi: Fili mi, in omnibus prophetis expectabam te, ut venires et requiescerem in te. Tu es enim requies mea, tu es filius meus primogenitus, qui regnas in sempiternum.* The account in the Gospel of the Ebionites, on the other hand, is a worthless conglomeration of the three synoptic gospels (in Epiphanius, *Haer.* XXX 13.7f. [GCS 25, 350f.; Hennecke-Schneemelcher-Wilson I 157f.]).

[3] There is no need to go into recent discussion about the age and provenance of the Testaments here. It is at least certain that they contain Jewish-Christian as well as Jewish (including Qumran) traditions, and that the final redaction by which they reached their present form took place in a Greek-speaking milieu. The variety of echoes of the New Testament, which extend throughout the context, make it probable that the two passages quoted have been influenced by Jewish Christianity. I would differ from R. H. Charles, *The Greek Versions of the Testaments of the Twelve Patriarchs*, Oxford 1908 = Hildesheim/Darmstadt 1960, an edition which has not been surpassed for the completeness of its presentation of the material, over the restoration of the extremely illegible text. The best strand of tradition is not manuscript group α, but β (best witness: *b*). However, the differences between the manuscripts in the two passages quoted here are only small. Cf.

All the texts agree in reporting two things: the descent of the spirit and a proclamation associated with it.[1]

(ii) The baptism of Jesus

The conventional idea of Jesus' baptism is of his standing in front of John the Baptist while John pours water over his head from his hand or from some vessel. This idea is hardly appropriate. In the first place, the corresponding Aramaic to the Greek passive βαπτισθῆναι (Mark 1.9 par. Matt. 3.16; Luke 3.21) is the intransitive active qal ṭᵉbal, which means 'undergo immersion, immerse oneself', rather than 'be baptized'.[2] Thus ἐβαπτίσθη in Mark 1.9 goes back to a tradition which implied that Jesus 'immersed himself'. This idea is also present in Luke 3.7 D it, where it is said that those who were baptized immersed themselves ἐνώπιον αὐτοῦ, 'in the presence' of the Baptist. Accordingly, John the Baptist had the function of a witness, as in proselyte baptism. Secondly, it is illegitimate to picture Jesus' baptism as an act which took place between him and John in private. Luke will be nearer the truth (ἐγένετο δὲ ἐν τῷ βαπτισθῆναι ἅπαντα τὸν λαὸν καὶ Ἰησοῦ βαπτισθέντος 3.21) in depicting Jesus' baptism as part of a collective baptism.[3] Jesus stood among the people, who immersed themselves in the Jordan at a sign or a call from John, as one who did not distinguish himself from those who were being baptized with him (John 1.26, 31).

We are told that at Jesus' baptism *the spirit of God descended upon him*. All the accounts agree on this statement. The individual details which go further may well be elaborations.

Luke mentions that Jesus prayed at his baptism (3.22), but the early Christian rite of baptism may have exerted some influence here. The synoptic gospels and the Testaments of the Twelve Patriarchs make an opening of the heavens precede the descent of the spirit, and later traditions speak of a sudden blaze of light[4] or

---

M. de Jonge, *Testamenta XII Patriarcharum edited according to Cambridge University Library MS Ff* 1.24 *fol.* 203a–262b, Pseudepigrapha Veteris Testamenti Graece 1, Leiden 1964, and the review of it by C. Burchard, *Revue de Qumran* 5, 1964–66, 281–84.

[1] In Test. Judah 24.2f., the proclamation is concealed behind the sentence: 'You will be sons to him in truth'.
[2] J. Wellhausen, *Das Evangelium Marci*[2], Berlin 1909, 4; ‡Sahlin, 130–33.
[3] ‡Sahlin, 62.
[4] Gospel of the Ebionites in Epiphanius, Haer. XXX 13.7 (GCS 25, 351;

fire,[1] but these are illustrative clarifications: God opens the closed doors of heaven to reveal his glory. The phrase 'like a dove' (Mark 1.10 par.) also represents an attempt at clarification. It is quite remarkable, because the comparison of the spirit with a dove is quite unknown to early Judaism.[2] The strangest parallels from the history of religion have been adduced in attempts at explanation.[3] All these theories presuppose that the spirit is imagined as a dove. In reality, however, the ὡς περιστερά (Mark 1.10) was originally quite a simple comparison, like that, for example, in Luke 22.44: καὶ ἐγένετο ὁ ἱδρὼς αὐτοῦ ὡσεὶ θρόμβοι αἵματος καταβαίνοντες ἐπὶ τὴν γῆν. The latter does not, of course, mean that Jesus' sweat turned into blood, but that it broke out so intensively that it fell to the ground like drops of blood in quick succession. Similarly, ὡς περιστερά did not originally mean that the spirit became a dove or appeared in the form of a dove, but that it descended with a gentle sound 'like a dove'. An identification of the spirit and the dove came about only at a secondary stage (it is clearest in Luke 3.22: σωματικῷ εἴδει); it follows a more material idea of the pneuma which can also be observed elsewhere in the Hellenistic milieu. Finally, we will also have elaboration when the Fourth Gospel (1.32) and the Gospel of the Nazareans emphasize the unique significance of the event by stressing (on the basis of Isa. 11.2) that the spirit 'remained' on Jesus (ἔμεινεν ἐπ'αὐτόν, requievit).[4] The Gospel of the Nazareans (see p. 50, n.2) makes this additionally clear by the motif of the restless spirit of God which looked in vain for a resting place in one prophet after another until it found it in Jesus: tu enim es requies mea.

In the Judaism of the time, the imparting of the spirit almost always means prophetic inspiration:[5] a man is grasped by God, who authorizes him to be his messenger and preacher and speaks through him. Thus when it is said that the spirit descends on Jesus, the meaning is that Jesus is called in this way to be God's messenger. However,

---

Hennecke-Schneemelcher-Wilson I, 157f.); further instances are given by W. Bauer, *Das Leben Jesu im Zeitalter der neutestamentlichen Apokryphen*, Tübingen 1909 (= Darmstadt 1967), 134–37.

[1] Justin, *Dial.* 88.3.
[2] Billerbeck I 125.
[3] As in folk-tales the choice of a king is occasionally decided by a bird which chooses the rightful claimant, the dove is said to bring about the choice of Jesus as king. Or: as the dove is the sacred bird of Ishtar and Atargatis, the goddess is said to choose a man as her son (Mark 1.11 par. υἱός) or her lover (Mark 1.11 par. ἀγαπητός) by means of her holy creature. Bultmann, *Synoptic Tradition*, 249f., has said all that is necessary about these fantastic combinations. But he himself has to resort to Persia to explain the dove, where there is evidence of the dove as a figure for the power of God that fills the king (p. 250), because he, too, equates spirit and dove.
[4] See also Test. Levi 18.7: 'the spirit of understanding and sanctification will rest on him'.
[5] Billerbeck II 127–38.

as we shall see later,[1] there is a fundamental difference between the call of Jesus and that of the Old Testament prophets. The return of the spirit that had been quenched gives the event its eschatological character.

The eschatological significance of the baptism of Jesus is expressed particularly clearly in the two passages from the Testaments of the Twelve Patriarchs quoted above on p. 50: the opening of the heavens, the revelation of holiness from the temple of glory, the heavenly voice of the Father, the uttering of the glory of the Most High, the pouring out of the spirit of grace, understanding and sanctification and the 'resting' after its descent, the gift of sonship – all this is a many-sided periphrasis for the fullness of the eschatological gifts of God and the dawn of the time of salvation.

The second statement on which all the accounts are agreed is that the descent of the spirit was followed by a *proclamation*. Here again, the accounts differ over the details. According to the synoptic gospels, the proclamation was made by a heavenly voice; according to the Gospel of the Nazareans (see p. 50, n.2) it was made by the spirit, and according to the Fourth Gospel by John the Baptist. According to Mark, Luke and the Gospel of the Nazareans it took the form of an address and was directed to Jesus; according to Matthew and the Gospel of the Ebionites it was made to John the Baptist, and according to the Fourth Gospel it was public. The most important difference, however, concerns the wording of the proclamation, or, more exactly, its relationship to scripture.

In the synoptic gospels (Mark 1.11; Matt. 3.17; Luke 3.22: σὺ εἶ [Matt. οὗτός ἐστιν] ὁ υἱός μου ὁ ἀγαπητός, ἐν σοὶ [Matt.: ᾧ] εὐδόκησα), we seem to have a composite quotation consisting of Ps. 2.7 ('*You are my son*, today I have begotten you') and Isa. 42.1 ('Behold my servant, whom I uphold, my chosen, *in whom I delight*').[2] In John (1.34) the wording in the manuscripts fluctuates between οὗτός ἐστιν ὁ υἱός τοῦ θεοῦ[3] and οὗτός ἐστιν ὁ ἐκλεκτὸς τοῦ θεοῦ.[4] The testimony to the second reading is certainly considerably weaker, but the reading is attested by very early (𝔭5 vid sa ℵ*), if not the earliest (a b e ff.2 sysin cur), witnesses in Egypt, in Syria and in the west. Not only does antiquity give considerable weight to the reading

---

[1] See below, pp. 82ff.

[2] The western text of Luke 3.22 (D it Just Cl Or Hil) υἱός μου εἶ σύ, ἐγὼ σήμερον γεγέννηκά σε is a secondary assimilation to the wording of Ps. 2.7 LXX (cf. the assimilation of the Western text of Mark 15.34D par. Matt. 27.46D to Ps. 22.2 [Heb.]) and therefore has to be left out of account.

[3] 𝔭66 75 and most MSS.

[4] 𝔭5 vid ℵ* 77 218 b e ff2 sysin cur Ambr.; cf. ὁ ἐκλεκτὸς υἱός sa a ff2c (sypal).

οὗτός ἐστιν ὁ ἐκλεκτὸς τοῦ θεοῦ, but also the difficulty of its content. On the one hand, the title 'the elect of God' occurs only here in the Fourth Gospel, a fact which must have led to assimilation to the synoptic voice at the baptism (ὁ υἱός μου); on the other, as early as Justin,[1] the idea that Jesus was a man who was 'chosen' to be Messiah was regarded as an Ebionite heresy. This must have been a reason for deleting the offensive ἐκλεκτός. If the more difficult reading οὗτός ἐστιν ὁ ἐκλεκτὸς τοῦ θεοῦ may have been the older,[2] then according to the Gospel of John the proclamation at Jesus's baptism will have referred *exclusively* to Isa. 42.1. But if that is the case, it may possibly also have been true of the voice in the synoptic accounts of the baptism. This conclusion suggests itself if we compare their wording with Isa. 42.1:[3]

Mark 1.11 = *Luke* 3.22	*Isa.* 42.1 *acc.* to *Matt.* 12.18	*Isa.* 42.1 *acc.* to Θ (Q *sy*[h])
σὺ εἶ (Matt. οὗτός ἐστιν)	ἰδού	ἰδού
ὁ υἱός μου	ὁ παῖς μου	ὁ παῖς μου
	ὃν ᾑρέτισα	ἀντιλήψομαι αὐτοῦ
ὁ ἀγαπητός	ὁ ἀγαπητός μου	ὁ ἐκλεκτός μου
ἐν σοί (Matt. ᾧ) εὐδόκησα	ὃν εὐδόκησεν ἡ ψυχή μου	ὃν εὐδόκησεν ἡ ψυχή μου
(10: τὸ πνεῦμα καταβαῖνον)	θήσω τὸ πνεῦμά μου ἐπ'αὐτόν	Not preserved.

The three texts largely correspond: the only difference of any importance is: ὁ υἱός μου/ὁ παῖς μου. As παῖς is ambiguous ('servant', 'son'), and as the designation of Jesus as ὁ παῖς θεοῦ was avoided in a Hellenistic milieu from an early date,[4] it is reasonable to suppose that ὁ υἱός μου in the voice at the baptism represents the christological development of an original ὁ παῖς μου.

Thus we have to reckon with the possibility that the voice at the baptism in the synoptic account is not a composite quotation of Ps. 2.7 and Isa. 42.1, but is limited to Isa. 42.1, in the same way as perhaps John 1.34.[5] The conjecture that the proclamation refers to Isa. 42.1, and only to this passage, is given considerable support if we look at the continuation of Isa. 42.1. The immediate sequel is (cf. Matt. 12.18): θήσω τὸ πνεῦμά μου ἐπ'αὐτόν. This clause brings us directly into the situation depicted in the account of the baptism. At this point we must remember that in the Judaism of this period, when large parts of scripture were known off by heart, it was regularly the custom to quote only the beginning of a passage, even if

---

[1] *Dial.* 48.3; 49.1.

[2] Thus emphatically ‡von Harnack, 552–556 = 127–32.

[3] As Isa. 42.1 LXX differs in many ways from the Hebrew text, the translations of Isa. 42.1 by Matt. 12.18 and Theodotion have been presented for comparison.

[4] J. Jeremias, παῖς θεοῦ C-D, *TDNT* V, 1967, 700–704; revised version in: 'παῖς (θεοῦ) im Neuen Testament', *Abba*, 192–98.

[5] ‡Vögtle, 660f., concludes on the basis of other considerations that 'the voice from heaven may originally have had nothing to do with Ps. 2.7'. Further representatives of this view since Dalman, *Words of Jesus*, 277, are given in J. Jeremias, 'παῖς (θεοῦ) im Neuen Testament', *Abba* 193, n.350 and I. H. Marshall, 'Son of God or Servant of Yahweh? – A reconsideration of Mark 1.11', *NTS* 15, 1968/9, 327 n.3. Most recently, Flusser, *Jesus*, 28.

its continuation were kept in mind.[1] The voice from heaven in Mark 1.11/Luke 3.22 may be one such case of an abbreviated quotation. The really decisive clause from Isa. 42.1 : θήσω τὸ πνεῦμά μου ἐπ' αὐτόν does not appear in the quotation. Thus in all probability the proclamation means that what Isa. 42.1 promised, that God would lay his spirit on his servant, has just been fulfilled.

Now if the proclamation interprets the descent of the spirit as a fulfilment of Isa. 42.1, far-reaching consequences follow for understanding the story of the baptism of Jesus. First, it becomes clear that all the emphasis lies on the event of the communication of the spirit: the interpretation has only a subsidiary function. Second, it becomes clear that the proclamation originally had nothing to do with the enthronement of the king or adoption rites or anything like that; it does not take us into the realm of conceptions of the Messiah as king, but into that of scriptural statements about the servant of God.

(iii) The significance of Jesus' experience at his baptism

We saw on p. 45 above that there is no reason for doubting the historicity of the baptism of Jesus. Even the report that at his baptism Jesus had an experience which was determinative for his career has probability on its side. Such a view is supported by the fact that Jesus was close to John, yet adopted a fundamentally different position from him. This presupposes that some event opened up a gulf between the two men. The accounts of the baptism suggest that this event took place at Jesus' baptism.

If we attempt to make more precise what it was that Jesus experienced at his baptism, we might say that from that time he knew that he was in the grasp of the spirit. God was taking him into his service, equipping him and authorizing him to be his messenger and the inaugurator of the time of salvation. At his baptism, Jesus experienced his call.

According to Isa. 42.1, the spirit was to be given to God's elect, his servant. There is nothing to exclude the possibility that the thought of this passage, as it is expressed in the proclamation, occurred to Jesus and that from the time of the baptism he was conscious of being God's servant promised by Isaiah. We shall have to return to this point in §24.

Be that as it may, it is clear that Jesus attached supreme importance to the moment of his baptism. The puzzling and, by that token, early

[1] Rom. 3.4b is a New Testament example.

pericope Mark 11.27–33 par. is evidence of that. Jesus is asked about the basis of his authority. His counter-question, whether the baptism of John was or was not from God (v. 30) is hardly an evasion, a move by which Jesus seeks to avoid a direct answer. Now if his counter-question is meant seriously,[1] it means: 'My authority rests on John's baptism', and that again will mean in concrete terms: 'My authority rests on what happened when I was baptized by John'.

We were concerned with the starting point for our account of the message of Jesus. It is here: the call which Jesus experienced when he was baptized by John.

But perhaps we can say even more.

§ 6 · HANDING ON THE REVELATION

Dalman, *Words of Jesus*; W. L. Knox, *Some Hellenistic Elements in Primitive Christianity*, Schweich Lectures 1942, London 1944; F. Hahn, *Christologische Hoheitstitel*, FRLANT 83, Göttingen 1963, ²1964, 319–33 (there is an abridged ET, *The Titles of Jesus in Christology*, London 1969); Jeremias, 'Abba', in: *The Prayers of Jesus*, SBT II 6, 1967, 45–52 (what follows is closely related to this discussion); further literature in G. Schrenk – G. Quell, – G. Schrenk, πατήρ κτλ, *TDNT* V, 1967, 945–1014: 992f. (Schrenk).

A second passage which gives us some idea of what preceded Jesus' appearance on the scene is Matt. 11.27 par. Luke 10.22:

πάντα μοι παρεδόθη ὑπὸ τοῦ πατρός μου
καὶ οὐδεὶς ἐπιγινώσκει τὸν υἱὸν εἰ μὴ ὁ πατήρ,
οὐδὲ τὸν πατέρα τις ἐπιγινώσκει εἰ μὴ ὁ υἱὸς
καὶ ᾧ ἐὰν βούληται ὁ υἱὸς ἀποκαλύψαι.

(i) Matt. 11.27 (par. Luke 10.22): Is this a Hellenistic, Johannine revelation saying?

Karl von Hase, who was professor of church history at Jena, made the famous remark that this synoptic *logion* 'gives the impression of a thunderbolt fallen from the Johannine sky'.[2] Two things, above all, appeared Johannine: (a) the mutual knowledge, which seemed to be

[1] E. Lohmeyer, *Das Evangelium des Markus*, MeyerK 1.2, Göttingen 1937 = ¹⁷1967, 242.
[2] *Die Geschichte Jesu²*, Leipzig 1876, 422.

a technical term of Hellenistic mysticism, and (b) Jesus' designation of himself as ὁ υἱός, used absolutely. This absolute usage is characteristic of Johannine christology,[1] whereas there are only quite isolated instances before John.[2]

These objections have been repeated constantly. For a long time it was considered certain that Matt. 11.27 par. was a late product of Hellenistic Christianity. In the last four decades, however, the tide has begun to turn.[3]

In fact, the explicitly Semitic character of the saying, which is clear from both its language and style, tells against the description of it as a 'Hellenistic revelation saying'.[4] As far as the *vocabulary* is concerned, the un-Greek οὐδείς/εἰ μή or οὐδέ/εἰ μή corresponds to *lēt/'ēllā'*, which in Aramaic is a paraphrase for 'only'; the meaning 'reveal' for ἀποκαλύπτειν is also not Greek.[5] The only development in the direction of Greek is in the construction παρεδόθη ὑπό.[6] For *style*, it should first be noted that in structure, Matt. 11.27 par. is a four-line stanza which is exactly paralleled in Matt. 11.25f.: line 1 gives the theme; lines 2 and 3 elaborate it with parallel clauses (despite the formal parataxis, in each case the second line is subordinated to the third); line 4 brings an emphatic conclusion. In addition, Matt. 11.27 par. has asyndeton at the beginning; repetition of the verb in the second and third lines, which Greek taste found ugly (Luke therefore avoided it); and the replacement of the reciprocal pronoun, which is defective in Semitic languages, with the synthetic parallelism in lines 2 and 3 (see below).

Language, style and structure thus clearly assign the saying to a Semitic-speaking milieu. The two arguments for an allegedly Hellenistic, Johannine origin mentioned initially ('mystical' knowledge and the use of ὁ υἱός as a title) can be answered on linguistic grounds.

True, Hellenistic mysticism offers expressions for 'mystic' knowledge similar to (ἐπι)γινώσκειν used twice in the active, but so far no exact parallel has been demonstrated. There is, however, one in a Jewish milieu:

αὐτὸς οὐ γινώσκει με
καὶ ἐγὼ οὐ γινώσκω αὐτόν[7]

[1] Fifteen times in the gospels and eight in the epistles.

[2] First in Paul, but only once (I Cor. 15.28), then in Mark 13.32 par. Matt. 24.36, in the baptismal formula Matt. 28.19 and Heb. 1.8.

[3] English scholars, above all, have objected here: Manson, *Sayings*, 79: 'The passage is full of Semitic turns of phrase, and certainly Palestinian in origin'; *Teaching*[2], 109–12; ‡Knox, 7: 'If we reject it, it must be on the grounds of our general attitude to the person of Jesus, not on the ground that its form or language are 'hellenistic' in any intelligible sense.'

[4] So Bultmann, *Synoptic Tradition*, 166.

[5] A. Oepke, καλύπτω κτλ, *TDNT* III, 1965, 556–92: 566, 22f.

[6] Dalman, *Words of Jesus*, 284, n.1.

[7] Tobit 5.2 ℵ (noted by Dr. C. Burchard).

This sentence appears in a quite secular context: Tobias is to reclaim a sum of money left in trust by his father, and says that he cannot carry out the request because the man who has the money and he do not know each other. Thus it should be translated 'We do not know each other'. We may feel that 'He does not know me and I do not know him' is an extraordinarily roundabout way of saying this, but this way to express reciprocity is idiomatic in Semitic languages, for the simple reason that they have no reciprocal pronoun ('one another', 'mutual'). If the Semite wants to describe a reciprocal relationship, he must resort either to periphrases[1] or, as in this case, to repetition.[2] As G. Dalman recognized,[3] the monotony of the parallel lines

$$οὐδεὶς ἐπιγινώσκει τὸν υἱὸν εἰ μὴ ὁ πατήρ,$$
$$οὐδὲ τὸν πατέρα τις ἐπιγινώσκει εἰ μὴ ὁ υἱός,$$

is simply an oriental periphrasis for a mutual relationship: only father and son really know each other.

This recognition also puts a question-mark against the second argument in support of the view that this *logion* derives from a Johannine, Hellenistic milieu, namely, that ὁ υἱός is used as a title. Once again, attention must be drawn to a characteristic of Semitic languages: the Semite is fond of using the definite article in a generic sense in metaphors, similes and parables, as can be seen, e.g., in Mark 4.3–8.[4] If the article also originally had a generic sense in Matt. 11.27, lines 2 and 3 would have to be translated:

Only a father knows his son,
and only a son knows his father.

In other words, we would have here a quite general statement about human experience: only a father and a son really know each other. There is a completely analogous statement in John 5.19–20a, if C. H. Dodd is right. He believes that this passage is 'une parabole cachée', i.e., that it was originally an everyday metaphor of the son as his father's apprentice.[5] The absolute ὁ υἱός in such cases was only understood as a title at a later stage.

It would, in fact, be quite unparalleled if a Johannine *logion* had found its way into the synoptic corpus in the form of Matt. 11.27 par. Moreover, the fact that both ἐπιγινώσκειν (so Matthew) and

[1] E.g. ἕκαστος τῷ ἀδελφῷ αὐτοῦ 'one another', Matt. 18.35. Thus already Gen. 26.31; Ex. 25.20; 37.9.
[2] There are further instances of repetition to express a mutual relationship in Jeremias, *Prayers of Jesus*, 47. Also Gen. 45.14; Jub. 23.19; 1 QS 4.17; Fragment Targ. Ex. 15.2 (cod. Vat. 440, ed. M. Ginsburger, Berlin 1899, 83); Fragment Targ. Num. 21.15 (twice); Sanh. 3.1; Test. Napht. 7.3.
[3] *Words of Jesus*, 284.
[4] ὁ σπείρων 'a sower' (v. 3) etc. See Jeremias, *Parables*[2], 11, n.2.
[5] 'Une parabole cachée dans le quatrième Évangile', *RHPR* 24, 1962, 107–15; seen at the same time and evidently independently of Dodd by P. Gaechter, 'Zur Form von Joh 5, 19–30', in: J. Blinzler – O. Kuss – F. Mussner (eds.), *Neutestamentliche Aufsätze*, J. Schmid-Festschrift, Regensburg 1963, 65–68: 67.

ἀποκαλύπτειν are not Johannine words,[1] and that παραδιδόναι is never used with God as subject in John, tells against the presence of a *logion* of a Johannine character. On the other hand, we can easily see how Matt. 11.27 par. could have been an important stimulus to Johannine christology and its remarks about knowledge, once the absolute ὁ υἱός was taken as a title. Thus we may have here one of the *logia* of Jesus from which Johannine theology grew. Indeed, without such points of departure in the synoptic tradition it would be a complete puzzle how Johannine theology could have originated at all.

If, then, there is nothing against the authenticity of Matt. 11.27, the intrinsic connection it has with the way in which Jesus addressed God as *'Abbā*[2] is decisively in its favour.

(ii) The meaning of the logion Matt. 11.27 (par. Luke 10.22)

As we saw, Matt. 11.27 par. Luke 10.22 is a four-line stanza.[3] The first line introduces the theme: 'My Father has given me all things'. παραδιδόναι (*māsar/mᵉsar*) is a technical term for the transmission of doctrine, knowledge and holy lore.[4] Thus πάντα, like ταῦτα in v. 25, designates the mystery of revelation, and the first line means: 'My Father has given me a full revelation'.

Lines 2 and 3 elaborate the theme with a synthetic parallelism. It should be noted that although the form of the two lines is paratactic, their logic is hypotactic,[5] and that the definite article has a generic sense,[6] so we must translate:

Just as only a father (really) knows his son,
so only a son (really) knows his father.[7]

The final line, 'and any one to whom the son chooses to reveal him', suggests: because only a son really knows his father, he alone is in a position to pass this knowledge on to others.

---

[1] ἀποκαλύπτειν occurs in the Johannine writings only in the LXX quotation John 12.38 (Isa. 53.1), ἐπιγινώσκειν does not occur at all.

[2] See below, pp. 61ff.

[3] The Lucan version (10.22) betrays slight Greek influence through the omission of the verb in the third line, but it has not lost its four-line structure.

[4] Jeremias, *Eucharistic Words*[2], 101, 202.

[5] See above, p. 57.

[6] See above, p. 58.

[7] For the translation 'as . . . so' see John 10.15: καθὼς γινώσκει με ὁ πατήρ, κἀγὼ γινώσκω τὸν πατέρα.

Thus Jesus is explaining the communication of revelation (line 1) with the aid of a comparison between father and son (lines 2f.). This comparison also occurs elsewhere. 'Every secret did I (God) reveal to him (*Meṭaṭron*)[1] as a father.'[2] 'He (*Meṭaṭron*) said to me: "Come, I will show you the curtain of God which is drawn before the Holy One (blessed be He), on which all the generations of the world and all their doings . . . are woven." And . . . he showed me with the fingers of his hands – like a father who is teaching his son the letters of the Torah.'[3] Evidence that the father-son comparison is used in connection with the transmission of revelation before the Hebrew book of Enoch, which was edited in the fourth/fifth century AD, comes from John 5.19–20a, the metaphor of the son as a pupil, if it is taken in what was presumably its original sense:[4]

Truly, truly, I say to you: the (= a)[5] son can do nothing of his own accord, (but) only what he sees the father doing; for whatever he does, that the son does likewise. For the father loves the son, and initiates him into all that he himself is doing.

It was customary for the son to learn his father's craft. Many trades had their secret processes, which were carefully guarded, and into which the son was initiated by his father. In the same way, this metaphor of the pupil suggests, Jesus' Father has initiated him into the revelation.[6] Jesus explains his theme in exactly the same way in Matt. 11.27 par.: 'My Father has given me all things' (line 1) is developed by means of the father-son comparison (lines 2 and 3): 'Only father and son really know one another'. What Jesus wants to convey in the guise of an everyday simile is this: Just as a father talks to his son, just as he teaches him the letters of the Torah, just as he initiates him into the well-prepared secrets of his craft, just as he hides nothing from him and opens his heart to him as to no-one else, so God has granted me knowledge of himself.

The fourth line, 'and any one to whom the son chooses to reveal him', is the one that is stressed. It remains within the framework of everyday experience (because only a son really understands the intention and actions of his father, only he can make them under-

---

[1] The chief of the angels round God's throne.
[2] Hebrew Enoch 48C.7.
[3] Hebrew Enoch 45.1f. Ms E.
[4] See above, p. 58.
[5] *Ibid.*
[6] Cf. also Test. Levi 17.2: the anointed priest of the first Jubilee will 'speak with God as with his father'.

standable to others), and leaves the hearer to draw the consequences for Jesus' claim for his mission.

Matthew 11.27 is a central statement about the mission of Jesus. His Father has granted him the revelation of himself as completely as only a father can disclose himself to his son. Therefore only Jesus can pass on to others the real knowledge of God.

Jesus' awareness of his mission, his consciousness of being in a singular way the recipient and mediator of knowledge of God, is not expressed solely in Matt. 11.27 par. Despite fundamental differences in the message of the Teacher of Righteousness,[1] the latter's awareness of his mission provides an impressive analogy in a Palestinian setting.[2] This awareness has also found expression in many other places in the gospels, and particularly in *logia* whose lack of christological titles shows them to be ancient tradition: Mark 4.11 (the μυστήριον τῆς βασιλείας is disclosed to the disciples); Matt. 11.25 par. Luke 10.21 (Jesus possesses and teaches ταῦτα; God reveals it through him); Matt. 13.16f. par. Luke 10.23f. (the disciples can see and hear what has not been granted to prophets and righteous men [Luke: kings]); Matt. 5.17 (Jesus brings the final revelation);[3] Luke 15.1–7, 8–10, 11–32 (Jesus' actions reflect God's attitude to sinners),[4] etc.

We are not told when and where Jesus received this revelation in which God disclosed himself to him like a father to his son. The aorist παρεδόθη does, however, give us a hint. It suggests one particular occurrence. It is striking, because (as in e.g. John 5.19–20a) we would expect the present. Perhaps, therefore, we should take παρεδόθη to refer to Jesus' baptism.

Matthew 11.27 par. gives only a hint at the content of the revelation which was granted to Jesus. It lies in the word 'my Father'. At this point, we have to extend our enquiry further.

§ 7 · '*Abbā* AS AN ADDRESS TO GOD

Dalman, *Words of Jesus*; G. Kittel, ἀββᾶ, *TDNT* I, 1964, 5–6; W. Marchel, *Abba, Père! La prière du Christ et des chrétiens. Étude exégétique sur les origines et la signification de*

[1] G. Jeremias, *Lehrer der Gerechtigkeit*, 336–353, esp. 327f., 334–36.
[2] *Ibid.*, 319–336.
[3] See below, pp. 82ff.
[4] See below, p. 120.

l'invocation à la divinité comme père, avant et dans le Nouveau Testament, Analecta Biblica 19, Rome 1963; J. Jeremias, 'Abba', in: *The Prayers of Jesus*, SBT II 6, London 1967, 11–65.

(i) The sources

All five strata of tradition in our gospels (Mark, *logia* material, Matthaean special material, Lucan special material, John) are unanimous in affirming that Jesus addressed God as 'my Father'.[1] The instances are distributed as follows (parallels are only counted once):

Mark	1[2]
Material common to Matthew and Luke	3[3]
Additional instances in Luke only	2[4]
Additional instances in Matthew only	1[5]
John	9[6]

Not only do the five strata agree that Jesus used 'Father' as a form of address; it is also their unanimous witness that Jesus used this address in *all* his prayers. (The one exception is Mark 15.34 par. Matt. 27.46, the cry from the cross: 'My God, my God, why hast thou forsaken me?', and here Ps. 22.2 already provided the form of address.)[7] The essential point of this assertion is the unanimity of the tradition.

Quite apart from the question of the authenticity of individual prayers, this shows that 'Father' as an address to God was firmly rooted in the tradition about Jesus.

Furthermore, in the Gethsemane story Mark records that when Jesus addressed God as 'my Father', he used the Aramaic form *'Abbā*:[8] καὶ ἔλεγεν· 'Αββὰ ὁ πατήρ, πάντα δυνατά σοι · παρένεγκε τὸ ποτήριον τοῦτο ἀπ' ἐμοῦ (14.36).

[1] A distinction must be made between 'my Father' as an *address* to God and the *designation* of God as Father on the lips of Jesus (cf. ‡Jeremias, 35–59). This section is concerned only with the address.

[2] 14.36.

[3] Matt. 6.9 (par. Luke 11.2); 11.25f. (par. Luke 10.21, twice).

[4] 23.34, 46.

[5] 26.42.

[6] 11.41; 12.27f.; 17.1, 5, 11, 21, 24f.

[7] See above, p. 5, n.2.

[8] Accent on the closing syllable. In what follows, *'Abbā* is capitalized where it is an address to God, otherwise written lower case.

(ii) The uniqueness of 'Abbā as an address to God

Judaism had a great wealth of forms of address to God at its disposal. For example, the 'Prayer' (*T^ephilla*, later called the Eighteen Benedictions), which was already prayed three times a day in the New Testament period,[1] ends each benediction with a new form of address to God. In what is presumably its earliest form, the first benediction runs as follows:[2]

Blessed art thou, Yahweh,
God of Abraham, God of Isaac and God of Jacob (cf. Mark 12.26 par.),
the most high God,
Master[3] of heaven and earth (cf. Matt. 11.25 par.),
our shield and the shield of our fathers.
Blessed art thou, Yahweh, the shield of Abraham.

It can be seen here that one form of address to God is put after another. If we were to collect together all the forms of address that appear in early Jewish prayer literature, we would find ourselves with a very extensive list.

Nowhere, however, in the Old Testament do we find God addressed as 'Father'. The cry of despair *'ābīnū 'attā*[4] or *'ābī 'attā*[5] and the king's privilege of saying *'ābī 'attā* to God[6] certainly come very near to it, but they are statements and not addresses to God using the name 'Father'. In post-canonical Jewish literature there are isolated examples of the use of πάτερ as an address to God;[7] these, however, come from Diaspora Judaism, which is here following the influence of the Greek world. In Palestine, it is only in the early Christian period that we come across two prayers which use 'Father' as an address to God, both in the form *'ābīnū malkēnū*.[8] But it should be

---

[1] J. Jeremias, 'Daily Prayer in the Life of Jesus and the Primitive Church', *The Prayers of Jesus*, 66–81: 70–72.

[2] Following Dalman, *Worte Jesu*[1], Leipzig 1898, 299 (unfortunately not in the second edition). What are probably additions have been omitted.

[3] For this translation of *qōnē*, see Jeremias, 'Daily Prayer', 74, n.33.

[4] Isa. 63.16 (twice); 64.7.

[5] Jer. 3.4.

[6] Ps. 89.27, taken up in Sirach 51.10 (Hebrew).

[7] Sirach 23.1, 4 LXX; III Macc. 6.3, 8; Apocryphon Ezek. Fragm.3 (ed. K. Holl, in: *Gesammelte Aufsätze zur Kirchengeschichte II*, *Der Osten*, Tübingen 1928, 36); Wisdom 14.3.

[8] ‡Jeremias, 27–29; the prayers are the *'^ahābā rabbā* (the second of the two benedictions which introduced the *Sh^ema^c* in the morning and which probably

noted that these are liturgical prayers in which God is addressed as the Father of the community, that the language used is Hebrew, and that 'ābīnū is associated with malkēnū: the Father to whom the community calls is the heavenly king of the people of God. On the other hand, we look in vain for the personal address 'my Father'. It occurs for the first and only time in *Seder Eliyyahu Rabbah*, a writing which originated in Southern Italy about AD 974, in the form 'ābī šebbaššāmayīm (i.e. in Hebrew and with the addition of 'who art in heaven')[1] – the original text of Sirach 23.1, 4 to be inferred from a Hebrew paraphrase ran 'el 'ābī and therefore is to be translated 'God of my Father', and not 'God, my Father'.[2] That means that in the literature of Palestinian Judaism *no evidence has yet been found* of 'my Father' being used by an individual as an address to God. It first appears in the Middle Ages, in Southern Italy.

It is quite unusual that Jesus should have addressed God as 'my Father'; it is even more so that he should have used the Aramaic form *'Abbā*. True, the actual word has only been handed on in Mark 14.36 but two things suggest that Jesus used this *'Abbā* as an address to God elsewhere in his prayers. First, there is a remarkable variation of forms in the tradition of 'Father' as an address to God. On the one hand, we find the correct Greek vocative form πάτερ,[3] which Matthew provides with a personal pronoun πάτερ μου;[4] on the other hand, we find the nominative with the article (ὁ πατήρ) as a vocative.[5] It is particularly striking that we find πάτερ and the vocative ὁ πατήρ side by side in one and the same prayer (Matt. 11.25f. par. Luke 10.21). This remarkable variation points to an underlying *'abbā* which, in the time of Jesus, was used in colloquial language at the same time as an address, for the emphatic state ('the Father') and for the form with the first person suffix ('my, our Father').[6] Second, we learn from Rom.

even belonged to the ancient priestly liturgy of temple worship) and the New Year Litany (the basic elements of which are already attested by R. Akiba, died after AD 135).

[1] I have listed the instances *op. cit.*, 28, n.65.
[2] *Op. cit.*, 28f.
[3] Matt. 11.25 par. Luke 10.21a; Luke 11.2; 22.42; 23.34, 46; John 11.41; 12.27f.; 17.1, 5, 11, 24f.
[4] Matt. 26.39, 42.
[5] Mark 14.36; Matt. 11.26 par. Luke 10.21b (Rom. 8.15; Gal. 4.6). πατήρ without the article as a vocative, which has been transmitted by some witnesses at John 17.5, 11, 21, 24f., is an inner-Greek variation (vulgarism).
[6] ‡Jeremias, 59f.

8.15 and Gal. 4.6 that the cry 'Αββὰ ὁ πατήρ, uttered in the spirit, was widespread in the early church. Indeed, Paul presupposes that it is not only to be heard in his own congregations (Gal. 4.6) but that it also rings out as cry of prayer in congregations which he has not founded, like that in Rome (Rom. 8.15). The unusual character of this form of address (see below) shows that it is an echo of the prayer of Jesus. Thus we have every reason to suppose that an 'Abbā underlies every instance of πάτερ (μου) or ὁ πατήρ in his words of prayer.

There may be a few sparse instances of πάτερ as a form of address to God in the milieu of Hellenistic Judaism[1] – probably under Greek influence – but it can certainly be said that there is no instance of the use of 'Abbā as an address to God in all the extensive prayer-literature of Judaism, whether in liturgical or in private prayers.[2]

As we can learn from the Targum, Jews deliberately avoided applying the word 'abbā to God even outside prayers. In the three passages of the Old Testament where God is called 'ābī, the Targum twice renders the word ribbūnī ('my Lord') (Jer. 3.4, 19); only in the Targum on Ps. 89.27 did the translator feel himself compelled by the sense to translate 'ābī as 'abbā. Otherwise, 'abbā is applied to God elsewhere in the Targum only at Mal. 2.10 (Hebrew 'āb); here, too, the translator saw no other possible rendering in view of the content. Outside the Targum there is only a single passage in Rabbinic literature in which 'abbā is used with reference to God. It is a story which was told of Hanin ha-Nehba, famous for his prayers for rain, who lived about the end of the first century BC;

Hanin ha-Nehba was the son of the daughter of Onias the Circle-drawer.[3] When the world needed rain, our teachers used to send school-children to him, who seized the hem of his coat[4] and said to him, 'abbā, 'abbā, hab lan miṭrā ('Daddy,

---

[1] See above, p. 63, n.7.

[2] Nor can E. Haenchen, *Der Weg Jesu*, Berlin 1966, 492–94, n.7a produce any evidence. Neither of the two passages to which he refers contains 'Abbā as an address to God. His next remarks, 'It is quite clear that the form 'Abbā, which occurs only in Aramaic, is not to be found in the Mishnah (c. AD 200), which is written in pure Hebrew', betray an inadequate conception of Mishnah Hebrew. For the situation is precisely the opposite. The Hebrew form 'ābī does not stand for 'my father' in any passage in the Mishnah; without exception the Aramaic form 'abbā is used, more than fifty times. (All these passages are instances of secular usage; 'my father' does not occur at all in the Mishnah as an address to God or a designation of God.)

[3] See ‡Jeremias, 61.

[4] A gesture of urgent request, cf. Mark 5.27.

66 THE MISSION OF JESUS

daddy, give us rain!'). He said to Him (God): 'Master of the world, grant it for the sake of these who are not yet able to distinguish between an '*Abbā* who has the power to give rain and an '*abbā* who has not.'[1]

Ḥanin appeals to God's mercy by using the trustful "*abbā*, '*abbā*' which the school-children cry out to him and describes God – in contrast to himself – as the "*Abbā* who has the power to give rain'. The little story can be regarded as a prelude to Matt. 5.45, where God is described as the heavenly Father who grants the gift of rain without discrimination to both righteous and unrighteous – but it does not provide the missing Jewish example of '*Abbā* used as an address to God. For we must remember that Ḥanin does not in any way address God himself as '*Abbā*; his address is 'Master of the world'.

All this confronts us with a fact of fundamental importance. *We do not have a single example* of God being addressed as '*Abbā* in Judaism, but Jesus *always* addressed God in this way in his prayers. The only exception is the cry from the cross (Mark 15.34 par. Matt. 27.46), and the reason for that is its character as a quotation.

There is a linguistic explanation for the striking silence of the Jewish prayer literature. In origin, '*abbā* is a babbling sound, so it is not inflected and takes no suffix. 'When a child experiences the taste of wheat (i.e. when it is weaned), it learns to say '*abbā* and '*immā* (i.e. these are the first sounds that it prattles).'[2] Originally an exclamatory form, '*abbā* had gained considerable ground in Palestinian Aramaic even before the New Testament period. It suppressed the 'Imperial Aramaic' and biblical-Hebraic form of address '*ābī* all along the line, and even took its place in statements; in addition, it took the place of the emphatic '*ābā* and largely established itself as an expression for 'his father' and 'our father'.[3] By the time of Jesus, '*abbā* had long had a wider use than in the talk of small children. Even grown-up children, sons as well as daughters, now addressed their father as '*abbā*.[4] The story of Ḥanin ha-Neḥba (see above, pp. 65f.), which is set in pre-Christian times, is an example of the way in which older, respected people other than fathers might be addressed as '*abbā*. A newly-discovered Jewish-Christian source[5] says that it is a peculiarity of the

---

[1] b. Taan. 23b.
[2] b. Ber. 40a Bar. par. b. Sanh. 70b Bar.
[3] Instances are collected in ‡Jeremias, 58ff.
[4] ‡Jeremias, 58 n.32, 60 n.43.
[5] Worked over in ʿAbd el-Jabbār, *Erweis der Prophetenschaft unseres Herrn Mohammed*, preserved in Istanbul, Sammlung Shehid Ali Pasha, no.1575 (cf. S. Pines,

Hebrew language that 'son' can designate a true and upright slave and 'father' the lord and master.[1] The Midrash confirms this: 'as the disciples are called sons, so is the master called father'.[2] In the house of R. Gamaliel II (c. AD 90), even the slave Ṭabi was called ''abbā Ṭabi'.[3]

If we keep in mind this setting for 'abbā, it will be clear why Palestinian Judaism does not use 'abbā as a form of address to God. 'abbā was a children's word, used in everyday talk, an expression of courtesy. It would have seemed disrespectful, indeed unthinkable, to the sensibilities of Jesus' contemporaries to address God with this familiar word.[4]

Jesus dared to use 'Abbā as a form of address to God. This 'Abbā is the ipsissima vox Jesu.

(iii) The significance of 'Abbā as an address to God

The complete novelty and uniqueness of 'Abbā as an address to God in the prayers of Jesus shows that it expresses the heart of Jesus' relationship to God. He spoke to God as a child to its father: confidently and securely, and yet at the same time reverently and obediently.

At this point it is necessary to issue a warning against two possible misunderstandings. First, the fact that 'abbā was originally a child's exclamatory word has occasionally led to the mistaken assumption that Jesus adopted the language of a tiny child when he addressed God as 'Father'; even I myself believed this earlier. However, the discovery that even in the period before the New Testament, grown-up sons and daughters addressed their fathers as 'abbā, stands in the way of any such limitation. Secondly, the fact that the address 'Abbā expresses a consciousness of sonship should not mislead us into ascribing to Jesus himself in detail the 'Son of God' christology, e.g. the idea of pre-existence, which developed very early in

---

The Jewish Christians of the Early Centuries of Christianity According to a New Source, The Israel Academy of Sciences and Humanities, Proceedings, II no.13, Jerusalem 1966).

[1] f.55b–56a (according to Pines, The Jewish Christians, 8).
[2] Siphre Deut. 34 on 6.7.
[3] j. Nidd. 49b 42f. Bar.
[4] ‡Kittel, 5. E. Haenchen's objection against Kittel (Der Weg Jesu, 59 n.19), 'It is pure supposition that Jesus' way of expressing himself caused offence to his contemporaries', is not to the point, as is shown by what is said on p. 65 above about the terminology of the Targum; cf. also Taan. 3.8 (familiarity towards God which is expressed in childlike urgency deserves to be punished by the ban).

the primitive church. This over-interpretation of the address *'Abbā* is prohibited by the everyday sound of the word.

Jesus regarded *'Abbā* as a sacred word. When he instructs the disciples to 'Call no man your father on earth, for you have one Father, who is in heaven' (Matt. 23.9),[1] he certainly does not mean to prohibit them from addressing their physical fathers as 'father'. He is thinking, rather, of the custom of addressing distinguished people, especially older men, as *'abbā*. The disciples are not to do this, because that would be a misuse of the word. He wanted to reserve the honour of the name 'father' for God alone. This prohibition shows the degree to which Jesus felt that the address *'Abbā* should be revered.

'Abbā as a form of address to God expresses the ultimate mystery of the mission of Jesus. He was conscious of being authorized to communicate God's revelation, because God had made himself known to him as Father (Matt. 11.27 par.).

§ 8 · YES TO THE MISSION

J. Jeremias, 'Ἀδάμ, *TDNT* I, 1964, 141–43; id., 'Die "Zinne" des Tempels (Mt. 4, 5; Lk. 4, 9)', *ZDPV* 59, 1936, 195–208; E. Lohmeyer, 'Die Versuchung Jesu', *ZsystT* 14, 1937, 619–50 (= in E. Lohmeyer, *Urchristliche Mystik. Neutestamentliche Studien*, Darmstadt 1955, 83–122); E. Fascher, *Jesus und der Satan. Eine Studie zur Auslegung der Versuchungsgeschichte*, Hallische Monographien 11, Halle 1949; R. Schnackenburg, 'Der Sinn der Versuchung Jesu bei den Synoptikern', *TQS* 132, 1952, 297–326; K. P. Koppen, *Die Auslegung der Versuchungsgeschichte unter besonderer Berücksichtigung der Alten Kirche*, Beiträge zur Geschichte der biblischen Exegese 4, Tübingen 1960; N. Hyldahl, 'Die Versuchung auf die Zinne des Tempels (Matth. 4, 5–7 par. Luk. 4, 9–12)', *StTh* 15, 1961, 113–27; H.-G. Leder, 'Sündenfallerzählung und Versuchungsgeschichte. Zur Interpretation von Mc 1, 12f.', *ZNW* 54, 1963, 188–216; J. Jeremias, 'Nachwort zum Artikel von H.-G. Leder', *ZNW* 54, 1963, 278f.; E. Fascher, 'Jesus und die Tiere', *TLZ* 90, 1965, cols. 561–70; J. Dupont, 'L'origine du récit des tentations de Jésus au désert', *RB* 73, 1966, 30–76 (lit.).

(i) The sources

In the synoptic gospels, the account of Jesus' baptism is followed by the so-called 'temptation story' (Mark 1.12f.; Matt. 4.1–11 par. Luke 4.1–13). The version of it in Mark is quite different from that in Matthew and Luke. Mark offers only a few mysterious hints and says

[1] On the passage see ‡Jeremias, 41f.

nothing about the nature of the temptation; Matthew and Luke, on the other hand, fill this gap by describing the temptation in a form reminiscent of debates between scribes, in which both sides make use of scriptural proof-texts. The debate between Jesus and Satan takes its course by means of three conversations, set in three different places, in each of which Satan has the initiative. Consideration of individual details confirms that the Matthaean/Lucan version reflects a later stage of the tradition.[1]

The *earliest account*, Mark 1.12f., is astonishingly obscure. It consists of statements which bear the stamp of symbolic biblical language.

(*a*) The spirit 'drives' (ἐκβάλλει) Jesus into the wilderness. The wilderness is the dwelling-place of evil spirits (Matt. 12.43 par.), but it also has eschatological significance: the Messiah is to come from the wilderness (Isa. 40.3). Jesus stays there for forty days. Forty is a common symbolic number, which denotes times of oppression and of curse.[2] During this time Jesus is tempted by Satan.

(*b*) Jesus 'was with the wild beasts' (ἦν μετὰ τῶν θηρίων). This phrase is not meant to be a description, say, of the desolation of the landscape or the danger to Jesus; it is a theme from the idea of paradise. This is perhaps already suggested by the εἶναι μετά, which in Mark designates close community (3.14; 5.18; 14.67); even if that is not the case, the parallel content of Luke 10.19 supports such an interpretation.[3] The expectation was that just as, according to Gen. 2.19, Adam lived among the wild animals in paradise, so in the last days peace would again prevail between man and beast. Isaiah 11.6–9 depicts how the wolf will dwell with the lamb and the leopard will lie down with the kid; how the calf and the lion will graze together and a little child shall lead them; how the sucking child will play safely over the hole of the asp.[4] Paradise is restored, the time of

---

[1] The title 'Son of God' reflects the christology of the community; biblical quotations follow the Septuagint, etc.

[2] The flood lasted forty days and nights (Gen. 7.12); Israel was in the wilderness for forty years (Ps. 95.10); Moses fasted on Sinai for forty days and nights (Ex. 34.28; Deut. 9.18); Israel was in the hands of the Philistines for forty years (Judg. 13.1); Elijah travelled through the wilderness to Horeb for forty days and nights (I Kings 19.8).

[3] E. Fascher, 'Jesus und die Tiere', *TLZ* 90, 1965, cols. 561–70. Cf. also W. A. Schulze, 'Der Heilige und die wilden Tiere. Zur Exegese von Mc. 1, 13b', *ZNW* 46, 1955, 280–83.

[4] The same theme also appears in Hos. 2.18[20]: 'And I will make for them a

salvation is dawning: that is what ἦν μετὰ τῶν θηρίων means. Because the temptation has been overcome and Satan has been vanquished, the gate to paradise is again opened.

(c) The angels 'did him table-service' (διηκόνουν αὐτῷ). This feature, too, is part of the idea of paradise and can only be understood in that light. Just as, according to the Midrash, Adam lived on angels' food in paradise,[1] so the angels give Jesus nourishment.[2] The table-service of angels is a symbol of the restored communion between man and God.

This earliest report must be our starting point.

(ii) A historical nucleus?

It might seem obvious that Mark 1.12f. is a legend by means of which the community acknowledged Jesus as the consummation of the world. He vanquishes Satan, restores paradise, repairs the breach in communion between God and man. It is true that not only the language, but the images and ideas which the text uses assign it to a stage in the tradition at which there was a Jewish influence.[3] Nevertheless, at first sight it seems that the account does not have any historical usefulness whatsoever. However, at this point we have to be careful. Three considerations compel a cautious judgment.

(a) The first is a quite general one, and concerns the *symbolic language* of the Bible, study of which has been unduly neglected.[4] The symbolic triad of Mark 1.13 (unsuccessful tempting by Satan, docility of the wild beasts, table-service by the angels), discussed on pp. 69f. above, has a counterpart in Luke 10.18–20. In the latter passage, it takes the following form: the fall of Satan from heaven, escape unharmed from poisonous beasts, the writing of names in the book of life. In both instances, the same symbolic triad is used to describe an event which cannot adequately be expressed in everyday

---

covenant on that day with the beasts of the field, the birds of the air, and the creeping things of the ground; and I will abolish the bow, the sword, and war from the land; and I will make them lie down in safety'; see also Isa. 65.25; Ps. 91.13.

[1] Vita Ad. 4; ARN 1 (1c, 3); b. Sanh. 59b (Tannaitic).
[2] According to Matt. 4.4 it consisted in the word of God. Cf. also John 6.32.
[3] The forty days (see p. 69, n.2); σατανᾶς (not διάβολος); the Old Testament allusions.
[4] My work *Jesus als Weltvollender*, BFCT 33, 4, Gütersloh 1930, represents a first attempt.

language: the conquest of evil and the dawning of God's new world. Reverence for the ultimate mysteries demands that they shall be spoken of in veiled terms. But this veiled language is no more than a hint at the mystery; its use is in no way an argument against the presence of a historical nucleus of a narrative or a logion. This is as true in the case of the return of the disciples (Luke 10.17) or the narrative of Jesus' baptism (see § 5 above) as it is in the case of the temptation story.

(b) We come a stage further if we analyse the Matthaean/Lucan version. There is much to suggest that the three conversations reported here, and set in different localities, did not originally form a unity. First of all, it is clear from Mark that the temptation in the wilderness circulated as an independent tradition; secondly, the Gospel of the Hebrews, of which only a fantastic fragment has been preserved at this point,[1] seems to have described the temptation on the high mountain as a separate event; finally, in the case of the temptation at the temple, the different sequences of temptations in Matthew (wilderness-temple-mountain) and Luke (wilderness-mountain-temple) point in the same direction (if they are not redactional). All of this suggests that the temptation story originally circulated in three different, independent versions.[2] Such a view is supported by the fact that all three versions may have had the same content. The temptation in the wilderness is probably that Jesus, as the second Moses, should repeat the miracle of the manna.[3] Worshipping Satan on the mountain of the world is clearly concerned with Jesus' emergence as a political leader. Finally, jumping from the lintel of the temple gateway[4] may have been meant as a public miracle to legitimate Jesus' mission.[5] This means that all three variants of the story are concerned with one and the same temptation: *the emergence of Jesus as a political Messiah.*

Now we can say with absolute certainty that this temptation of a

[1] In Origen, *Commentary on John* II, 12.87 (E. Klostermann, *Apocrypha* II³, KlT 8, Berlin 1929, 7): ἄρτι ἔλαβέ με ἡ μήτηρ μου τὸ ἅγιον πνεῦμα ἐν μιᾷ τῶν τριχῶν μου καὶ ἀπήνεγκέ με εἰς τὸ ὄρος μέγα Θαβώρ. The text might refer to the story of the transfiguration, but the 'carrying off' fits the temptation story better; cf. Matt. 4.8 par. Luke 4.5.

[2] ‡Lohmeyer, 622 = 87.

[3] See John 6.15.

[4] ‡Jeremias, 'Die "Zinne" des Tempels'.

[5] ‡Hyldahl differs: by jumping, Jesus is to prove his readiness to suffer martyrdom as a false prophet.

political messiahship simply did not exist for the early church. It never thought for a moment of being a movement with political aims. The question of a political Messiah has no 'Sitz im Leben' in the early church. On the other hand, it was a burning issue in the lifetime of Jesus, not only for the disciples, who came from Galilee, the home of the Zealot movement, and had at least one Zealot among their number,[1] but also for Jesus himself. This political temptation, which brought with it the possibility of avoiding the way of suffering, accompanied Jesus like a shadow throughout his whole ministry.[2] Thus the nucleus of the temptation story goes back to a *pre-Easter* tradition.[3]

(c) In fact, the gospels report that Jesus repeatedly spoke to his disciples about his struggle with Satan. Mark 8.33, where Jesus repulses Peter with ὕπαγε ὀπίσω μου, σατανᾶ, is an early saying that mentions Jesus' battle with Satan. It is hardly conceivable that the early church should have invented so sharp a saying, which addresses the leading apostle directly as 'Satan'.

In addition to this, we even have a saying of Jesus which alludes directly to a victory over Satan that has *preceded* his own activity. It is the little parable of the duel, which has been handed down in two forms: first, by Mark (3.27 par. Matt. 12.29), and secondly in an independent version by Luke (11.21f.), in which the picture is painted even more vividly than in Mark:

[1] Σίμωνα τὸν καλούμενον Ζηλωτήν Luke 6.15; the parallels Mark 3.18; Matt. 10.4 call him Καναναῖος, i.e. Zealot. Cf. also the designation of the sons of Zebedee as Βοανηργές (Mark 3.17, on which see above, p. 6, n.8) and their behaviour in Luke 9.51–56. On the other hand, it is doubtful whether the surname Ἰσκαριώθ goes back to sicarius.

[2] Mark 8.32 par.; 11.9f. par; 12.13–17 par.; John 6.15. Perhaps 7.53–8.11 also belongs here, as the question 8.5 may be meant as a political issue: if Jesus says that the woman should be stoned, he is inciting the men to commit a revolutionary act (cf. Jeremias, 'Zur Geschichtlichkeit des Verhörs Jesu vor dem Hohen Rat', ZNW 43, 1950–51, 148f. = Abba, 143). The political temptation may also lie behind the demand for a sign as a legitimation with which Jesus is regularly confronted (Mark 8.11f. par.; Matt. 12.38f. par.; Luke 11.16; 23.8; Mark 15.29–32 par.); this demand, too, is pre-Easter, for whereas the primitive church was familiar with the sign to authenticate missionaries, the idea of a sign to legitimate Jesus himself did not occupy its attention. God had already given this sign in the form of the resurrection of Jesus (‡Dupont, 63). Finally, the degree to which the Zealot temptation faced the disciples can be seen from anti-Zealot sayings of Jesus like Mark 4.26–29; 12.17; 13.22, etc. Cf. pp. 228f.

[3] The recollection that Jesus was tempted during his life has been preserved outside the gospels in the Epistle to the Hebrews (2.18; 4.15).

When a strong man, fully armed, guards his own palace,
his goods are in peace;
but when one stronger than he assails him and overcomes him,
he takes away his armour in which he trusted,
and divides his (possessions as) spoil (Luke 11.21f.).[1]

The context, in Mark as well as in the Lucan special tradition, in which this little parable stands, is important for understanding the passage. Jesus is charged by his opponents with driving out demons with the help of Satan. He rejects this charge as preposterous: how can one Satan drive out another? No, Jesus continues, his power over the demons has another basis: he has overcome the strong man armed, fettered Satan; now he can rob him of his possessions. The message of the parable of the duel is thus that Jesus drives out demons, not as Satan's instrument but as his vanquisher. This remark by Jesus about his might must be assigned to the earliest tradition. On the one hand, the charge of being allied with the devil, i.e. of magic, is an old one. On the other hand, there is a degree of tension between the parable and the early Christian christology, according to which Jesus is the vanquisher of Satan by virtue of his crucifixion and resurrection (thus I Cor. 15.24; Col. 2.15; Eph. 1.20f.).[2] Thus it is highly probable that here, too, we have a piece of pre-Easter tradition. In this parable of the duel, the binding of the strong man evidently alludes to a particular event: Jesus can only mean the overcoming of the temptation depicted in Mark 1.12f.

It is particularly remarkable that two *logia* which speak of a vision of Satan have been handed down as sayings of Jesus in the *first person*. In Luke 22.31f., Jesus describes Satan as the accuser of the disciples before the throne of God and his own intervention as advocate for Simon (ἐγὼ ἐδεήθην), and in 10.18 Jesus cries out for joy that he has seen (ἐθεώρουν) Satan cast headlong from heaven and falling to earth like lightning.[3] Furthermore, the Gospel of the Hebrews shows that there was a tradition according to which Jesus spoke in the first person of his being taken up into the mountain.[4]

[1] In Luke the 'strong man' is not just a householder, but the master of a strongly armed citadel; his fortress is stormed by his opponents and his 'armour' (mail, helmet, shield, sword) is stripped from him (as from dead enemies elsewhere); his possessions are divided as 'spoil'.
[2] Cf. W. Grundmann, *Die Geschichte Jesu Christi*, Berlin 1957 = ³1960, 274.
[3] πεσόντα = Heb. *nāpal*, Aram. *nᵉpal*, is a Semitic-type quasi-passive, cf. Rev. 12.9 ἐβλήθη ὁ δράκων ὁ μέγας; John 12.31 ὁ ἄρχων τοῦ κόσμου τούτου ἐκβληθήσεται.
[4] See p. 71, n.1 above.

These traditions preserved in the first person suggest that Jesus spoke to his disciples about his temptation by Satan, his struggle against him and his victory over him.

It is not difficult to imagine why he should have done this. During the time of Jesus' ministry, the disciples were constantly subject to the same temptation as Jesus (Luke 22.28); the temptation that lay in the hope for the political Messiah was also theirs. Jesus will have told them of his own experience and of his overcoming of the temptation in order to strengthen them against it.

This may be the historical nucleus that lies behind the temptation story.

(iii) The meaning of the accounts

According to an early, pre-Easter tradition, then, the first appearance of Jesus was preceded not only by the experience at his baptism, with the revelation that is echoed in the use of the word '*Abbā* as an address to God in prayer, but also by a quite different event: his rejection of the temptation of a political messiahship. In other words, the mission of Jesus includes not only the divine commissioning, but also Jesus' own acceptance of his mission in the form of his victory over temptation.

So far we have retained the traditional expression 'temptation story'. That must now be put right. 'Temptation' is a misleading designation. The word πειρασμός occurs twenty-one times in the NT. In no less than twenty of them, however, it has the meaning 'trial, testing, ordeal'; only in one passage does it clearly denote 'temptation to sin' (I Tim. 6.9).[1] It is to be rendered 'testing, ordeal' even in Luke 4.13.[2] For the meaning of the so-called 'temptation story' is not that Jesus was put in the way of sin and resisted it; rather, the story is about Jesus' acceptance of his mission. It is better, therefore, to avoid the term 'temptation story', the moralizing tone of which can easily be misunderstood. The Jesus who confronts us is not the one who has been tempted, but the *one who has emerged from his ordeal.*

All the great figures of the Old Testament had to prove their faith by ordeal. The New Testament cites Abraham and Job as the most outstanding examples of faith that has stood the test.[3] Paul says

[1] M. H. Sykes, 'And Do Not Bring Us to the Test', *ExpT* 73, 1961/2, 189f.: 189.
[2] The same is true of the verb πειράζειν in Mark 1.13; Matt. 4.1, 3; Luke 4.2.
[3] Cf. K. H. Rengstorf, *Das Evangelium nach Lukas*, NTD 3¹³, Göttingen 1968, on 4.2.

of the trial of Abraham that 'in hope he believed against hope' (Rom. 4.18), and the Epistle of James says of Job: 'You have heard of the steadfastness of Job, and you have seen the purpose of the Lord, how the Lord is compassionate and merciful' (James 5.11). Jesus was tested in just the same way, to see whether he was prepared to renounce the easy way of public success and obediently to tread the hard road marked out by Isa. 42.1ff., the passage of scripture to which the call at the baptism had directed him (see pp. 53–55 above):

> He (my servant) will not cry or lift up his voice,
>   or make it heard in the street;
> a bruised reed he will not break,
> and a dimly burning wick he will not quench (vv. 2f.).

But we shall hardly do justice to the account of Jesus' ordeal if we limit its significance to the fact that Jesus resisted the allurement of gaining political power and external success. For in the light of the total picture presented to us by the sources, it is inconceivable that political ambition should have been a serious temptation for Jesus. The ὕπαγε ὀπίσω μου, σατανᾶ (Mark 8.33) with which Jesus rejected Peter's well-meaning counsel to avoid the way of suffering as being of the devil takes us further here. The quite unusual agitation expressed in this sharp remark shows that Jesus faced an ordeal which tried him to the uttermost. We may draw our own conclusions from this. The so-called 'temptation story' can only be understood if it has as its background and as the substance of Jesus' ordeal not only what is said in Isa. 42.1ff., but also what is said in the subsequent chapters of Isaiah, 52.13–53.12, about the servant of God. We shall be returning to the questions associated with this issue in §24.

Jesus attached eschatological significance to the time of his ordeal. The parable of the duel shows that he interpreted his testing as the vanquishing of Satan and that he derived his authority over the evil spirits from it. For victory over Satan means the dawning of the time of salvation.

IIII

THE DAWN OF THE TIME OF
SALVATION

MUCH WILL always remain obscure in any inquiry into the mystery of the mission of Jesus. On the other hand, we should not undervalue the fact that we do have clear information about his words and actions during his ministry.

§ 9 · THE RETURN OF THE QUENCHED SPIRIT

R. Meyer, *Der Prophet aus Galiläa*, Leipzig 1940; O. Cullmann, *The Christology of the New Testament*, London and Philadelphia ²1963; W. Foerster, 'Der Heilige Geist im Spätjudentum', *NTS* 8, 1961/62, 117–34; F. Hahn, *Christologische Hoheitstitel*, FRLANT 83, Göttingen 1963, ²1964; M. Hengel, *Nachfolge und Charisma, Eine exegetisch-religionsgeschichtliche Studie zu Mt 8, 21f. und Jesu Ruf in die Nachfolge*, BZNW 34, Berlin 1968. See also the dictionaries s.v. πνεῦμα and προφήτης.

(i) *The prophet*

In the manner in which he appeared on the scene, there was some similarity between Jesus and the scribes. He gave his teaching surrounded by a group of pupils; he debated the interpretation of the Law; he was approached for decisions on points of law:[1] he preached at synagogue services; he was addressed as 'Rabbi'.[2] So it was common during the nineteenth century for people to speak of Jesus as the 'Rabbi of Nazareth' – as even did Bultmann (with some emphasis)

[1] Luke 12.13f.; Mark 12.13–17 par. John 7.53–8.11 also belongs here (see above, p. 72, n.2).
[2] Mark 9.5; 11.21; 14.45; Matt. 26.25; often in John, also the address διδάσκαλε (Mark 4.38; 9.17, 38; 10.17, 20, 35 etc.) may go back to ῥαββί.

in his book on Jesus.[1] That is hardly correct.[2] For, as far as we know, Jesus was lacking in the basic requirement for the profession of a scribe: theological study.

There were strict regulations for the course of scribal education in the time of Jesus.[3] From about the age of 7–10, the budding Rabbi first lived permanently with a scribe as a pupil (*talmīd*). He heard his lectures and observed him exercising his profession and fulfilling the precepts of the law in practice. When the pupil had mastered the substance of the tradition and knew how to apply it, he was declared *talmīd ḥākām*, i.e. ready for ordination. Then, eventually, he was ordained[4] and entrusted with an office. There is no indication that Jesus underwent an education of this kind. On the contrary, Mark 1.22 par. shows that from the start there was a striking contrast between Jesus and the scribes, and he was accused of teaching without being authorized (Mark 6.2; John 7.15). He was indeed addressed as 'Rabbi', but this was not a theological title; 'Rabbi' ('Sir'), was commonly used as a mark of respect in the first century AD (cf. Matt. 23.8).[5] The fact that Jesus preached in synagogues does not mean that he was a trained theologian; there is no evidence that the exposition of scripture which followed the reading from the prophets was reserved for theologians as early as the time of Jesus.[6]

Jesus, then, was regarded as a *charismatic* rather than as a professional theologian (Mark 1.22 par.). The unanimous verdict on him was that he was a prophet. There was a constant echo to this effect among the people (Mark 6.15 par.; 8.28 par.; Matt. 21.11, 46; Luke 7.16; John 4.19; 6.14; 7.40, 52; 9.17) and even – though coupled with some scepticism – in Pharisaic circles (Luke 7.39; Mark 8.11 par.).[7] According to Luke 24.19, Jesus' disciples, too, saw him as a prophet. Finally, it was as a false prophet that Jesus was arrested and accused. This is clear from the account of the mockery under Jewish confinement.

The gospels record three quite different mockings of Jesus. The watchmen of the

---

[1] *Jesus and the Word*, London 1958, 48ff. But see below, p. 255, n.2.

[2] ‡Hengel, 46–55: 'Jesus was no "Rabbi"'.

[3] Jeremias, *Jerusalem*, 233–45, esp. 244f.; E. Lohse, ῥαββί, ῥαββουνί, *TDNT* VI, 1968, 962–66: 963.

[4] E. Lohse, *Die Ordination im Spätjudentum und im Neuen Testament*, Göttingen-Berlin 1951.

[5] Dalman, *Words of Jesus*, 334; Billerbeck I 916; E. Lohse, *TDNT* VI, 1968, 962; Jeremias, *Prayers of Jesus*, 42.

[6] I. Elbogen, *Der jüdische Gottesdienst in seiner geschichtlichen Entwicklung*[3], Breslau [4]1931 = Hildesheim 1962, 197; only in the second century AD did preaching become the exclusive domain of the scribes.

[7] The demand for a sign presupposes that Jesus is a prophet, and looks for him to legitimate himself as such.

78   THE DAWN OF THE TIME OF SALVATION

Sanhedrin (thus, rightly, Luke 22.63) played a kind of blind man's buff with him.[1] The guards covered his eyes, boxed his ears and with the cry προφήτευσον challenged him to tell who had struck him (Mark 14.65 par.). According to the special Lucan source, the bodyguard of the tetrarch, Herod Antipas, dressed Jesus in a white robe, which was the characteristic garb of the national Jewish king (Luke 23.11).[2] Finally, the Roman soldiery used a red soldier's cloak and a crown of thorns with which to mock him (Mark 15.16–20 par.): purple chlamys and garland were the insignia of the Hellenistic princes.[3] On each occasion the mockery was a travesty of the charge. This is particularly clear in the case of the second and third incidents: the mummery with the white and red robes reflects the political character of the accusation made by the Roman governor. In the present context we are concerned with the first mockery, which took place either before (Luke 22.63–65) or after (Mark 14.65 par.) the hearing by the Sanhedrin. The blind man's buff itself is some indication that Jesus was accused before the supreme council of being a false prophet; the cry προφήτευσον, which was not part of the game, makes that quite certain. As a false prophet, according to Deut. 18.20 (cf. 13.6), he had to die, and the execution had to take place during the feast (see Deut. 17.13) in order to deter others from this crime.[4] The vivid scene of the rough game which the Sanhedrin watch plays with Jesus is a very credible tradition, as it has been handed down by Mark and Luke independently, is recounted in an unbiassed way, and is in each case free from christological elaboration.[5] Its very insignificance gives the little episode considerable historical value as an incidental piece of information about the charge levelled against Jesus before the supreme Jewish authority.

Jesus himself did not reject the judgment that he was a prophet. 'Prophet' was not a full description of the task for which he had been sent (see below), but he included himself among the ranks of the prophets (Luke 13.33; Matt. 23.31f., 34–36 par., 37–39 par. cf. Mark 6.4 par.; Luke 4.24; John 4.44). He does this not only in the passages in which he uses the term 'prophet', but also in those in which he claims to possess the spirit. For the synagogue regarded the possession of the holy spirit, i.e. the spirit of God,[6] as *the* mark of prophecy. To possess the spirit of God was to be a prophet.[7]

In fact, Jesus repeatedly made an explicit claim that he himself *possessed the spirit*. This can be seen in the very first of the thirteen Marcan Ἀμήν sayings: Ἀμὴν λέγω ὑμῖν . . . ὃς δ'ἂν βλασφημήσῃ εἰς τὸ

[1] W. C. van Unnik, 'Jesu Verhöhnung vor dem Synhedrium (Mc 14, 65 par.)', *ZNW* 29, 1930, 310f.
[2] R. Delbrueck, 'Antiquarisches zu den Verspottungen Jesu', *ZNW* 41, 1942, 124–45; 140–42.
[3] Delbrueck, *op. cit.*, 138, 144.
[4] Jeremias, *Eucharistic Words*[2], 78f.
[5] Matt. 26.68, χριστέ, differs.
[6] In the phrase rūḥā dequdšā, qudšā is in fact a periphrasis of the divine name.
[7] See above, p. 52.

πνεῦμα τὸ ἅγιον, οὐκ ἔχει ἄφεσιν εἰς τὸν αἰῶνα (Mark 3.28f. par.).[1] According to Matt. 12.28 (par. Luke 11.20), Jesus also attributed his driving out of demons to the spirit of God. Luke 4.18–21; Matt. 5.3 par. and 11.5 par. indicate that he applied the promise of the spirit in Isa. 61.1 to himself; in view of the remarkable statements made by the Teacher of Righteousness about himself, this no longer seems as inconceivable as it did a short time ago.[2] In addition, there are the sayings which presuppose that the possession of the spirit has been communicated to the disciples. The principal relevant passages are Mark 6.7 (cf. Matt. 10.8), where Jesus confers on the disciples ἐξουσίαν τῶν πνευμάτων τῶν ἀκαθάρτων (cf. Matt. 12.28); Mark 13.11, where the spirit is promised to the disciples as a support when they come to judgment; and *logia* like Luke 6.23, 26 par. Matt. 5.12, which put the disciples in the ranks of the prophets. All these passages show that after the call at his baptism (see above, pp. 55f.), Jesus claimed *prophetic authority*. Taken as a whole, the sayings of Jesus which refer to his possession of the spirit are not very numerous; one reason for this is that Jesus, in contrast, say, to Paul, spoke more in figurative language than in theological terms. For example, in Luke 11.20 (the earlier version of Matt. 12.28, quoted above), Jesus speaks of his possession of the spirit without using the words 'spirit of God'. The words he does use are ἐν δακτύλῳ θεοῦ, in which the 'finger of God' is an image for the direct intervention of God, but the Matthaean parallel, ἐν πνεύματι θεοῦ, shows that this intervention of God is thought of as being accomplished through the spirit. The *logion* John 7.37 (cf. v. 39) speaks similarly of the spirit under the image of the water of life; the claim to inspiration is also expressed in the unique use of ἀμήν.[3] The extensive use of parallelism and rhythm which was described at length in §2, and Jesus' predilection for paronomasia and the sound patterns associated with it show how strongly his prophetic consciousness of mission influenced his ministry, even to the way in which he spoke. For in these elevated forms of expression, which have largely been lost in the process of translation into Greek, Jesus follows the pattern of the prophets.

The tradition in which Jesus appears as prophet and bearer of the spirit must be an old one, as it cannot be traced back to the early church. Where possible, the

---

[1] See below, p. 150.

[2] G. Jeremias, *Lehrer der Gerechtigkeit*, 319–53 ('Der Lehrer der Gerechtigkeit und der historische Jesus'): 325.

[3] See above, pp. 35f.

earliest church avoided 'prophet' as a christological title, because it felt it to be inadequate. Moreover, glossolalia makes no appearance in the picture of Jesus as the bearer of the spirit that is handed on to us by the gospels; so the early Christian pneumatic did not serve as a model.[1] Finally, the bestowing of the spirit on the disciples during the lifetime of Jesus is in tension with the later view, according to which the spirit first came down at Pentecost. We can see from John 7.39 how keenly this difficulty was felt. Here the saviour's cry at the Feast of Tabernacles,

If any one thirst, let him come,
and let him drink who believes in me

(vv. 37f.; to be divided in this way, see Rev. 22.17b), is first interpreted appropriately[2] with reference to the offer of the spirit (τοῦτο δὲ εἶπεν περὶ τοῦ πνεύματος v.39a). Afterwards, however, in flagrant contradiction to the cry and the interpretation, there follows: οὔπω γὰρ ἦν πνεῦμα, ὅτι Ἰησοῦς οὐδέπω ἐδοξάσθη (v.39b).

(ii) The quenched spirit

That Jesus was conscious of being a prophet and bearer of the spirit and was regarded as such does not, however, mean that he simply took his place as a link in the chain of the many Old Testament messengers of God. For this prophetic sequence had been broken off; it was the conviction of the synagogue that the spirit had been quenched. It is very much open to question whether this view is already to be found in the later parts of the Old Testament (e.g. in the lament, Ps. 74.9);[3] it is certainly present in I Maccabees (4.46; 9.27; 14.41),[4] in the apocalyptic literature (whose very pseudonymity expresses the conviction that there is no prophecy in the present),[5] in Josephus[6] and then at length in Rabbinic literature. This view took the following form:[7] In the time of the patriarchs, all pious and upright men had the spirit of God. When Israel committed sin with the golden calf, God limited the spirit to chosen men,

---

[1] E. Schweizer, πνεῦμα κτλ. E, TDNT VI, 1968, 396–451: 402: the community consistently avoided 'depicting Jesus simply as the first pneumatic'.

[2] Rabbinic instances of the interpretation of the pouring of water at the Feast of Tabernacles as the 'drawing of the holy spirit' (cf. Isa. 12.3) are collected in J. Jeremias, Golgotha, Angelos-Beiheft 1, Leipzig 1926, 82f.

[3] 'There is no more a prophet; none among us knows for how long.'

[4] R. Meyer προφήτης κτλ. TDNT VI, 1968, 812–28: 816f., differs. But his proposal to interpret I Macc. 4.46; 9.27; 14.41 with reference to John Hyrcanus is not convincing.

[5] Explicitly in Syr. Apoc. Bar. 85.3: 'The prophets have lain down to sleep'.

[6] Contra Ap. 1.41.

[7] Billerbeck I 127–34; II 128–34.

prophets, high priests and kings.[1] With the death of the last writing prophets, Haggai, Zechariah and Malachi, *the spirit was quenched*[2] because of the sin of Israel.[3] After that time, it was believed, God still spoke only through the 'echo of his voice' (*bat qōl* = echo),[4] a poor substitute.[5]

Now this view did not completely win the field. True, the pieces of isolated testimony to the present working of the spirit from Hellenistic Jewish writings[6] tell us little about Palestine. But even in Palestine, eschatological enthusiasm[7] repeatedly led to the hope that the spirit was again at work.[8] Qumran, too, should be mentioned as an exception. In the hymns of thanksgiving (mainly in the later 'community hymns'),[9] the worshipper repeatedly speaks of the 'spirit that thou (God) hast given in me',[10] i.e. on his entry into the community. He adds that he has been purified[11] and has received knowledge of God[12] through God's holy spirit. It is in agreement with this that Josephus twice reports that an Essene possessed the gift of prophecy,[13] though it is striking that he avoids the words προφήτης/ προφητεύειν, evidently on purpose. Still, it is not said that the spirit was understood by the Essenes as the anticipated eschatological gift of salvation; it appears, rather, as a continuing possession of the Essene community in their position as the true people of God.

Qumran is no more than an exception. The dominant view of orthodox Judaism was the conviction that the spirit had been quenched.[14] Such a view is also generally taken for granted in the New Testament, too. This is true, above all,

[1] E.g. David, Mark 12.36.
[2] Tos. Sota 13.2.
[3] Billerbeck I 127, under *b*.
[4] Billerbeck I 125, 127 under *a*.
[5] Billerbeck I 126.
[6] Wisdom 9.17, cf. 7.7 and Joseph and Asenath 8.11 (ed. M. Philonenko, 1968, 144, 158).
[7] Or the veneration of significant learned men (Billerbeck I 127 under *b*; II 128f.).
[8] R. Meyer, προφήτης C, *TDNT* VI, 1968, 812–28: 824f., 826f.
[9] The literary-critical distinction between Teacher-psalms and community psalms was first carried out by G. Jeremias, *Lehrer der Gerechtigkeit*, 168–77.
[10] I QH 12.11f.; 13.19; 14.13 (supplemented); 16.11; Fragm. 3.14. Cf., however, already I QH 7.6f.
[11] I QH 16.12.
[12] I QH 12.11f. Cf. H.-W. Kuhn, *Enderwartung und gegenwärtiges Heil. Untersuchungen zu den Gemeindeliedern von Qumran*, SUNT 4, Göttingen 1966, 130–39.
[13] *Antt.* 13.311–13; 15.373–79. Cf. 17.345–48: interpretation of a dream by an Essene; *B.J.* 2.159: general remark that the Essenes predict the future.
[14] I. Heinemann, 'Die Lehre vom heiligen Geist', *MGWJ* 66–67, 1922–23, 177; E. Sjöberg, πνεῦμα κτλ. C III, *TDNT* VI, 1968, 373–87: 383f.; ‡Foerster, 117–22; A. Nissen, 'Tora und Geschichte im Spätjudentum', *NovT* 9, 1967, 241–77. H.-W. Kuhn, *op. cit.*, 130–39, 117–20 is more restrained. For R. Meyer, προφήτης C, *TDNT* VI, 1968, 813–28, see above, p. 80, n.4.

of John the Baptist (Mark 1.8 par.) and his community. The remark of the disciples of John in Ephesus ἀλλ'οὐδ'εἰ πνεῦμα ἅγιον ἔστιν ἠκούσαμεν (Acts 19.2) does not, of course, mean 'we have never heard that there is such a thing as holy spirit', but, 'we have not yet heard anything about its being present again'. As far as the sayings of Jesus are concerned, the sharp antithesis in Mark 3.28f. is only comprehensible in the light of the idea that the spirit has been quenched (see below, p. 150). In the early church, this idea is presupposed in Acts 2.17, where ἐν ταῖς ἐσχάταις ἡμέραις is added to the quotation of the biblical text (Joel 3.1 LXX); see also Rom. 8.23 (ἀπαρχή); II Cor. 1.22; 5.5; Eph. 1.14 (ἀρραβών); I Thess. 4.8 (cf. Ezek. 36.27; 37.14); Heb. 6.4f. (. . . δυνάμεις τε μέλλοντος αἰῶνος); John 7.39 (οὔπω γὰρ ἦν πνεῦμα).

The idea of the quenching of the spirit is an expression of the consciousness that the present time is alienated from God. Time without the spirit is time under judgment. God is silent. Only in the last days will the disastrous epoch of the absence of the spirit come to an end and the spirit return again. There is abundant evidence of the degree to which people longed for the coming of the spirit.[1]

(iii) The concluding revelation

Jesus saw in John the Baptist a prophet, indeed περισσότερον προφήτου (Matt. 11.9 par. Luke 7.26). Similarly, he said of himself ἰδοὺ πλεῖον Ἰωνᾶ ὧδε (Matt. 12.41 par. Luke 11.32). Only now can we grasp what these remarks mean. The time of barrenness and judgment is coming to an end. The quenched spirit is returning after a long absence. God is breaking his silence and is speaking again, as he once did in the days of the prophets.

But that is not everything. There is something 'more', 'more than a prophet', 'more than Jonah'. This 'more' indicates that the salvation history of the past has not only been taken up, but has been transcended; in other words, this 'more' has an eschatological ring. Things have come so far. With the new activity of the spirit the time of salvation has begun. God is speaking for the last and final time. The eschatological return of the spirit means that God will remain with his community for ever, to complete his saving work. The eschatological presence of the spirit thus represents a new creation. Τὸ πνεῦμά ἐστιν τὸ ζωοποιοῦν (John 6.63).[2]

Jesus says that the time of salvation, the time of the spirit, has already begun with the activity of John the Baptist. But this does not

[1] Billerbeck II 134, under t: 615f.
[2] J. Jeremias, Jesus als Weltvollender, BFCT 33, 4, Gütersloh 1930, 16f.

mean that he puts himself on the same level as John (see above, p. 49). More than the Baptist is here (Matt. 11.11 par. Luke 7.28); here is the dawn of the *basileia*, here is more even than Moses (Matt. 5.21–48; Mark 10.5 par.). This consciousness of authority is expressed most sharply in Matt. 5.17:

μὴ νομίσητε, ὅτι ἦλθον καταλῦσαι τὸν νόμον ἢ τοὺς προφήτας·
οὐκ ἦλθον καταλῦσαι ἀλλὰ πληρῶσαι.

It has been argued against the authenticity of the *logion* that ἦλθον looks back on the activity of Jesus as already completed.[1] But, as Matt. 11.19 shows, this assertion does not even apply to the Greek wording; it is quite inappropriate for the underlying Aramaic *'atayit*, which can simply mean 'I am there', 'I will', 'it is my task'.[2] On the other hand, the fact that this is one of the very few sayings of Jesus[3] which have been handed down to us in Aramaic is a pointer to its age.

The crux of the saying is the word πληρῶσαι. The Greek might be translated 'fulfil (through action)', 'keep' (cf. Matt. 3.15; Rom. 8.4 etc.), which would apply only to the law and not to the prophets. Alternatively, it might mean 'fulfil (promises)' (see Matt. 2.17, 23 etc.): that, on the other hand, would fit the prophets, but not the law. To escape this dilemma, Dalman conjectured as the underlying Aramaic equivalent the word *lim*^{e}*qayyāmā* (= 'confirm', 'make valid') with the meaning 'bring into effect'.[4] This would make good sense, but there is a linguistic difficulty. Forms of *qūm* are never rendered in LXX by πληροῦν, and for 'to bring into effect' the New Testament tends to use ἱστάναι instead (Rom. 3.31; Heb. 10.9). Here the Aramaic wording, as transmitted by b. Shab. 116b, is of more help. We need not be concerned here with the context of the quotation, a mockery of the Christian message; the only important thing is the explicit statement that the quotation comes from a gospel.[5] It runs:[6]

'^{a}*nā lā l*^{e}*miphat min 'ōrāy*^{e}*tā d*^{e}*mōšē '*^{a}*tayit*
'ellā le'ōsope 'al 'ōrāy^e*tā d*^{e}*mōšē '*^{a}*tayit*
I did not come to take away from the law of Moses,
rather,[7] I came to add to the law of Moses.

---

[1] Bultmann, *Synoptic Tradition*, 164f.
[2] I gave instances of *'*^{a}*tā (bā) l*^{e} meaning 'intend', 'will', 'shall', 'have the task' in: 'Die älteste Schicht der Menschensohn-Logien', *ZNW* 58, 1967, 159–72: 167.
[3] See above, pp. 4f.
[4] *Jesus-Jeshua*, 61.
[5] Cf. Billerbeck I 241. K. G. Kuhn, 'Giljonim und sifre minim', in: W. Eltester (ed.), *Judentum, Urchristentum, Kirche*, BZNW 26, Berlin 1960 = ²1964, 24–61, here 54 n.110, has made an incisive and illuminating interpretation of the context, and shown that the anecdote mocking Christianity, in the framework of which the saying has been transmitted, is to be assigned to the third century AD. That does not, however, mean that the text of the *logion* also arose so late.
[6] Text: L. Goldschmidt, *Der babylonische Talmud* I, den Haag 1933, 599.
[7] *'ellā* cod.M. (preferred by Franz Delitzsch, Merx, Chwolson, Jastrow, Goldschmidt, Laible, Resch, A. Meyer, Zahn, Strack, Aufhauser, J. Weiss,

Thus according to b. Shab. 116b, καταλῦσαι corresponds to the Aramaic *miphat* ('take away') and πληρῶσαι to the Aramaic *'ōsopē* ('increase, add, enlarge').[1] This understanding of πληρῶσαι as 'fill up' matches the usual exegesis of Matt. 5.17b in Jewish Christianity, as we learn from the pseudo-Clementine Recognitions[2] and, recently, from a Jewish-Christian source worked over by a Mohammedan author, which renders Matt. 5.17b as follows:[3]

I did not come to diminish,
but, on the contrary, to complete.[4]

On linguistic grounds then there is every probability that the Jewish-Christian tradition has retained the original sense of πληρῶσαι.

Jesus, then, is countering the insinuation (μὴ νομίσητε) that he is an antinomian: his task is not the dissolution of the *Torah* but its fulfilment. The rendering of *'ōsopē* ('add') by πληρῶσαι in Greek aptly expresses the fact that the purpose of the 'fulfilling' is the reaching of the complete measure. We have here the idea of the eschatological measure, which Jesus also uses elsewhere;[5] πληρῶσαι is thus an eschatological technical term. In other words, in Matt. 5.17, Jesus is

---

Billerbeck, Fiebig, Klostermann, Ljungman, Stauffer, K. G. Kuhn, Grundmann), *wᵉlā* cod.B. (preferred by Güdemann, Graetz, Chajes, Levy, Herford, Klausner, Dalman, Baeck, Schoeps), cf. E. Stauffer, *Die Botschaft Jesu damals und heute*, Dalp-Taschenbücher 333, Bern-München 1959, 34f., 162f. The two readings give opposite senses. The reading *'ellā* ('I came not to take away . . . but to add . . .') means that Jesus brings something new; the reading *wᵉlā* ('I came neither to take away . . . nor to add . . .') that Jesus leaves everything as it was. The reading *'ellā* is supported by the fact that its content agrees with what Jesus says elsewhere about the Old Testament, as with the evidence of the newly-discovered Jewish source to be mentioned. The reading *wᵉlā* is a reshaping of the *logion* which takes up the canonization formula of Deut. 4.2; 13.1; cf. Rev. 22.18f., which forbids alterations to the sacred text by deletions or expansions.

[1] The Aramaic equivalents of καταλῦσαι and πληρῶσαι would also be significant if the quotation b. Shab. 116b did not go back to independent tradition, but were derived from a translation of the Gospel of Matthew along the lines of the Gospel of the Nazareans. In that case, they would show how the *logion* was understood by the tradition in a Semitic-speaking milieu.

[2] I 39.1 (GCS 51 p. 31 Rehm): *Ut autem tempus adesse coepit, quo id quod deesse Moysei institutis diximus impleretur . . .*

[3] S. Pines, *The Jewish Christians of the Early Centuries of Christianity According to a New Source*, Israel Academy of Sciences II 13, Jerusalem 1966, 5.

[4] Arabic *mutammiman*.

[5] Matt. 23.32 (full measure of sin); Mark 13.20 (shortening of the measure of the time of distress); 4.29 (harvest as the full measure of time); cf. Mark 1.15 πεπλήρωται ὁ καιρός. Elsewhere in the New Testament: Rom. 11.25 (full number of Gentiles); Gal. 4.4 (fullness of time); Rev. 6.11 (full number of martyrs) etc.

claiming to be the *eschatological messenger of God*, the promised prophet like Moses (Deut. 18.15, 18),[1] who brings the final revelation and therefore demands absolute obedience. In fact, this claim of Jesus that he brings the concluding revelation is to be found throughout his sayings. It is expressed particularly clearly in the antithetic pattern of Matt. 5.21–48. This pattern belongs to the bedrock of the tradition, since it involves a conflict with the *Torah*, something unheard of in the atmosphere of the period.[2] Jesus proclaims that the divine will in the *basileia* stands above the divine will as expressed in the time of the Old Testament (Mark 10.1–12).

To sum up: The presence of the spirit is a sign of the dawn of the time of salvation. Its return means the end of judgment and the beginning of the time of grace. God is turning towards his people. As bearer of the spirit, Jesus is not only one man among the ranks of the prophets, but God's last and final messenger. His proclamation is an eschatological event. The dawn of the consummation of the world is manifested in it. God is speaking his final word.

Now wherever the spirit of God is revealed in the biblical sphere, this happens in a twofold way, ἐν ἔργῳ καὶ λόγῳ (Luke 24.19; cf. Mark 1.27; I Thess. 1.5 etc.). The two belong indissolubly together. The word is never without its accompanying deed and the deed is never without the word that proclaims it. So too with Jesus: the concluding revelation is manifested in two ways (see Matt. 11.5f. par.): in acts of power (§10) and in words of authority (§11–12).

§ 10 · OVERCOMING THE RULE OF SATAN

O. Weinreich, *Antike Heilungswunder*, Religionsgeschichtliche Versuche und Vorarbeiten VIII, 1, Giessen 1909; P. Fiebig, *Rabbinische Wundergeschichten des neutestamentlichen Zeitalters*, KlT 78, Bonn 1911 = ²Berlin 1933; id., *Jüdische Wundergeschichten des neutestamentlichen Zeitalters*, Tübingen 1911; A. Schlatter, *Das Wunder in der Synagoge*, BFCT 16, 5, Gütersloh 1912; Dibelius, *Tradition*, index s.v. 'Miracle'; Bultmann, *Synoptic Tradition*, 218–44; A. Fridrichsen, *Le problème du miracle dans le christianisme primitif*, Strasbourg 1925; O. Bauernfeind, *Die Worte der*

---

[1] Cf. John 6.14; 7.40. The article (ὁ προφήτης) points to Deut. 18.15, 18.

[2] On the question of the authenticity of the antitheses, especially the widespread view that the introductory reference to the *Torah* is original in only a few of them, see §22 below.

Dämonen im Markusevangelium, BWANT 3, 8, Stuttgart 1927; W. Foerster, δαίμων κτλ, *TDNT* II, 1964, 1–19; A. Oepke, ἰάομαι κτλ, *TDNT* III, 1965, 194–215; H. van der Loos, *The Miracles of Jesus*, NovTestSuppl 9, Leiden 1965.

(i) The miracle stories of the gospels

'God anointed him with holy spirit and power. He went about doing good and healing all that were oppressed by the devil, for God was with him,' says Acts (10.38). And the four gospels report numerous healings by Jesus of sicknesses of every kind,[1] three raisings of the dead[2] and seven nature miracles.[3] A critical investigation of these accounts leads to four results.

1. When it is subjected to a critical literary and linguistic analysis, the content of the miracle stories diminishes quite considerably.

A *literary-critical* investigation of the miracle stories reveals a tendency to heighten the element of miracle. Numbers increase.[4] The miracles are elaborated.[5] Doublets are handed down.[6] Summaries generalize on the wonder-working activity of Jesus.[7] In several instances we can see, or at least imagine, how a miracle story grew out of a *linguistic* misunderstanding. Thus one factor behind the origin of the legend of the departure of demons into a giant herd of two thousand swine (Mark 5.12f. par.) may be the ambiguity of the Aramaic word *ligyonā'*, which means (1) 'legion', (2) 'legionary'. The original meaning of the reply of the evil spirit in the possessed man to the question 'What is your name?', λεγιὼν ὄνομά μοι,

[1] Possession (Mark 1.21–28 par.; 5.1–20 par.; 7.24–30 par.); fever (1.29–31 par.); leprosy (see note 6); lameness (Mark 2.1–12 par.; Matt. 8.5–13 par.; John 5.1–18); consumption (Mark 3.1–6 par.); haemorrhage (5.25–34 par.); deafness and dumbness (see note 6); blindness (see note 6); epilepsy (9.14–29 par.); deformation (Luke 13.10–17); dropsy (14.1–6); sword wound (22.51).
[2] See note 5.
[3] See p. 88, n.1.
[4] Mark 10.46 one blind man/Matt. 20.30 two; Mark 5.2 one possessed man/ Matt. 8.28 two; Mark 8.9 four thousand/6.44 five thousand (+Matt. 14.21 χωρὶς γυναικῶν καὶ παιδίων); Mark 8.8 seven baskets/6.43 twelve.
[5] Cf. Mark 5.35 with Luke 7.12f. and John 11.39.
[6] Five healings of the blind (Mark 8.22–26; 10.46–52 par.; Matt. 9.27–31; 12.22; John 9.1–34); two healings of a deaf and dumb man (Matt. 9.32–34; Luke 11.14 par. Matt. 12.22, where he is blind in addition); two healings of lepers (Mark 1.40–45 par.; Luke 17.12–19); two feedings (Mark 6.34–44: five thousand; 8.1–9: four thousand); two miraculous catches (Luke 5.1–11; John 21.1–11).
[7] Mark 1.32–34 par., 39 par.; 3.7–12 par.; 6.55f. par. Matthew has inserted summaries of healings into the Marcan original (Matt. 14.14, contrast Mark 6.34; Matt. 19.2, contrast Mark 10.1; also Matt. 9.35; 21.14f.) and generalized from Mark's information about Jesus' healings (Matt. 4.23f., contrast Mark 1.39; Matt. 15.30, contrast Mark 7.32).

ὅτι πολλοί ἐσμεν (Mark 5.9) may have been: 'My name is "soldier", because there are many like me (and we resemble one another as soldiers do)'. The word *ligyōnā* was wrongly understood as 'legion': 'My name is "legion", because our number is great (and a whole regiment of us is billeted in the sick man)' – and this alone produced the idea of the sick man being possessed by thousands of evil spirits.[1] From that point it was only a short step to the legend of the departure of the demons into the swine, taking up v.11 (originally continued in v.14) and making use of the theme of the devil deceived.

The story of the cursing of the fig tree (Mark 11.12–14, 20) is another miracle that may have grown up from a linguistic misunderstanding. The Aramaic imperfect *yēkōl*, which underlies φάγοι in v.14, was ambiguous. It could originally have had a future sense, and then could have been understood wrongly as an optative.[2] Once we allow this possibility, we can see how an announcement of the nearness of the end ('No one *will* ever eat fruit from you again [because the end will have come before it is ripe]')[3] might have become a curse ('*May* no one ever eat fruit from you again') and then a cursing miracle.

Even the story of Jesus walking on the water (Mark 6.45–52 par.; John 6.16–21) might have grown out of a story of the stilling of the storm (cf. Mark 4.35–41 par.) as the result of a linguistic misunderstanding.[4]

Finally, in the context of this critical analysis, it should also be said that some miracle stories may owe their origin *to delight in the elaboration* of a story or a saying. In the account of the arrest of Jesus it is reported that one of the servants of the high priest had his ear cut off (Mark 14.47 par.). It must have been a great temptation to have it healed by Jesus (Luke 22.51). Furthermore, once the signs of the time of salvation (Luke 7.22, see below, pp. 103f.) had been wrongly understood as an enumeration of the miracles Jesus had done, it was an obvious move to insert a picture of the healing Lord before the saying (v. 21). It is a great help towards understanding the story of the coin in the fish's mouth (Matt. 17.24–27) if we assume that v. 27 originally meant: 'Cast your hook into the sea, sell your catch and pay the temple tax with the proceeds'. The widespread occurrence of the fairy-tale theme of the precious object in the fish (Polycrates' ring, the valuable pearl), which also occurs in Jewish legend,[5] makes it easy to see how the words ἀνοίξας τὸ στόμα αὐτοῦ εὑρήσεις στατῆρα (v. 27) could have found their way into the story and could have changed it into a miracle story. Finally, the story of Peter's fishing expedition also belongs here (Luke 5.1–11; cf. John 21.1–11). It may be a 'preliminary symbolic representation' of the saying about 'fishers of men' (Luke 5.10; Mark 1.17 par.).[6]

[1] J. Jeremias, *Jesus' Promise to the Nations*, SBT 24, ²1967, 30 n.3.
[2] J. Jeremias in H. W. Bartsch, 'Die "Verfluchung" des Feigenbaums', *ZNW* 53, 1962, 256–60: 258.
[3] Bartsch, *op. cit.*, 257f.
[4] ἐπὶ τῆς θαλάσσης (Mark 6.48f.; Matt. 14.26; John 6.19) is ambiguous and can mean (*a*) 'on the sea (shore)' (cf. John 21.1); (*b*) 'on the sea'. The first meaning will be original and the accent of the story will have been on Mark 6.51 (ἐκόπασεν ὁ ἄνεμος).
[5] Billerbeck I 614, 675.
[6] Bultmann, *Synoptic Tradition*, 218.

We can see from this how the material in the miracle stories dwindles considerably when it is subjected to a critical literary and linguistic investigation. It is particularly worth noting that, if what has been said is right, plausible grounds can be advanced for supposing no less than four of the six synoptic nature miracles to be secondary in origin.[1] It is hardly coincidental that it is the nature miracles that prove to be secondary.

2. The material is reduced further if we make a comparison with *Rabbinic* and *Hellenistic* miracle stories.

We also find accounts of the expulsions of demons, healings, raisings of the dead, stillings of the storm, miracles with wine, in contemporary popular literature, especially from a Hellenistic milieu. Some of these miracle stories display such close contacts with those in the gospels that we can hardly avoid the conclusion that the Christian tradition borrowed from its environment and at the least took over some individual themes from it. Thus we have a story ascribed to Apollonius of Tyana (first century AD) of the raising of a young bride which is similar, even down to points of detail, to the raising of the young man of Nain (Luke 7.11–17);[2] it is reported that Vespasian healed a blind man by the use of spittle (cf. Mark 8.23);[3] we hear of one cured man who carries off the bed on which he had been brought (cf. Mark 2.11 par.; John 5.8),[4] and the changing of water into wine is a widespread feature of the myth and cult of Dionysus. The context of Luke 7.11–17 suggests what may have been the reason for taking over a story about the raising of a dead man. John the Baptist makes an inquiry, which Jesus answers by listing the marks of the time of salvation (7.18–23, see below, pp. 103f.). As soon as this list was wrongly understood as a list of five miracles which Jesus performed in the presence of the messengers (Luke 7.21f.; Matt. 11.4, see above, p. 87), the desire must have arisen to have an example of each of these miracles, even of the νεκροὶ ἐγείρονται; Matthew, too, provides instances of all five miracles in chs. 8–9, but in a different sequence.

The early church shared with its time a delight in miracles; this is confirmed by the miracle stories in Acts. To understand this, we must be sympathetic to the general atmosphere of the environment. Ancient man, especially in the east, had great powers of imagination; he loved large numbers and unusual happenings. Not only the simple

[1] Walking on the water (Mark 6.45–52); cursing the fig-tree (Mark 11.12–14, 20 par.); the coin in the fish's mouth (Matt. 17.24–27); Peter's catch (Luke 5.1–11). The other two are the stilling of the storm (Mark 4.35–41 par.) and the feeding in the wilderness (Mark 6.34–44 par.; 8.1–9 par.); there is a seventh nature miracle in the Gospel of John (2.1–11).

[2] Philostratus, *Vita Apollonii* 4.45. Similarities: a young person is to be buried, a particularly tragic case; the whole town joins the cortège: the helper meets them and brings the young girl back to life.

[3] Tacitus, *Hist.* 4.81; Suetonius, *Vespasian* 7.21f.

[4] Lucian, *Philopseudes* 11, cf. Bultmann, *Synoptic Tradition*, 227.

man was uncritical about miracle stories. Ancient man had no difficulties about much that seems extraordinary to us. So it is not surprising that the early church transferred miracle stories to Jesus. It saw them as an aid towards depicting the glory and authority of its Lord and towards proclaiming this to men of the time in a language that they could understand.

3. A *form-critical analysis* of the miracle stories of the gospels takes us one step further; it helps us to distinguish a later Hellenistic stratum of tradition from an earlier Palestinian one.

The most brilliant section of Bultmann's *History of the Synoptic Tradition* is the chapter on miracle stories.[1] He demonstrated here that the *pattern* of accounts of miracles which had developed in antiquity[2] recurs in numerous New Testament miracle stories. Characteristic features of this pattern are, for example, the way in which the accounts of healings begin with an exposition (the seriousness of the illness, vain attempts at its cure, etc.), the description of the cure itself (it takes place through a gesture, a word, spittle, etc.), a demonstration by the person cured of his miraculous healing (the lame man carries his bed, the blind man sees, etc.) and a note about the impression made by the miracle (a conclusion in chorus, i.e. shouts from eyewitnesses expressing astonishment or fright).

This gives us an important aid in analysing the miracle stories of the gospels. But Bultmann ran into error in supposing that the stylistic narration of a miracle story represented the earlier stage of the tradition (p. 219). *De facto*, it is the other way round: absence of the pattern is a sign of age. At this point Dibelius saw more clearly. He showed that we find two types of miracle story in the gospels, on the one hand stories which put the inner aspect of the happening right in the centre, and on the other those which are concerned to elaborate the miracle.[3] This apt observation caused Dibelius to divide the miracle stories into two categories, one group characterized by a simple mode of narration and one group working with secular themes. To the first group he assigned a number of narratives including the following miracle stories: Mark 2.1–12; 3.1–6; and, as a 'less pure type',[4] 1.23–28; 10.46–52; Luke 14.1–6;[5] to the second he assigned miracle stories exclusively, namely Mark 1.40–45; 4.35–41; 5.1–20, 21–43; 6.35–44, 45–52; 7.32–37; 8.22–26; 9.14–29; Luke 7.11–17 and the great miracle stories of the Gospel of John: John 2.1–11; 4.46–54; 5.1ff.; 9.1ff.; 11.1ff.[6] The two groups, he went on to argue, are so different that they must each have had a different 'Sitz im Leben'; he suggested that the simple descriptions, i.e. the first group, were used as

---

[1] *Op. cit.*, 209–44.
[2] Fundamental for the phenomenology of the miracle stories of antiquity is: ‡Weinreich. Texts in ‡Fiebig; G. Delling, *Antike Wundertexte*, KlT 79[2], Berlin 1960. There is a survey in Bultmann, *Synoptic Tradition*, 220–26; cf. also Dibelius, *From Tradition to Gospel*, London 1934, 71–103.
[3] *Jesus*, London 1963, 25–29; *Tradition*, 37–103.
[4] *Tradition*, 43.
[5] *Ibid.*
[6] *Tradition*, 71f.

illustrations in sermons; the second group he derived from story-tellers or (since the sources, as Dibelius himself conceded,[1] say nothing about early Christian story-tellers) from teachers. Accordingly he designated the first group 'paradigms', calling the second group (rather unfortunately) 'Novellen'. But this division cannot be carried through. Indeed, on closer inspection it proves to be an arbitrary one. Certainly, we possess a number of miracle stories which are free from the regular pattern, like Mark 10.46–52; Luke 14.1–6, but there are stylistic features in other miracle stories which Dibelius includes among the paradigms. For example, Mark 2.1–12 has the demonstration (ἄρας τὸν κράβατον v.12a) and the choral conclusion (v.12b), and Mark 1.23–28 the theme of the battle with the demon (see p. 94). The pattern cannot be used to carry through a distinction between 'paradigms' and 'Novellen'. Rather, the dividing lines are blurred; the stylistic features are slow to make an appearance and then become more and more intensive in the miracle stories. The pattern does not help us so much to distinguish two different types, paradigm and Novelle, as two different strata in oral tradition: the stories which are free from the pattern prove to be Palestinian in many ways. The pattern certainly begins to make an appearance in the Palestinian milieu, but the essential change only takes place in the Hellenistic sphere. This difference becomes clear if we compare the two healings of blind men in Mark 10.46–52 and 8.22–26. The pattern is completely absent from the healing of the blind beggar Bartimaeus. We are given no exposition (telling us, say, how old the blind man was, whether he had been blind from birth or whether the blindness was the result of some disease of the eyes, why it was particularly oppressive in his case, etc.); there is no description of the miracle, which is only stated with the utmost brevity: καὶ εὐθὺς ἀνέβλεψεν; there is no demonstration and no choral conclusion. It is not the performance of the miracle that stands in the centre of the story, but Jesus, who hears the cry for mercy (10.47f.) and recognizes the faith of the blind man (v. 52). There are a number of indications that the story has a Palestinian origin: we find two Aramaic words (bar v. 46; rabbūnī v. 51); the address υἱὲ Δαυίδ (vv. 47f.) points to a Jewish context; the scene described is a typical oriental one (the fact that the blind man is begging; the change in the attitude of the crowd, which first tells him to be quiet and then calls him; the excitement expressed in the throwing away of the indispensable cloak). Mark 8.22–26 is quite different. Here the pattern is all-pervasive: the exclusion of the public;[2] the manipulations (the use of spittle, to which popular medicine ascribed healing powers, and the laying on of hands);[3] the difficulty of the healing, which required hands to be laid on the eyes for a second time;[4] the recovery of the power to see by stages;[5] the successful healing, described by three verbs; and then the exclusion of the public again at the end. The pattern recurs again in a varied form in 7.32–37, the story of the deaf and dumb man. The accumulation of stylistic features indicates the Hellenistic sphere.[6]

---

[1] Tradition, 69f.   [2] Bultmann, Synoptic Tradition, 213.

[3] Op. cit., 221.   [4] Ibid.   [5] Op. cit., 228.

[6] It is very significant that the story of the healing of Bartimaeus is free of stylistic features in the Marcan version, but that the pattern immediately appears, though only to a degree, in the parallels. Matthew adds a short stylistic description of the performance of the miracle: ἥψατο τῶν ὀμμάτων αὐτῶν (20.34), Luke adds a word of command ἀνάβλεψον (18.42) and a stylistic choral conclusion (v. 43b).

In this way we have come up against an earlier Palestinian and a later Hellenistic version of the miracle stories; the second of these depicts Jesus as a wonder-worker, whereas the simple narrative of the first brings his authority into the centre. That means that a form-critical analysis of the miracle stories results in a further reduction of their substance.

4. But even when critical methods have been applied with the utmost strictness and the material has been reduced accordingly, a *nucleus of tradition* still stands out which is firmly associated with the events of the ministry of Jesus.

The charge that Jesus drives out demons with the help of the prince of the demons (Mark 3.22b par.; Matt. 9.34; Luke 11.15; cf. Matt. 10.25), i.e. that he makes use of magic, belongs to the earliest material in the tradition. That is clear from its malice and offensiveness, which excludes the possibility of invention. Such a charge is inconceivable without having been preceded by events to provoke it. We can see from this suspicion that the healings performed by Jesus could not be disputed by his opponents, and this is confirmed by both Rabbinic and early Christian accounts.[1] The story of the strange exorcist (Mark 9.38–40 par.) may also represent early material, because it brings out plainly the contrast between the intolerance of the disciples and the tolerance of Jesus; it is not coincidence that Matthew omits it. The same conclusion can be drawn once again: it is inconceivable that anyone should have used Jesus' name to drive out demons had Jesus not shown himself to have power over the spirits. The disciples are shown up even more sharply in Mark 9.14ff.; their attempts at exorcism fail. This is an indication of the age of the narrative, because the tradition has a tendency to spare the disciples. Indeed, in Mark 6.5a, Jesus himself is said to be powerless. We are told that he could perform no mighty act (οὐκ ἐδύνατο) in Nazareth because of their unbelief. The offence, which the addition in v. 5b and the rephrasing in Matt. 13.58 attempt to mitigate, guarantees the trustworthiness of the account, which presupposes that δυνάμεις were the norm for Jesus. Jesus' disputes over the sabbath ought also to be mentioned. They have a firm place in the tradition, and Jesus' healings on the sabbath have an intrinsic connection with them. For example, the first healing that Mark reports after the call of the disciples, in an early complex of tradition (Mark 1.16–39) that possibly goes back to Peter himself,[2] is an exorcism in the

---

[1] b.Shab.104b Bar. (Billerbeck I 39) should be added to the instances in Billerbeck I 631; cf. further M. Hengel, *Nachfolge und Charisma*, BZNW 34, Berlin 1968, 44 n.14.

[2] The reasons can only be hinted at: (*a*) Mark 1.21b–38 depicts the events of a twenty-four hour day; (*b*) among them is a relatively large number of insignificant individual details; (*c*) they are presented in an unbiassed topographical-chronological connection (as happens elsewhere in Mark only in the Passion narrative); (*d*) this is achieved through the figure of Peter; (*e*) Peter is given his original name Σίμων (1.16, 29, 30, 36, which occurs elsewhere in Mark only at 3.16 and 14.37), which is a characteristic of the earliest stratum of the Peter tradition; (*f*) the

synagogue on the sabbath (1.23–28). Part of the same complex is the account of the healing of Peter's mother-in-law, ill with fever (1.29–31 par.). This is told in a matter-of-fact way, briefly, with detailed information and without bias. The *logion* in which Jesus threatens Chorazin and Bethsaida (Matt. 11.20–22 par.), because they rejected him despite his mighty acts (v. 21), must also be early. We do not hear elsewhere of any activity of Jesus in Chorazin. The healing of the leper in Mark 1.40–44 might also be assigned to early traditional material; we need only recall the mysterious 'snorting' (ἐμβριμησάμενος v. 43), which presumably paraphrases the oriental sign-language for a command to be silent,[1] and the no less remarkable *dativus incommodi* εἰς μαρτύριον αὐτοῖς (v. 44),[2] which stamps the healing as a piece of evidence brought against the unbelieving people. Finally, sayings like Matt. 7.22 and Luke 10.20 may be early, because in them Jesus plays down the exorcisms and mighty acts which the early church so treasured; they do not guarantee entry into the *basileia*.

Thus even when strict critical standards have been applied to the miracle stories, a demonstrably historical nucleus remains. Jesus performed healings which astonished his contemporaries. These were primarily healings of psychogenous suffering, especially what the texts describe as the driving out of demons,[3] which Jesus performed with a brief word of command.[4] There were also, however, healings of lepers (in the broad sense of the word as understood at that time),[5] of the paralysed and the blind. These are happenings along the lines of what doctors call 'overpowering therapy'.

It was not just the tradition that felt these healings to be important; they were particularly important to Jesus himself. So important, in fact, that he could sum up the whole of his work in one of the ancient 'three days' sayings[6] in the words ἐκβάλλω δαιμόνια καὶ ἰάσεις ἀποτελῶ (Luke 13.32). But why was this so?

---

striking phrase Σίμων καὶ οἱ μετ'αὐτοῦ finally looks like the transposition of an account given in the first person into the third.

[1] While the hand is placed on the lips, air is blown in puffs through the teeth, cf. E. E. Bishop, *Jesus of Palestine*, London 1955, 89. Verse 44 supports this interpretation. The east loves sign language.

[2] H. Strathmann, μάρτυς κτλ, *TDNT* IV, 1967, 474–514: 503.

[3] Exorcisms by Jesus are reported or presupposed in Mark alone at the following places: 1.23–27, 32–34, 39; 3.11f., 14f., 22–27; 5.1–20; 6.7, 13; 7.24–30; 9.14–29, 38–40.

[4] Mark 1.25, 27; 5.8; 9.25; Luke 4.41 (ἐπιτιμᾶν).

[5] Leprosy in the modern sense of the word was first defined by the Norwegian doctor A. Hansen in 1872. In ancient times other psychogenic diseases of the skin were also described as 'leprosy'.

[6] See below, pp. 285f.

(ii) The power of evil[1]

An extraordinarily strong fear of demons prevailed in the time of Jesus,[2] as it still does, even today, in Islamic Palestine. Illnesses of all kinds were attributed to demons, especially the different forms of mental illness, whose external manifestations already betrayed the fact that the victim was no longer his own master. We shall understand the extent of this fear of demons better if we note that the absence of enclosed mental hospitals meant that illnesses of this kind came much more before the public eye than they do in our world. We have a vivid picture of the way in which a deranged person began to rave in the middle of a synagogue service (Mark 1.26); I myself remember as a boy seeing a mentally ill person running through the streets of Jerusalem, roaring and foaming at the mouth (cf. Mark 5.5b).[3] In the time of Jesus, the oriental was familiar with such occurrences and saw in the healing of such a sick person a victory over the demon who had him in its power. There is therefore nothing surprising in the fact that the gospels, too, portray mental illness as being possessed by demons. They speak in the language and conceptuality of their time. In one respect, however, Jesus seems to have transformed contemporary ideas. In Judaism, the demons were regarded predominantly – but not exclusively (Mark 3.22b) – as individual beings. They were named and known one by one, as the countless names for demons show.[4] Jesus, however, stressed the connection between the appearance of the demons and Satan. He expressed this connection with a variety of pictures. Satan appears as a commander of a military force (Luke 10.19: δύναμις) or even rules over a kingdom (Matt. 12.26 par. Luke 11.18: βασιλεία); the demons are his soldiers (see pp. 86f. on Mark 5.9). In Matt. 10.25, Jesus makes

---

[1] W. Foerster in: G. von Rad – W. Foerster, διαβάλλω, διάβολος, TDNT II, 1964, 71–81; W. Foerster – K. Schäferdiek, σατανᾶς, TWNT VII, 1964, 151–65.

[2] Billerbeck IV 501–35 (Excursus 21: on Jewish demonology).

[3] In Samaria, the deranged were concentrated in public round the graves of the prophets Elijah and Obadiah and that of John the Baptist, which were to be found there. Paula saw them on her pilgrimage in AD 385: '. . . demons screaming under different tortures before the tombs of the saints, and men howling like wolves, baying like dogs, roaring like lions, hissing like serpents and bellowing like bulls. They twisted their heads and bent them backwards until they touched the ground' (Jerome, Ep. 108.13); cf. J. Jeremias, Heiligengräber in Jesu Umwelt, Göttingen 1958, 132.

[4] Billerbeck IV 501–35 passim.

use of a word-play to describe Satan as master of the house (*be'ēl zebūl*, see above, p. 7) with control over his servants. This shows that Jesus does not have an atomistic view of the world of evil, but sees it as a unity. In this way evil is no longer something isolated and fortuitous; the problem is made more radical.[1] Behind its various manifestations stands *the* ἐχθρός, the disrupter of creation. Men are delivered over helpless to his host of evil spirits. This knowledge of the reality of evil finds its peak in the certainty that the power of evil has yet to reach its climax: Satan will set himself up as God and demand worship (Mark 13.14). Only then, at the end of days, will Pseudo-god be cast down: *tunc Zabulus[2] finem habebit* (Ass. Mos. 10.1).

(iii) The vanquishing of Satan

Jesus enters this world enslaved by Satan with the authority of God, not only to exercise mercy, but above all to join battle with evil. O. Bauernfeind[3] has shown how the Gospel of Mark depicts Jesus' exorcisms as battles (see e.g. Mark 1.23–28). We find the following pattern: the possessed man approaches Jesus with a remark intended to ward him off (v. 24a, to be read as two questions); the parrying becomes an attack, for next the demon utters a solemn adjuration (οἶδά σε τίς εἶ, ὁ ἅγιος τοῦ θεοῦ v. 24b). The demon puts up a final resistance against Jesus' command to be silent and to depart (v. 25) before it obeys (v. 26). The same pattern recurs in Mark 5.6–10. The idea of the exorcisms as battles against evil powers is also shared by Jesus, as is shown by the parable of the duel (Mark 3.27 par. Luke 11.21).[4] It makes use of the image of the eschatological war, which the Essene texts (especially 1 QM) show to have been widespread. Jesus uses this parable to interpret his exorcisms as a battle, or rather, as the spoiling of the strong man after he has been vanquished. Isaiah 53.12 ('he shall have the strong men as spoil') may perhaps be in the background here. In Luke 13.16 he uses the image of the shattering of the bonds of Satan's victims to describe his healings.

These victories over the power of evil are not just isolated invasions of Satan's realm. They are more. They are manifestations of the dawn of the time of salvation and of the beginning of the annihilation of Satan (cf. Mark 1.24 ἀπολέσαι). This is said in Luke 11.20: εἰ δὲ ἐν

---

[1] ‡Foerster, 18.
[2] = (*Beel-*) *Zebulus* (suggested by the Rev. E. Synofzik).
[3] *Die Worte der Dämonen im Markusevangelium*, BWANT 3, 8, Stuttgart 1927.
[4] See above, pp. 72f.

δακτύλῳ (Matt. 12.28 πνεύματι) θεοῦ ἐκβάλλω τὰ δαιμόνια, ἄρα ἔφθασεν[1] ἐφ᾽ ὑμᾶς ἡ βασιλεία τοῦ θεοῦ. Every occasion on which Jesus drives out an evil spirit is an anticipation of the hour in which Satan will be visibly robbed of his power. The victories over his instruments are a foretaste of the eschaton.

Jesus interprets the exorcisms which the disciples do at his bidding in the same terms. He sends them out to proclaim the kingdom and gives them authority over the powers of evil (Mark 3.14f.). Authority over the spirits recurs constantly in the mission sayings and is virtually a characteristic of them (Mark 6.7 par.; Matt. 10.7f.; Luke 10.19f.; cf. Mark 6.13 par.; Matt. 7.22; Luke 10.17). This is early tradition, as the mission charge to the early Christian missionaries was put in other terms: it had a christological content. Why Jesus attributes such importance to the authority over the spirits exercised by his disciples is to be seen from the cry of joy with which he greets the report of the disciples on their return, that the spirits had to yield to their commands: ἐθεώρουν τὸν σατανᾶν ὡς ἀστραπὴν ἐκ τοῦ οὐρανοῦ πεσόντα (Luke 10.18). πίπτειν here must be regarded as a Semitic-type quasi-passive,[2] and be rendered 'be cast out'. Thus the *logion* means, 'I watched Satan cast headlong from heaven like lightning'. The casting of Satan out of the heavenly world presupposes an earlier battle in heaven, like that described in Rev. 12.7–9. Jesus' visionary cry of joy leaps over the interval of time before the final crisis and sees in the exorcisms performed by the disciples the dawn of the annihilation of Satan. This stage has already been reached: the evil spirits are powerless, Satan is being destroyed (Luke 10.18), paradise is opening up (v. 19), the names of the redeemed stand in the book of life (v. 20).[3]

There is no analogy to these statements in contemporary Judaism; neither the synagogue nor Qumran knows anything of a vanquishing of Satan that is already beginning in the present. Of course, everything is said paradoxically, and all this is visible only to the believer. Satan still exercises his power. Therefore the ἔργα are no legitimation;

---

[1] In Daniel Θ, φθάνω serves eight times to render *me̥ṭā*, 'reach', 'arrive'.

[2] See p. 73, n.3 above.

[3] We already saw on p. 70 that the triad: fall of Satan – not being able to be hurt by poisonous beasts – entering of name in the book of life (Luke 10.18–20) corresponds to the eschatological triad: victory over Satan – not being hurt by wild beasts – table service by angels (Mark 1.13), and that these are paradise themes.

they can even be understood as the devil's work (Mark 3.22). But where men believe Jesus, the cry of joy rings out that permeates the whole of the New Testament: the power of Satan has been broken! *Satana maior Christus* (Luther).

§ 11 · THE DAWN OF THE REIGN OF GOD

Dalman, *Sayings of Jesus*; Billerbeck I, 1922, 172–84, 418f.; H. Kleinknecht, G. von Rad, K.-G. Kuhn, K.-L. Schmidt, βασιλεύς κτλ, *TDNT* I, 1964, 564–593; R. Schnackenburg, *God's Rule and Kingdom*, 1963; N. Perrin, *The Kingdom of God in the Teaching of Jesus*, New York and London 1963 (for a history of scholarship); id., *Rediscovering*.

(*i*) *The* basileia *as the central theme of the public proclamation of Jesus*

The return of the spirit of God is manifested not only in actions, but also in words of authority, to which we now turn. Our starting point is the fact that the central theme of the public proclamation of Jesus was the kingly reign of God. At any rate, the first three gospels sum up his message in this concept, Mark in the summary verse 1.15, placed at the begining of his gospel, Matthew and Luke in the phrases κηρύσσειν τὸ εὐαγγέλιον τῆς βασιλείας (Matt. 4.23; 9.35) or εὐαγγελίζεσθαι τὴν βασιλείαν (Luke 4.43; 8.1, cf. 9.2, 60). We can see that these formulations really represent the central theme of the proclamation of Jesus from the frequency of the occurrence of βασιλεία in the synoptic sayings of Jesus, which forms a striking contrast to the relatively sparse number of examples in contemporary Judaism and the rest of the New Testament.[1] Above all, however, a large number of new phrases about the *basileia* appear which have no parallels in the literature of the world of Jesus, a fact to which sufficient attention has not yet been paid.[2] Finally, there is the recurrence of the expression in a great variety of types of sayings and contexts. Numerous parables deal with the reign of God, as do apocalyptic sayings (Mark 9.47; Luke 17.20f.), especially sayings about entry into the *basileia* (Mark 10.23–25 par. etc.) and the feast in the time of salvation (Mark 14.25 par.; Matt. 8.11f. par.), sayings about the nearness of the reign of God (Mark 1.15 par.; 9.1 par.; Matt. 11.12 par.; Luke 10.11),

[1] See above, pp. 32, 34 n.4.   [2] See above, pp. 32–34.

the request for its coming (Luke 11.2 par.), the many paradoxical *mešālim* about those who belong to it (above all Matt. 5.3 par.; cf. Mark 10.14f. par. 23–25 par.; Matt. 5.10, 19; 11.11 par.; 21.31; Luke 12.32), admonitions (Matt. 6.33 par.; 19.12; Luke 9.62), mission sayings (Matt. 10.7 par. Luke 10.9; 9.2, 60), and the saying about the mystery of the *basileia* (Mark 4.11; cf. Luke 11.20 par. Matt. 12.28).

Terminology

In the gospels, ἡ βασιλεία τοῦ θεοῦ alternates with ἡ βασιλεία τῶν οὐρανῶν. Both expressions have the same meaning, for οἱ οὐρανοί is merely a periphrasis for God.

There is still dispute as to which expression Jesus used. One point of reference for answering this question is that the term 'kingdom of heaven' appears for the first time in Jewish literature half a century after Jesus' ministry, with R. Johanan ben Zakkai, *c.* AD 80.[1] The complete silence of the Jewish inter-testamental literature makes it highly improbable, if not completely inconceivable, that the expression 'kingdom of heaven' was already current language at the time of Jesus and was taken up by him. On the other hand, there is nothing to suggest that Jesus did not say 'kingdom of God'. He certainly paraphrased the divine name quite frequently (see above, pp. 9f.), but according to the synoptic tradition he by no means consistently avoided the word 'God'.[2] The Qumran texts confirm that in the pre-Christian period there was no hesitation about using *'ēl* or *'elōhīm*. Thus the expression 'kingdom of heaven' may be secondary. It is native to a Jewish-Christian milieu (Matthew thirty-one times, Gospel of the Nazarenes once),[3] where it falls in with the increasing tendency in Judaism to avoid the word 'God' altogether, except in biblical quotations.

(*ii*) ἡ βασιλεία τοῦ θεοῦ *with a future meaning in the sayings of Jesus*

If we are to understand the sayings of Jesus which deal with the *basileia*, it is extremely important that we should know what ideas the people of his time associated with the expression 'reign of God'.[4] We have seen[5] that it was not a common way of speaking in pre-

---

[1] j. Kidd. 59d 28.

[2] Mark has 35, Matthew 33, Luke 65 instances in the sayings of Jesus.

[3] Elsewhere only in an agraphon (quoted by Tertullian, *De baptismo* 20.2), three times in the Gospel of Thomas (20, 54, 114, as compared with 'reign of the Father' seven times and 'reign' in the absolute twelve times) and six times in the Gospel of Philip.

[4] Dalman, *Words of Jesus*, 96–101; *Worte Jesu*[2], 310–14, 361–63; Billerbeck I 172–84; ‡K. G. Kuhn, 570–73. P. Billerbeck told me that the impulse to embark on his monumental work came at a time when, as a young pastor, he had to preach on a text in which 'kingdom of God' appeared. Nowhere in the commentaries could he find any information about what people of Jesus's time understood by the expression.

[5] See above, p. 32.

Christian Judaism; there are relatively few examples, even if we include the passages in which the verb *mālak* and the noun *melek* are applied to God.

One thing is certain: the word *malkūtā* did not have for the oriental the significance that the word 'kingdom' does for the westerner. Only in quite isolated instances in the Old Testament does *malkūt* denote a realm in the spatial sense, a territory; almost always it stands for the government, the authority, the power of a king.[1] But this does not mean that *malkūt* is understood in an abstract way; it is always in process of being achieved. Thus the reign of God is neither a spatial nor a static concept; it is a *dynamic concept*.[2] It denotes the reign of God in action, in the first place as opposed to earthly monarchy, but then in contrast to all rule in heaven and on earth. Its chief characteristic is that God is realizing the ideal of the king of righteousness, constantly longed for, but never fulfilled on earth. From earliest times, the oriental conception of kingly righteousness – and indeed that held in the Israel of Jesus's time – was not primarily one of dispassionate adjudication, but of the protection which the king extends to the helpless, the weak and the poor, widows and orphans.[3]

Another important fact is that there were two expressions of the conception of the reign of God in Judaism.[4] Just as there were two aeons, present and future, so too people spoke of a (lasting) reign of God in this age and a (future) reign of God in the new age. This distinction goes back to the Old Testament, where it only emerges at a late stage, at least in an explicit way.[5] The distinction is made

[1] E.g. Daniel 6.29 *bᵉmalkūt dāryāweš*, 'under the rule of Darius'; cf. Rev. 17.12, where βασιλεία is parallel to ἐξουσία ὡς βασιλεῖς.

[2] This can be recognized particularly clearly in the synoptic passages in which βασιλεία is linked with a temporal ἐν (Jeremias, *Eucharistic Words*², 184): Matt. 20.21 ἐν τῇ βασιλείᾳ σου does not mean 'in your kingdom', but must, as the parallel Mark 10.37 ἐν τῇ δόξῃ σου shows, be translated in personal terms, 'when you are king'; Matt. 16.28 ἐρχόμενον ἐν τῇ βασιλείᾳ αὐτοῦ 'coming as king'; Mark 14.25 ἐν τῇ βασιλείᾳ τοῦ θεοῦ 'when God has established his reign'; Luke 22.30 ἐν τῇ βασιλείᾳ μου 'when I am king'; 23.42 ἐν τῇ βασιλείᾳ σου (to be preferred with ℵ C Θ s pl as the more difficult reading to εἰς τὴν βασιλείαν σου (BL *lat*) 'when you come (again) as king'.

[3] J. Dupont, *Les Béatitudes II. La bonne nouvelle*², Paris 1969, 53–90. Cf. also H.-T. Wrege, *Die Überlieferungsgeschichte der Bergpredigt*, WUNT 9, Tübingen 1968, 13–15.

[4] It was one of the main concerns of T. W. Manson's regularly reprinted (unaltered) standard work, *Teaching*², to work out this twofold aspect.

[5] The distinction was already present implicitly at an earlier stage; one need think only of Jer. 31.31–34.

clearly for the first time in Daniel. 4.34 speaks of the reign of God in the present age:

> I praised and honoured him who lives for ever; for his dominion is an everlasting dominion, and his kingdom endures from generation to generation.

2.44 speaks of his future rule:

> And in the days of those kings the God of heaven will set up a kingdom which shall never be destroyed, nor shall its sovereignty be left to another people. It shall break in pieces all these kingdoms and bring them to an end, and it shall stand for ever.

This distinction remains fundamental for the following period. For Judaism, God's lasting reign is his *lordship over Israel*. He is the creator of the whole world and of all people, but the nations have turned away from him. When he offered them his kingdom once again on Sinai, Israel alone submitted to him, and since then he has been Israel's king. This kingdom, then, was established through the proclamation of the royal will in the Law, and God's reign can be seen wherever men subject themselves in obedience to the Law by a decision of the will. The Jew who recites the Sh*ma*ʿ, the confession of belief in the one God, in public prayer, is proclaiming God's reign over Israel; the Gentile who is converted takes the yoke of the reign of God upon himself. But in the present age, the reign of God is limited and hidden, because Israel is in slavery to the Gentile nations who reject the reign of God. God's reign and the reign of the Gentiles over Israel are an intolerable contradiction. But the time is coming when this dissonance will be resolved. Israel will be freed, the reign of God will be revealed in all its glory, and *the whole world* will see and acknowledge God as king. 'When idolatry has been rooted out together with all who worship idols . . ., then Yahweh will be king over the whole earth (cf. Zech. 14.9)', remarks Mek. Ex. on 17.14. 'Then shall the m*e*lūkā belong to the God of Israel, and he will evince his power among the sacred hosts', runs 1 QM 6.6. Israel entreated for the coming of this longed-for hour at the end of each service, even in the time of Jesus, in the Kaddish,[1] which begins with a twofold petition for the hallowing of the divine name and the ruling of the reign of God.[2]

[1] See below, p. 198.   [2] For the wording, see below, *ibid.*

86884

To sum up: Judaism acknowledged God as king. In the present age his reign extends only over Israel, but in the end-time he will be acknowledged by all nations.

How did Jesus understand the expression? Was he thinking of the present or the future reign of God, or did he combine both conceptions? The answer to this question is easy. The second petition of the Lord's Prayer, which takes up the Kaddish (Matt. 6.10; Luke 11.2), shows quite certainly that Jesus used the term *malkūtā in its eschatological sense*. This is in fact confirmed by his words at every step.

According to a very early saying, Mark 9.1, he promises some of his disciples that they will not die ἕως ἂν ἴδωσιν τὴν βασιλείαν τοῦ θεοῦ ἐληλυθυῖαν ἐν δυνάμει. Here Jesus is speaking of a future event. The numerous sayings about entering the *basileia*,[1] like e.g. Mark 9.43–48, also speak of the eschatological *basileia*. They show that its coming will be introduced by the last judgment. Indeed, we might even say that when Jesus speaks of the *basileia*, he almost always includes the notion of the last judgment that is to precede it.

The *basileia* is also clearly understood in an eschatological way in the metaphors associated with the feast of salvation, which say that Jesus himself (Mark 14.25), Abraham, Isaac and Jacob and the prophets (Luke 13.28), and the Gentiles streaming in from every direction (v. 29), will recline at table 'in the *basileia* of God'.

Finally, we should mention the sayings about the nearness of the *basileia*. Jesus himself proclaimed its nearness with the words ἤγγικεν ἡ βασιλεία, and he sent his disciples out with the same message.[2]

As a last example, mention should be made of Luke 17.20f., a passage at which we must look rather more closely, as its meaning is disputed:

οὐκ ἔρχεται ἡ βασιλεία τοῦ θεοῦ μετὰ παρατηρήσεως,
οὐδὲ ἐροῦσιν· ἰδοὺ ὧδε ἤ · ἐκεῖ·
ἰδοὺ γὰρ ἡ βασιλεία τοῦ θεοῦ ἐντὸς ὑμῶν ἐστιν.[3]

It is important to note the construction of this saying. It is occasioned

---

[1] H. Windisch, 'Die Sprüche vom Eingehen in das Reich Gottes', *ZNW* 27, 1928, 163–92.

[2] Jesus: Mark 1.15 par.; the disciples: Matt. 10.7; Luke 10.9, 11. For the expectation of an imminent coming see §13.

[3] Dalman, *Words of Jesus*, 143–47; A. Rüstow, "Ἐντὸς ὑμῶν ἐστιν. Zur Deutung von Lukas 17, 20–21', *ZNW* 51, 1960, 197–224 (lit.).

by a question from the Pharisees about the time of the coming of the reign of God.[1] Jesus answers this question, which takes up a central theme of Jewish apocalyptic that is discussed again and again by the scribes, in a sentence with three clauses. Two are negative and one positive. The two negative statements run: no time[2] can be calculated in advance for the revelation of the *basileia*. By the same token, it is impossible to determine a place, say, in the wilderness (Matt. 24.26), where it will appear. Rather – and this is the positive statement – the reign of God ἐντὸς ὑμῶν ἐστιν (note, however, that the ἐστίν has no equivalent in Aramaic, as Aramaic does not have a copula). But what does ἐντὸς ὑμῶν mean?

The difficulty is that ἐντός is ambiguous. In secular Greek ἐντός means 'in the realm of', 'within', 'in the midst of'; in Septuagint Greek it can also mean 'indwelling in' (e.g. Ψ 108.22). Now the meaning 'indwelling in' can certainly be excluded. Neither in Judaism nor elsewhere in the New Testament do we find the idea that the reign of God is something indwelling in men, to be found, say, in the heart; such a spiritualistic understanding is ruled out both for Jesus and for the early Christian tradition. There remains, then, the meaning 'in the midst of'. But this immediately raises a new difficulty. The statement that 'the reign is in your midst' can be interpreted in two ways: the *basileia* can be thought to be either present (in which case the 'in your midst' would refer to the presence of Jesus) or future. We can solve this question if we note that in the following verses (17.23f.) there is a parallel to v. 21.[3] Both times a positive statement is set over against the negative assertion that the dawning of the *basileia* cannot be localized (v. 21a/23). Just as the negative statement in v. 21a corresponds to that in v. 23, so the positive statement in v. 21b corresponds to that in v. 24. That means that v. 21b is to be interpreted along the lines of v. 24; the two statements are parallel. It follows that just as the future ἐροῦσιν in the negative statement has the same meaning in vv. 21a and 23, so too the ἐστίν in v. 21b belongs in the same temporal sphere as the ἔσται in v. 24. Neither the ἐστίν nor the ἔσται had an equivalent in Aramaic, so the difference in tense only arose when the sayings were translated into Greek. Verse 21b must therefore, like v. 24, be understood eschatologically and be translated: '. . . . will (suddenly) be in your midst'.

Thus even in the ἐντὸς ὑμῶν ἐστιν saying (Luke 17.21b), the *basileia* is understood eschatologically; it is coming suddenly.

We are confronted with an assured result: nowhere in the message

[1] ἔρχεται, which corresponds to an atemporal Aramaic participle, the time reference of which is determined by the context, must be translated as future in both instances in v. 20 (in the question 20a, as well as in the answer 20b, cf. the future ἐροῦσιν v. 21).

[2] παρατήρησις denotes e.g. astronomical calculation or diagnosis.

[3] The reason for the twofold tradition lies in the different audiences: vv. 20f. are directed to the Pharisees, vv. 23f. to the disciples.

of Jesus does the *basileia* denote the lasting reign of God over Israel in this age (this idea is, in fact, present in Matt. 21.43, ἀρθήσεται ἀφ' ὑμῶν ἡ βασιλεία τοῦ θεοῦ, but the verse is absent from Mark, and is therefore an addition). Rather, the *basileia* is always and everywhere understood in eschatological terms; it denotes the time of salvation, the consummation of the world, the restoration of the disrupted communion between God and man. Jesus in particular takes up Dan. 2.44, according to which the God of heaven will establish an eternal rule, and Dan. 7.27, according to which the kingdom will be given to the people of the saints of the most high (cf. Luke 12.32)[1] – we shall see later that the book of Daniel was especially important to him.[2] So when Jesus proclaims ἤγγικεν ἡ βασιλεία τοῦ θεοῦ and has it proclaimed by his disciples (Mark 1.15 par. Matt. 4.17; 10.7; Luke 10.9, 11), the meaning is that the eschatological hour of God, the victory of God, the consummation of the world, is near. Indeed it is very near.

We can sum up the result of this section by giving a last precision to the sentence ἤγγικεν ἡ βασιλεία τοῦ θεοῦ. We saw earlier that Jesus largely followed the pious custom of his time in paraphrasing the divine name.[3] Now in Judaism the term *malkūtā* (*delāhā*) can be used as a periphrasis for God as ruler.[4] This meaning can be detected in the sayings of Jesus which speak of the coming of the reign of God. So when Jesus announces ἤγγικεν ἡ βασιλεία τοῦ θεοῦ, his meaning is virtually, 'God is near'.[5] This is what people will have heard in the call of Jesus: 'God is coming, he is standing at the door, indeed (ἔφθασεν),[6] he is already there'.

[1] See below §21 (The Consummation of the People of God).
[2] See below, p. 205.
[3] See above, pp. 9f.
[4] *yēred yhwh ṣebā'ōt*, Isa. 31.4, is rendered by the Targum *titgelē malkūtā deyhwh ṣebā'ōt*; in the same way, *hinnē 'elōhēkem* 40.9 is rendered by the Targum *'itgelī'at malkūtā de'elāhakōn*. Cf. further Targ. Isa. 24.23; 52.7; Micah 4.7; Zech.14.9. Outside the Targum e.g. 1 QSb 4.25f.; 'And you will be a servant (*behēkāl malkūt*) in the temple of the kingly reign (i.e. of God)'; Kaddish (see below, p. 198); Wisdom 10.10 (of Jacob's dream at Bethel, Gen. 28.12): ἔδειξεν (wisdom) αὐτῷ (Jacob) βασιλείαν θεοῦ; Midr. Sam. 13.4 (ed. S. Buber, Krakau 1893, 42b 13f.) on I Sam. 8.7, where R. Simeon ben Yohai (about AD 150) renders the *'ōtī* of the text ('they have rejected me') as 'kingly reign of God, kingly reign of David and building of the sanctuary'.
[5] For the idea of God's 'coming' see Isa. 59.20; Micah 1.3; Eth. Enoch 1.3f., 9; Ass. Mos. 10.3, 7; Rabbinic instances in Billerbeck I 164; IV 966, 981.
[6] Luke 11.20 par. Matt. 12.28.

(iii) *The dawning consummation of the world*

Only now that we have established that ἡ βασιλεία τοῦ θεοῦ had an eschatological significance in the sayings of Jesus and denoted the last, final revelation of the glory of God, can we estimate the new element in the message with which Jesus appeared. This new element was certainly not the assurance that the coming of the new age was near; Jesus shared this assurance with apocalyptic and especially with John the Baptist. No, what must be set down as the original work of Jesus is that he made the rarely used term *malkūtā*[1] the central concept of his public preaching. With this word he associated such a wealth of otherwise uninstanced phrases, that we must regard these linguistic creations as a characteristic of his way of speaking (see above, pp. 32–35). But the really new element in his proclamation of the *basileia* is something different.

The sixfold parallelism in two-beat rhythm[2] in Luke 7.22f. par. Matt. 11.5f. brings out this new element very clearly:

> τυφλοὶ ἀναβλέπουσιν,
> χωλοὶ περιπατοῦσιν,
> λεπροὶ καθαρίζονται,
> καὶ κωφοὶ ἀκούουσιν,
> νεκροὶ ἐγείρονται,
> πτωχοὶ εὐαγγελίζονται·
> καὶ μακάριός ἐστιν ὃς ἐὰν μὴ σκανδαλισθῇ ἐν ἐμοί.

Matthew and Luke understood this saying as an enumeration of miracles which Jesus performed before the eyes of John's messengers.[3] But originally the *logion* had another meaning. To understand it we must start from the fact that it represents a free combination of quotations from Isa. 35.5ff. and 29.18f. (both representations of the time of salvation) with 61.1f. (glad tidings for the poor):

> 5 Then the eyes of the *blind* shall be opened,
> and the ears of the *deaf* unstopped;
> 6 then shall the *lame man* leap like a hart,
> and the tongue of the dumb sing for joy.

---

[1] Billerbeck I 178–80 has collected the instances of the eschatological use of *malkūt*/βασιλεία.

[2] For the division see p. 21, n.1; we are following Luke.

[3] Luke 7.21f.; Matt. 11.4. Cf. also the miracle stories, which Matthew puts first in chs. 8f.

> For waters shall break forth in the wilderness,
> and streams in the desert;
> 7 the burning sand shall become a pool,
> and the thirsty ground springs of water . . . (Isa. 35.5ff.)

> 18 In that day the *deaf* shall hear the words of a book,
> and out of their gloom and darkness the eyes of the *blind*
> shall see.
> 19 The *meek* shall obtain fresh joy in the Lord,
> and the *poor* among men shall exult in the Holy One of
> Israel . . . (Isa. 29.18f.)

> 1 The Spirit of the Lord God is upon me,
> because the Lord has anointed me
> to bring *good tidings to the afflicted*;
> he has sent me to bind up the broken-hearted,
> to proclaim liberty to the captives,
> and the opening of the prison to those who are bound;
> 2 to proclaim the year of the Lord's favour . . . (Isa. 61.1f.)[1]

In respect of its form, Luke 7.22f. par., like all the three Isaiah passages, has the character of a list. The images that they use, light for the blind, hearing for the deaf, shouting for joy by the dumb, etc., are all age-old phrases in the east for the time of salvation, when there will be no more sorrow, no more crying and no more grief. Thus in Luke 7.22f. we have an eschatological cry of joy uttered by Jesus. To tune our ear to its contents we should, say, contrast the Tannaitic list which says: 'Four are compared with a dead man: the lame, the blind, the leper and the childless'.[2] According to the thinking of the time, the situation of such men was no longer worth calling life: in effect, they were dead. But now help is extended to those in the depths of despair, now those who were as good as dead are raised

---

[1] Agreements between Isaiah's and Jesus' enumeration are italicized. Isa. 26.19 also has a place here:

> Thy *dead* shall live,
> my bodies shall rise,
> O dwellers in the dust, awake and sing for joy!
> For thy dew is a dew of light,
> and on the land of the shades thou wilt let it fall.

But the significant form of an enumeration by means of a list, which characterizes the three Isaiah texts cited above, does not appear in this passage.

[2] b. Ned. 64b Bar.

to life. The water of life flows, the time of the curse is at an end, paradise is opened. Even now, *the consummation of the world is dawning.* The sixfold list merely picks out examples of the fullness of its gifts; it could continue endlessly, as the continuation of the three Isaiah passages shows. It should be noted that the lepers and the dead are not mentioned in the three lists in Isaiah.[1] That Jesus mentions them means that the fulfilment goes far beyond all promises, hopes and expectations. Of course, there is still a closing sentence to follow: 'And blessed is he who takes no offence at me'. All this is said paradoxically; it is true despite the stumbling-block,[2] true only for him who believes.

Closely associated with this cry of joy is Luke 4.16–21. Here Isa. 61.1f. is quoted as the text of a sermon by Jesus. Now this is the text which Luke 7.22f. par. ended (see above). The sermon itself is summed up in the sentence σήμερον πεπλήρωται ἡ γραφὴ αὕτη ἐν τοῖς ὠσὶν ὑμῶν (v. 21). Here ἐν τοῖς ὠσὶν ὑμῶν does not mean '(the text of scripture which is still ringing) in your ears (is now being fulfilled)', but, '(the text of scripture is being fulfilled) before your ears', i.e. you are ear-witnesses that the promise that the time of God's grace is dawning, is being fulfilled *today* – that is where the stress lies.

Mark 2.18f. provides a further example of this message. Jesus is charged implicitly, in the question why his disciples do not fast voluntarily,[3] like the disciples of John and the Pharisees,[4] with a lack of religious seriousness and readiness to repent. He replies with the counter-question: μὴ δύνανται οἱ υἱοὶ τοῦ νυμφῶνος, ἐν ᾧ ὁ νυμφίος μετ' αὐτῶν ἐστιν, νηστεύειν; (n.b.: as the comparison between the Messiah and the bridegroom is unknown to Judaism of this period,[5] ἐν ᾧ ὁ νυμφίος μετ'αὐτῶν should be translated 'at the wedding').[6] The wedding has begun, the bridegroom has been received, the rejoicing rings out far and wide over the land, the guests are reclining at the festal meal – who could fast in those circumstances? The wedding is a

---

[1] But cf. p. 104, n. 1 above on the dead.

[2] For the offence, see pp. 118f., 245 below.

[3] Only on the Day of Atonement was fasting a universal obligation.

[4] Cf. Luke 18.12.

[5] J. Jeremias, νύμφη, νυμφίος, *TDNT* IV, 1967, 1099–1106: 1101f.; cf. J. Gnilka, '"Bräutigam" – ein spätjüdisches Messiasprädikat?', *TTZ* 69, 1960, 298–301 (on 1 Q Isaᵃ. 61.10). An isolated and late instance, *Pesiqta de Rab Kahana* 149a, ed. S. Buber, Lyck 1868, which interprets Isa. 61.10 as referring to the Messiah (Jeremias, *Parables*², 52 n.14), does not alter the general picture.

[6] Dodd, *Parables*, 116 n.2.

106	THE DAWN OF THE TIME OF SALVATION

common symbol of the time of salvation. It has dawned, it is already here.

Thus Jesus uses the symbolic language of the Bible to proclaim the dawn of the time of salvation. He does it with repeatedly new pictures. The *light* shines. The whole house (which at that time usually consisted only of one room) becomes bright when the oil-lamp is lit, and the darkness has to yield (Mark 4.21 par.). The brightness of the city of God[1] on the summit of the hill is already shining into the darkness of the world (Matt. 5.14).

The *harvest* time has come. In the parables of Jesus, harvest is a symbol for the time of salvation and its abundant riches – thirty-fold, sixty-fold, a hundred-fold (Mark 4.8 par.). It is ripe (Matt. 9.37 par.); the fields are white (John 4.35). Seedtime and harvest arrive together (v. 36). Jesus sends out the disciples, not to sow (nowhere is that said) but to reap,[2] and he bids them ask the Lord of the harvest to send labourers into his harvest (Matt. 9.38 par.).

The *fig-tree* shoots: spring is here (Mark 13.28f.). Whereas almost all trees in Palestine keep their leaves in winter, those of the fig tree fall. With its bare branches it then looks as if it is dead. So it is particularly appropriate as a symbol of the change from death to life: when it shoots, that means that God is creating new life from death.[3]

The *new wine* is offered. From earliest times in the East, vine and wine have been symbols of the new age.[4] It would be senseless to put the young wine into old skins, as it would burst them (Mark 2.22 par.).

The *best robe* is given to the lost son (Luke 15.22). The wedding garment is put on (Matt. 22.11). In Mark 2.21 the garment is a symbol of the cosmos (cf. Heb. 1.11f.; Acts 10.11 par. 11.5):[5] it is senseless to sew a piece of untreated, new cloth on an old garment – the old times have passed away.

---

[1] G. von Rad, 'The City on the Hill', *The Problem of the Hexateuch and other Essays*, Edinburgh and London 1966, 232–42.

[2] Dodd, *Parables*, 187.

[3] Jeremias, *Parables*[2], 119f.

[4] Gen. 9.20; 49.11f.; Num. 13.23f.; Amos 9.13; Joel 3.18; Syr. Apoc. Bar. 39.7; John 2.1–11, cf. 15.1ff.; many Rabbinic instances. Cf. J. Jeremias, *Jesus als Weltvollender*, BFCT 33, 4, Gütersloh 1930, 27–29.

[5] R. Eisler, *Weltenmantel und Himmelszelt*, München 1910; J. Jeremias, *op. cit.*, 24–27.

The *bread of life* is given to the children (Mark 7.24–30 par.).[1] Bread of life and water of life[2] are the gifts of paradise. Its gates are opening.

At this very moment the *peace of God* is offered and judgment decreed (Matt. 10.11–15 par. Luke 10.5–11). Even now there is binding and loosing (Matt. 16.19; 18.18).

The Gospel of John stresses the 'even now' that Jesus proclaimed with special emphasis. 'The hour is coming and *now is*', in which those who are spiritually dead will be raised to life (John 5.25) and worship will be offered to God in spirit and in truth (4.23). So dominant is the present eschatology in the Fourth Gospel that Bultmann claims that there is no future eschatology in it at all, and ascribes the few passages in which it is expressed to an ecclesiastical redaction.[3]

Jesus announced the 'even now' of salvation not only in words, but also *in deeds*. In driving out the merchants from the profaned sanctuary he is fulfilling Zech. 14.21: 'And there shall no longer be a trader in the house of the Lord of hosts on that day'. The day has come, the sanctuary is being renewed, the new age is dawning.[4] Mention should also be made of Mark 7.24–30 and Matt. 8.5–13 (par. Luke 7.1–10). Elsewhere Jesus limits his help in principle to Israel; the advent of the Gentiles in the eschatological pilgrimage of the nations is God's own act at the end of things (see below, pp. 245ff.). The help for the two Gentiles depicted in the two stories is an anticipation, a proleptic sign of the breaking in of the kingdom.

Jesus' disciples can experience all this with him, and so Jesus calls them blessed (Luke 10.23f. par. Matt. 13.16f.). What was it that prophets and righteous men longed to experience, what did kings like David and Solomon desire? The dawn of the time of salvation!

---

[1] The faith of the Gentile woman does not consist in the fact that she gives Jesus a quick answer, but in the fact that with her 'Yes, sir, but' she acknowledges him as the giver of the bread of life (v.28).

[2] Cf. John 4.10, 14; 7.37f.

[3] The weakness of this production of a de-eschatologized Gospel of John is that it presupposes Bultmann's source theories not only for the Gospel, but also for I John. That seems impossible to me on grounds of both style and language. Cf. J. Jeremias, 'Johanneische Literarkritik', *ThBl* 20 2/3, 1941, cols. 34–46; E. Ruckstuhl, *Die literarische Einheit des Johannesevangeliums*, Freiburg in der Schweiz 1951.

[4] C. H. Dodd, *According to the Scriptures*, London 1952, 66f.; C. Roth, 'The Cleansing of the Temple and Zechariah XIV.21', *NovTest* 4, 1960, 174–81; F. Hahn, *Christologische Hoheitstitel*, FRLANT 83, Göttingen 1963=[3]1966, 172 n.2; N. Q. Hamilton, 'Temple Cleansing and Temple Bank', *JBL* 83, 1964, 365–72: 372.

The disciples may not only experience it but also, like Jesus himself, proclaim it in word and deed:

κηρύσσετε λέγοντες ὅτι ἤγγικεν ἡ βασιλεία τῶν οὐρανῶν.
ἀσθενοῦντας θεραπεύετε,
νεκροὺς   ἐγείρετε,
λεπροὺς   καθαρίζετε,
δαιμόνια   ἐκβάλλετε   (Matt. 10.7f.)

John appeared as the preacher of repentance in the wilderness (Isa. 40.3); Jesus is the *mᵉbasśēr*, the messenger of peace, anointed with the spirit, who proclaims the time of salvation (Isa. 52.7).[1] The time of expectation is at an end; the time of fulfilment has dawned.

With what has just been said we are on the threshold of the earliest tradition, quite independently of any decision on the authenticity of each individual saying. For Jesus' proclamation of the dawn of the time of salvation is without analogy. With regard to his environment, he is the 'only Jew known to us from ancient times', who proclaimed 'that the new age of salvation had already begun'.[2] With regard to the early church, the message of the first Christian missionaries ran differently: Jesus, the crucified and risen one, is the Christ. The proclamation of the present dawning of the transfiguration of the world comes from before Easter; it does not yet have the stamp of the christology of the early church.

§ 12 · GOOD NEWS FOR THE POOR

J. Jeremias, 'Zöllner und Sünder', *ZNW* 30, 1931, 293–300; a revised version appeared in *Jerusalem*, 303–12; E. Gulin, *Die Freude im Neuen Testament*, Helsinki 1932; G. Friedrich, εὐαγγελίζομαι κτλ., *TDNT* II, 1964, 707–37; R. Pesch, 'Levi-Matthäus (Mc 2, 14/Mt 9, 9; 10, 3). Ein Beitrag zur Lösung eines alten Problems', *ZNW* 59, 1968, 40–56; O. Michel, τελώνης, *TWNT* VIII, 1969, 88–106.

To say that Jesus proclaimed the dawn of the consummation of the world is not a complete description of his proclamation of the *basileia*; on the contrary, we have still to mention its most decisive feature. This becomes clear if we turn once again to the sixfold

---

[1] 11Q Melch 18, expounding Isa. 52.7, 'The bringer of joyful news, he is the one anointed by the spirit' (read *hrw*[*ḥ*] with Yadin, Flusser, van der Woude).

[2] Flusser, *Jesus*, 87.

parallelism in Matt. 11.5 par. Luke 7.22, which enumerates the signs of the time of salvation.[1] In lines 1–5 it speaks of God's acts, and in line 6 of his word: πτωχοὶ εὐαγγελίζονται. That this sixth clause carries the stress emerges not only from its position at the end but also from the saying that is attached to it: καὶ μακάριός ἐστιν ὃς ἐὰν μὴ σκανδαλισθῇ ἐν ἐμοί (Matt. 11.6 par. Luke 7.23). Why should anyone be offended at the blind seeing, the lame walking, the lepers being cleansed, the deaf hearing and the dead being raised? The closing remark about the offence cannot refer to these first five clauses, at least at first glance[2] – but in practice Jesus' offer to the poor proved to be highly offensive. In pronouncing those who overcame this stumbling-block blessed, Jesus underlines the importance of the phrase πτωχοὶ εὐαγγελίζονται. That this in fact expresses the heart of Jesus' proclamation is confirmed from yet another side: the same statement, put in the form of a promise, opens the powerful eschatological proclamation of the beatitudes: μακάριοι οἱ πτωχοί (Luke 6.20).

(i) Who are 'the poor'?

If we are to gain a clear picture of the people to whom Jesus brought the good news, our starting point must be the fact that, when we look at the various designations of the followers of Jesus as they are given in the gospels, we come to know these people from a double perspective. They are repeatedly called 'publicans and sinners' (Mark 2.16 par.; Matt. 11.19 par.; Luke 15.1), 'publicans and prostitutes' (Matt. 21.32), or simply 'sinners' (Mark 2.17; Luke 7.37, 39; 15.2; 19.7). The deep contempt expressed in such designations shows that these phrases were coined by *Jesus' opponents*; Matt. 11.19 par. Luke 7.34 confirms that explicitly. In the world of Jesus, the term 'sinner' had a quite definite ring. It was not only a fairly general designation for those who notoriously failed to observe the commandments of God and at whom, therefore, everyone pointed a finger, but also a specific term for those engaged in despised trades. We have lists in which proscribed trades are collected.[3] These are in part trades which were generally thought to lead to immorality, but above all those which by experience led to dishonesty: the second

---

[1] See above, pp. 103f.
[2] We shall see in §21 that the first five clauses also contain a stumbling block, though only indirectly (cf. p. 246, n.2).
[3] ‡Jeremias.

category included gamblers with dice, usurers, tax collectors, publicans and herdsmen (these last were suspected of leading their herds on to other people's land and pilfering the produce of the herd). When the gospels talk of 'sinners', they are thinking of those occupied in despised trades as well as those whose way of life was disreputable. This is clear from their terminology, especially the composite phrase 'robbers, deceivers, adulterers, publicans' (Luke 18.11), which is paralleled by analogous collections in Rabbinic literature, e.g. 'tax collectors, robbers, money changers and publicans' (Derek ereṣ 2); 'murderers, robbers and publicans' (Ned. 3.4); cf. 'tax collectors and thieves' (John 7.6). The publicans are the typical ἁμαρτωλοί in the gospels.[1] They, in particular, were outlawed.

A distinction must be made here between tax collectors (*gabbāyā*) and toll collectors (*mōkᵉsā*). In New Testament times, the tax collectors, who had to take in the direct taxes (poll-taxes and land-taxes), were state officials.[2] They were usually drawn from the ranks of well-to-do families, and had to apportion the taxes to those citizens who were liable to pay them. They had to guarantee the receipt of the taxes from their own resources.[3] The toll collectors, on the other hand, were sub-tenants of the rich toll farmers (Luke 19.2 ἀρχιτελώνης), who had successfully made the highest bid for the toll income of a district for a fixed period.[4] The rule that tolls were to be farmed out, which seems to have been usual in Palestine both in the areas under the Herodian princes and in those occupied by the Romans, explains why the publicans were particularly hated by the people.[5] The police who accompanied the tax collectors to protect them could indeed also be guilty of abuses (Luke 3.14),[6] but the publicans were to a much greater degree open to the temptation to deceive, because whatever the circumstances they had to extract the agreed sum plus their additional profit. They therefore exploited public ignorance of the scale of tolls[7] to administer duties unscrupulously into their own pockets during their tax season (Luke 3.12f.). Because of this they were regarded as utter deceivers, and this contempt also extended to their families.[8] Civil rights were denied publicans: no honorary offices could be conferred on them, and they were not admitted as witnesses

---

[1] ‡Michel.   [2] ‡Michel, 97.8f.   [3] Jeremias, *Jerusalem*, 228.

[4] ‡Michel, 97.20f. The toll-farmers looked after larger areas (Luke 19.2 ἀρχιτελώνης) and sub-let to lesser contractors.

[5] In b. Sanh.25b the tax-collectors are exonerated, but not the publicans.

[6] See p. 48, n.3.   [7] ‡Michel, 99.18ff.   [8] Instances in ‡Michel, 102.15–17.

in trials.[1] If they had belonged to a Pharisaic community before they entered office, they were expelled.[2] 'Repentance is hard for tax collectors and publicans',[3] for that meant not only giving up their profession but making good in the same way as a thief (restoration plus a fifth). How could they know everyone whom they had deceived?[4]

On the other hand, the assertion that the publicans were regarded as levitically unclean[5] is inaccurate. This was true only of the tax collectors (Hag. 3.6; Toh. 7.6; Tos.Toh. 8.5f.); they were unclean because to collect the tax or to check information they had to go into houses which could have become unclean (e.g. by the presence of a corpse). The publican, on the other hand, was not himself unclean. All that was unclean was the crook of his staff with which he rummaged through baggage, because there might be levitically unclean clothing inside it (Kel. 15.4). This fact is important if we are rightly to assess the offence caused to Pharisaic circles by Jesus' associations with publicans. It did not lie in the ritual or even in the political realm (collaboration); its basis was exclusively moral.

Jesus' followers are also often described as 'the little ones' (Mark 9.42; Matt. 10.42; 18.10, 14) or – as Semitic languages have no superlatives – 'the least' (Matt. 25.40, 45) or 'the simple ones' (Matt. 11.25 par.; οἱ νήπιοι). The 'simple ones' are contrasted with the 'wise and understanding' (ibid.).[6] The expression νήπιος (Hebrew petī, Aramaic šabrā) designates the disciples of Jesus as men who have had no religious education, i.e., as the only education in Palestinian Judaism was religious, as uneducated, backward and at the same time irreligious people. Once again we can hear the note of contempt attached to the designation 'little, immature', which suggests that it was coined by Jesus' opponents.

The explanation of the much discussed saying Matt. 11.12: ἡ βασιλεία τῶν οὐρανῶν βιάζεται καὶ βιασταὶ ἁρπάζουσιν αὐτήν par. Luke 16.16: ἡ βασιλεία τοῦ θεοῦ εὐαγγελίζεται καὶ πᾶς εἰς αὐτὴν βιάζεται is possibly also to be sought in the same direction. What is the meaning of 'violent men rob the basileia', or 'every man makes his way into

[1] Jeremias, Jerusalem, 311f.
[2] Tos.Dem. 3.4: 'They expelled an associate who became a tax-collector'. This also applied, of course, to the publicans (cf. the way in which the two groups are taken together in note 3).
[3] Tos.B.M. 8.26; b. B.K. 94b.
[4] Tos.B.K. 10.14. A later expedient was to use the sum owed to unknown persons for purposes which served the common good, in particular for providing cisterns (b. B.K. 94b). But this rule does not appear to have existed as early as in the days of Jesus; at any rate, Zacchaeus acted differently (Luke 19.8).
[5] ‡Michel, 101.13f.; Perrin, Rediscovering, 94.
[6] For the age of the logion see below, p. 190.

it violently'? F. W. Danker[1] has made the illuminating suggestion that here, too, we have a designation of the followers of Jesus which derived from his opponents: these sinners who follow Jesus force their way into the holy precincts reserved for the pious. They are βιασταί 'violent intruders'; the basileia βιάζεται 'suffers violence'. This could be the solution of the riddle posed by this obscure saying.

Summing up, then, we can now say that Jesus' following consisted predominantly of the disreputable, the 'ammē hā-'āreṣ, the uneducated, the ignorant, whose *religious* ignorance and *moral* behaviour stood in the way of their access to salvation, according to the convictions of the time.

But alongside this there is a quite different perspective. If we look at the same people through the eyes of Jesus, they appear in another light. He calls them 'the poor', those who 'labour and are heavy laden' (Matt. 11.28).

The term '*the poor*' has been understood by Luke and Matthew in different senses, as the first beatitude shows. Its very wording is different in the two gospels. Luke 6.20 has a short form: μακάριοι οἱ πτωχοί, Matt. 5.3 a long form: μακάριοι οἱ πτωχοὶ τῷ πνεύματι. The short οἱ πτωχοί is surely original. This is suggested by the fact that Matt. 11.5 par. Luke 7.22 similarly speaks only of πτωχοί (without any addition). Furthermore, the first woe in Luke 6.24, which runs parallel to the first beatitude, speaks only of οἱ πλούσιοι (without any addition). To the different wording corresponds a different meaning which the context shows Luke and Matthew to attach to the word πτωχοί. The Lucan tradition has in mind those who are really poor, just as in the continuation of the beatitudes it is thinking of those who are really hungry, who really weep and are really persecuted (Luke 6.21–23). That is not, of course, to say that by οἱ πτωχοί it means simply those who have no material possessions, the proletariat; rather, Luke 6.22f. shows that the Lucan tradition is thinking of the disciples, who have to suffer poverty, hunger and persecution because of their discipleship. The Matthaean tradition, on the other hand, understands the first beatitude in a purely religious way, as the addition τῷ πνεύματι shows, taking up Old Testament formulations.[2] In this view, οἱ πτωχοί means the humble, those who are poor before God, who stand before God as beggars, with empty hands, conscious of their spiritual poverty. So we find quite different understandings of οἱ πτωχοί in Matthew and in Luke. How did Jesus intend the word?

In answering this question, we must start from the fact that the statement πτωχοὶ εὐαγγελίζονται (Matt. 11.5 par.; cf. Luke 4.18) is a quotation, indeed a quotation of the prophetic saying Isa. 61.1, understood as a prediction: 'He has

---

[1] 'Luke 16.16 – An Opposition Logion', *JBL* 77, 1958, 231–43. F. Mussner, 'Die Mitte des Evangeliums in neutestamentlicher Sicht', *Catholica* 15, 1961, 271–92: 277, agrees.

[2] Isa. 57.15: 'humble spirit'; 66.2: 'contrite spirit'; Ps. 34.18 [19] 'broken-hearted'. From the Qumran literature compare 1 QM 14.7 ʿnwy rwḥ, 'humble in spirit', in contrast to 1 QS 11.1 rmʿy rwḥ, 'proud in spirit'.

sent me to bring good tidings to the poor (*lᵉbaśśēr ʿᵃnāwîm*)'.[1] It is helpful to establish this, as in the context of Isa. 61.1, the term 'poor' is explained by a whole series of parallel expressions. The following phrases alternate with it: 'the broken-hearted', 'the captives (to guilt?)', 'those who are bound' (v.1), 'those who mourn' (v. 2), 'those who are of a faint spirit' (v. 3). This makes it certain that the 'poor' are those who are oppressed in quite a general sense: the oppressed who cannot defend themselves, the desperate, the hopeless. *ʿānī/ʿānāw* is also used elsewhere in prophetic preaching in this comprehensive sense. Originally a designation for the desolate, in the prophets the word embraces the oppressed and the poor who know that they are thrown completely on God's help. Jesus used 'the poor' in this wide sense that the term had acquired in the prophets. Certainly all those in need, the hungry and the thirsty, the unclothed and the strangers, the sick and the captives, belong to the 'least': they are his brothers (Matt. 25.31-46).[2] But the circle of the 'poor' is wider. That becomes clear when we collect the designations and imagery with which Jesus characterizes them. He calls them the hungry, those who weep, the sick, those who labour, those who bear burdens, the last, the simple, the lost, the sinners.

The reason why Luke and Matthew each emphasize a different feature of the complex meaning of the word 'poor', in that Luke thinks of outward oppression and Matthew of inner need, is that the tradition at their disposal had applied the designation 'poor' to different church situations and controversies: the Matthaean tradition of the beatitudes was formulated in a church which was fighting against the Pharisaic temptation to self-righteousness, the Lucan tradition in a church which was in deep distress and needed to be comforted.

Jesus looks with infinite mercy on these beggars before God when in Matt. 11.28 he calls them 'those who labour and are heavy laden'. Their burden is doubly hard: they have to bear public contempt from men and, in addition, the hopelessness of ever gaining God's salvation.

(ii) The good news

The good news that Jesus proclaims to the πτωχοί is said in the first beatitude to be ὑμετέρα ἐστὶν ἡ βασιλεία τοῦ θεοῦ 'You share in God's reign' (Luke 6.20). Mark 2.17 paraphrases the proclamation of the good news as καλέσαι ἁμαρτωλούς; the good news consists in the fact the Jesus invites sinners to God's festive meal. The poor are promised that God will intervene; nor are they put off with hopes for an indefinite future; the time of salvation is manifested, realized, actualized for them even now. The parables of the two debtors (Luke 7.41-43), the unmerciful servant (Matt. 18.23-25) and the love of the father (Luke 15.11-32) show that in the good news what

---

[1] See above, p. 108.
[2] For the authenticity of the nucleus of Matt. 25.31-46 see Jeremias, *Parables*[2], 207f.

happens is the remission of debts. Now it is in fact only reported twice that Jesus promised the *forgiveness of sins* in so many words (Mark 2.1–12 par.; Luke 7.36–50), and therefore there has been some doubt whether he ever did so.[1] In reality, however, the number of indications that Jesus promised God's forgiveness is much greater. (Note that the passive in Mark 2.5; Luke 7.47f. is a periphrasis for the divine action: *God* is the one who forgives.) This becomes clear as soon as two points are established. First, counting words in the proclamation of Jesus always leads to confusion. ἄφεσις meaning forgiveness may occur on Jesus' lips only in isolated instances,[2] and ἀφιέναι (= forgive) slightly more often, but still to a limited degree. However, such statistical statements mean nothing. Jesus does not speak in an abstract theological way as Paul does later, but in pictures, and there the subject of 'forgiveness' is constantly present. Jesus speaks of the remission of a giant debt (Matt. 18.27), of debts great and small (Luke 7.42), of the sinner being heard (18.14),[3] of the stray being brought home (15.5), of the lost being found (15.9), of the prisoners being freed and the badly treated being released (4.18), of acceptance of the child into the father's house (15.11–32). He pictures the father running to meet the lost child and kissing him (Luke 15.20), putting on him the best garment, the ring and the shoes which in the east are a mark of the free man (v. 22), having a feast prepared, to be celebrated with music and dancing in honour of the lost one who has returned (v. 25). And then Jesus makes the father speak in two metaphors about what has happened: the lost ἀνέζησεν, i.e. (noting that Aramaic-type avoidance of the passive, cf. p. 12) 'has been raised from the dead', and εὑρέθη, i.e 'he has been brought home' (like a stray animal) (vv. 24, 32). All these metaphors and parables are pictures of forgiveness and the restoration of communion with God. So forgiveness is not mentioned only in those passages in which the words ἀφιέναι or ἄφεσις occur.

This discovery is confirmed by a second, even more important observation: Jesus promised forgiveness not only in words, but *in actions*. The form of proclamation of forgiveness in action that most

---

[1] E. Linnemann, *Parables of Jesus*, London 1966, 178.

[2] Mark 3.29 ('never has forgiveness'); Matt. 26.28 (addition to Mark 14.24); Luke 24.47 (Easter story).

[3] For δικαιοῦσθαι 'having one's prayers heard' (*iustificari*, IV Ezra 7.12), cf. J. Jeremias, *The Central Message of the New Testament*, New York and London 1965, 52; id., 'Die Gedankenführung in Röm. 4. Zum paulinischen Glaubensverständnis' (to be printed among the papers from the *Colloquium Paulinum*, 16–21 April 1968, held in Rome).

impressed the men of his time was his table-fellowship with sinners. Jesus invited them into his house (Luke 15.2 προσδέχεται) and reclined at table with them (Mark 2.15f. par.)[1] in festive meals.[2] The taunt recorded in Matt. 11.19 par. Luke 7.34, which certainly comes from the time of Jesus' ministry, shows vividly that these reports are historical:[3]

ἰδοὺ ἄνθρωπος φάγος καὶ οἰνοπότης,

τελωνῶν φίλος καὶ ἁμαρτωλῶν.

The mocking exaggeration should not give us the wrong idea that Jesus' normal company at table with his followers was limited to 'sinners'; it was quite enough to offend Jesus' opponents that he excluded no-one from it.[4] The fact that this course of action has not left even stronger traces in our sources reminds us that sadly the great interval of time that separates the gospels from the events they describe has dimmed some of their essential features.[5] Nevertheless, it is worth noting that we know by name no less than three publicans who were numbered among the followers of Jesus.[6]

To understand what Jesus was doing in eating with 'sinners', it is important to realize that in the east, even today, to invite a man to a meal was an honour. It was an offer of peace, trust, brotherhood and forgiveness; in short, sharing a table meant sharing life. The report in II Kings 25.27–30 (par. Jer. 52.31–34) that Jehoiachin was brought by the king of Babylon from prison to the royal *table* is a public proclamation of his rehabilitation. In a similar way, king Agrippa I had the supreme commander Silas, who had fallen out of favour, invited to his table as a sign that he had forgiven him.[7] In Judaism in particular, table-fellowship means fellowship before God, for the eating of a piece of broken bread by everyone who shares in the meal brings out the fact that they all have a share in the blessing which the master of the house had spoken over the unbroken bread. Thus Jesus' meals with the publicans and sinners, too, are not only events on a social level, not only an expression of his unusual humanity and

---

[1] ἐν τῇ οἰκίᾳ αὐτοῦ (Mark 2.15) could also have referred to Jesus' house here (E. Lohmeyer, *Das Evangelium des Markus*, Meyer K 1, 2, Göttingen 1937 = [17]1967, 55).

[2] The festive character of the meal emerges from the κατακεῖσθαι 'recline'. For ordinary meals, people sat at table (see Jeremias, *Eucharistic Words*[2], 48f.).

[3] Jeremias, *Parables*[2], 161.   [4] Perrin, *Rediscovering*, 107.

[5] Perrin, *op. cit.*, 102.   [6] Levi, Matthew, Zacchaeus (see p. 116, n.1).

[7] Josephus, *Antt.* 19.321.

social generosity and his sympathy with those who were despised, but had an even deeper significance. They are an expression of the mission and message of Jesus (Mark 2.17), eschatological meals, anticipatory celebrations of the feast in the end-time (Matt. 8.11 par.), in which the community of the saints is already being represented (Mark 2.19). The inclusion of sinners in the community of salvation, achieved in table-fellowship, is the most meaningful expression of the message of the redeeming love of God.

Jesus had other ways of expressing the proclamation of forgiveness in action, as well as eating with publicans and sinners. He did it, for example, by lodging quite openly with the chief toll-farmer in Jericho (Luke 19.5), or by summoning publicans into the group of disciples that accompanied him (Mark 2.14; Matt. 9.9; 10.3).[1] Everyone was to see that these people had been accepted by God.

At this point we must make a little sharper the content of the phrase πτωχοὶ εὐαγγελίζονται (Matt. 11.5), which was brought out in the preceding remarks. When the first beatitude says μακάριοι οἱ πτωχοί, ὅτι ὑμετέρα ἐστιν ἡ βασιλεία τοῦ θεοῦ (Luke 6.20; Matt. 5.3 in the third person), the emphasis lies on the ὑμετέρα (Luke) or αὐτῶν (Matthew) which is put at the beginning of the subordinate clause: the reign of God belongs *to the poor alone*. Semitic languages often omit a qualifying 'only', even where we feel it to be indispensable; it must therefore often be supplied in translation.[2] So too here; the first beatitude means that salvation is destined *only* for beggars and sinners. This is what we read explicitly in Mark 2.17 οὐκ ἦλθον καλέσαι (viz. to the eschatological meal) δικαίους ἀλλὰ ἁμαρτωλούς. Jesus said again and again that salvation was for sinners, not for the righteous (it should be noticed that 'the righteous' seems to have been a self-designation of the Pharisees, cf. Ps. Sol. 13.11; 15.6f.). God does not give his revelation to learned theologians, but to the uneducated (Matt. 11.25f. par. Luke 10.21); he opens the *basileia* to children (Mark 10.14) and to those who can say '*Abba* like a child (Matt. 18.3).[3] So the wedding

---

[1] In the First Gospel, the publican Levi, whom (according to Mark) Jesus summons to follow him (Mark 2.14) is replaced by Matthew (Matt. 9.9); this evidently happened because the name Levi did not occur in the list of the twelve (‡Pesch). From this exchange of names we can see: 1. The pre-literary tradition reported of both Levi and Matthew that they were publicans; 2. The report that both Levi (Mark 2.14) and Matthew (Matt. 10.3) were among the disciples who accompanied Jesus is similarly pre-literary.

[2] Cf. Matt. 5.18f., 28, 43, 46 and very frequently.

[3] For the exegesis of Matt. 18.3 cf. Jeremias, *Parables*[2], 190f.

banquet is full, even if all the invited guests refuse to come (Matt. 22.1–10 par. Luke 14.16–24). The lost son is restored to his rights, the one who stayed at home is alienated from his father (Luke 15.11–32). Publicans and prostitutes will 'precede' the righteous into the *basileia* (Matt. 21.31). (The προάγουσιν ὑμᾶς = *mᵉqaddᵉmîn lᵉkôn* does not denote a priority in time, but an exclusive displacement of the others.)[1] The sentence means: 'Publicans and prostitutes will enter the *basileia* of God, and not you'. Similarly an exclusive *min* underlies the παρ' ἐκεῖνον in Luke 18.14:[2] the publican 'went home δεδικαιωμένος παρ' ἐκεῖνον as one whose prayer had been heard by God,[3] whereas the other's had not'.[4]

The end-time brings with it a reversal of conditions. This is an old eschatological theme which recurs frequently in the gospels.[5] It expresses not only the unlimited sovereignty of God, but also his unbounded mercy.

This goodness of God, passing all understanding, means joy and gladness for the poor.[6] They have received riches before which all other values fade (Matt. 13.44–46). They experience more than they could ever have hoped for: God accepts them, although they are empty-handed. Jesus himself rejoices with them: Matt. 11.25f. par. Luke 10.21 and Matt. 11.12 par. Luke 16.16 are probably shouts of of joy rather than laments.[7]

The promise of Ezek. 34.16 is being fulfilled:

I will seek the lost,
and I will bring back the strayed,
and I will bind up the crippled,
and I will strengthen the weak   (cf. Mark 2.17).

Isaiah 29.19 is being fulfilled:

The meek shall obtain fresh joy in the Lord
and the poor among men shall exult in the Holy One of Israel.

[1] Cf. Jeremias, *Parables*², 125 n.48.
[2] There is a survey of the possible renderings of exclusive *min* in Greek in J. Jeremias, *Unknown Sayings of Jesus*, London 1957, 78 n.1 (not included in ²1964).
[3] See above, p. 114, n.3.
[4] Jeremias, *Parables*², 140f.
[5] See below, p. 248.
[6] ‡Gulin.
[7] J. Schmid, *Das Evangelium nach Matthäus*², Regensburg 1965, 193; cf. above, pp. 111f.

Even more, Isaiah 65.19 is being fulfilled, where God says:

I will rejoice in Jerusalem
and be glad in my people,

and Zeph. 3.17f., where it is said of God:

He will rejoice over you with gladness,
he will renew you in his love;
he will exult over you with loud singing as on a day of festival.

So God exults over the returning sinners (Luke 15.7, 10).
This good news is *the* gift of the dawning time of salvation.

(iii) *The vindication of the good news*

The proclamation of the good news was received with a storm of indignation. It was primarily the Pharisaic circles that sharply rejected Jesus' message. We can almost read a scale of rejection out of the tradition: incomprehension (Luke 15.29f.); dismay (15.2; 19.7; Matt. 20.11); abuse (Matt. 11.19 par. Luke 7.34); charge of blasphemy (Mark 2.7);[1] invitation to the disciples to part company with this corrupter (Mark 2.16).[2]

This reaction is not surprising. The good news was a slap in the face to all the religious feelings of the time. The supreme religious duty for contemporary Judaism was to keep away from sinners. Table-fellowship in Qumran was open only to the pure, to the full members.[3] For the Pharisee, 'dealings with sinners put at risk the purity of the righteous and his membership within the realm of the holy and the divine'.[4] 'A Pharisee does not dwell with them (the *'ammē hā-āreṣ*) as a guest, nor does he entertain one of them at home in his garments.'[5] 'It is forbidden to have mercy on one who has no knowledge.'[6]

---

[1] Even the promise of God's forgiveness (see above, p. 11) was enough for Jesus' opponents to feel that he was encroaching on the area reserved for God alone.

[2] The question ὅ τι BL*pc* (= τί ὅ τι AG*pl* = 'So?') μετὰ τῶν τελωνῶν καὶ ἁμαρτωλῶν ἐσθίει καὶ πίνει; is not a harmless request for information, but an invitation to the disciples to reject Jesus.

[3] O. Betz, *What do we know about Jesus?*, London 1968, 74.

[4] *Ibid.*, 32.   [5] Dem. 2.3.

[6] Midr.Sam. 5 §9 (ed. S. Buber, Krakau 1893, 31a 1) par. b. Ber. 33a; b. Sanh. 92a. Cf. 1 QS 10.20f.: 'I (the person praying) will have no pity on all who depart from the way. I will offer no comfort to the smitten until their way becomes perfect.'

'This crowd which does not know the Law stands under the divine curse.'[1] Certainly, Judaism knew that God was merciful and could forgive. But his help was for the righteous; judgment was the destiny of the sinner. Even the sinner could be saved, but only when he had proved the earnestness of his repentance by making good and altering his way of life. Then, and only then, did the Pharisee see him as the object of the love of God. First he had to have become a righteous man.

For Jesus, the love of the Father was directed even towards the despised and lost children. That he called them, and not the righteous (Mark 2.17), was apparently the dissolution of all ethics; it seemed as if moral conduct meant nothing in God's eyes. The world around Jesus based man's relationship with God on his moral conduct. Because the gospel did not do that, it shook religion to its foundations. Thus the stumbling block arose from the good news – and not primarily from Jesus' call to repentance (Matt. 11.6 par.). The message that God wanted to have dealings with the πτωχοί, the sinners, and that they were nearer to God than the righteous, provoked a passionate protest from the Pharisees. At every turn Jesus was compelled to give an answer to the offence taken by the Pharisees to the gospel. He did this above all in the form of parables. The parables which deal with the reprieving of sinners are not a presentation but a *vindication of the good news*.[2]

Jesus gives three reasons in his vindication of the gospel.

(a) He points to the ἁμαρτωλοί. They are like sick men, and sick men need a doctor (Mark 2.17). They are not only poor, sick and in need, but they are also grateful. For unlike the righteous, only those laden with debts can really know the meaning of remission, and as a result their gratitude is boundless (Luke 7.36–50).

(b) Jesus directs the attention of the δίκαιοι to their own remoteness from God. In truth they are further from God than the ἁμαρτωλοί, because they think well of themselves and rely on their piety (Luke 18.9–14); because they claim to be obedient, but really are not (Matt. 21.28–31); because they are unwilling to follow God's call (Luke 14.16–24 par. Matt. 22.1–10) and resist his messenger (Mark 12.1–9); because they have no love for their poor brothers (Luke 15.25–32); because they know about forgiveness, and yet have no idea of what forgiveness really is (Luke 7.47: the one who has been

[1] John 7.49. [2] Jeremias, *Parables*[2], 124–46, etc.

forgiven little, loves little). In Jesus' view, nothing separates people so completely from God as a self-assured religiosity.

(c) Jesus' most decisive vindication is, however, his almost monotonous reference to the nature of God. God is infinitely gracious (Matt. 20.1–15). He rejoices when one who has strayed finds his way home (Luke 15.4–10).[1] He hears the cries of those in distress, unlike the judge who allows himself to be mollified by a complainant (Luke 18.1–8). He grants the request of the despairing publican (Luke 18.9–14). He is like the father who runs to meet his lost son and stops him from following his plan to ask to be treated as a day-labourer (Luke 15.19–21). This is what God is like. The fact that Jesus justifies his *own* mercy upon sinners, his *own* preaching of forgiveness in word and action by referring to God's mercy on sinners has one important consequence: in his scandalous conduct, Jesus is claiming to be realizing the love of God; he is claiming to act as God's representative.[2] God's love for the poor is made real in his proclamation.

This good news divides the spirits. Jesus himself does not think that this is surprising: ὑμῖν (the disciples) τὸ μυστήριον δέδοται τῆς βασιλείας τοῦ θεοῦ, ἐκείνοις δὲ τοῖς ἔξω ἐν παραβολαῖς τὰ πάντα γίνεται (Mark 4.11). This much-discussed saying has a strong Palestinian colouring.[3] In the present context it gives the reason why Jesus spoke in parables; by so doing, it was his aim to harden the hearts of those outside. But that is surely not the purpose of the parables. Rather, Mark 4.11 has only been put in its present context at a later stage because of the word παραβολή. In the original *logion*, παραβολή, behind which lies an Aramaic *matlā*, did not have the meaning 'parable', but 'riddle', as is shown by the parallel μυστήριον. 'God has disclosed the mystery of his reign to you, but to those outside everything happens in riddles, . . . unless[4] they return and God forgives them' (Mark 4.11f. quoting Isa. 6.9f.). This is a saying which applies to all Jesus' proclamations (τὰ πάντα), and not just the parables. Jesus ascribes a twofold effect to it: on the one hand it opens eyes to see the mystery of God, namely that something of the future kingdom is breaking into the present in the gospel of God's mercy upon the poor; on the other,

---

[1] The 'soteriological joy of God' (‡Gulin, 99).

[2] E. Fuchs, *Studies of the Historical Jesus*, SBT 42, London 1964, 20f.

[3] Antithetic parallelism (see §2.ii above), divine passive (see §2.i above), superfluous ἐκείνοις, close relationship of v.12 to Targ. Isa. 6.9f. For exegesis, see Jeremias, *Parables*[2], 14–18.

[4] For this translation of μήποτε = *dilᵉmā*, see Jeremias, *op. cit.*, 17f.

the gospel again and again makes men blind. The disciples will have the same experience (Matt. 10.13–15): in one house men accept the 'peace', i.e. God's peace of the end-time, that they bring, while in the next they are turned away and have to proclaim judgment. These opposite reactions on the part of people are grounded in the nature of the good news. Because the gospel offers the greatest salvation, at the same time it can bring about the greatest disaster. Guilt arises from grace.

Two things show that all this is part of the bed-rock of the tradition. First, the message that God wants to have dealings with sinners and only with sinners and that his love extends to them is without parallel at the time. It is unique. The literature of Qumran has confirmed this uniqueness. Indeed, the chief significance of the newly-discovered texts for understanding the proclamation of Jesus and the early church lies in this very fact, that they confirm that nothing comparable is to be found in contemporary Judaism.[1] Nor is this lack of an analogy to the message of Jesus the only indication of its authenticity. The offence taken at him, which permeates all the strata of the synoptic tradition to about the same degree (as is shown by the numerous parables which are concerned with the vindication of the good news),[2] and which finds its most striking expression in the mocking description of Jesus as a 'glutton and a drunkard, a friend of publicans and sinners' (Matt. 11.19 par. Luke 7.34; cf. Mark 2.16 par.), dates from before Easter. For the offence after Easter was Jesus' accursed death on the cross – his table-fellowship with sinners was the pre-Easter scandal. In other words, the gospel accounts of Jesus's proclamation of the good news for the poor cannot be derived either from Judaism or from the earliest church. They reproduce the *ipsissima vox* of Jesus.

---

[1] J. Jeremias, *Die theologische Bedeutung der Funde am Toten Meer*, Vortragsreihe der Niedersächsischen Landesregierung zur Förderung der wissenschaftlichen Forschung in Niedersachsen 21, Göttingen 1962.

[2] Jeremias, *Parables²*, 124–46.

IV

THE PERIOD OF GRACE

The true prophetic message has two sides which belong in-dissolubly together: it is proclamation of salvation and proclamation of condemnation. There are profound reasons for this: grace and judgment belong together. So Jesus, too, announced not only the gracious dawn of the time of salvation, but also the catastrophe that would precede its full revelation. The good news is announced in the final respite before the judgment.

§ 13 · IN THE FACE OF CATASTROPHE

Albert Schweitzer, *The Quest of the Historical Jesus*, London ³1954; J. A. T. Robinson, *Jesus and his Coming*, London and Philadelphia 1957; W. G. Kümmel, *Promise and Fulfilment*, SBT 23, London 1957; E. Grässer, *Das Problem der Parusieverzögerung in den synoptischen Evangelien und in der Apostelgeschichte*, BZNW 22, Berlin 1957, ²1966; L. Gaston, 'Sondergut und Markusstoff in Luk. 21', *ThZ* 16, 1960, 161–72; B. Rigaux, 'La seconde venue de Jésus', in: *La venue du Messie. Messianisme et Eschatologie*, Recherches Bibliques VI, Bruges 1962, 173–216; W. G. Kümmel, 'Die Naherwartung in der Verkündigung Jesu', in: *Zeit und Geschichte, Dankesgabe an R. Bultmann zum 80. Geburtstag*, Tübingen 1964, 31–46 (lit.); O. Cullmann, *Salvation in History*, London and New York 1967; L. Hartman, *Prophecy Interpreted*, Coniectanea Biblica, Lund 1966; J. Lambrecht, *Die Redaktion der Markus-Apokalypse*, Analecta Biblica 28, Roma 1967.

(i) The two synoptic apocalypses

It is of fundamental importance in understanding Jesus' remarks about the imminent events of the end to recognize that we have not one – as the usual terminology asserts – but two synoptic apocalypses.[1]

---

[1] ‡Robinson, 122; W. Grundmann, *Die Geschichte Jesu Christi*, Berlin 1957 = ³1960, 208–20.

The *Marcan apocalypse* (13.1–37) provides the fullest statement in the gospels of what is to come. It has been expanded to twice its original length in Matthew (24.1–25.46) by the addition of new material at the end; in Luke (21.5–36), its content has been considerably changed. Mark 13 is a great prophecy of disaster which depicts the time of the curse and the time of distress before the last great crisis in three stages:

(1) Verses 5–13: the beginning of the ὠδῖνες (the 'birth pangs' of the Messiah): false Messiahs, wars, earthquakes, famines, persecutions;
(2) Verses 14–23: the appearance of the 'abomination of desolation' in the temple, eschatological flight, false Messiahs and false prophets;
(3) Verses 24–27: final revolt and collapse of the cosmos, which ushers in the parousia of the Son of man. This is followed by a solemn conclusion (vv. 28–37): the end is near, but no-one knows the time and the hour, so watch!

We have *a second apocalypse* in the synoptic gospels, Luke 17.20–37. Like Mark 13.4 par., it begins with Jesus being asked when the end will come. The difference is that in Luke 17.20 this question is put by Pharisees, whereas in Mark 13.4 par. it is put by the disciples. As in Mark 13, in Luke 17 Jesus refuses to give a time. For the rest, however, his answer turns out to be quite different from that in Mark 13. In Mark it runs, no-one knows the hour; all that can be said is that first the extended period of distress must be lived through. The preliminary signs must be fulfilled first. The eschatological drama must run its course, scene by scene. Watch for the first signs! In Luke 17.20–37, on the other hand, the answer to the question about the date of the great crisis takes another form. No one knows it. Only one thing is certain: the end will come suddenly, at a time no-one expects. This one notion is made sharper and sharper, verse by verse, in a chain of sayings and metaphors: the end will come suddenly, like lightning (v. 24), like the flood (vv. 26f.), like the rain of fire on Sodom and Gomorrha (vv. 28–33). Before you notice it, the hour of the great division will be upon you (vv. 34f.). The conclusion is formed by the question 'Where will it be?'. Jesus' answer again by-passes the question: 'Where the carcase is, there are the eagles gathered together'. You will see it when it comes (v. 37).[1]

[1] Matthew has inserted the material from Luke 17.20–37, as far as it was known to him, into the Marcan apocalypse (Matt. 24.26f., 37–41, 28).

Thus the two synoptic apocalypses have quite different themes. In Mark 13 all the emphasis is on the preliminary signs; in Luke 17.20–37 it is on the suddenness of the end. There can be no doubt as to which of the two themes is the earlier. We need only look at the analogies. Alongside the synoptic apocalypse with the preliminary signs in Mark 13 stands the Pauline apocalypse in II Thess. 2.1–12 and the Apocalypse of John, in which the preliminary signs occupy the most room, in the form of a series of sevens arranged one after another (seven seals, seven trumpets, seven bowls of wrath). The early church, which had to deal with the problem of the delay of the parousia, found an answer by referring to the series of preliminary signs which still had to be fulfilled first. There is also an analogy to the theme of Luke 17.20–37, but that is in the numerous parables and metaphors used by Jesus which stress the sudden and unexpected coming of the end: the burglar, the returning householder, the ten virgins, the servant left in charge, the talents left on trust, the rich farmer, the journey to the judge, the children in the street, the weather forecast, the signs of the time, the bird-catcher's snare, and so on. Both answers to the question 'When?' are mutually exclusive. It is beyond question that the theme of Luke 17.20–37 is a nucleus of the proclamation of Jesus, whereas Mark 13 is a theme that belongs to the early church.

There is a widespread view that Mark 13 is a Jewish apocalypse which was put on the lips of Jesus in a modified and extended form by the early church. R. Bultmann might be seen as a representative of this view. In vv. 7f., 12, 14–22, 24–27 he finds Jewish apocalyptic sayings which had already been collected together before they were worked over by Mark; he regards vv. 5f., 9–11, 13a, 23 as Christian additions.[1] In fact the pattern and theme of the synoptic apocalypse largely speak the language of contemporary Jewish apocalyptic. There, too, we read of fearful preliminary signs announcing the end: the earth quakes, blood drops from trees, fire spreads itself over the earth, famines break out, the heavens withhold rain, all moral bonds are broken and a battle of all against all breaks out.[2] Without question, the discourse in Mark 13 makes use of traditional apocalyptic themes to a greater degree than is the case elsewhere in the sayings of Jesus.[3]

[1] *Synoptic Tradition*, 122f.
[2] Billerbeck IV 977–86; P. Volz, *Die Eschatologie der jüdischen Gemeinde im neutestamentlichen Zeitalter*, Tübingen 1934 = Hildesheim 1966, 147–63.
[3] Verses 7f. (wars, famines, earthquakes, 'birth-pangs'); 9, 11 (persecutions);

It is also true that at least the mention of the Gentile mission in v. 10 reflects the situation of the church.[1] These suspicions about the authenticity of Mark 13 occasioned by the content are given greater weight by observations about its language. According to N. Perrin's reckoning, of the 165 words used in Mark 13.5–27, 35 do not occur elsewhere in Mark (i.e. over 20 per cent), a very high proportion, and of these 35 words, 15 (almost half) recur in Revelation.[2] This linguistic evidence confirms that traditional apocalyptic diction has influenced Mark 13.

Nevertheless, it would be uncritical if we were to overlook the fact that Mark 13 differs fundamentally from contemporary apocalyptic in that decisive themes of the apocalyptic of the time are absent: the holy war, the annihilation of Rome, the feelings of hate and vengeance, the gathering of the Diaspora, the sensual, earthly portrayal of salvation, the renewal of Jerusalem as the capital of a mighty realm, rule over the Gentiles, the luxuriance of life in the new age, etc. None of this is to be found in Mark 13. On the contrary, it is said here that the catastrophe will affect Israel itself. This is particularly clear in v. 14, where the appearance of the abomination of desolation (Dan. 11.31; 12.11; plural 9.27) in the holy place is announced. No Jewish apocalyptist ventured to take up this prophecy in the way that Mark 13.14 does; rather, it was thought to have been fulfilled in the time of the Maccabees.[3] Jewish apocalyptic expected the temple to flourish, not to go under.[4] In view of these differences, we must

---

12 (dissolution of all moral ordinances); 13b (enduring); 24f. (dissolution of order in nature).

[1] See below, p. 247.

[2] N. Perrin, *The Kingdom of God in the Teaching of Jesus*, London 1963, 131. On the other hand, we can only draw limited conclusions from the allusions to the scriptures. It is certainly correct that in Mark 13 we find a whole series of references to the Septuagint (v. 14: Dan. 12.11 LXX τὸ βδέλυγμα τῆς ἐρημώσεως; v. 19: Dan. 12.1 Θ θλῖψις οἵα οὐ γέγονεν; v. 25: Isa. 34.4 LXX τὰ ἄστρα . . . πεσεῖται; v. 27: Zech. 2.6 LXX ἐκ τῶν τεσσάρων ἀνέμων . . . συνάξω, cf. T. F. Glasson, 'Mark XIII and the Greek Old Testament', *ExpT* 69, 1957–58, 213–15); but an equally large number of instances can be adduced in which Mark 13 does not follow the Septuagint (v. 8 βασιλεία ἐπὶ βασιλείαν: Isa. 19.2, Hebrew text; v. 22 ψευδοπροφῆται: Deut. 13.2 Targ.; v. 22 ποιήσουσιν: Deut. 13.2 Hebrew text, as LXX reads δῷ; v. 26 ἐν νεφέλαις: Dan. 7.13, again diverging from LXX ἐπὶ τῶν νεφελῶν and Θ μετὰ τῶν νεφελῶν; cf. T. W. Manson, 'The Old Testament in the Teaching of Jesus', *BJRL* 34, 1952, 314–18).

[3] I Macc. 1.54; b. Taan. 28b.

[4] That it was a common conviction that the Temple was indestructable is to be

reckon with the possibility that there is genuine material among the individual *logia* of which Mark 13 is made up.

Scholars have even ventured to speak of a *third synoptic apocalypse* alongside Mark 13.1–37 and Luke 17.20–37.[1] If we analyse Luke's treatment of Mark 13, we see that he altered what he found partly by substitution, and partly by the addition of individual verses. Now if we collect the *logia* which are new in Luke 21.5–28 in comparison with Mark (Luke 21.18, 20, 21b, 22, 23b–26a, 28), we shall see that they are characterized formally by parallelism, and in content by a pattern of thought which is to some degree coherent in itself. There is therefore much to be said for the conclusion that Luke incorporated a special apocalyptic tradition into his Marcan original.[2] This third synoptic apocalypse must have been compiled round about Easter AD 70, at a time when Titus was preparing to lay siege to Jerusalem (Luke 21.20), but flight from the holy city had not yet been made impossible (v. 21b). In that case it would be the latest of the three synoptic apocalypses, only a few weeks earlier than the prophecy in Rev. 11.1f., which presupposes that the Roman attack on the outer court of the temple had already begun. The little apocalypse would have expected the sacking of the holy city (v. 24) and would have seen in the Jewish-Roman war the beginning of the horrors preceding the end (vv. 22ff.), but also, at the same time, the sign of God's great new beginning (v. 28). Of course, we should not forget that the reconstruction of such buried sources remains a pure hypothesis. In this instance, the fact that the verses ascribed to the 'third' apocalypse bear an explicitly Lucan linguistic stamp is a warning that we should be particularly cautious.[3] The reason for these Lucanisms

---

seen from Josephus, *BJ* 6.283, 285. Eth. Enoch 90.27f. indeed expects that the 'old house' will be 'folded up', but this is only so that it can be replaced by a new, more glorious house. This is not quite the same thing as the abomination of desolation. Besides, the 'old house' seems to stand for Jerusalem, not for the Temple. Only in the period shortly before the first Jewish revolt does a man whom everyone regards as being of a deranged mind go through the streets of Jerusalem crying, 'Woe to the city, the people, the temple' (Josephus, *B.J.* 6.309, cf. 301). Later tradition affirmed that R. Johanan ben Zakkai knew in advance that the Temple was going to be burnt (j. Yom. 43c 60 Bar. par. b. Yom. 39b).

[1] ‡Robinson, 122.

[2] ‡Robinson, 123f.; ‡Gaston; H.-T. Wrege, *Die Überlieferungsgeschichte der Bergpredigt*, WUNT 9, Tübingen 1968, 151 n.8.

[3] Luke 21.20: Ἰερουσαλήμ (Luke/Acts sixty-six times, elsewhere only twice in the Gospels); ἐγγίζω (favourite Lucan word: Luke/Acts twenty-four times); v. 22: τοῦ with infinitive in a final sense (without being attached to a noun or verb governing the genitive, Blass-Debrunner-Funk 400.5: Luke/Acts twenty-four times); πίμπλημι (Luke/Acts twenty-two times, elsewhere in the New Testament only at Matt. 22.10; 27.48); πάντα τὰ γεγραμμένα (Luke/Acts five times, elsewhere in the New Testament only at Gal. 3.10); v. 23b λαός (favourite Lucan word: Luke/Acts eighty-four times); v. 24: Ἰερουσαλήμ (see v. 20); ἄχρι favourite Lucan word: Luke/Acts twenty times); πληρόω (of time: Luke/Acts five times, elsewhere only Mark 1.15; John 7.8); v. 25b: ἦχος (Luke/Acts three times, elsewhere only Heb. 12.19);

might be that Luke had worked over a source, but in that case the question would remain why Luke took over the intermediary verses which come from Mark 13 (Luke 21.21a, 23a, 26b, 27) in an almost slavishly literal way, and yet had worked over the verses from the 'third' apocalypse to such a degree. That seems highly improbable. For that reason, it is probably better to refrain from conjecturing a third apocalypse and to regard Luke 21.18, 20, 21b, 22, 23b–26a, 28 as a Lucan revision of Mark.

(ii) What did Jesus expect?

Any attempt to sketch out what Jesus expected in the future will have to start from his conviction that his mission was the prelude to the coming of the eschatological time of distress. Let no one imagine that he had come to bring peace – no, he brought a sword (Matt. 10.34), fire on the earth (Luke 12.49), the cosmic baptism of suffering (v.50).[1] For the murdering of the last divine messenger by Jerusalem the prophet-killer[2] will exceed the measure of guilt appointed by God (Matt. 23.32), exhaust his patience (Mark 12.9 par.) and introduce the hour of darkness (Luke 22.53). Jesus was convinced that the suffering of his disciples was indissolubly connected with his own; he saw that his followers would be involved in a collective suffering, introduced by his passion.[3] The fact that this expectation was not fulfilled in such a precise form[4] indicates that the sayings dealing with it belong to the period before Easter.

But people will live on heedless, right up to the day itself (Luke 17.26–29 par. Matt. 24.37–39), blind to the sword of Damocles that hangs over their heads and can fall at any time, because the measure of guilt has been accomplished. Horrors will descend upon them like lightning from a clear sky, as astounding as the flood, the rain of fire on Sodom, a burglar, the snare, death. The (Roman) sword is coming, says Matt. 10.34. Streams of blood will flow. Pilate's blood-bath among the Galileans and the collapse of the tower of Siloah (Luke 13.1–5) will seem child's play in comparison to what will

---

v. 26: ἐπέρχομαι (Luke/Acts seven times, elsewhere only Eph. 2.7; James 5.1); οἰκουμένη (Luke/Acts eight times, seven times elsewhere in the New Testament); γάρ (instead of καί Mark 13.25: Luke avoids parataxis); v. 28: δέ with the genitive absolute (used thirteen times by Luke in contrast to Mark); ἐγγίζω (see v. 20); the construction a∥b+c.

[1] Jeremias, Parables[2], 163f.
[2] On the question whether Jesus expected a violent death, see below, pp. 278–80.
[3] See below, p. 241.
[4] See below, p. 284.

break out over Israel. Everything will be so fearful that Jesus calls to the women who bewail him to sing even now the death lament for themselves and their children (Luke 23.28–31). They will have to share the dreadful fate that will fall upon the last generation. In Luke 11.49–51 (par. Matt. 23.34f.), Jesus quotes a divine saying[1] which announces that God will punish all the evil that befalls his messengers, from the blood of Abel to the blood of the priestly prophet Zechariah who was slain in the most holy place – between the altar of burnt offering and the Temple building (II Chron. 24.20–22). He adds: ναὶ λέγω ὑμῖν, ἐκζητηθήσεται ἀπὸ τῆς γενεᾶς ταύτης (v.51b). Why must 'this generation' pay the blood debt? What have the people of the present to do with the murder of Abel and Zechariah? They are the last generation; they have accomplished the measure. The last generation will have to pay the full debt that has been accumulated.

Nevertheless, all this is only the beginning. Something else will be much more fearful. God will leave the Temple (Luke 13.35 par.) and the 'abomination of desolation' will appear (Mark 13.14 par.). What is meant by this expression, taken from Dan. 11.31; 12.11? Here Mark has the remarkable *constructio ad sensum* ὅταν δὲ ἴδητε τὸ βδέλυγμα τῆς ἐρημώσεως ἑστηκότα (with a masculine, not a neuter participle) ὅπου οὐ δεῖ. Matthew took the masculine to be a grammatical mistake and therefore changed it to the neuter ἑστός (24.15), but its presence shows that the earliest tradition interpreted the Danielic 'abomination of desolation' as referring to a person, to the false Christ. He will reveal himself ὅπου οὐ δεῖ, in the sanctuary. False prophets will glorify him (Mark 13.22 par.). But his time is limited.[2] In the end the Temple will fall in ruins, and not one stone will be left standing on another (Mark 13.2).[3] The fall of the Temple will at the same time be the signal for the intervention of God: within three days[4] the new Temple will rise (14.58 par.).

The abomination of desolation in the holy place, demanding worship and reverence, glorified by false prophets through word and miracle – that is the last great temptation. It is characteristic of Jesus – and a sign of the antiquity of the tradition, that he does not elaborate it. Only half a verse is devoted to it (Mark 13.14a). A

[1] Verse 49: ἡ σοφία τοῦ θεοῦ εἶπεν.

[2] For the idea see Rev. 12.12: ὁ διάβολος . . . ἔχων θυμὸν μέγαν, εἰδὼς ὅτι ὀλίγον καιρὸν ἔχει.

[3] See the Gospel of Thomas 71: 'Jesus says: I will de(stroy) (this) house and no one will be able to build it (again)'.

[4] On this, see below, pp. 285f.

description would do no one any good. Jesus says only one thing: flee (Mark 13.14b–20). Eschatological flight from the danger zone is the only thing left for friend (Luke 17.31) and foe (Matt. 23.33). Every minute will be precious: woe to those who want to go quickly into the house to fetch a cloak, indispensable at night (Luke 17.31; Mark 13.15f.). That could ruin everything. For it is no longer a matter of earthly life, but of the soul. This is the meaning of an ancient *agraphon*, which makes Jesus utter the warning: Save yourself, your life is at stake (cf. Gen. 19.17).[1] Only those who endure the 'three days'[2] before the rebuilding of the temple will be saved (Mark 13.13b). In respect of these 'three days' of utmost distress, the conclusion of the Lord's Prayer asks, 'Let us not be put to the test'.[3] The petition for protection from succumbing to the πειρασμός is the desperate cry of faith on trial: preserve us from apostasy, keep us from going wrong.

This is the last and final catastrophe in history that Jesus sees coming. He was certain that the kingdom of God comes through suffering and only through suffering.

Fearful as all this is, it is still only the prelude to the last disaster of all that is to follow. This last thing of all transcends history. The angels of God accomplish the division. Two men will be at the plough (thus Matt. 24.40) or in bed (so Luke 17.34), each like the other and indistinguishable to human eyes, but one will be saved and the other rejected. Two women will be working at the mill in the morning, before daybreak, one grinding and the other throwing on the corn, each like the other (Matt. 24.41 par. Luke 17.35), but the one will be a child of peace and the other a child of death. At this hour, when the angels of God are bringing about the divine judgment, γέεννα is opening up, the eternal hell of fire.[4] When the gospels speak of it,

---

[1] Theodotus in Clement of Alexandria, *Exc. ex Theod.* 2.2; on this see Jeremias, *Unknown Sayings of Jesus*[2], London 1964, 77–80.

[2] Mark 14.58 par. For the 'three-day' sayings see below, pp. 285f.

[3] For exegesis see below, pp. 201f.

[4] γέεννα (appears in the New Testament for the first time, and outside James 3.3 to be found only in synoptic sayings of Jesus) is a Greek form of the Aramaic *gēhinnām* (Hebrew *gēhinnōm*). Since ancient times it has been the name of the valley west and south of Jerusalem, which runs into the Kidron valley on the south-east of the city (the present *wādī er-rabābī*). From the woes pronounced by the prophets on the valley (Jer. 7.32 = 19.6; cf. Isa. 31.9; 66.24) because sacrifices to Moloch took place here (II Kings 16.3; 21.6), there developed in the second century BC the idea that the valley of Hinnom would be the place of a fiery hell (Eth. Enoch 26f.; 90.26f.). To this hell it therefore gave its name. It is distinguished from ᾅδης (*šeʾōl*), which, according to Jewish ideas, was the place where the souls of the godless were punished before the resurrection. Gehenna makes an appearance

they do so with deliberate realism which is meant to express all the fearfulness of judgment. It is a place ὅπου ὁ σκώληξ αὐτῶν οὐ τελευτᾷ καὶ τὸ πῦρ οὐ σβέννυται (Mark 9.48 quot. Isa. 66.24). It is pre-existent in the same way as the *basileia* (Matt. 25.41), and therefore its coming is inevitable. It embraces the whole man (Mark 9.43-48). It is eternal (Mark 3.29; 9.48; Matt. 25.46). But there is no elaboration of the different torments of hell such as are to be found in the apocalyptic of contemporary Judaism and the early church (e.g. in the Apocalypse of Peter). Jesus is simply concerned to express the fearful seriousness of the divine judgment, against the pronouncement of which there is no appeal. For Jesus, the word γέεννα has a twofold content: (*a*) γέεννα is darkness (Matt. 8.12; 22.13; 25.30); it therefore means the exclusion of God's light. (*b*) In γέεννα there will be κλαυθμὸς καὶ βρυγμὸς τῶν ὀδόντων (Matt. 8.12 par. Luke 13.28). This 'weeping and gnashing of teeth' at the table fellowship of the Gentiles with the patriarchs is an expression of despair of those who have forfeited salvation through their own fault. That is what hell is.

According to Luke 13.23, Jesus is asked εἰ ὀλίγοι οἱ σῳζόμενοι; He refuses to give an answer, and instead warns his audience to strive to enter through the narrow gate (v. 24). In another passage, however, Jesus spoke of, or at least hinted at, the number of the saved: πολλοὶ γάρ εἰσιν κλητοί, ὀλίγοι δὲ ἐκλεκτοί (Matt. 22.14). This saying about the great number of those who are called and the small number of those who are chosen might be interpreted as a predestinarian remark. Both πολλοί and ἐκλεκτοί seem to point in this direction: God calls many, though still only a limited number; only a few are saved, namely, those whom God chooses from the number of those who are called. But neither of these is Jesus' meaning. To understand this *crux interpretum* we must first note that πολλοί here, as often in Semitic languages, has an inclusive meaning ('the many', 'the great crowd', 'all'); connected with this is the fact that Semitic languages have no words which describe totality and plurality at the same time (like our 'all').[1] A key instance is IV Ezra 8.3: *multi quidem creati sunt, pauci autem salvabuntur.* Here to render *multi* as 'many' would be nonsense.

---

only after the resurrection and the final judgment, to embrace not only the souls but the souls and bodies of the condemned for ever. Cf. J. Jeremias, ᾅδης, *TDNT* I, 1964, 146-49; γέεννα, *ibid.*, 655f.

[1] J. Jeremias, πολλοί, *TDNT* VI, 1968, 536-45: 542. The Hebrew *kōl*/Aramaic *kōllā* denotes the totality, not the plurality.

Not many, but all have been created; thus the meaning is: 'The number of the created is incalculable, but the number of those who are saved will be small.' In a similar way, Matt. 22.14 does not speak of many, but, in a Semitic way, of the totality, which embraces many, i.e. all. ἐκλεκτοί, too, has nothing to do with predestination; it is a fixed technical term for the messianic community of salvation (thus in Eth. Enoch, in the New Testament and the Qumran literature). The appropriate translation of Matt. 22.14 is therefore: 'The number of those who have been invited (to the festal meal) is (incalculably) great, but only a few will belong to the community of salvation'. The saying is not about predestination, but about guilt. The call is unlimited, but the number of those who follow it and are saved is only small.

(iii) *When will the catastrophe come?*

That Jesus refused to give a definite date for the dawning of the last things (Luke 17.20f.; Mark 13.4ff., 32 par.)[1] does not mean that no general conception of the time of the end can be seen from his sayings. This conception is firmly rooted in the tradition, as it emerges in every strata of the tradition and in sayings of quite different categories, as the following instances show.

(a) *The announcement of the* basileia

The dead fig-tree is turning green, the summer is coming, the consummation is dawning, says the parable in Mark 13.28f. par.[2] *Ἤγγικεν ἡ βασιλεία τῶν οὐρανῶν*, 'God is near',[3] runs the message of the disciples who are sent out (Matt. 10.7 par. Luke 10.9; Luke 9.2, 60; 10.11). 'Thy kingdom come' is the prayer that Jesus teaches his disciples, and that can only mean (as in the Kaddish):[4] 'May it come soon'. For the subject of all actual eschatological preaching is the imminent intervention of God,[5] and not an intervention after thirty[6] or forty[7] years.

---

[1] See p. 123 above. In Mark 13.32, at least, the words οὐδὲ ὁ υἱός are secondary because of the absolute use of ὁ υἱός, which is alien to Palestine; on the other hand, the absolute use of ὁ πατήρ is assured as a rendering of *'Abbā* (cf. Jeremias, *The Prayers of Jesus*, 36f.).

[2] Jeremias, *Parables*[2], 119.   [3] For this translation, see above, p. 102.

[4] See below, p. 198.   [5] ‡Rigaux, 190.   [6] For γενεά see below, p. 135.

[7] Destruction of Jerusalem AD 70.

The nearness of the *basileia* is also presupposed in the numerous parables and metaphors mentioned on p. 124 which deal with the sudden and unexpected coming of the end and issue a summons to watchfulness. The sayings about the 'three days' also belong among those which expect an imminent end (see pp. 285f.), as does Luke 17.20f., if our eschatological interpretation of ἐντὸς ὑμῶν (see pp. 100f.) is the right one. If, too, it is right to suppose that the Aramaic imperfect *yēkōl* which underlies the φάγοι of Mark 11.14 originally had a future meaning ('no one will eat your fruit again'),[1] then it would be a particularly vivid presentation of the expectation of an imminent end; the crisis will be there even before the figs become ripe.[2]

In this connection, we should also mention sayings which describe John the Baptist as *Elijah redivivus* (Mark 9.13 par. Matt. 17.12; Matt. 11.10 par. Luke 7.27; Matt. 11.14), that is, if they go back to Jesus, which is disputed. The three passages refer to the expectation of a forerunner, which grew up from Mal. 3.23f. (LXX 4.4f.), where the sending of the prophet Elijah before the great and terrible day of the Lord is announced. This prophecy of Malachi was understood to say that the forerunner would bring about the ἀποκατάστασις directly[3] – three days,[4] one day[5] – before the great crisis. Mark 9.13 is intended to be understood against this background: ἀλλὰ λέγω ὑμῖν ὅτι καὶ Ἠλίας ἐλήλυθεν (cf. Matt. 11.10, 14). The forerunner has already been here – that is how near the end is.

(b) The call to the disciples

Jesus put his call to join the group of disciples which accompanied him in terms of the utmost urgency. Elisha was allowed to say farewell to his family (I Kings 19.20), but Jesus does not grant this permission (Luke 9.61f.). Indeed, he refuses the request of a son to be allowed to fulfil the most elementary duty of a child, to bury his father. In Palestine, burial took place on the day of death, but it was followed by six days of mourning on which the bereaved family received expressions of sympathy. Jesus cannot allow so long a delay. Why this urgency? Jesus justifies it by the harsh sentence: ἄφες τοὺς νεκροὺς θάψαι τοὺς ἑαυτῶν νεκρούς (Matt. 8.22 par. Luke 9.60). Outside the *basileia* there is only death and dead bodies. Existence in the old age, existence under guilt, does not deserve the name of life. Life has begun to enter the world of death, and soon it will reveal itself in its fulness. Every hour is precious. The dead must be called into the world of life before it is too late.

This is how we are also to understand Mark 1.17. Jesus calls Simon and Andrew while they are in the midst of their work of catching fish: δεῦτε ὀπίσω μου, καὶ ποιήσω ὑμᾶς γενέσθαι ἁλεεῖς ἀνθρώπων. This is

---

[1] See above, p. 87.
[2] Early figs are ripe at the end of May, late figs from the middle of August.
[3] Billerbeck IV 785, under *l*.   [4] *Ibid.*, under *m*.   [5] *Ibid.*, under *n*.

an allusion to Jer. 16.16, which describes the bringing home of Israel from every country (vv. 14f.). God promises: 'Behold, I am sending for many fishers, says the Lord, and they shall catch them'. Thus the designation of the disciples as 'fishers of men' means that they have an eschatological task, to bring home the people of God, and this task does not allow the smallest delay.

(c) Mission sayings

In Luke 10.4 (special material) Jesus commands the messengers whom he sends out: μηδένα κατὰ τὴν ὁδὸν ἀσπάσησθε. This is a command which would be extremely offensive. In the east, greetings have a deeper significance than they do with us, because they have a religious meaning. They represent not only a good wish, but a real communication of the peace of God (cf. Matt. 10.13 par. Luke 10.5). This explains the solemnity of the ceremonial greeting which, e.g. among the Bedouins today, requires as the answer to the question 'Where are you going?', the words 'to the gates of God'. There is no analogy in the literature of the time of Jesus to the way in which he prohibits greetings on the journey. Why this prohibition? Probably the word ἀσπάζεσθαι includes not only the greeting ceremonial itself, but also joining company with travellers going in the same direction, say in a caravan. That means a slower pace, but it does guarantee protection against robbers. In no circumstances, however, may the messengers involve themselves in any loss of time. Their duty, to proclaim the nearness of the reign of God, must be fulfilled with the utmost speed. Every minute is precious.[1]

Matthew 10.23 is equally urgent (see below, pp. 135f.).

Two mission sayings contrast strangely with the extreme urgency of the other sayings connected with the call and the sending out of the disciples, Mark 13.10 (par. Matt. 24.14): καὶ εἰς πάντα τὰ ἔθνη πρῶτον δεῖ κηρυχθῆναι τὸ εὐαγγέλιον and 14.9 (par. Matt. 26.13): ἀμὴν δὲ λέγω ὑμῖν, ὅπου ἐὰν κηρυχθῇ τὸ εὐαγγέλιον εἰς ὅλον τὸν κόσμον, καὶ ὃ ἐποίησεν αὕτη λαληθήσεται εἰς μνημόσυνον αὐτῆς. Both sayings speak of a missionary preaching to the whole world before the end comes. A long interval of time is presupposed. But this raises a number of questions. Jesus limited his own activity to the borders of Israel. The two stories in which he helps Gentiles each begin with a refusal of Jesus, because he is conscious of being sent only to Israel (cf. Matt. 15.24). The fact that he nevertheless helps is an anticipation of the consummation. Even more, Jesus instructed his disciples to limit their activity to Israel and expressly forbade them to go to the Gentiles, or even to the Samaritans (Matt.

---

[1] Only in the Old Testament is there a similar command to that of Jesus: II Kings 4.29. Here, too, as in Luke 10.4, the reason is the haste that is enjoined.

10.5f.). That does not mean that Jesus exluded the Gentiles from the *basileia*. It does, however, mean that Jesus did not expect a mission among the Gentiles; rather, he expected the eschatological pilgrimage of the peoples to Zion (Matt. 8.11 par. Luke 13.28f.) as God's mighty act at the coming of his reign.[1] It is impossible to reconcile Mark 13.10 par.; 14.9 par. with all this.

Not only does the content of Mark 13.10; 14.9 arouse suspicions about their authenticity; there is also a linguistic difficulty. Both passages use the word εὐαγγέλιον. Now it is a remarkable fact that while the verb *biśśar* had acquired a religious significance since the time of Deutero-Isaiah ('to announce God's victory'), the substantive (without any addition), in Hebrew *b*ᵉ*śōrā* and in Aramaic *b*ᵉ*śōrā*, always has an exclusively secular meaning. On the other hand, the Greek equivalent εὐαγγέλιον had become a religious term in the Hellenistic world, in the emperor cult.[2] That means that whereas the use of the verb by Jesus is incontestable (especially the phrase πτωχοὶ εὐαγγελίζονται in Matt. 11.5, which is a quotation from Isa. 61.1), it is improbable that he used the substantive in a religious sense. If we add to this the fact that ὅπου ἐάν with the aorist subjunctive in Mark 14.9 is a favourite phrase of Mark's,[3] we shall have to conclude that neither Mark 13.10 nor Mark 14.9 goes back to Jesus, at any rate in their present form.[4]

(d) The call to repentance

In Luke 13.1–5, Jesus proclaims to his audience: Unless you repent, you will all, without exception, perish, like those killed by Pilate's legionaries and those who were buried under the tower of Siloah. The urgency of this appeal shows that in thinking of the catastrophe that threatened, Jesus does not have in mind a national misfortune lying in the far distance, but a danger which immediately threatens the people standing before him. For the flood is at hand (Matt. 24.37–39 par.; cf. 7.24–27), the axe is laid to the root of the unfruitful fig tree (Luke 13.6–9). Repent! There is still a last respite, but it will not last long. Soon it will be too late, urge the parables of the ten virgins (Matt. 25.1–12)[5] and the great supper (Luke 14.15–24 par. Matt. 22.1–10). Then the doors to the banqueting hall will finally be closed. The parables of the journey to the judge (Matt.

[1] J. Jeremias, *Jesus' Promise to the Nations*, SBT 24, London ²1967, 55–73.

[2] G. Friedrich, εὐαγγέλιον A, *TDNT* II, 1964, 721–27.

[3] ὅπου ἐάν with the aorist subjunctive occurs only in the New Testament at Mark 6.10; 9.18; 14.9 (par. Matt. 26.13), 14.

[4] This qualification is necessary because there is much to suggest that Mark 14.9 without the intermediary clause ὅπου ἐὰν κηρυχθῇ τὸ εὐαγγέλιον εἰς ὅλον τὸν κόσμον is an early eschatological saying of Jesus (cf. J. Jeremias, 'Markus 14, 9', in *Abba*, 115–20): 'Truly I say to you . . . that what she has done they (the angels) will say (before the judgment seat of God), so that he thinks (graciously) of her'.

[5] For interpretation cf. J. Jeremias, 'ΛΑΜΠΑΔΕΣ Mt 25, 1, 3f., 7f.', *ZNW* 56, 1965, 196–201.

5.25f. par. Luke 12.57–59), the unjust steward (Luke 16.1–8) and many others have the same note. Act immediately! There is still one last final chance of reprieve.

(e) *The ἡ γενεὰ αὕτη sayings*

The fourteen sayings about 'this generation'[1] are (with the exception of Mark 13.30 par.) all sayings of extreme rebuke. The γενεά is evil (Matt. 12.39 par.; 16.4) and unfaithful (Mark 9.19 par.), and breaks faith with God like an adulterous woman (Mark 8.38; Matt. 12.39; 16.4). It complains, like peevish children, at both the call to repentance and the good news (Matt. 11.16f.). It entrenches itself, with its unbelief, behind the demand for a sign (Mark 8.12; Luke 16.31), and will have to watch Gentiles like the Queen of Sheba and the Ninevites, who granted men of God a hearing, mounting the witness stand to testify against it (Matt. 12.41f. par.).[2] Because it is on the point of murdering the last divine messenger (Luke 11.48 par.; Mark 12.8 par.), the generation will have to bear the sum total of guilt from Abel to Zechariah (Matt. 23.34–36 par.). The eschatological point of all these sayings cannot be blunted either by interpreting γενεά as 'race' and referring to it to the Jewish people (for that is linguistically impossible),[3] or by understanding γενεά as 'generation', extending the term to a period of about forty years and referring the threats against the γενεά to the destruction of Jerusalem in AD 70. For γενεά always denotes those in Jesus' presence, whom he has there before him and to whom he is actually speaking, his 'contemporaries'. Destruction faces them. Soon roles will be exchanged, and those who now sit in judgment on Jesus will stand before his judgment-seat (Luke 22.69).

(f) *Sayings about suffering and consolation*

In Matt. 10.23b (special material), Jesus promises his messengers: ἀμὴν γὰρ λέγω ὑμῖν, οὐ μὴ τελέσητε τὰς πόλεις τοῦ Ἰσραὴλ ἕως ἔλθῃ ὁ υἱὸς τοῦ ἀνθρώπου.[4] There are two contrasting interpretations. One takes

---

[1] Mark 8.12a, 12b, 38; 9.19; 13.30; Matt. 11.16 par.; 12.39 par., 41f. par. 45; 22.36; Luke 11.30, 50; 17.25.

[2] For ἐγερθήσεται, ἀναστήσονται = 'appear in court' and κατακρινεῖ, κατακρινοῦσιν = 'provide the standard for condemnation', cf. J. Wellhausen, *Das Evangelium Matthaei*, Berlin 1904, 65.

[3] The Greek γενεά can have the meaning 'race', but not the Hebrew dōr or Aramaic dār.

[4] Note that this is one of the few Son of man sayings handed down 'without

v. 23 as a unity and relates the *logion* to the situation of persecution:[1] before the disciples have used the last possible refuge in Palestine, the Son of man will appear to save them. The other interpretation regards v. 23b as an isolated *logion*[2] and refers the word to the proclamation of the gospel by the disciples:[3] the parousia will arrive before they have finished proclaiming the *basileia* to the cities of Israel. The debate seems rather to have come to a halt with these alternatives. Perhaps it may help to reflect that v. 23a is hardly likely to have had a separate existence (it would have no point), but that it does not look like a redactional composition by Matthew either (the demonstrative hanging in the air and the unskilful article before ἑτέραν tell against that). It therefore seems better to leave v. 23 as a unity and to refer the *logion* to the persecution of the disciples. But in that case, we have to explain how it is that v. 23b restricts the area of flight to Palestine. Why do the disciples not go outside the country? The answer can only be that their commission binds them to Israel. We may therefore see v. 23 as a word of consolation not for the persecuted disciples in general but for the persecuted messengers: the Son of man will intervene before they have completed their task – as soon as that. The crisis is near, and that is a spur to the utmost haste.

Mark 9.1 also belongs in this context: καὶ ἔλεγεν αὐτοῖς · ἀμὴν λέγω ὑμῖν ὅτι εἰσίν τινες ὧδε τῶν ἑστηκότων οἵτινες οὐ μὴ γεύσωνται θανάτου ἕως ἂν ἴδωσιν τὴν βασιλείαν τοῦ θεοῦ ἐληλυθυῖαν ἐν δυνάμει. There should never have been any dispute that this *logion*, which has had to suffer more than others under laborious apologetic reinterpretations, deals with the visible revelation of the reign of God (cf. par. Matt. 16.28). καὶ ἔλεγεν αὐτοῖς is a Marcan connecting formula;[4] thus we have here an

---

rivals' (see below, pp. 263f.). Further important indications of age are the number of Semitisms and the offence caused both by the limitation of the saying to Israel and the fact that it was not fulfilled (cf. J. Jeremias, *Jesus' Promise to the Nations*, SBT 24, London 1967[2], 19f.; C. Colpe, ὁ υἱὸς τοῦ ἀνθρώπου *TWNT* VIII, 1969, 439f.).

[1] H. Schürmann, 'Zur Traditions und Redaktionsgeschichte von Mt. 10, 23', *BZ* 3, 1959, 82–88 = in: Schürmann, *Traditionsgeschichtliche Untersuchungen zu den synoptischen Evangelien*, Düsseldorf 1968, 150–56 ('A word of comfort for the persecutions in the last tribulation'); E. Bammel, 'Matthäus 10.23', *Studia Theologica* 15, 1961, 79–92, but he assumes Christian reshaping in a number of ways, 92.

[2] Thus first E. Klostermann, *Das Matthäusevangelium*, HNT 4, Tübingen 1919, 227 ([2]1927, 89).

[3] ‡Kümmel, *Promise*, 62–64; id., *Naherwartung* 42f. (literature).

[4] Jeremias, *Parables*[2], 14.

originally isolated *logion*. A distinction is made between a majority of those present, who will die before the revelation of the *basileia*, and some (τινές), who will still be alive then. John 21.21–23 has given rise to the false impression that the minority of those who will not taste death are the last survivors of the circle of disciples. In that case, Mark 9.1 would mean that the revelation of the *basileia* will be postponed until almost all the personal disciples of Jesus have died and only a few grey-haired ones are still alive. But the expectation expressed in John 21.23a (ὁ μαθητὴς ἐκεῖνος οὐκ ἀποθνῄσκει) is a reinterpretation of the Marcan saying influenced by the delay of the parousia. It comes from a time when a fervent hope still clung to the last surviving disciples; this false interpretation should not still be repeated today. For it cannot be thought that the fate of the majority who will have to taste death will be that they will die peacefully; rather, they will be martyred (Mark 8.35 par.; 10.38f. par.; 13.12 par.; Matt. 10.21, 28 par., 34 par.; etc.). Before the tribulation introduced by the passion of Jesus (see below, p. 241) has reached its climax, the intervention promised by Mark 13.20 par.; Matt. 10.23 will occur, so that at least some disciples will escape a violent death.

The parable in Luke 18.1–8 also belongs among the sayings of consolation: even if God puts the patience of his elect to the test (v. 7),[1] he will see that they get their rights ἐν τάχει (v. 8).

(g) Jesus' avowal of abstinence and the petition in Gethsemane

One last indication that Jesus saw the dawning of the reign of God in the immediate future is provided by the passion narrative. First, mention should be made in this connection of Jesus' avowal of abstinence at the last supper.[2] If Jesus refuses to taste wine 'until the kingly reign of God comes' (Luke 22.18),[3] then this coming must be really near.

This is also presupposed in the Gethsemane pericope (Mark 14.32–

---

[1] For translation see H. Riesenfeld, 'Zu μακροθυμεῖν (Lk 18, 7)', in: *Neutestamentliche Aufsätze*, Festschrift für J. Schmid, Regensburg 1963, 214–17.

[2] For the avowal of abstinence see Jeremias, *Eucharistic Words*[2], 207–17. That it is old is shown not only by the Semitisms (173f.), but also by Jesus' favourite phrases: ἀμήν, the divine passive and the phrase 'the reign of God comes' (not attested outside Christianity). For the meaning of the avowal of abstinence see below, pp. 189f.

[3] Par. Mark 14.25. According to Luke 22.16 Jesus also abstained from sharing in the eating of the passover lamb.

42 par.). There is vigorous dispute as to its trustworthiness, as the disciples' sleep (Mark 14.37, 40 par.) seems to exclude the possibility that they might have heard Jesus' words. But the text hardly means to say that all those who accompanied Jesus fell into a deep sleep at the same time; indeed, it is not inconceivable that the picture of the sleeping disciples simply grew up out of a misunderstanding of the imperative γρηγορεῖτε (vv. 34, 37), intended in a metaphorical but understood in a physical sense.[1] At all events, the offensive character of the christology makes it very difficult to regard the pericope as a free invention.

It is hardly a correct interpretation of Jesus' prayer that the cup should pass away from him (Mark 14.36 par.) if we merely see in it the wish that a way out of his hopeless situation might present itself; indeed, were that the case, Jesus could have attempted to escape. Rather, the petition has an eschatological reference: it considers the possibility that God might bring in his reign even without suffering to precede it.[2] The summons to watch and pray also has an eschatological reference; the reason which Jesus gives for it is that the time of testing is imminent (v. 38). Finally, the closing *logion* of the Gethsemane pericope ἦλθεν ἡ ὥρα (v. 41) also has an eschatological ring.

These announcements of the approaching catastrophe seem to conflict with the so-called 'watching parables', as they envisage a delay of the end: Matt. 24.48 par.: χρονίζει μου ὁ κύριος; Matt. 25.5 χρονίζοντος δὲ τοῦ νυμφίου; Mark 13.35 'You do not know when the master of the house will come, in the evening or at midnight, or at cockcrow, or in the morning' (cf. Matt. 24.43 par.); Matt. 25.19: the Lord will only return μετὰ πολὺν χρόνον. The evangelists do, in fact, relate these four parables to the delay of the *parousia*: Be ready, even if the Lord delays! But C. H. Dodd has recognized that this was hardly the original sense of these parables.[3] They have undergone a change of audience, like so many others. They were originally addressed to Jesus' enemies, and applied secondarily to the disciples. We therefore have to ask what these parables sound like if they are taken as words to the enemies of Jesus or to the crowd. In the case of the parable of the servant left in charge (Matt. 24.45–51 par.), the answer is that it was originally a call to the religious leaders of Israel, and above all the scribes: The catastrophe is at hand; before you know where you are, you will be having to give an account of yourselves. Here the delay of the master (Matt. 24.48) is merely intended as an explanation of how it was possible for the servant to abuse his office in such a carefree way. Originally the parable did not refer to the delay of the *parousia*, but to the suddenness with which it would come. It is exactly the same with the three other parables mentioned above. Old as it is, the interpretation of them as referring to the delay of the *parousia* is not

[1] C. K. Barrett, *Jesus and the Gospel Tradition*, London 1967, 47.
[2] *Ibid.* [3] *Parables*, 154–74.

the right one. Originally they were all parables of crisis, aimed at giving the warning, 'Take care, disaster is hanging over your head!', before it is 'too late'.[1]

We have no saying of Jesus that postpones the end into the distant future. That is the result of our investigation. On the contrary, when we analyse the synoptic gospels, we keep coming up against an earliest stratum in which the eschatological time of distress and the revelation of the *basileia* that follows it are expected *soon*. In this there is no difference between Jesus and John the Baptist or the Teacher of Righteousness – at most, the difference is that Jesus puts the nearness of the end in even more pointed terms than the people of Qumran do. Certainly, there are sayings of Jesus which presuppose a last period of grace between the announcement of the final catastrophe and its coming,[2] but this intermediate period is by no means thought of as a period of time of an incalculable length. The age of the *logia* that express this expectation of an imminent end is not only vouched for by the fact that, as we saw, they belong to a great variety of categories and therefore are firmly rooted in the tradition. There is a second argument which carries considerable weight: these *logia* were a particular stumbling block for the early church, when the *parousia* was delayed.

That raises an extremely serious question: must we not concede that Jesus' expectation of an imminent end was one that remained unfulfilled? Honesty and the demand for truthfulness compel us to the answer 'Yes'. Jesus expected that the end would come soon. But in conceding this quite frankly, we must immediately go on to make two further points. First, the sayings of Jesus in which there is a note of the expection of an imminent end are not apocalyptic speculations, forecasts of a date – Jesus rejected that quite firmly – but spiritual judgments. Their basic theme is: the hour of fulfilment has dawned, the reign of God is already being manifested here and now; soon the catastrophe introducing its definitive coming will arrive. Make use of the time before it is too late; it is a matter of life or death. If we want to sum up these spiritual judgments in one sentence, we might say that God has granted a last period of grace. The most important function of eschatology is that it keeps alive knowledge of this respite. The second point is even more important. Jesus himself added an

---

[1] Further justification in Jeremias, *Parables*[2], 48–66 (following Dodd).

[2] Clearest in Mark 9.1 par. (see pp. 136f.), further I Cor. 11.25b, 26b par. Luke 22.19b. (cf. Jeremias, *Eucharistic Words*[2], 254f.). On the other hand, Mark 13.30 should be left out of consideration in view of the fact that ἡ γενεὰ αὕτη is used in a different way from elsewhere in the Synoptics (cf. above, p. 135).

astounding qualification to the sayings which presuppose that the end is near: God can *shorten* the time of distress for the sake of the elect who cry to him day and night (Luke 18.7f.); he can hear the cry 'Thy kingdom come'. And not only can God do that, he will do it. If he were to keep to the length of the time of distress originally appointed, no-one would be able to survive, 'but for the sake of the elect, whom he chose, he shortened the days' (Mark 13.20 par.). On the other hand, however, God can also hear the request, 'Let it alone this year also', and *lengthen* the period of grace (Luke 13.6–9). Thus Jesus takes into account the possibility that God may rescind his own holy will. These sayings are among the most powerful spoken by Jesus. God has ordered the course of history and appointed the hour of judgment. The measure of sin is full. Judgment is due, but God's will is not unalterable. The Father of Jesus is not the immovable, unchangeable God who in the end can only be described in negations. He is not a God to whom it is pointless to pray. He is a gracious God, who hears prayers and intercessions (Luke 13.8f.; 22.31f.), and is capable in his mercy of rescinding his own holy will. Jesus sets God's grace above his holiness. It can shorten the time of distress for his people and lengthen the opportunity for the unbelievers to repent. All human existence, hourly threatened by the catastrophe, lives in the interval of grace: 'Let it alone this year also, in case it perhaps bears fruit' (Luke 13.8f.).

The sayings of Jesus about God's rescinding of his own will take up the Old Testament idea of *God's repentance*, which is developed most fully in the antithetical parallelism of Jer. 18.7f.//9f.:

7 If at any time I declare concerning a nation or a kingdom, that I will pluck up and break down and destroy it,

8 And if the nation, concerning which I have spoken, turns from its evil, I will repent of the evil that I intended to do to it.

9 And if at any time I declare concerning a nation or a kingdom, that I will build and plant it,

10 And if it does evil in my sight, not listening to my voice, then I will repent of the good which I had intended to do to it.[1]

We should not, however, overlook the profound difference. First, whereas Jer.18 recognizes God's repentance not only for salvation (vv. 7f.), but also for condemnation (vv. 9f.), Jesus knows only of a *gracious* action on the part of God, when he alters the times of the eschatological events. Secondly, whereas according to Jer. 18, God's gracious repentance is his answer to penitence (v. 8), Jesus makes no mention of previous human contributions as the basis of the correction of the appointed time; it happens as a result of pure mercy.

[1] An investigation of 'God's repentance' by Jörg Jeremias is in preparation.

Can it be pure chance that there is no parallel to God's rescinding of his holy will as a free act of mercy anywhere else in the world of Jesus?[1]

§ 14 · THE WOES

J. Wellhausen, *Die Pharisäer und die Sadducäer*, Greifswald 1874 (= Göttingen 1967), [2]Hannover 1924; L. Baeck, 'Die Pharisäer', in: *44.Bericht der Hochschule für die Wissenschaft des Judentums in Berlin*, Berlin 1927, 34–71 (an enlarged version has been published in Schocken Bücherei 6, Berlin 1934); L. Finkelstein, *The Pharisees. The Sociological Background of Their Faith*, two vols, Philadelphia 1938, [3]1962; Jeremias, *Jerusalem*, 246–67; H. Odeberg, *Pharisaism and Christianity*, St Louis 1964; A. Finkel, *The Pharisees and the Teacher of Nazareth*, AGSU 4, Leiden-Köln 1964; R. Meyer, 'Tradition und Neuschöpfung im antiken Judentum, dargestellt an der Geschichte

---

[1] IV Ezra 4.37 gives the conviction generally prevailing, that God's plan is unalterable, in apt terms:

> For he has weighed the age in the balance,
> And with measure has measured the times,
> And by number has numbered the seasons:
> Neither will he move nor stir things,
> till the measure appointed be fulfilled.

The discussion between R. Eliezer (ben Hyrcanus, *c.* AD 90) and R. Joshua (ben Hananiah, *c.* AD 90) on the question whether the time of redemption depended on penitence is significant: R. Joshua gives a negative answer to the question, because the term set by God is unalterable, but R. Eliezer gives an affirmative answer. His view, however, is (note!) that the time appointed by God has already passed, i.e. for him, too, the terminus appointed by God for the end is unshakable (j. Taan. 63d 50 par. b. Sanh. 97b, cf. Billerbeck I 162f.). Ps.-Philo, *Lib. ant.* 19.13, speaks of a shortening of the time before the end: *abbreviabuntur (tempora)*, but this has nothing to do with Mark 13.20, for the idea is of a faster course of the stars (*accelerabuntur astra*), because God impatiently looks forward to the resurrection of the dead (*quoniam festinabo excitare vos dormientes*). Similarly, the 'shortening' of the years (Eth. Enoch 80.2) which is combined with a tardiness of the seed is nothing but a symptom of the eschatological disorder of nature. When there is repeatedly mention of the 'hastening' of the times towards doomsday (Ecclus. 33.10; Syr. Bar. 20.1; 54.1; 83.1), the idea is similar to the 'abbreviation' (συντέμνειν cf. Isa. 10.22f. LXX, quoted by Paul in Rom. 9.28, and Dan. 5.25–28 LXX) which means that God is making short shrift. He is hearing the cry of his own for punishment of their oppressors (Eth. Enoch 10.43, Greek text ed. by C. Bonner, London 1937). In the third century AD we find expressions like, 'If you have merit I will hasten (the end); if not (it comes) at (the appointed) time' (j. Taan. 63d 58, R. Aha, *c.* 320, in the name of R. Joshua ben Levi, *c.* 250); but even this brings us only to Jer. 18.7–10, and not to Mark 13.20.

des Pharisaismus', and H.-F. Weiss, 'Der Pharisäismus in Lichte der Überlieferung des Neuen Testaments', in: *Sitzungsberichte der sächsischen Akademie der Wissenschaften zu Leipzig*, phil-. hist. Klasse, Band 110 Heft 2, Berlin 1965.

(i) Woes on contemporaries

The last troubled time is at hand. God is giving one final respite before the catastrophe. But 'this generation', the last generation before the end, refuses to believe (Mark 9.19). People are like the generation of the flood (Matt. 24.37–39 par. Luke 17.26f.) and the inhabitants of Sodom and Gomorrha (Luke 17.28–30); like them, they live in a carefree world, enjoying earthly pleasure: they have a good time at feasts, conclude business agreements, cultivate their fields, build houses (v. 28), celebrate weddings with rejoicing (v. 27), enjoy their possessions, exchange invitations; their laughter is easy and they sun themselves in the recognition that people accord to them (6.24–26).

Jesus does not censure them for their rejoicings. The one whom they call a glutton and a wine-bibber (Matt. 11.19 par. Luke 7.34) is no joyless ascetic. But he censures the light-heartedness with which they toss God's warnings aside and with which they enjoy their life in the face of catastrophe, as though nothing could happen to them. They are like birds who fly unsuspecting into a snare (Luke 21.35), like children who squabble while Rome burns (Matt. 11.16–19 par. Luke 7.31–35).[1] They are blind; that is, they are hardened (Luke 11.34–36 par. Matt. 6.22f.). That is why Jesus pronounces a fourfold 'woe' over them:

Woe to you that are rich!
Woe to you that are full!
Woe to you that laugh!
Woe to you when you are sure of yourselves! (Luke 6.24–26)

(ii) Woes on priests, scribes and Pharisees

Infinitely worse than the thoughtlessness and indifference of the crowd is the self-assurance of the responsible and the religious. There are three groups of people in this sphere which Jesus sought to shake into alertness: the priests, the scribes and the Pharisees.

---

[1] For this sense of Matt. 11.19b par. Luke 7.35, cf. Dodd, *Parables*, 28f.; Jeremias, *Parables*,[2] 160–62.

It is important to know the difference between these three groups.[1] The *priests* are easiest to describe.[2] Essentially, they had to carry on public worship in Jerusalem. Being a priest was a hereditary position. In order to be consecrated, a man needed no theological training; he simply had to prove his descent and show that he was physically unblemished. There was a great social distinction between the bulk of the priesthood that lived scattered over the country and was divided into twenty-four courses of priests, and the rich priestly nobility of Jerusalem.

The *scribes*[3] were a class which had only developed in the period after the exile. In contrast to the priests, they came from all levels of society, like the prophets before them. As we have already seen (see p. 77), they were trained theologians who had to have completed a period of study with a teacher lasting many years before they themselves became scribes through ordination. Ordination[4] took place through a powerful pressure (*sāmak*) from both hands (and is to be distinguished from a laying on of hands that merely made contact [*śîm/śît*], as in blessing or healing). It conferred on them the right to work as theological teachers and as judges and to make binding decisions on questions of religious and penal law.[5] The great respect enjoyed by scribes rested exclusively on their theological knowledge.

Finally, the *Pharisees*[6] were a lay movement which had been formed in the first half of the second century BC in the struggle against the Hellenization of the Jewish religion. Its members came from all groups of strata of the populace. Mostly they were merchants and craftsmen. Only their leaders were scribes. Their numbers were always small. According to Josephus' estimate[7] there were at the time of Herod the Great no more than about six thousand Pharisees in Palestine out of a total population of about half a million.[8] All over the country they gathered together in conventicles as religious laity. Above all, there were two duties which they laid on their fellow members and which would-be members had to prove they had performed before being accepted for a probationary period: strict fulfilment of the duty of paying the tithe, which had been neglected

---

[1] Jeremias, *Jerusalem*, 147–267.   [2] *Op. cit.*, 147–221.   [3] *Op. cit.*, 233–45.
[4] Billerbeck II 647–61; E. Lohse, *Die Ordination im Spätjudentum und im Neuen Testament*, Göttingen-Berlin 1951.
[5] The age of the rite of ordination can be deduced from I Tim. 4.14; 5.22; II Tim. 1.6; Acts 6.6; 13.3.
[6] Jeremias, *Jerusalem*, 246–67.   [7] *Antt.* 17.42.   [8] Jeremias, *Jerusalem*, 205.

among the people, and conscientious adherence to the regulations for purity. In addition, characteristic features were their charity, through which they hoped to secure God's good pleasure, punctilious adherence to the three daily hours of prayer, and a twice-weekly fast, which was presumably kept vicariously for Israel. The concern of the Pharisaic movement becomes clearest in one of the regulations for purity laid on all its members, i.e. the washing of hands before meals (Mark 7.1–5). This washing was not just a hygienic measure but originally a ritual duty which was incumbent only on priests whenever they ate the tithe or the priestly heave offering.[1] The fact that the Pharisees bound themselves to observe this priestly regulation about purity although they were laymen shows that they set out to represent the priestly people of salvation at the end-time (following Ex. 19.6). This is also indicated by the titles which they used. They called themselves the pious, the righteous, the God-fearers or the poor;[2] their favourite title was 'the separated ones' (pᵉrīšayyā).[3] The meaning of the last-mentioned designation emerges when we note that in the Tannaitic midrashim, pārūš and qādōš are used synonymously.[4] Thus they wanted to be the holy ones, the true Israel, the priestly people of God.

A sharp distinction must be made between Pharisees and scribes, though this does not happen even in all parts of the New Testament. The chief reason for the confusion is that in his collection of the seven woes in Matt. 23, Matthew constantly has scribes and Pharisees addressed at the same time (except in v.26), so that the distinction between the two groups disappears (rightly, in his view, in that after AD 70 Pharisaic scribes had taken over the leadership of the people). Fortunately, the parallel tradition in Luke provides help. Here the same material is divided between two composite discourses, woes against the scribes (11.46–52; also 20.46f.), and woes against the Pharisees (11.39–44). Only one mistake has found its way into the Lucan tradition, at 11.43: the ambition to get the best seats in the synagogue and to be greeted with respect in the market places here ascribed to the Pharisees really characterizes the scribes, as Luke himself rightly says in another passage (20.46 par. Mark 12.38f.). Following this division of the material in Luke, we also have to distinguish two collections of material in Matt. 23. Verses 1–13, 16–22, 29–36 are directed against the theologians; vv. 23–28 (and probably also v. 15)[5] are

---

[1] Payment to the priests of about two per-cent of all the fruits of the field and the trees, cf. Billerbeck IV 646–50.
[2] ὅσιοι, δίκαιοι, φοβούμενοι τὸν κύριον, πτωχοί (Ps. Sol.).
[3] Sot. 9.9. The earliest instance is Phil. 3.5.
[4] ‡Baeck, 34–41.
[5] The assignment of Matt. 23.15 (woes on the makers of proselytes) to Pharisaic polemic is supported by the fact that Eleazar, who was instrumental in leading king

directed against the Pharisees. We can perceive a similar distinction in the sermon on the mount: Matt. 5.21–48 is directed against the scribes and 6.1–18 against the Pharisees.

Just as there are three different groups, priests, theologians and Pharisees, so Jesus has three different sets of charges to level against them.

Jesus' charge against the *priests* is expressed in the cleansing of the temple (Mark 11.15–17). There is nothing like it in the history of the time, and it was the immediate occasion for the measures taken against him by the authorities.[1] The cleansing of the temple was a prophetic symbolic action, and was also understood to be such, as is shown by the accusation that Jesus was a false prophet (see above, pp. 77f.). In it, Jesus realizes the promise of Zech. 14.21: 'And there shall no longer be a trader in the house of the Lord on that day' (see above, p. 107). At the same time, he threatens judgment on the caste of the priestly nobility, which had organized the haggling in the holy place:[2] οὐ γέγραπται ὅτι ὁ οἶκός μου οἶκος προσευχῆς κληθήσεται πᾶσιν τοῖς ἔθνεσιν (Isa. 56.7); ὑμεῖς δὲ πεποιήκατε αὐτὸν σπήλαιον λῃστῶν (Mark 11.17). This vivid picture comes from Jer. 7.11: the priests have made the temple a lair from which they go out again and again on new sorties. They misuse their calling, to celebrate public worship to the glory of God, by carrying on business to make profit. And in so doing they commit something frightful: they put God at the service of sin.

Jesus lays quite different charges against the learned *theologians* (Matt. 23.1–13, 16–22, 29–36). They lay heavy burdens on men, but do not lay (even a little) finger on them themselves (vv. 2–4, 13).

Izates of Adiabene *c.* AD 50 to have himself circumcised, is described by Josephus as a Pharisee (*Antt.* 20.43, and on this Billerbeck I 926).

[1] The connection between the cleansing of the temple and the trial of Jesus asserted by Mark 11.18 is confirmed if we bracket out Mark 12–13 as a block of tradition which obscures the original connection between Mark 11.15–33 and 14.1ff. (for the complexes of tradition from which the Gospel of Mark is built up, see above, p. 38). Specific individual features speak for the historicity of the cleansing of the temple, quite apart from this. 'The tables of the money-changers' (Mark 11.25) were not to be found in the temple courtyard all the year round, but only in the three weeks from the 25 Adar to the feast of Passover (Shek. 1.3); the account in the gospels is thus based on good information. That Jesus would not tolerate the way through the temple court to be used (by water carriers) as a short cut between the Ophel and the eastern suburbs (that is what is meant by 'carrying vessels through' in v.16) does not look like invention.

[2] Jeremias, *Jerusalem*, 48f.

They want to be respected; they strive for places of honour, for greetings and titles, and in so doing make God's honour their own (vv. 5–12). Their virtuoso theology, acutely perceptive, lacks reverence for God (vv. 16–22).[1] They call on the people with earnest words to expiate their fathers' murder of the prophets with tokens of atonement,[2] while they themselves are in process of committing the murder of a prophet far more dreadful than anything that their fathers did (vv. 29–36). They exploit their knowledge of the law to take advantage of the helpless (Mark 12.40 par.). All these sins of the theologians are connected with their theological education, their judicial office and their social status. The woes against the scribes can be summed up in one charge: they rely on their theological knowledge; they know and preach the will of God, but they do not fulfil it. In Jesus' eyes, this is *the* besetting sin of the theologians.

The content of the woes against the *Pharisees* is quite different again. Jesus charges them with over-conscientiously giving a tithe of all their crops, even down to herbs from the kitchen garden, but setting at nought the great demands of God, righteousness, mercy and faithfulness (Matt. 23.23f.); they fulfil the regulations for purity with the utmost scrupulosity, whereas within they are unclean, though the one and only thing that matters before God is inward cleanliness (vv. 25f.). The works of supererogation of the Pharisees no more stand before Jesus' judgment than does their missionary zeal (v. 15). They offer money for the poor, they carefully observe the hours of prayer, they fast vicariously for the people twice a week (Matt. 6.1–18), but all their piety is at the service of their need to assert themselves and their ambition, and is therefore hypocrisy. So they are like graves which are whitewashed in the spring so that no one incurs impurity by coming into contact with them: outside they are bright, but inwardly they are dead bones (Matt. 23.27f.). All the charges against the Pharisees are connected with their claim to represent the true Israel and the community of the time of salvation, through strict fulfilment of the commandments and works of supererogation.

The factor common to all three groups is that they have to do with God, his service and his worship. But it is they more than others who are, in Jesus' eyes, in danger. How can that be?

---

[1] For the rejection of the Rabbinic *Halakah* by Jesus, see below, pp. 208ff.

[2] For the so-called 'tomb renaissance' which flourished at the time of Jesus, see J. Jeremias, *Heiligengräber in Jesu Umwelt*, Göttingen 1958.

(iii) The piety that separates from God

Where is it that Jesus sees the cancer that is not recognized by the pious men of his day? This becomes clearest in his sayings against the Pharisees, with whom he had most to do. He did not mistake the seriousness of their concern for obedience to God's will. He saw their delight in giving, their fasting, their economic sacrifice. He did not try to correct the rich young man when he claimed to have fulfilled all the commandments (Mark 10.20), and the fact that he calls the pious δίκαιοι (Mark 2.17; Luke 15.7) should not be dismissed lightly as irony.[1] On the contrary, even in Jesus' eyes the Pharisees are upright men who really try to do God's will. We have no right to impute to him a distorted picture of the Pharisees. Nevertheless, it is the pious whom Jesus regards as being in special danger and at a special remove from God: *they do not take sin seriously.* Certainly, Judaism had a markedly vivid consciousness of sin. A profound ethical pessimism prevailed (cf. IV Ezra). Sin is not regarded as a natural necessity, but each man is thought to be responsible for his failings. In Paul, consciousness of sin is one of the best legacies of Jewish piety. But in Pharisaic Judaism, sin is made innocuous by two things: by casuistry and by the idea of merit.

Casuistry views the individual sin in isolation. Sin, it is said, consists in transgressing one or more of the 613 commandments or prohibitions of the *Torah*,[2] or the prescriptions of tradition, the *Halakah*. Gradations are made of conscious and unconscious sins, greater and lesser sins. The main thing is not to commit any greater sins. The result of this casuistry is that sin is not seen as rebellion against God.

The *idea of merit* makes sin innocuous in that a counter-balance is set over against it. Merits compensate for sins. There are numerous merits to which the pious man can appeal. First, there are the merits of the fathers, in which Israel shares by descent; second, there are a man's own merits which he acquires by fulfilling the commandments and in addition by good works, * maʿᵃśîm ṭōbîm,* i.e. works of love[3] and

[1] A. Schlatter, *Das Evangelium des Lukas aus seinen Quellen erklärt*, Stuttgart 1931 = ²1960, 349f.

[2] 248 commandments and 365 prohibitions (instances in Billerbeck I 900f.; III 542; IV 438f.).

[3] Matt. 25.31–46 enumerates six of them: to feed the hungry, give drink to the thirsty, provide hospitality for the stranger, clothe the naked, take care of the sick, visit the prisoners. Further works of love are given in Billerbeck IV 599–610 and in

gifts of love. According to a commonly used picture, merit is like capital that accumulates in heaven and is laid up there for the pious.[1] The only important thing is that in the final judgment merits should outweigh transgressions. The Pharisee was convinced that this would be so in his case, but not in that of the sinner.

This devaluation of sin by casuistry and the idea of merit has a disastrous consequence. Where sin is not taken seriously, men think too well of themselves. They become self-assured, self-righteous and loveless. The Pharisee was convinced that he belonged to the true people of salvation. He did not doubt for a moment that God's good pleasure rested on him and he was conscious of being superior to the sinner (Luke 18.11f.).

This self-assurance, in Jesus' view, destroyed the whole of a man's life. The man who thinks too well of himself no longer takes God seriously. Because he is sure of God's positive judgment on his life, he only asks what men think of him. All his piety is directed to the one sole purpose that others should regard him as pious. It thus becomes hypocrisy (Matt. 6.1–18). Similarly, the man who thinks too well of himself no longer takes his brother seriously. He believes himself to be better, and despises him (Luke 15.25–32; 7.39).

Jesus attacks this evil at the root by putting an end to the casuistic devaluation of sin.

Again, we should not make the mistake of being misled by the concordance here. Jesus used words like 'sin', 'to sin', relatively rarely.[2] But we should not conclude from this that he spoke of sin only incidentally. Even though he uses the words relatively rarely, the subject has as central a position in his message as the words do in Paul. The only difference is that Jesus speaks in a kaleidoscopic variety of *pictures* (evil fruit, graves full of dead bones, lost sheep, lost coins, profligate son), whereas Paul makes use of theological language.

Our statement that Jesus rejects the *casuistic devaluation* of sin could seem to be

---

my article 'Die Salbungsgeschichte Mk 14, 3–9', *ZNW* 35, 1936, 75–82=*Abba*, 107–15.

[1] Instances in Billerbeck I 429–31, 822d.

[2]

ἁμαρτάνειν	Synoptic *logia* 4	Paul 17
ἁμάρτημα	Synoptic *logia* 2	Paul 2
ἁμαρτία	Synoptic *logia* 8	Paul 64
ὀφείλημα	Synoptic *logia* 1	Paul —
παράπτωμα	Synoptic *logia* 2	Paul 16

Synoptic parallels are counted as one. Paul uses ὀφείλημα once in Rom 4.4, but there the word does not mean 'debt', but 'merit'.

contradicted by one passage in which there is a gradation of sin even in the teaching of Jesus: Matt. 5.22.[1] Here it looks as if he is speaking of a heightening of transgressions (anger, calling a brother ῥακά, and calling him μωρέ), with a parallel heightening of the penalties. But the *logion* is not meant in this way. To take the transgressions first: ῥακά (Aramaic *rēqā*: 'numskull') and μωρός (Aramaic *šaṭeyā*: 'idiot') are equivalent – both are harmless insults – and ὁ ὀργιζόμενος may equally mean an expression of anger in an insult. So there is no heightening in the protases which name the transgressions. The apodoses certainly build up to a formal climax (death penalty, death penalty by the supreme authority,[2] punishment in hell), but it is purely rhetorical.

Although Jesus deliberately chooses the *form* of the casuistic legal clause, he in fact puts an end to all casuistry when he teaches that not just murder, but even an offensive insult is worthy of death. Elsewhere, too, Jesus repeatedly condemns sins of the tongue, which his contemporaries regarded as mere bagatelles, with the utmost sharpness. The statement of principle in Mark 7.15b is particularly radical: οὐδέν ἐστιν ἔξωθεν τοῦ ἀνθρώπου εἰσπορευόμενον εἰς αὐτὸν ὃ δύναται κοινῶσαι αὐτόν· ἀλλὰ τὰ ἐκ τοῦ ἀνθρώπου ἐκπορευόμενά ἐστιν τὰ κοινοῦντα τὸν ἄνθρωπον. This *logion*, the first half of which Paul knew and quoted as a saying of Jesus (Rom. 14.14), and which is without analogy in Judaism for its radical character, means that sins of the tongue are the only kind that make a man unclean at all.[3] The same radical treatment of sin applies, for example, to the sphere of sex. Even the slightest transgression, a covetous look at a married woman, is sin which delivers the one who commits it to God's judgment (Matt. 5.28).

Taking even the smallest sin seriously was not the only way in which Jesus expressed his hostility to Jewish casuistry and the radical way in which he understood sin. He did it in another way, too. He knows only one sin which cannot be forgiven. Rabbinic casuistry pronounces a whole series of grave sins to be unforgivable: murder, unchastity, apostasy, contempt for the Law, etc. In Mark 3.28f., Jesus says otherwise:

[1] J. Jeremias, ῥακά, *TDNT* VI, 1968, 973–76; on the question of authenticity 976.13–23.

[2] The Aramaic *'iṭhayyab* underlying ἔνοχος ἔσται is not followed by a mention of the court of justice, but by mention of the punishment. The translation in v. 22, as in v. 21 ἔνοχος ἔσται τῇ κρίσει, must therefore be: 'he shall incur the penalty (of death)'. Similarly, in v. 22b ἔνοχος ἔσται τῷ συνεδρίῳ means 'he shall incur (the penalty of death through the) supreme council'.

[3] For the subject, see also pp. 219f. below.

28 God[1] can[2] forgive men all sins,
    indeed even[3] whatever blasphemies they utter;
29 but whoever blasphemes against the spirit of God,
    God will never forgive him.

What is so special about the sin against the spirit? How is it different from blasphemy that can be forgiven (v. 28)? The answer appears when we remember that the contemporary view was that the spirit had been quenched. Jesus,[4] on the other hand, knows that God's spirit is at work again. In other words, Mark 3.28 speaks of sin against the God who is still hidden, v. 29 of sin against the God who is revealing himself. The former can be forgiven, the latter is unforgivable. Thus the unforgivable sin is not a particular moral transgression, as it is in the sphere of Rabbinic casuistry (this has, of course, been a recurrent misunderstanding of Mark 3.29); rather, it is the sin that arises in connection with the revelation. Only the rejection of forgiveness is unforgivable (cf. Matt. 11.20–24).[5] Casuistry shatters on the gospel.

Not only does Jesus reject casuistry in assessing sin; he also puts an end to the *idea of merit*.[6] There are no merits at all before God: 'When you have done all that God has commanded you, you should think, "We are just poor (ἀχρεῖος here does not mean 'unprofitable' but 'miserable') slaves; we have only done our duty"' (Luke 17.10).

In parting from the devaluation of sin by casuistry and the idea of merit, Jesus inescapably brings to light the way in which the pious man, above all, is totally removed from God. Because the pious devalue sin and think too well of themselves, they are infinitely further from God than the notorious sinners. It was the son in the parable who stayed at home who alienated himself from the father, not the one who returned home from a wretchedness that he had brought upon himself (Luke 15.11–32); Simon the Pharisee knows of

[1] Like ἅγιον and the impersonal construction οὐκ ἔχει ἄφεσιν, the passive ἀφεθήσεται speaks in a veiled way of the divine action.
[2] The future ἀφεθήσεται corresponds to an imperfect in Galilean Aramaic, which almost always has virtual and not future significance.
[3] καί is meant intensively.
[4] See above, pp. 78–80.
[5] H. W. Beyer, βλασφημέω κτλ, TDNT I, 1964, 621–25: 624. In Mark 9.42, Jesus puts alongside the rejection of forgiveness as an unforgivable sin all seduction into such rejection, into unbelief.
[6] See below, pp. 216f.

forgiveness, yet does not really know what forgiveness is (Luke 7.36–50). Astonishingly enough, we have only one saying of Jesus against a man who transgressed the sabbath commandment, and that is only transmitted as an *agraphon* (Luke 6.5D);[1] but we have most vehement sayings against those who observe the sabbath strictly. The numerous words of judgment in the gospels are, almost without exception, not directed against those who commit adultery, cheat, etc., but against those who vigorously condemn adultery and exclude cheats from the community. It is not the sinners, but the pious who are called a generation of vipers in Matt. 12.34; 23.33, and in Luke 18.9–14 it is not the zealous Pharisee who finds God's good pleasure, but the publican. Why? Because the pious are separated from God by their theology and their piety. For a piety that leads men astray to pride and self-assurance is an almost hopeless thing. It was the view of the time that repentance was particularly difficult for the publican, because first he had to make good, and it was impossible for him to know all those whom he had cheated. It was Jesus' view that repentance was hardest for the pious man, because he was separated from God not by crude sins, but by his piety. Nothing separates a man from God so radically as self-assured piety. Jesus had such painful experiences in this sphere that he was ultimately convinced that his call would be in vain, 'But you would not' (Matt. 23.37 par. Luke 13.34; cf. Matt. 21.31f.).

This is the situation of those confronted with the catastrophe: they are stubborn and indifferent, and the pious live in self-righteous blindness, which makes them deaf to the gospel.

§ 15 · THE CHALLENGE OF THE HOUR

H. Windisch, 'Die Sprüche vom Eingehen in das Reich Gottes', *ZNW* 27, 1928, 163–92; E. K. Dietrich, *Die Umkehr (Bekehrung und Busse) im Alten Testament und im Judentum bei besonderer Berücksichtigung der neutestamentlicher Zeit*, Stuttgart 1936; H. S. Nyberg, 'Zum grammatischen Verständnis von Mt 12, 44f.', *Arbeiten und Mitteilungen aus dem neutestamentlichen Seminar zu Uppsala* 4, Lund 1936, 22–35; J. Schniewind, 'Was verstand Jesus unter Umkehr?', in: H. Asmussen (ed.), *Rechtgläubigkeit und Frömmigkeit* II, Berlin 1938, 70–84 (= in: J. Schniewind, *Die Freude der Busse*, Kleine Vandenhoeck Reihe 32, Göttingen 1956, 19–33).

[1] See Jeremias, *Unknown Sayings of Jesus*, London ²1964, 61–65.

(i) Repentance

Jesus sees men rushing to their destruction. Everything is on a knife-edge. It is the last hour. The respite is running out. He unwearyingly points to the threatening nature of the situation. Can't you see, he says, that you are in the position of an accused man on the steps of the court, whose case is hopeless? Now is the last moment for you to settle with your opponent (Matt. 5.25f. par. Luke 12.58f.). Can't you see that you are in the position of the administrator with a knife at his throat, because his deceptions have been uncovered? Learn from him. He does not let things take their course; he acts resolutely, where everything is at risk (Luke 16.1–8a, expanded by the comment vv. 8b–13).[1] At any moment the cry may ring out: the bridegroom is coming; then the wedding procession will go with torches[2] into the banqueting hall and the doors will be shut, irrevocably. Take care that you have oil for your torch (Matt. 25.1–12).[3] Put on your wedding garment before it is too late (Matt. 22.11–13).[4] In a word, repent, while there is still time. Repentance, that is the challenge of the hour. Repentance is necessary not only for so-called sinners but also, indeed even more, for those who in the world's view 'need no repentance' (Luke 15.7), for the upright and the pious, who have committed no great sins. Repentance is most urgent for them.

But what does Jesus mean when he says 'Repent'? Again, it is typical that the words μετάνοια and μετανοεῖν provide no exhaustive picture of what Jesus understands by repentance.[5] The parables speak a clearer language; the parable of the lost son expresses it most clearly of all.[6] The turning point in his life is described by the words εἰς ἑαυτὸν δὲ ἐλθών (Luke 15.17). Underlying this may be an Aramaic *hᵃdar bēh*, which does not mean, like the Greek phrase, 'he returned to a rational state of mind',[7] but 'he repented'.[8] The first thing here

---

[1] Cf. Dodd, *Parables*, 29f.; Jeremias, *Parables²*, 45–48, 181f.

[2] J. Jeremias, 'ΛΑΜΠΑΔΕΣ Mt 25, 1.3f. 7f.', ZNW 56, 1965, 196–201.

[3] Jeremias, *Parables²*, 171–75.　　[4] *Op. cit.*, 187–90.

[5] μετάνοια occurs on the lips of the earthly Jesus only at Luke 15.7 (5.32 is a Lucan addition to Mark 2.17), μετανοεῖν somewhat more frequently (Mark once, Luke nine times, but a number of these instances are certainly secondary).

[6] Jeremias, *Parables²*, 128–32.

[7] Thus e.g. Test. Joseph 3.9 (of Joseph after the attempt by Potiphar's wife to seduce him) ἦλθον εἰς ἐμαυτόν; further instances in Bauer–Arndt–Gingrich, 211, cf. Acts 12.11 ἐν ἑαυτῷ γενόμενος.

[8] Instances in Billerbeck I 165; II 215f.

is that he affirms his guilt (v. 18). The publican does the same: 'He did not dare[1] to raise his eyes to heaven', much less (we should add) his hands (Luke 18.13). Instead of the usual gesture of raising hands and eyes in prayer, he beats his breast in despair with the opening words of Ps. 51, which he expands by the dative τῷ ἁμαρτωλῷ (which is meant in an adversative sense): 'God, be gracious to me, although I am so sinful'. The meaning is probably that the publican prayed all the penitential psalm:

Have mercy on me, O God, according to thy steadfast love;
according to thy abundant mercy blot out my transgressions.
Wash me thoroughly from my iniquity,
and cleanse me from my sin.

For I know my transgressions,
and my sin is ever before me . . .

This affirmation of guilt has to be made not only before God, but also before man. It is expressed in the request for forgiveness towards the brethren (Matt. 5.23f.; Luke 17.4) and in the courage to make a public confession of sin (19.8).

But repentance is more than being sorry. It is a turning away from sin. Jesus demands this in a whole series of new pictures, always in concrete terms, of each in his situation. He expects the publican to stop cheating (Luke 19.8), the rich man to turn away from his service of Mammon (Mark 10.17–31), the conceited man to turn away from pride (Matt. 6.1–18).[2] If a man has dealt unjustly with another, he is to make good (Luke 19.8). From henceforward, life is to be ruled by obedience to the word of Jesus (Matt. 7.24–27), the confession of him (Matt. 10.32f. par.), the discipleship that comes before all other ties (v. 37 par.).

Repentance is not to be half-hearted. This is expressed by the little parable of the evil spirit who returns to his house with seven others (Matt. 12.43–45 par. Luke 11.24–26), for the interpretation of which research is indebted to H. S. Nyberg.[3] There is a difficulty in

[1] ἤθελεν = 'he dared'. Semitic languages have no word for 'dare'; cf. P. Joüon, *L'Évangile de Notre-Seigneur Jésus-Christ*, Verbum Salutis V, 1930, 216.

[2] In speaking of action ἐν τῷ κρυπτῷ/κρυφαίῳ (vv. 3f., 6, 17f.) Jesus means not only: conceal your almsgiving, your prayer, your fasting, but: give up your ambition, your urge to be praised by your fellow-men. For praying in secret see below, p. 192.

[3] ‡Nyberg.

v. 44b: a relapse is apparently seen as being unavoidable; in that case, what is the point of driving out the evil spirit? Nyberg saw that vv. 44b–45 provide an instance of formal parataxis with logical hypotaxis. That means that v. 44b is to be understood logically as a conditional sentence and should be translated: *if* the demon returns and finds the house empty, *in that case* he will return with sevenfold reinforcements (and here seven is the number of totality). Jesus is not, therefore, speaking of an inevitable consequence, as though every exorcized person were helplessly bound to suffer a relapse; rather, he is speaking of the consequences of a half-hearted repentance. Woe to anyone whose house stands empty! What does that mean? Even today in the east, the possessed person is regarded as the 'house' of the demon who possesses him. The 'house' was inhabited by a demon. Now that has been driven out, but the house is not to stand empty. A new master must take up residence in it, the shining light must take possession of it (Matt. 5.16; 6.22f. par.). Only then is repentance authentic, if it takes hold of the whole man and all his life.

True as all this is – that repentance means being sorry, that repentance means turning away from sin, that repentance means a complete surrender to a new master – we still have not reached the heart of the matter. The essence of repentance is something different.

In many passages in the Old Testament we find a mention of conditions which must be fulfilled for entry into the sanctuary, the so-called 'entry *tōrōt*'. Thus in Ps. 24, the 'entrance liturgy', the question is put to the pilgrims as they enter Jerusalem:

> Who shall ascend into the hill of the Lord?
> And who shall stand in his holy place? (v. 3)

The answer follows:

> He who has clean hands and a pure heart,
>   who does not lift up his soul to what is false,
> and does not swear deceitfully.
> He will receive blessing from the Lord,
>   and vindication from the God of his salvation (vv. 4f.).

Jesus repeatedly used entry-formulas of this kind.[1] Among the sayings which mention conditions for entering the *basileia* are Matt. 18.3

---

[1] εἰσέρχεσθαι: Mark 9.43 par., 45, 47 par.; 10.15 par., 23–25 par.; Matt. 5.20; 7.13f. par., 21; 19.17; 23.13 par.; John 3.5; 10.9. Cf. ‡Windisch and the numerous synonymous phrases there.

(par. Mark 10.15 par. Luke 18.17): ἀμὴν λέγω ὑμῖν, ἐὰν μὴ στραφῆτε καὶ γένησθε ὡς τὰ παιδία, οὐ μὴ εἰσέλθητε εἰς τὴν βασιλείαν τῶν οὐρανῶν.[1]

On interpreting the saying: First, a negative point must be made about the language. The common rendering of ἐὰν μὴ στραφῆτε as 'unless you are converted'[2] cannot be supported, as nowhere in secular Greek, the Septuagint or the Hexaplaric translation is στρέφεσθαι used with this meaning, the only exception being John 12.40.[3] We therefore have to look out for another explanation, and consider the possibility that στραφῆτε goes back to an Aramaic tūb, ḥazar or hᵃdar; these verbs are often used alongside another verb to express our 'again'.[4] In fact, in the Septuagint we have a whole series of double expressions which paraphrase an 'again' and are analogous in structure to the στραφῆτε καὶ γένησθε ὡς τὰ παιδία, e.g. ἐπιστραφήσεσθε καὶ ὄψεσθε (LXX Mal. 3.18: 'You will see again'); ἐπιστρέψωμεν καὶ ἀνοικοδομήσωμεν (1.4: 'We will build again'); ἐπιστράφητε ὑμεῖς καὶ ἀπάρατε εἰς τὴν ἔρημον (Num. 14.25; cf. Deut. 1.40; 2.1: 'Go back into the wilderness'); ἀνέστρεψεν καὶ ἐκάθευδεν (Ι Βασ. 13.5: 'He lay down to sleep again'); ἤγαγέν με καὶ ἔστρεψέν με (Ezek. 47.6 Θ: 'He led me back').[5] Matthew 18.3 should be translated in a similar way: 'Truly I say to you, unless you become like children again, you will not reach the basileia of God'.

What does 'become like a child again' mean? Is the point of comparison a child's humility (cf. Matt. 18.4)? Hardly, as we have no parallel from the world of Jesus for the idea that the child is a model of humility. Or is the point of camparison the purity of children?

[1] Linguistic considerations support the assumption that here Matthew provides an earlier version than Mark, who also introduces the saying in another place. On the one hand, Matt. 18.3 is more strongly of a Semitic type (for the predicate ὡς τὰ παιδία = substitute for an adjective = Semitism, cf. Bauer–Arndt–Gingrich, 906; on στραφῆτε see note 5); on the other, Mark 10.15 uses a term of Christian missionary language in the form of δέχεσθαι τὴν βασιλείαν τοῦ θεοῦ (J. Jeremias, 'Mc 10,13–16 Parr. und die Übung der Kindertaufe in der Urkirche', ZNW 40, 1941, 244f., cf. Billerbeck I 174–77). J. Dupont, Les Béatitudes II, Paris 1969, 167ff.; id., 'Matthieu 18:3', in: Neotestamentica et Semitica (Studies in Honour of M. Black), Edinburgh 1969, 50–60, differs and takes Matt. 18.3 as a revision of Mark 10.15.

[2] E. Percy, Die Botschaft Jesu, Lund 1953, 36 n.5; W. G. Kümmel, Promise and Fulfilment, SBT 23, London 1957, 126 n.77; W. Trilling, Das wahre Israel, Leipzig 1959, 87= ³München 1964, 108.

[3] P. Joüon, L'Évangile de Notre-Seigneur Jésus-Christ, Verbum Salutis V, Paris 1930, 112.

[4] R. Le Déaut, 'Le substrat araméen des évangiles: scolies en marge de l'Aramaic Approach de Matthew Black', Biblica 49, 1968, 388–99: 390.

[5] Also Deut. 24.4: οὐ δυνήσεται . . . ἐπαναστρέψας λαβεῖν αὐτήν ('he may not take her to himself again'); Ι Βασ. 3.5, 6, 9: ἀνάστρεφε κάθευδε ('go to sleep again'); Ψ 84[85].7: ἐπιστρέψας ζωώσεις ἡμᾶς ('you will restore us to life again'); 103 [104].9: οὐδὲ ἐπιστρέψουσιν καλύψαι τὴν γῆν ('they may never cover the earth again'); Hos. 2.11 [9]: ἐπιστρέψω καὶ κομιοῦμαι τὸν σῖτόν μου ('I will take my corn back again'); Micah 7.19: ἐπιστρέψει καὶ οἰκτιρήσει ἡμᾶς ('He will have mercy on us again').

This idea, too, is not current in early Palestinian Judaism.[1] T. W. Manson's suggestion that Matt. 18.3 could have something to do with the use of the address '*Abbā* may put us on the right track.[2] That will, in fact, be the solution. 'Become a child again' means: to learn to say '*Abbā* again.

This brings us to the heart of the meaning of repentance. Repentance means learning to say '*Abbā* again, putting one's whole trust in the heavenly Father, returning to the Father's house and the Father's arms. Luke 15.11–32 provides evidence that this understanding might not be completely wrong. The repentance of the lost son consists in his finding his way home to his father. In the last resort, repentance is simply trusting in the grace of God.

(ii) Motive

John the Baptist also issued a summons to repentance. But with Jesus, repentance is something quite different. Where does the distinction lie? One answer is given by the story of the conversion of the chief publican Zacchaeus (Luke 19.1–10). To this man it seems quite inconceivable that Jesus should want to look in on him, despised as he is and avoided by everyone else. Jesus restores the respect he has lost by staying in his house and breaking bread with him. He gives him his fellowship.[3] This kindness on the part of Jesus overcomes Zacchaeus. It achieves what all the insults and all the contempt from his fellow citizens could not do. He confesses his fault in public and promises to make good (v. 8). The story of the woman who was a sinner is along just the same lines (Luke 7.36–50 par.).[4] Jesus interprets her action in the parable of the two debtors. It was the remission of her great debt that led the woman to her open confession of sin through her actions and to a gratitude that is almost helpless because it does not know how it should be expressed. On the other hand, Jesus rebukes Chorazin and Bethsaida because the acts of God proclaiming the time of salvation were made visible in them, and yet they did not repent (Matt. 11.20–24 par.).

These stories and *logia* continually make clear the decisive difference between the Baptist's call to repentance and that of Jesus. The difference is one of *motive*. In the case of John, the motive is fear at the

---

[1] A. Oepke, παῖς κτλ., *TDNT* V, 1967, 636–54: 645–48.
[2] *Teaching*[2], 331.   [3] See pp. 115f. above.   [4] Jeremias, *Parables*[2], 126f.

threat of judgment; this is not lacking with Jesus (e.g. Luke 13.1–5), but in his case the decisive motive is experience of the incomprehensible goodness of God (e.g. Luke 13.6–9). Repentance springs from grace. God's goodness is the only power that can really lead a man to repentance.

Here Jesus takes up high points of the prophetic preaching, especially Deutero-Isaiah. 'I have swept away your transgressions like a cloud, and your sins like mist; return to me, for I have redeemed you' (Isa. 44.22). God's grace overwhelms the faithless. A note that is struck in the Old Testament – but only occasionally – becomes central to the proclamation of Jesus. Repentance is not an act of human humility or human self-mastery; it is being overwhelmed by the grace of God. With the prophets this grace is promised; with Jesus it is present and is already being offered. Repentance takes place in the light of the gospel; only the opening of his eyes to God's goodness makes a man recognize his guilt and the distance that separates him from God. In the end, Jesus himself and the New Testament as a whole know only one motive for repentance: the personal assurance of salvation.

(iii) The joy of repentance

Once we have understood that God's goodness is the motive for repentance, we can understand one last thing, that J. Schniewind has stressed: repentance is joy.[1]

Repentance is returning home to the Father's house. The joyful noise of dancing resounds over the land: a lost child has found his way home (Luke 15.25). A dead man has come alive again, a lost member of the herd has been found (vv. 24, 32). The return home is a resurrection from the dead, because there is life only in the sphere of the kingly reign of God. Anyone who belongs to it has even now attained the consummation of the world beyond the barrier of death (Matt. 8.22 par. and on it, see p. 132).

This note of joy keeps re-echoing in the pictures with which Jesus describes repentance. Repentance is putting on the wedding garment (Matt. 22.11–13, see p. 106 above; see the anticipation in Isa. 61.10); the festal robe is the mantle of righteousness. In a quite different picture, repentance is a head anointed with oil (Matt. 6.17), not as a

[1] ‡Schniewind 78f. (= 27f.).

new form of hypocrisy, but as an expression of joy at the salvation that has been given. Because repentance is joy, in Mark 2.15f. Jesus celebrates the meal of joy with those who have turned back.

Repentance is joy that God is so gracious. Even more, repentance is *God's* joy (Luke 15.7: χαρὰ ἐν τῷ οὐρανῷ or v. 10 χαρὰ ἐνώπιον τῶν ἀγγέλων τοῦ θεοῦ). God rejoices like the shepherd who rediscovers a stray animal, or the woman who rediscovers her lost coin, or the father who rediscovers his lost son. God 'exults with loud singing as on a day of festival' (Zeph. 3.17f., see p. 118), like 'the bridegroom over the bride' (Isa. 62.5). This is the 'soteriological joy of God'.[1]

Because repentance means being able to live from forgiveness, being able to be a child again, repentance is joy.

[1] E. G. Gulin, *Die Freude im Neuen Testament* I, Helsinki 1932, 99.

THE NEW PEOPLE OF GOD

THE PROCLAMATION of Jesus always comes to a climax in a personal appeal. This is true of his message of condemnation and all the more so of his offer of salvation. The invitation can be put in general terms: Δεῦτε πρός με πάντες οἱ κοπιῶντες καὶ πεφορτισμένοι (Matt. 11.28) or (as in Isa 55.1, taking up the cry of the water seller, so familiar to the people of the East):[1]

ἐάν τις διψᾷ, ἐρχέσθω
καὶ πινέτω ὁ πιστεύων εἰς ἐμέ (John 7.37f.).[2]

But the appeal can also be addressed to the individual: καθάρισον πρῶτον τὸ ἐντὸς τοῦ ποτηρίου (Matt. 23.26) or: μὴ φοβοῦ, μόνον πίστευε (Mark 5.36). It can be brought to a head in specific terms as a call to discipleship: δεῦτε ὀπίσω μου (Mark 1.17); ἀκολούθει μοι (2.14; 10.21). The answer to Jesus' challenge is faith.

§ 16 · FAITH

A. Schlatter, *Der Glaube im Neuen Testament*, Stuttgart 1927 = [5]1963; G. Ebeling, 'Jesus and Faith', in: *Word and Faith*, London and Philadelphia 1963, 201–46; E. Fuchs, 'Jesus and Faith', in: *Studies of the Historical Jesus*, SBT 42, London 1964, 48–64.

(i) The sources

If we consider the πίστις group of words in the synoptic gospels, we

---

[1] C. Westermann, *Isaiah 40–66*, Old Testament Library, London 1969, 218f., on Isa. 55.1–3a.

[2] Both the synonymous parallelism arranged chiastically and the comparison with Rev. 22.17b show that the last four words (ὁ πιστεύων εἰς ἐμέ) are not to be taken with what follows. (πιστεύειν εἰς is Johannine stylization: synoptics 1, Johannine literature 38, Paul 3; 3 other NT examples.)

are struck by the repeated occurrence of two formal phrases: ἡ πίστις σου σέσωκέν σε[1] and: ὡς ἐπίστευσας γενηθήτω σοι.[2] The second phrase is a peculiarity of Matthew; in 15.28 it is added by him to the Marcan text; Luke, too, in 8.12f. has expanded the Marcan text with two πιστεύειν sayings. All this raises the suspicion that the synoptic sayings about faith have been strongly influenced by the early church, which would not be surprising, considering the central significance faith had for it.[3]

There are, however, a number of observations to be made which warn against overestimating the influence of the early church in this particular question. The relatively *rare occurrence* of the words πίστις and πιστεύειν in the synoptic gospels itself suggests the need for care.

On an average, the two words occur on each page of the Nestle text of the New Testament the following number of times:

Synoptics	0·24
Acts	0·55
Catholic epistles	1·10
Paul	1·25
Hebrews	1·31
Gospel of John	1·48
Revelation	0·09[4]

If we count the parallels only once, and bracket off the instances of non-specific usage,[5] the count for the synoptic gospels falls as low as 0.14 per Nestle page. Thus the first three gospels are much further from early Christian usage – as far as the frequency of the words πίστις/πιστεύειν is concerned – than the whole of the rest of the New Testament, apart from the Apocalypse.

Another warning against overestimating the influence of the early church is the linguistic evidence. It appears that the usage of the word group in the synoptic sayings of Jesus often reflects the Aramaic equivalents hēmīn/hēmānūtā.[6] For example, there is no previous Greek

---

[1] Mark 5.34 par.; 10.52 par.; Luke 7.50; 17.19.

[2] Matt. 8.13; cf. 9.29 (κατὰ τὴν πίστιν ὑμῶν γενηθήτω ὑμῖν); 15.28 (μεγάλη σου ἡ πίστις· γενηθήτω σοι ὡς θέλεις).

[3] It is significant that R. Bultmann, πιστεύω κτλ. CD, *TDNT* VI, 1968, 197–228: 203ff. (D. The group of concepts in the NT) does not even raise the question whether Jesus could have used the group of words, but begins immediately with the kerygma of the primitive church.

[4] Thus only Revelation falls outside the framework; it has πίστις only four times on forty-five pages, and πιστεύω does not occur at all.

[5] πιστεύειν = 'entrust' (Luke 16.11); 'regard as possible' (Matt. 9.28); 'give credit (to a rumour)' (Mark 13.21 par.; Matt. 23.26); πίστις = 'faithfulness' (Matt. 23.23).

[6] ‡Schlatter, 585–94.

history to the composite ὀλιγόπιστος[1] (Matt. 6.30 par. Luke 12.28; Matt. 8.26; 14.31; 16.8; cf. 17.20 ὀλιγοπιστία), which only occurs in a Christian setting. There is, however, a Semitic equivalent,[2] as there is for the objective genitive πίστις θεοῦ (Mark 11.22),[3] which is unusual in Greek.[4] The article before the noun (Luke 18.8), which seems harsh to Greek linguistic sensibilities, reproduces the determination of hēmānūtā, which is idiomatic in Aramaic.[5] These observations show that the nucleus of the synoptic sayings of Jesus which deal with faith have their origin in an Aramaic-speaking milieu.

One saying which is illuminating for the question of authenticity is the *logion* about faith, which, even if it is only the size of a mustard-seed (Matt. 17.20 par. Luke 17.6), can nevertheless move mountains (Mark 11.23 par. Matt. 21.21; 17.20) or trees (Luke 17.6). It is evident that the saying uses Palestinian material: the grain of mustard-seed as the smallest object perceptible to the human eye,[6] the uprooting of trees as a spectacular miracle,[7] the moving of mountains as a proverbial expression for 'making possible what seems impossible'.[8] All this is specifically Palestinian. But the really remarkable thing has still to be mentioned. It is that in the Talmud, the uprooting of mountains is used as a periphrasis for hair-splitting acuteness in disputation ('he is an uprooter of mountains') and for irrefutable decisiveness ('I would (rather) root up mountains', viz. than change my mind).[9] On the other hand, the application of the phrase to the power of faith occurs *only* in the sayings of Jesus and in I Cor. 13.2. We must exclude the possibility that the synoptic tradition and Paul may have come upon this phrase independently of each other. Unless we want to resort to the hypothesis (without any support from a text) that Jesus and Paul go back to material that was known to both of them, we must reckon on the possibility that Paul's saying about faith that can move mountains takes up a *logion* of Jesus.

A consideration that weighs still more heavily than all this is that the use of the πιστεύειν/πίστις group in the synoptic gospels *differs funda-*

[1] It is true that ὀλιγόπιστος also occurs in the sayings of Sextus, a collection of 451 mostly non-religious sayings which owe their present form to a Christian redaction which took place about AD 200, as saying 6: ὀλιγόπιστος ἐν πίστει ἄπιστος. But saying 6 is to be ascribed to the Christian redaction; cf. H. Chadwick, *The Sentences of Sextus*, Texts and Studies, NS 5, Cambridge 1959, 139.

[2] qᵉṭannē 'ᵉmūnā (b. Ber. 24b; b. Sot. 48b).

[3] hēmānūt šᵉmayyā, Fragment Targum Gen. 16.5; 'ᵉmūnātō šel hqb'h (= haqqādōš bārūk hū'), Ex. R.15.7 on 12.2. The objective genitive is Jewish-Greek only (most significantly!) in the form πίστις τοῦ θείου (Josephus, *Antt.* 17.179); for this, IV Macc. has ἡ πρὸς (τὸν) θεὸν πίστις (15.24; 16.22). In the alleged place-name Θεοῦ πίστις, I. Bao. 21.3, θεοῦ is subjective genitive.

[4] ‡Schlatter, 586.

[5] hēmānūtā is regularly used in the determinative in Aramaic, cf. C. C. Torrey, *The Four Gospels*, London 1933, 312.

[6] Billerbeck I 669.   [7] *Ibid.* IV 313f., cf. I 127, 759.   [8] *Ibid.* I 759.   [9] *Ibid.*

162 THE NEW PEOPLE OF GOD

mentally from the terminology of the early church. Nowhere is it said *expressis verbis* that faith is an echo to the message; nowhere is the relationship of faith to the person of Jesus made explicitly clear. On the contrary, where synoptic sayings of Jesus make express mention of the point of reference of faith, it is God (Mark 11.22), John the Baptist (Matt. 21.32 three times), the gospel (Mark 1.15 summary). True, we hear twice of faith 'in Jesus': Matt. 18.6 τῶν πιστευόντων εἰς ἐμέ, and 27.42 πιστεύσομεν ἐπ' αὐτόν, but in both places the prepositional phrase is an addition by Matthew to the Marcan text (9.42; 15.32). The mockery directed at the *titulus* on the cross in Mark 15.32 is the only passage in which the context supplies a christological title as the object of an expression of faith. This situation makes it clear how exaggerated is the assertion that the synoptic gospels have been over-painted to the point of unrecognizability in the light of the kerygma. The absence of christological titles in the synoptic sayings about faith, indeed simply the express mention of its reference to Jesus, is an indication of age of the first rank, and a pointer to the origin of at least the nucleus of the synoptic statements of faith from the period before Easter.

(ii) The meaning of faith

The Old Testament word for 'to believe' is *he'emîn*. The basic meaning of the root *'mn* is 'firm, constant, reliable'. In the qal and sometimes in the niphal, *'mn* denotes the carrying of a child in the folds of a garment or on the hips, because it is safe and sheltered there. The hiphil ('gain or keep confidence, trust') is used only sparingly in the Old Testament in a religious sense (25 times), but in very significant expressions. If we consider the passages which have had an influence on the New Testament (Gen. 15.6; Isa. 28.16; 53.1; Ps. 116.10), we discover that *he'emîn* describes not so much reliance on God in daily life as searching for God in a crisis, fighting down temptation. What is meant is a faith that trusts God against appearances. Thus even in the Old Testament, the decisive basic significance of the concept of faith emerges clearly, as it also remains normative for the New Testament. Faith is a trust which does not allow itself to be dissuaded.

If we turn to the word-group πίστις/πιστεύειν/ὀλιγόπιστος/ἄπιστος in the synoptic gospels, it is striking how more than half the examples fall either in miracle stories or in *logia* dealing with miracles. This is remarkable, because faith does not play a role either in Jewish or in

Hellenistic miracle stories. There is a predilection for using the group of words in instances in which people come to Jesus in search of help;[1] here faith consists in the certainty that Jesus can help because he has power over spirits and diseases. This certainty is, however, *more than mere belief in miracles*, for it includes an attitude to Jesus' person and mission which is expressed, for example, in the addresses *rabbī*, *mārī*, *rabbūnī*, son of David. These are more than courtesy titles, as Luke 6.46 shows. People who speak in this way have great confidence in Jesus' goodness and compassion, which is sometimes expressed in a moving way, as in the story of the woman with a haemorrhage. According to Mark 5.28 par., she touches Jesus' robe because she hopes to be healed by mere contact. Probably, however, touching the hem of the robe originally had a different significance: it is a gesture requesting help, as the story of Ḥanin the Rain-maker shows (see p. 65). The woman is ashamed to talk about her affliction publicly. Modestly she touches the hem of Jesus' robe; her confidence in his kindness is so great that she is certain that this silent gesture will be enough. The stories of the centurion (Matt. 8.5–13 par. Luke 7.1–10) and the Syro-Phoenician woman (Mark 7.24–30 par. Matt. 15.21–28), too, show clearly that the attitude of both these Gentiles who sought for help embraced more than superstitious hope for a miracle.

In connection with the story of the centurion, three observations must be made about the text. They are intended to remove the following difficulties which are presented by the wording:

(*a*) Jesus declares himself ready to come, but the centurion strangely refuses (Matt. v. 8; Luke v. 6b);

(*b*) The remark that he is under authority (Matt. v. 9a; Luke v. 8a) makes no sense in view of the stress on his commanding position in the continuation of the verse;

(*c*) It is difficult to see the point of comparison for the 'too' in this verse ('for I too am under authority'): how is he like Jesus here?

The following comments may be made:

(*a*) Matt. 8.7 is to be read as a negative answer in the form of a question: 'Am I to come (into your home, an unclean Gentile) and make him (your servant) healthy?' Jesus is not saying that he is ready to come; on the contrary, he is refusing help.

(*b*) An unskilful translation has produced the contradiction in Matt. 8.9a (Luke 7.8a) between the statement of the centurion that he is under authority, i.e. that he has to obey, and the stress on his commanding position.[2] In reproducing Semitic parataxis, the translators have often translated the secondary statement with the finite verb and taken the stress from the primary statement by translating it with a

---

[1] Mark 2.5 par; 5.34 par., 36 par.; 9.19 par., 23f.; 10.52 par.; Matt. 8.10 par., 13; 9.28f.; 15.28; Luke 17.20.

[2] Cf. J. Jeremias, *Jesus' Promise to the Nations*, SBT 24, ²1967, 30 n.4.

164   THE NEW PEOPLE OF GOD

participle.[1] We have such an instance in v. 9a. The participial phrase ἔχων κτλ. contains the primary statement, whereas the main clause ἄνθρωπός εἰμι ὑπὸ ἐξουσίαν introduces a subsidiary comment (in this case meant in a concessive sense). It therefore means: 'Even I, although I am a subordinate officer, have authority'. (c) This sentence lacks its conclusion, to which the καὶ γὰρ ἐγώ, 'I too', points. The centurion omits it out of modesty. It can only run: 'how much more have you'. In view of what was said in (b) above, the comparison with Jesus does not refer to the subordinate position of the centurion, but to his authority.

If we take account of these three observations, the train of thought of the dialogue between Jesus and the centurion is clarified. The centurion does not quarrel with the fact that Jesus does not want to enter his house. Rather, with his answer (Matt. 8.8 par. Luke 7.6b) that he is not worthy that Jesus should enter his house, he indicates that his confidence in Jesus' power and will to help is unshakable. He is convinced that Jesus can heal his boy even without entering the house. 'If I,' he says, 'an insignificant man, can give orders to my soldiers and have them carried out to the letter, how much more can you give orders – to the evil spirit which is making my servant ill. You are the master, and you have power over the spirits.' This confidence, which refuses to be repulsed, is also expressed in the other story about a Gentile, that of the Syro-Phoenician woman (Mark 7.27). Once again the refusal is accepted, yet at the same time overcome by an expression of unconditional trust: ναί, κύριε, καὶ τὰ κυνάρια ὑποκάτω τῆς τραπέζης ἐσθίουσιν ἀπὸ τῶν ψιχίων τῶν παιδίων (v. 29).[2] With this saying the woman acknowledges Jesus to be the giver of the bread of life, and declares herself content with a crumb of what is really meant for Israel. In both stories the original note of the Old Testament concept of faith recurs: the faith of these two Gentiles is a confidence that will not be discountenanced.

The group of words has this meaning even when it is applied to the disciples of Jesus. In Jesus they have recognized the prophet of the time of salvation (pp. 76ff.), the vanquisher of Satan (pp. 85ff), the messenger of good news for the poor (pp. 108ff.), and their faith includes readiness to sacrifice family, possessions and even life.

[1] E.g. Mark 2.23 ἤρξαντο ὁδὸν ποιεῖν τίλλοντες τοὺς στάχυας literally means 'they began to make a way by rubbing ears of corn'; in fact, it means, 'they rubbed ears of corn on their way'. In Luke 13.28, the sense is, of course, 'when you see Abraham in the basileia, but you yourselves are cast out'; in Luke 23.34b, the meaning is, 'they cast lots for his clothes'.

[2] We are not to think of the 'crumbs' as crumbs in our sense, but as pieces of bread with which people used to wipe their fingers while eating, afterwards throwing them under the table; cf. Jeremias, Parables[2], 184, note on Luke 16.21.

(iii) Jesus' evaluation of faith

In the synoptic gospels, ὀλιγόπιστος, ὀλιγοπιστία, ἄπιστος occur exclusively on the lips of Jesus; so does πίστις with one[1] and πιστεύειν with very few[2] exceptions. From this concentration of the occurence of the word-group in the sayings of Jesus, it can be seen that the tradition was interested, not in believing or unbelieving men, but entirely in Jesus' verdict on their attitude. This is also true of the only passage in which the noun πίστις occurs in narrative: ἰδὼν ὁ 'Ιησοῦς τὴν πίστιν αὐτῶν (Mark 2.5).

If we ask what was Jesus' evaluation of faith, the fact noted on p. 160, that the words πίστις and πιστεύειν occur more rarely in the synoptic sayings of Jesus than, say, in Paul should not lead us to the false conclusion that faith had only peripheral significance for Jesus. Rather, we again have one of the numerous instances in which it is wrong to rely on the statistics of theological nouns, because Jesus, unlike Paul, did not use a theological vocabulary. In content, Jesus' whole message is one single summons to accept the offer of salvation, one single appeal to trust in his word and in God's grace; that is, it is a call to faith, even if that word does not occur very often. Jesus himself calls the attitude of his disciples faith (Luke 22.32; cf. Mark 4.40; 9.42 par. 11.22), and the passages in which he rebukes the disciples for their little faith (Matt. 6.30 par. Luke 12.28; Matt. 8.26; 16.8; 17.20) confirm that he expected faith from his disciples.

The saying about the faith that can move mountains, which is also known by the apostle Paul (I Cor. 13.2, p. 161), indicates the significance that Jesus attached to faith. It was current in two versions, of which one used the mountain as an illustration (Matt. 17.20), the other the sycamore (Luke 17.6).[3] Both miracles, moving mountains and uprooting trees, were for the world of Jesus the proverbial embodiment of unusual acts of power (see p. 161); but in the sayings of Jesus the stress does not lie on the unusual character of the event. The decisive feature for understanding it is that the disappearance of mountains (Isa. 40.4; 49.11; esp. Zech. 14.10) and their reappearance to support

[1] Mark 2.5 par.
[2] Mark 9.24; 11.31 par.; 15.32 par.; elsewhere only three times in Luke in the birth and resurrection narratives (1.20, 45; 24.25).
[3] Mark 11.23 (par. Matt. 21.21) offers a composite form. Mountains are certainly mentioned here, as at Matt. 17.20; I Cor. 13.2; but like the sycamore in Luke 17.6, they are to be thrown into the sea.

the mountain of God (Isa. 2.2 par. Micah 4.1) was expected as an eschatological event.[1] Even the weakest kind of faith, as tiny as a grain of mustard seed, will – so Jesus promises – not primarily perform spectacular miracles, so much as have a share in the eschatological consummation.[2]

This recognition of even weak faith, which is expressed in the comparison with the grain of mustard seed, is also characteristic of Jesus elsewhere. He does not despise the trust of those who expect a healing miracle from him, and he listens to the father who cries out, 'I believe; help me in spite of my unbelief!' (Mark 9.24).

There is a difficulty in the context of Mark 9.24. To the father's request εἴ τι δύνῃ, βοήθησον ἡμῖν σπλαγχνισθεὶς ἐφ'ἡμᾶς (v. 22), Jesus replies τὸ 'εἰ δύνῃ', πάντα δυνατὰ τῷ πιστεύοντι (v. 23). The question is: to what does the dative τῷ πιστεύοντι refer? For Greek sensibility the dative mentions the logical subject (like Mark 14.36 πάντα δυνατά σοι, 'you can do everything'), i.e.: as far as 'if you can' is concerned, the believer can do everything. In this case Jesus would be designating himself as the believer. As such he has the whole power of God at his disposal. But this saying would be strange, in that there is no mention of Jesus' own faith elsewhere in any of the four gospels. The real difficulty in referring τῷ πιστεύοντι (v. 23) to Jesus, however, lies in v. 24, for the πιστεύω that the father utters here (πιστεύω· βοήθει μου τῇ ἀπιστίᾳ)[3] shows clearly that he has referred the dative τῷ πιστεύοντι to himself ('all is possible for him who believes'). This is also the understanding of syr^sin v. 23 ('If you believe, all things can be yours'). Is the double meaning intended by the evangelist? In that case Jesus would at the same time be depicted both as the believer who has blind confidence, coupled with complete surrender to God, and as the one who summons others to believe, full of mercy on those who try to believe, but have to confess their unbelief.

Just as Jesus respects weak faith, so he allows the validity of representative faith;[4] he regards intercession as being of the same importance as petition.

[1] 'R. Phineas (c. 360) said in the name of R. Reuben (c. 300): One day the Holy One, blessed be he, will bring Sinai, Tabor and Carmel and build the Temple on their summits. And what is the proof-text? "And it shall come to pass in the latter days, that the mountain of the house of the Lord shall be established as the highest of the mountains, and shall be raised above the hills" (Isa. 2.2),' Pesiqta de Rab Kahana, ed. S. Buber, Lyck 1868, 144b 14. More in my work Golgotha, Leipzig 1926, 51–53.
[2] Cf. Luke 12.32 εὐδόκησεν ὁ πατὴρ ὑμῶν δοῦναι ὑμῖν τὴν βασιλείαν.
[3] The dative τῇ ἀπιστίᾳ is to be taken in an adversative sense, as the dative τῷ ἁμαρτωλῷ (Luke 18.13, see p. 153).
[4] The father's: Mark 5.22ff. par.; 9.14ff. par. John 4.45ff. The mother's: Mark 7.24ff. The friends': Mark 2.3ff.

§ 17 · GATHERING TOGETHER THE COMMUNITY OF SALVATION

J. Thomas, *Le mouvement baptiste en Palestine et Syrie (150 av. J. -Chr. – 300 ap. J.-Chr.)*, Gembloux 1935; L. Rost, *Die Vorstufen von Kirche und Synagoge im Alten Testament*, Stuttgart 1938; J. Jeremias, 'Der Gedanke des "Heiligen Restes" im Spätjudentum und in der Verkündigung Jesu', *ZNW* 42, 1949, 184–94 = *Abba*, 121–32; P. Nepper-Christensen, *Wer hat die Kirche gestiftet?*, Lund 1950; A. Oepke, *Das neue Gottesvolk*, Gütersloh 1950; J. Jeremias, *Die theologische Bedeutung der Funde am Toten Meer*, Vortragsreihe der Niedersächsischen Landesregierung zur Förderung der wissenschaftlichen Forschung in Niedersachsen, Göttingen 1962; B. F. Meyer, 'Jesus and the Remnant of Israel', *JBL* 84, 1965, 123–30.

Those who open themselves to the gospel gather round Jesus, so to speak, in concentric circles. Where Jesus appears, he leaves behind followers who, with their families, wait for the reign of God and accept him and his messengers. They are to be found throughout the country, above all in Galilee, but also in Judaea, e.g. in Bethany, and in the Decapolis (Mark 5.19f.). A group of disciples accompanies Jesus on his travels, men like Levi the son of Alphaeus (Mark 2.14), Joseph named Barsabbas and Matthias (Acts 1.23),[1] and also women (Luke 8.1–3; Mark 15.40f.); as the latter had control over their own property, they must have been widows. The nucleus is made up of the twelve messengers whom Jesus sends out.[2] Thus in the midst of this world there arises the community of those who belong to the reign of God. But was it really Jesus' intention to assemble a community of his own? This has been doubted.

(i) Terminology

Doubt arises from the remarkable fact that the word ἐκκλησία appears in only two passages in the gospels. Both occur in Matthew, and each has a different meaning: Matt. 16.18 refers to the whole church, 18.17 (twice) to the individual community. When one considers the great significance of the word ἐκκλησία in both meanings for the early church, the obvious conclusion seems to be that in the two passages from Matthew's gospel just mentioned we have the

---

[1] They fulfil the condition laid down in vv. 21f., that they had been συνελθόντες ἡμῖν (Peter is speaking) from the baptism of John to the Ascension.

[2] For the historicity of the group of twelve see below, pp. 232–34.

language of the early church. In other words, there is a widespread view that the sparseness and doubtful character of the instances rules out the possibility that Jesus intended to assemble an ἐκκλησία. In addition, it was pointed out that as Jesus expected the end in a short (indeed a very short) time, he could not have thought of founding a church.

Now there is no question that if by ἐκκλησία we understand an organization of the kind that developed in a later period, it would be an anachronism to ascribe to Jesus the intention of founding an ἐκκλησία. But that would be to misunderstand the meaning of ἐκκλησία. It helps to understand the word correctly if we note that the picture of building the ἐκκλησία (Matt. 16.18) also occurs in Qumran, at 4QpPs 37.III.16 (on Ps. 37.23b–24a, DJD V 44): '(God) has established him (the Teacher of Righteousness), libnōt lō ʿadat . . . to build for himself a congregation of . . .' As this passage is the 'only verbal parallel to the saying about building the community in Matt. 16.18',[1] it seems best to begin from ʿēdā in defining more closely what ἐκκλησία means in Matt. 16.18. At Qumran, the Hebrew ʿēdā, used in bonam partem, occasionally designates the angels as the heavenly host, but most often refers to the Essene community as the community of the members of the people of salvation (in contrast to the massa perditionis which refuses to repent). Thus it is more appropriate to translate ἐκκλησία 'people of God' than 'church'.

Now Jesus speaks constantly of a new people of God that he is gathering, and with a wealth of pictures (another confirmation that accounts of the proclamation of Jesus should not be limited to technical terms). He speaks of the new people of God as the flock (Luke 12.32; Mark 14.27 par. Matt. 26.31f.; John 10.1–29, cf. Matt. 10.16 par. Luke 10.3; John 16.32) which the shepherd frees from oppressive isolation and gathers together (Matt. 12.30 par. Luke 11.23; Matt. 15.24; John 10.1–5, 16, 27–30; cf. Ezek. 34.1–31; Jer. 23.1–8),[2] as the throng of wedding guests (Mark 2.19 par.); as God's planting (Matt. 13.24; 15.13, where it is constrasted with the planting that does not come from God);[3] as the net (Matt. 13.47; cf. Mark 1.17). Those who belong to the new people of God are God's building (Matt. 16.18 cf. Hagg. 2.6–9) or the city of God which is founded on mount Zion

---

[1] G. Jeremias, Lehrer der Gerechtigkeit, 148.

[2] See J. Jeremias, ποιμήν κτλ, TDNT VI, 1959, 485–502.

[3] The comparison of the community with the planting is common in the Qumran texts, cf. G. Jeremias, Lehrer der Gerechtigkeit, 183 (n.7), 249ff., 256ff.

(Matt. 5.14; cf. Isa. 2.2–4 par. Micah 4.1–3; Isa. 25.6–8; 60) and whose light is to be seen from afar, so that its inhabitants are called children of light (Luke 16.8; John 12.36). They are the members of the new covenant (Mark 14.24 par.; I Cor. 11.25), in whom the promise of the covenant is fulfilled: God is their teacher (Matt. 23.8; Jer. 31.33f.).[1] It is certainly no coincidence that the image of God's warriors, that plays such a role at Qumran (1 QM), does not appear in Jesus' preaching.[2] His favourite of all the images for the new people of God is the comparison of the community of salvation with the eschatological family of God.[3] It is the substitute for the earthly family which Jesus himself and the disciples accompanying him have had to give up (Mark 10.29f. par.). In the eschatological family God is the father (Matt. 23.9), Jesus the master of the house, his followers the other occupants (Matt. 10.25).[4] The older women who hear his word are his mothers, the men and youths his brothers (Mark 3.34 par.). And at the same time they are all the little ones, the children, indeed the νήπιοι of the family (Matt. 11.25) whom Jesus addresses as children, although in age they are adult.[5] The family of God appears above all in table-fellowship, which is an anticipation of the meal of salvation at the consummation.[6] In another passage Jesus extends the framework of the family of God more widely, beyond the circle of his followers: he calls all those who are in need, oppressed or in desolation his brothers (Matt. 25.40, where the demonstrative τούτων is used pleonastically, in a Semitic-type way, and therefore should not give rise to the wrong interpretation that ἀδελφοί applies

[1] An understanding of διδάσκαλος in Matt. 23.8 (εἷς γάρ ἐστιν ὑμῶν ὁ διδάσκαλος) has to begin from the fact that vv. 8 and 9 run in parallel. The progression of ideas lies in the transition from passive to active in the protases (8a: κληθῆτε/9a: καλέσητε): the disciples are not to allow themselves to be given the title 'sir' (v. 8), nor for their part are they to address any old man as 'my father' (v. 9a), because this honour is reserved for God. Both supporting clauses have God in mind; just as it is God who is meant by the heavenly father (v. 9b), so too is it with the teacher (v. 8b, cf. Jer. 31. 33f.). The interpretation of the teacher as Christ in v. 10 is secondary, as is already shown by ὁ Χριστός, which Jesus avoided (cf. Jeremias, *The Prayers of Jesus*, 42).

[2] Cf. W. Grundmann, *Die Geschichte Jesu Christi*, Berlin 1957, 157.

[3] J. Schniewind, *Das Evangelium nach Markus*, NTD 1[10], Göttingen 1963, on Mark 3.31ff.

[4] For the word play Βεελζεβούλ/οἰκοδεσπότης in Matt. 10.25, see above, p. 7.

[5] Mark 10.24 τέκνα, cf. 2.5 τέκνον; 5.34 θυγάτηρ.

[6] Mark 2.15–17 par.; 6.34–42 par.; 8.1–10 par.; 7.27 par.; 14.22–25; Luke 15.1f.; see above, p. 116. Cf. W. Grundmann, 'Die νήπιοι in der urchristlichen Paränese', *NTS* 5, 1958/59, 205.

only to the disciples).[1] In so doing he includes them in the family of God. There is no doubt that Jesus speaks repeatedly with the greatest variety of imagery about the gathering of the people of God that he is bringing about.

The expectation of an imminent end does not contradict this in any way. On the contrary. Precisely because Jesus believed that the end is near, it had to be his purpose to gather God's people of the time of salvation. For the people of God belong to the one whom God has sent; the group of disciples belongs to the prophet. Indeed, we must put the point even more sharply: the *only* significance of the whole of Jesus's activity is to gather the eschatological people of God. It follows from Luke 11.1 that the group of disciples, too, regarded themselves as a well-defined fellowship. The request, 'Lord, teach us to pray', does not mean that the disciples still had to learn the right way to pray;[2] on the contrary, as the reference to John the Baptist's example shows, they ask Jesus for a prayer to distinguish them and hold them together as his disciples. To have a distinctive order of prayer was an essential mark of fellowship for the religious groups in the time of Jesus.[3] It was true of the Pharisees,[4] it was true of Qumran,[5] and it was true of the followers of John the Baptist (Luke 11.1). The request of Jesus' disciples for a prayer shows that they understand themselves as his community.

(ii) The holy remnant[6]

Jesus was not the first to attempt to gather God's people of the time

---

[1] Jeremias, *Parables*[2], 207.

[2] This is the way in which Luke may have understood it; in Luke 11.1 he begins a *didache* on prayer meant for Gentile Christians which extends to v.13 (J. Jeremias, 'The Lord's Prayer in the Light of Recent Research', in: *The Prayers of Jesus*, SBT II 6, 1967, 88).

[3] K. H. Rengstorf, *Das Evangelium nach Lukas*, NTD 3[9], Göttingen 1962, 144.

[4] Praying the *Tephilla* three times daily, in the morning, afternoon and evening, seems originally to have been a characteristic of the Pharisees: Matt. 6.5f. refers to their strict observance of the afternoon hour of prayer, even in the turmoil of the market place (J. Jeremias, 'Daily Prayer in the Life of Jesus and the Primitive Church', *The Prayers of Jesus*, SBT II 6, 1967, 70–72).

[5] In Cave 4 there has been found a still unpublished papyrus manuscript with blessings for evening and morning prayer for each day of the month (cf. C. -H. Hunzinger, 'Aus der Arbeit an den unveröffentlichten Texten von Qumran', *TLZ* 85, 1960, col. 152).

[6] ‡Jeremias, 'Der Gedanke des "Heiligen Restes"'.

of salvation; there was a whole series of attempts in this direction. It is not an exaggeration to say that the whole of contemporary Jewish religious life was fundamentally determined by it. These attempts were based on Old Testament sayings according to which only a remnant would be saved. To many people, the most urgent task seemed to be for this remnant to be gathered in the present time.

The *locus classicus* for the promise of the remnant is the saying to Elijah in I Kings 19.18 (quoted by Paul in Rom. 11.4):

'Yet I will leave seven thousand in Israel,
all the knees that have not bowed to Baal,
and every mouth that has not kissed him.'

The prophet Isaiah was the great theologian of the remnant. He calls his son *še'ār yāšūb* (7.3), and interprets this name (10.21):

'A remnant will return, the remnant of Jacob, to the mighty God.' The believers are this remnant: 'He who believes will not be put to shame' (28.16). The remnant is the righteous, adds Zephaniah, 'a people humble and lowly' (Zeph. 3.12).

The *Pharisaic movement* shows most clearly the degree to which the prophetic message of the holy remnant[1] determined not only the religious life but also the history of ancient Judaism. As we have already seen (above, p. 144), they set out to represent the holy priestly community of God and in this way aimed to realize the idea of the remnant.

After the Pharisees, mention should be made of the baptist groups,[2] among which the *Essenes* are the best known; Philo[3] and Josephus[4] agree in putting their number at over 4000. They go beyond the principles of the Pharisees, the mother movement, in their concern to put into practice the promise of the remnant. The Pharisees separated themselves from other people's society, but in the monastic community of Essenes at Qumran (by the precipitious slopes of the barren Judaean hill-country close to the Dead Sea), the separation is carried to extremes. The Pharisees set out to represent the priestly people of God; the Essenes expressed this claim even in their clothing: each member of the order, even the laity, wore a white linen robe, the

---

[1] Cf. also Isa. 1.9; 4.2ff.; 6.13; 11.11ff.; 28.5; 37.32 (par. II Kings 19.31); 45.20ff.; Jer. 23.3; 31.7; 50.20; Ezek. 11.13; 14.21ff.; 36.36; Joel 3.5; Amos 4.11; 5.15; Obad. 17; Micah 2.12; 4.6f.; 5.6f.; 7.18; Zeph. 2.9; Zech. 13.7–9 etc. See V. Herntrich – G. Schrenk, λεῖμμα κτλ, *TDNT* IV, 1967, 194–214.
[2] ‡Thomas.   [3] *Quod omnis probus liber sit*, 75.   [4] *Antt.* 18.21.

ceremonial dress of priests in office. The Pharisaic movement demanded ritual washing of hands before meals from all its members; the Essenes accentuated this demand so that it became one for a full bath before every meal, in order to achieve the highest possible standards of purity. As God's priestly people of the end-time, the Essenes confer the highest attributes upon themselves. They call themselves 'the remnant',[1] 'the elect of Israel',[2] 'the simple ones of Judah',[3] 'the sons of grace',[4] 'the men of holiness',[5] the members of the new covenant',[6] 'the people of the perfect life',[7] 'the sons of his (God's)well-pleasing',[8] 'the poor of grace',[9] etc.[10] The great founder of the movement, the Teacher of Righteousness, compares the Essene community (among other things) with an impregnable city. In the Psalm of Thanksgiving I QH 5.20–7.5, which is to be regarded as his own composition,[11] he shows how God delivered him from the depths of despair by helping him to find refuge in a fortress, namely the community (6.24ff.):

. . . and [I journeyed] to the gates of death.
25 And I was like one who enters a fortified city,
      as one who seeks refuge on a high wall
          until deliverance (comes);
      and I [leaned on] thy truth, O my God,
26 For thou didst set the foundation on rock
      and the framework by correct measuring-cord and reliable
          balance
      and [. . .] tried stones for a strong building,
27 So that it does not sway,
      and all entering there shall not stagger,
   and no stranger shall enter,
      [and] its [gates] are shielding doors,
      so that there is no access;
28 And strong bars (are there),
      which cannot be shattered.[12]

The language used here is the symbolic language of the eschatological

---

[1] CD 1.4f.; 2.6.; 1 QH 6.8; 1 QM 13.8; 14.8f.   [2] CD 4.3f.   [3] 1 QpH 12.4.
[4] 1 QH 7.20.   [5] 1 QS 5.13.   [6] CD 6.19.   [7] 1 QS 4.22.
[8] 1 QH 4.32f.; 11.9.   [9] 1 QH 5.22.
[10] Further self-designations of the Essenes e.g. in ‡Jeremias, *Die theologische Bedeutung der Funde am Toten Meer*, 22f.
[11] G. Jeremias, *Lehrer der Gerechtigkeit*, 168ff.
[12] Translation follows G. Jeremias, *op. cit.*, 235f.

Jerusalem; the individual features with which the suppliant depicts
the city of refuge are 'stereotypes from the portrait of the heavenly
Jerusalem'.[1]

Alongside the comparison of the community with the city of God,
and coupled with it, we find a comparison with the temple – not from
the Teacher himself, but in a later period (1 QS 8.5ff.).[2] The
community is 'a house of holiness for Israel and a foundation of the
holy of holies for Aaron' (5f., cf. 8f.). Thus the laity belonging to it
are compared with the temple building and the priests with the holy
of holies. This temple symbolism,[3] beloved at Qumran, also designates the community as the eschatological people of salvation. The
Essene psalms, their interpretation of scripture and their rule are
impressive evidence of the deep seriousness with which this community attempted in the present to prepare the community of the
saints of the end-time for their God.

John the Baptist towers alone above the numerous founders of
remnant communities. He, too, gathers the holy remnant (as we saw
in §4): that is the meaning of his preaching of judgment, his call to
repentance, his baptism. But this remnant is not like that of the
Pharisees or the Essenes. Both Pharisees and Essenes gathered a
'closed' remnant, a little group of those who were worthy to belong
to the people of God because of their piety, their obedience to the
Law, their strict observance of purity, their asceticism. John the
Baptist gathers an 'open' remnant;[4] he destroys trust in the prerogatives of Israel (Matt. 3.9 par.), he calls even the sinners to him if they
are ready to repent (Luke 3.12–14; 7.29f.). It is characteristic of this
most powerful expression of the idea of the remnant in the pre-
Christian period that it reverts to the prophetic preaching of the
remnant in two ways: it takes God's judgment seriously, and it
summons 'a people humble and lowly' (Zeph. 3.12) – a prelude to
the gospel.

(iii) Boundless grace

There have been those who tried to understand Jesus, too, against
this background and to include his community among the 'remnant'

[1] G. Jeremias, *op. cit.*, 248, cf. the list on p. 247.
[2] As reported by my son Gert.
[3] B. Gärtner, *The Temple and the Community in Qumran and the New Testament*,
Society for New Testament Studies Series 1, Cambridge 1965.
[4] ‡Meyer, see §4 above.

groups. Thus K. L. Schmidt, in his article ἐκκλησία in the *Theological Dictionary*, has made the remark that Jesus, too, wanted to gather a 'special *kᵉništā*' in a 'process of separation'.[1] Some evidence could be produced for such a view. Jesus rallied groups of followers around him everywhere; he laid strict demands upon them (entry *tōrōt*, see pp. 154f. above); his followers were conscious of being a community with a distinguishing sign, the Lord's Prayer.

In particular, the movement aroused by Jesus has some striking features in common with the Essenes. The Essenes prohibited marriage (at least to those of their members who lived in the monastery at Qumran), and this was unusual;[2] Jesus was not married. The Essenes of Qumran demanded the renunciation of all property and shared their goods in common; Jesus expected the rich young man to give up his possessions (Mark 10.17–31) and, at least according to John, the inmost group of disciples shared their possessions (John 12.6; 13.29). The Essenes forbade their followers to swear oaths; Jesus, too, prohibited the misuse of the divine name by too light-hearted swearing (Matt. 5.33–37; 23.16–22).[3] Must we conclude from similarities of this kind that Jesus intended to form a remnant group like that of the Essenes?

This would truly be to misunderstand the message of Jesus completely. The contrast between Jesus and all attempts at forming a 'remnant' group emerges at one quite definite point: *separation from outsiders*.

One of the Essene psalms of thanksgiving sounds as though it might have come out of the New Testament:

> that to the humble he might bring
> glad tidings of thy great mercy.[4]

But we should not overlook the fact that 'the humble' means the members of the community, the small group of penitents who have resolved upon radical obedience to the *Torah* and have separated themselves from the impenitent horde by joining the community. On entry they must take it upon themselves 'to love all that he (God) has chosen and hate all that he has rejected'.[5] Part of the entrance ceremonial is the fearful cursing of impenitent sinners:

---

[1] K. L. Schmidt, καλέω κτλ, *TDNT* III, 1965, 487–536: 526f.
[2] Gen. 1.28 was regarded as an obligatory command (Billerbeck II 372f.).
[3] See below, p. 220.   [4] 1 QH 18.14.   [5] 1 QS 1.3–4, cf. 9–11.

Be cursed without mercy
because of the darkness of your deeds!
Be damned in the shadowy place of everlasting fire!
May God not heed when you call on him,
nor pardon you by blotting out your sin!
May he raise his angry face towards you for vengeance!
May there be no 'Peace' for you in the mouth of all the angels
of intercession![1]

Certainly the Essenes are to 'requite no evil',[2] not to 'be zealous in the spirit of wantonness',[3] rather to 'pursue men with good';[4] but this does not alter the 'eternal hatred against all men of corruption',[5] the 'anger' against the 'men of wickedness'[6] and the mercilessness towards the apostates.[7] It merely means that vengeance is left to God, who will accomplish it on the 'day of vengeance'.[8]

The regulations for the assembly of full members are even more exclusive than the conditions for acceptance. Even the physically handicapped members of the community are excluded from it. The Essenes regarded themselves as the priestly people of the end-time, and therefore applied to themselves the precept that only physically unblemished priests could carry out their office in the temple (Lev. 21.18–20). 'No madman, or lunatic, or simpleton, or fool, no blind man, or maimed, or lame, or deaf man, and no minor, shall enter into the community, for the angels of holiness are with them' (and the presence of deformed or mentally deficient men would be offensive to the angel).[9]

In the same way, it is said of the community of the messianic time of consummation: 'No-one who is afflicted with any human impurity may come into the assembly of God. . . . Anyone who is afflicted in his flesh, maimed in hand or foot, lame or blind or deaf or

---

[1] 2.7–9, cf. 9.16, 21–24; 10.19–21. P. Wernberg-Møller, *The Manual of Discipline*, Studies on the Texts of the Desert of Judah 1, Leiden 1957, 53f., recognized that in the last words of the quotation *beṗī kol 'ōḥ^azē 'ābōt* the phrase *'ḥz 'bwt* means 'make intercession', as in Syriac.

[2] 1 QS 10.17f.   [3] 10.18f.   [4] 10.18.   [5] 9.21f.   [6] 10.19f.

[7] 10.20f.: I will 'have no pity on all who depart from the way. I will offer no comfort to the smitten until their way become perfect.'

[8] 10.18f.

[9] 4 QDb (J. T. Milik, *Ten Years of Discovery in the Wilderness of Judaea*, SBT 26, ²1963, 114f. gives the translation of the text; the original Hebrew has not yet been published) = CD 15.15–17 (here the text is badly damaged).

dumb or with a visible mark on his flesh or who is a helpless old man who cannot stand upright in the assembly of the community – these may not enter to take their place in the midst of the community of the men of the name, for the holy angels are in their community.'[1] The Essenes are concerned for the holiness of God. This holy God hates sinners, and just as his holiness will not permit a physically blemished man to do priestly service, so too the holiness of the heavenly hosts will not allow a physically blemished man to belong to the assembly of the community.

We have now reached the point at which the way of Jesus diverges from that of the Essenes.[2] With its joy at salvation, its earnestness, its sacrifice and its particular self-understanding, this revival movement stands nearer to Christianity than any other group, with the possible exception of the movement started by John the Baptist, about which, however, we know very little (but see e.g. Luke 1.13–17). The founder of the Essene movement, the Teacher of Righteousness, was convinced that judgment or salvation depended on his message, an intensified interpretation of the *Torah*. He surrendered the prerogatives of Israel and taught that the division would go through the midst of Israel. Unlike the rest of the Judaism of his time, he knew, as we saw earlier,[3] that the eschatological Jerusalem and the eschatological temple were being announced in the very present, in the form of his community. He is 'the only figure of later Judaism known to us whose awareness of his status might be compared with that of Jesus'.[4] But his message, with the all-embracing earnestness of its call to repentance and its jubilation at the salvation that had been given, culminated in the separation of the penitent from the great horde which the Essenes believed to be hopelessly given over to corruption.

It does not take long to show how sharply Jesus rejected all attempts to realize the community of the remnant by means of human striving or separation. He called those who had been proscribed by the 'remnant' groups. His command to his disciples to invite the poor, the crippled, the lame and the blind to their table (Luke 14.13), and the way in which in the parable he makes the householder summon

---

[1] 1 QSa 2.3–9. Similar regulations apply to the men of the army, to which only the unblemished may belong: 1 QM 7.3–7.

[2] For what follows see ‡Jeremias, *Die theologische Bedeutung der Funde am Toten Meer*, 22–28; G. Jeremias, *Lehrer der Gerechtigkeit*, 319–53 (Ch. 9: 'The Teacher of Righteousness and the Historical Jesus. An Attempt at a Comparison').

[3] See above, pp. 172f.   [4] G. Jeremias, *Lehrer der Gerechtigkeit*, 335.

the poor, the cripples, the blind and the lame into his house (v. 21), amount to a direct declaration of war on the Essene 'remnant' group. At the same time he declares war on the Pharisees, not only where he makes explicit mention of them (as at Luke 11.37–44, see above, pp. 144f.), but also e.g. at Matt. 6.1–18 and in many parables.

Jesus even differs from the Baptist, though the latter towers high above all other founders of 'remant' groups, by shattering all self-confidence and announcing judgment even upon the people of God (Matt. 3.7–12) and not turning away the penitent publicans (Luke 3.12). The difference becomes visible when we observe that John the Baptist accepts the guilty *after* they have declared their readiness to lead a new life, whereas Jesus offers salvation to sinners *before* they repent, as is particularly clear from Luke 19.1–10.

Again and again in the first three gospels it is said how offensive, provocative and disturbing was Jesus' rejection of Pharisaic and Essene special claims to be realizing the holy remnant. It was the same with the way in which he turned precisely to those who had been excluded by the 'remnant' groups. What distinguishes him from these groups, and even from John the Baptist, is his message of the *boundlessness* and unconditional character of *grace*. The God whom Jesus preaches is the Father of those who are small and lost, a God whose purpose it is to have dealings with sinners and who rejoices when a sinner finds his way home (Luke 15.7, 10). Because God is so boundlessly gracious, because God loves sinners, Jesus does not gather the holy remnant, but the all-embracing community of salvation of God's new people. Jesus has opened the doors wide, he has called all without exception, as a hen calls all her chickens under her wings (Matt. 23.37 par. Luke 13.34). 'All (inclusive πολλοί) have been invited (to the feast)', and Jesus is not to blame if only a few reach the goal (Matt. 22.14).[1]

Certainly, even Jesus is aware that there will be a division between sinners and the elect. Five virgins are wise, five are foolish. Table-fellowship with Jesus does not in itself guarantee salvation (Luke 13.26f.). So it is understandable that he should be asked why he does not remove the sinners from the number of his followers. Jesus replied to this question with the parable of the wheat and the tares (Matt. 13.24–30):[2] the time has not yet come. There is still a respite.

[1] For the exegesis of Matt. 22.14 see above, pp. 130f.

[2] The interpretation of the parable to be found in vv. 36–43 is secondary, cf. Jeremias, *Parables*[2], 81–85.

When the moment arrives, God himself will bring about the separation. It is not a thing that men can do. Only God can see into men's hearts.

In conclusion, the decisive element may be summarized briefly: the chief characteristic of the new people of God gathered together by Jesus is their awareness of the boundlessness of God's grace.[1]

§ 18 · BEING A CHILD

A. Seeberg, *Die vierte Bitte des Vaterunsers*, Rostock 1914; J. Jeremias, 'Das Gebetsleben Jesu', *ZNW* 25, 1926, 123–40; J. Leipoldt, *Das Gotteserlebnis Jesu im Lichte der vergleichenden Religionsgeschichte*, Leipzig 1927; I. Elbogen, *Der jüdische Gottesdienst in seiner geschichtlichen Entwicklung*[3], Frankfurt a. Main 1931 = [4]Hildesheim 1962; J. Herrmann, 'Der alttestamentliche Urgrund des Vaterunsers', in: *Festschrift für Otto Procksch*, Leipzig 1934, 71–98; Manson, *Teaching*[2], 89–115; K.-G. Kuhn, *Achtzehngebet und Vaterunser und der Reim*, WUNT 1, Tübingen 1950; H. Schürmann, *Das Gebet des Herrn*, Die Botschaft Gottes II 6, Leipzig 1957; K.-H. Rengstorf, '"Geven ist seliger denn Nehmen"'. Bemerkungen zu dem ausserevangelischen Herrenwort Apg. 20, 35', in: *Festschrift für Adolf Köberle*, Hamburg 1958, 23–33; J. Jeremias, 'The Lord's Prayer in the Light of Recent Research', in: *The Prayers of Jesus*, SBT II 6, London 1967, 82–107; P. Billerbeck, 'Ein Tempelgottesdienst in Jesu Tagen'; id., 'Ein Synagogengottesdienst in Jesu Tagen', *ZNW* 55, 1964, 1–17, 143–61; J. Jeremias, 'Abba'; id., 'Daily Prayer in the Life of Jesus and the Primitive Church', in: *The Prayers of Jesus*, 11–81.

Wherever people are won over by the good news and join company with the new people of God, they leave the world of death for the world of life (Matt. 8.22 par. Luke 9.60; John 5.24; cf. Luke 15.24, 32). Now they belong under the reign of God; a new life is beginning which consists in a new relationship to God (§18) and a new relationship to man (§19).

(i) *The Father*

The most important characteristic of the new life, more important than anything else, is *the new relationship to God*. For Judaism, God was primarily the Lord. As the Psalm says:

[1] For the manifestation of boundless grace, cf. also §21 (iii), pp. 245ff.: 'The eschatological pilgrimage'.

Let all the earth fear the Lord,
  let all the inhabitants of the world stand in awe of him!
For he spoke, and it came to be;
  he commanded, and it stood forth (Ps. 33.8f.).

He is the Creator, the Lord of life and death, who demands obedience. In no circumstances should one forget that the Lordship of God and all that that means remains fundamental, in the sphere of the gospels, too. The periphrases for God collected on pp. 9f. by their very variety make an impressive demonstration of the natural way in which Jesus also lived with this idea. His hesitation at using the divine name is not just an unconscious adaptation to the pious custom of the time. First, we can see how Jesus develops a way of speaking of his own, in that he accords an unusually wide scope to the paraphrasing of the divine name with the passive ('divine passive'). Secondly, we can see this hesitation from his passionate protest against light-hearted swearing (Matt. 5.33–37; 23.16–22).[1] In the sphere of the gospels, too, reverence and hesitation form the basis of man's relationship with God. God is the one who is utterly unfathomable (Matt. 11.25f.), the ruler who demands unqualified obedience; the disciple is his servant (Luke 17.7–10; Mark 13.34–37), indeed his slave (Matt. 6.24 par. Luke 16.13). God is the king who has sovereign power over life and death (Matt. 18.23–35). He is the judge whom man has to fear.[2] He is the one who can destroy body and soul in hell (Matt. 10.28).

Reverence before God, the unconditional Lord, is an essential part of the gospel – but it is not its centre. There is seldom mention of God the Creator (Mark 2.27; 10.6; 13.19). The picture of God as King is used predominantly in the traditional way,[3] but in the context it can change its significance (cf. Matt. 18.27). At the centre stands something else: for the disciples of Jesus, God is the Father.

At this point it is important to look at the sources carefully, as false ideas are often rampant. Astonishingly enough, the designation of God as 'your Father' occurs only rarely in the different strata of tradition. Only in Matthew is 'your Father' to be found more often.

---

[1] See below, p. 220.
[2] The sayings about eternal punishment only acquire their full weight when one sees how often the passive is a periphrasis for the divine action, cf. e.g. Matt. 7.1f. par.; 7.19; 12.31f., 37.
[3] ἡ βασιλεία τοῦ θεοῦ, ὁ μέγας βασιλεύς, parables about the king.

Mark   I
Common to Matthew and Luke   2
Additional instances peculiar to Luke   I
Additional instances peculiar to Matthew   12 (+ 'your [sing.]
                                               Father' five times)
John   I[1]

The accumulation of instances in Matthew puts him quite out of the
picture; a critical analysis confirms that the majority of the instances
peculiar to him are secondary.[2] On the other hand, the sparse
instances in the rest of the synoptic strata[3] show that linguistically,
traditionally and in point of content, they are the earliest material.[4]
Thus Jesus spoke of 'your Father' *only rarely*. It follows further that,
according to the earliest tradition, Jesus addressed the designation of
God as 'your Father' *only to his disciples*, and never to outsiders. That
indicates that Jesus did not see the Fatherhood of God as something
to be taken for granted, a common possession of all men, but as a
privilege enjoyed by his disciples, of which he spoke only when
teaching them, and then only on special occasions. Only in the sphere
of the *basileia* is God the Father.

According to the earliest stratum of tradition,[5] God is called the
Father as the one who has mercy (Luke 6.36), who forgives (Mark
11.25) and gives the glory (Luke 12.32); he alone has claim to the
name of Father (Matt. 23.9). The nearest parallel to this in the Old
Testament is Ps. 103.13:

> As a father pities his children,
> so the Lord pities those who fear him.

But the Father of the disciples is greater: he does not have mercy
only on those who fear him, but his mercy is boundless; he bestows
his goodness even on the ungrateful (Luke 6.35).

If God is the Father, the disciples are his children. Being a child

---

[1] John 20.17; 8.42, where to the Jews who want to kill him Jesus denies that
God is 'your Father', does not belong here.

[2] Jeremias, *The Prayers of Jesus*, SBT II 6, London 1967, 39.

[3] Mark 11.25; Matt. 5.48 par. Luke 6.36; Matt. 6.32 par. Luke 12.30; Luke
12.32. From the Matthaean special material 23.9 at least (cf. p. 169, note 1) may be
set alongside these passages. The Johannine instance (20.17), on the other hand, is
a saying of the Risen Lord.

[4] Jeremias, *The Prayers of Jesus*, 39–43.

[5] See above, n.3.

is *the* characteristic of the kingly rule: 'You will never be admitted to the *basileia*' unless you become like children again (Matt. 18.3).[1] Children can say '*Abbā*.[2] It should, however, be noted that the expression 'children (*υἱοί*) of God' occurs only three times in the synoptic gospels (Matt. 5.9, 45 par. Luke 6.35; Luke 20.36) and has eschatological significance in all three passages.[3] Thus in Jesus' eyes, being a child of God is not a gift of creation, but an eschatological gift of salvation. Only the one who belongs under the kingly rule of God may call God '*Abbā* (see below, p. 197), *already* has God as his Father, is *even now* a child of God. For the disciples, being children means sharing Jesus' sonship. It is an anticipation of the consummation.

This gift of being a child of God stamps the whole life of Jesus' disciples. This becomes clear in three ways:

1. Being a child of God brings the certainty of *a share in future salvation*. That is the most important thing. The disciples of Jesus know that it is God's will that none of the little ones should be lost (Matt. 18.10, 14).[4] He bestows on them the gifts of the time of salvation with more than fatherly love (Matt. 7.9–11 par.).[5] They will share in God's kingly glory. *Μὴ φοβοῦ, τὸ μικρὸν ποίμνιον, ὅτι εὐδόκησεν ὁ πατὴρ ὑμῶν δοῦναι ὑμῖν τὴν βασιλείαν*, says Luke 12.32 in a *logion* that takes up Dan. 7.27. This is put in a paradoxical way. Jesus' disciples are a little group of poor and despised men, and that they belong to the family of God makes their fate at the hands of men even worse. Like the master of the house, so too the family of God is misunderstood and mocked (Matt. 10.25).[6] Nevertheless, they are not to fear.

---

[1] See above, pp. 154f.

[2] See above, p. 156.

[3] Only Matt. 5.45 *ὅπως γένησθε υἱοί* . . . seems to mean 'that you (now) *show* yourselves to be sons . . .', but the parallel Luke 6.35 has *καὶ ἔσεσθε υἱοί* . . ., parallel to *καὶ ἔσται ὁ μισθὸς ὑμῶν πολύς*. Thus here being a child is understood eschatologically. Cf. Wisdom 5.5 (*κατελογίσθη ἐν υἱοῖς θεοῦ*), where 'children of God' also has eschatological significance.

[4] On the translation of Matt. 18.14 (*οὕτως οὐκ ἔστιν θέλημα ἔμπροσθεν τοῦ πατρὸς ὑμῶν τοῦ ἐν οὐρανοῖς ἵνα ἀπόληται ἓν τῶν μικρῶν τούτων*): in a Semitic-type way of speaking, the negative is introduced into the first half of the sentence, whereas in fact it belongs to the second half. *τούτων* is a superfluous demonstrative (Semitism). Thus: 'It pleases God if even one of the least of all escapes destruction'. The content agrees with Luke 15.7a.

[5] *ἀγαθά* (v.11) are the gifts of the time of salvation (cf. Isa. 52.7); at any rate, these are included.

[6] See below, pp. 239f. and 241–44 on the persecution of the disciples.

Their Father has made ready his reign, a salvation that surpasses all understanding:

And the kingdom and the dominion
and the greatness of the kingdoms under the whole heaven
shall be given to the people of the saints of the Most High;
their kingdom shall be an everlasting kingdom,
and all dominions shall serve and obey them (Dan. 7.27).

This certainty of salvation extends so far that the disciples may be sure that God will shorten the time of distress at the end (Mark 13.20) by himself rescinding his holy will, so that they can withstand (v. 13b).[1] To understand all these sayings rightly, we must understand them against the background of contemporary ideas. For the time of Jesus, salvation was inconceivable without merit. Certainty of salvation was completely dependent on pious achievement. Jesus' disciples, on the other hand, know that God means to grant them salvation, even if they stand before him as beggars. Even more, it is *because* they stand before him as beggars that they will be saved.

2. Being a child brings *everyday security*. The Father knows what his children need (Matt. 6.8, 32 par. Luke 12.30). His goodness and care is boundless (Matt. 5.45 par.). Nothing is too small for God. The Rabbis explicitly prohibited prayers that God's mercy should extend 'even to a bird's nest';[2] it was disrespectful to associate God with something as small as a tiny bird. In contrast, Jesus says that God's care embraces even sparrows, although two can be bought for an *as*, a tiny worthless copper coin (Matt. 10.29f.).[3] It is to the smallest that God extends his special protection; in the heavenly world built up in circles round God's throne, the guardian angels of the μικροί stand in the innermost circle (*m^eḥīṣā*), immediately before God (Matt. 18.10).

The messengers, above all, are to draw confidence from the knowledge of the Father's care. It may be to them that the three-line verse Matt. 6.34 is directed:

[1] See above, pp. 139–41.
[2] Ber. 5.3. Anyone who introduced this prayer in public worship exposed himself to the suspicion of being a heretic and therefore had to withdraw. Possibly the prohibition reflects the controversies between the synagogue and Jewish Christianity.
[3] The parallel in Luke 12.6 says 'five for two pennies' – they are cheaper by the dozen.

μὴ οὖν μεριμνήσητε¹ εἰς τὴν αὔριον,
ἡ γὰρ αὔριον μεριμνήσει ἑαυτῆς·
ἀρκετὸν τῇ ἡμέρᾳ ἡ κακία αὐτῆς.

Here not only does the day become an independent entity (line 2);
it almost amounts to a religious concept: today is the task appointed
by God, and tomorrow the future is that is looked after.

3. This certainty of salvation and security gives the disciples
courage to submit to what is unpredictable in the divine will. The riddles of
life and its inexplicable features remain. It is incomprehensible that
the gospel is rejected by the wise and learned (Matt. 11.25f. par.).
And it is hard to understand why so much of the sower's work
is in vain (the enumeration in Mark 4.4–7 par. gives examples
which could be increased at will).² Jesus does not trouble to vin-
dicate God. The word 'Father' (Matt. 11.25f. par.) says everything.

In particular, it is *suffering* that appears in a new light where men
are conscious of being children of God. At this point Judaism is quite
brutal. All suffering is punishment for particular individual sins.
That is the firm conviction of the time (cf. John 9.2).³ God keeps a
look-out to see that guilt and punishment correspond exactly,
'measure for measure'.⁴ If one meets a man who is maimed, lame,
blind or a leper, it is a pious duty to murmur, 'Praised be the reliable
judge'.⁵ If a small child dies, the parents must have committed
particular sins which God is punishing.⁶ Thus suffering is seen as the
scourge of God. Jesus strictly forbids any entering upon such calcula-
tions. In Luke 13.1–5 he expressly attacks the dogma that misfortune
is a punishment for the definite sins of particular people. Rather,
suffering is a call to repentance, a call which goes out to all. Whereas
his contemporaries ask, '*Why* does God send suffering?', the disciples
of Jesus are to ask, '*For what* does God send suffering?'. In addition
to God's purpose of summoning to repentance (vv. 3, 5), Jesus knows
of another purpose for which God uses suffering: there is suffering
which serves God's glory. Not only is this said in John 9.3; 11.4, but
such a purpose is also implicitly contained in the statements in all
four gospels which deal with Jesus' way of suffering⁷ and the persecution of the disciples.⁸ Suffering for Jesus' sake is an occasion for joy,

¹ See below, p. 236. ² The Gospel of Thomas, 9, also adds the worm.
³ Billerbeck II 193–97. ⁴ *Ibid.* I 444–46. ⁵ Tos. Ber. 7.3.
⁶ Billerbeck II 194f. ⁷ See below pp. 286ff. ⁸ See below pp. 239f.

because it serves to glorify God and is therefore recompensed by God (Matt. 5.11f.; Luke 6.23).

When one is a child of God, even *death* appears in a different light. Two *logia* may be mentioned, first Matt. 10.29-31 par. The saying is three-membered in construction:

(*a*) No sparrow dies without God; he has a hand even in that (v. 29);

(*b*) He has counted the hairs on the disciples' heads;[1] his concern for his children includes even the tiniest detail (v. 30);

(*c*) Jesus draws the conclusion with an argument *a minori ad maius*: μὴ οὖν φοβεῖσθε· πολλῶν στρουθίων διαφέρετε ὑμεῖς (v. 31: the πολλοί is to be understood inclusively[2] in the sense of 'all' the sparrows of the world): if no sparrow perishes without God's permission, how much more is it the case that he holds the life and death of his people in his hands! This certainty frees them from anxiety, so Jesus can demand: μὴ φοβεῖσθε. The other saying to be mentioned here, Mark 12.27 par., goes still further: οὐκ ἔστιν θεὸς νεκρῶν ἀλλὰ ζώντων. With unsurpassable brevity this sentence says that faith in God includes the certainty of conquering death.[3]

Above all, when one is a child of God the eternally unfathomable riddle of *evil* is left in God's hands. Even Satan's action is bounded by God's will. Satan has to request scope for his activity from God if he wants to 'sieve' the disciples, 'as one sieves grain' (Luke 22.31f.).

Nothing happens without God. Jesus believes that unconditionally. Stronger than all questions, riddles and anxieties is the one word *'Abbā*. The Father knows.

(*ii*) *The new way of praying*

Children talk with their father. 'The reign of God is inconceivable

---

[1] Cf. b. B.B. 16a: For every hair, God makes a little hole from which it drinks (Billerbeck I 584).

[2] See above, pp. 130f.; J. Jeremias, πολλοί *TDNT* VI, 1968, 536-45.

[3] The favourite recourse of assigning the dialogue with the Sadducees in Mark 12.18-27 par. to the community seems to me to be inconclusive for two reasons: 1. In vv. 24f. the mode of the resurrection state is described by means of a comparison with the angels; however, the primitive church did not refer to angels, but to the Risen Lord (Rom. 8.29; I Cor. 15.49; Phil. 3.21); 2. In vv. 26f. the question as to the fact of the resurrection is answered by means of Ex. 3.6.; the primitive church grounded it in the resurrection of Jesus (I Cor. 15.12ff.). Both considerations indicate that the pericope about the Sadducees dates from before Easter.

without prayer' (E. Fuchs). Just as everything else is new in the reign, so too here a new way of praying appears. In it, how one belongs to the *basileia* becomes clear. Indeed, more: in this new way of praying the power of the *basileia* is already at work in the life of the disciples.

(a) The liturgical heritage

Jesus and his disciples came from a people who knew how to pray. Whereas there was a crisis of prayer in the Hellenistic world,[1] in Judaism prayer was an uncontested force, thanks to a fixed order of prayer.

Generally the day began at dawn and ended after dusk with a gaze upwards to God. Morning and evening the boys and men of the people of Israel recited the creed, the so-called *Sh^ema^* (Deut. 6.4–9; 11.13–21; Num. 15.41),[2] set within its framework of benedictions. It was followed, at any rate in Pharisaic circles, by the so-called *T^ephilla, the* prayer, a prayerlike hymn made up of benedictions. In addition the Pharisees observed yet a third prayer time, in the afternoon (Dan. 6.11, 14): the *T^ephilla* was prayed throughout the country at 3 p.m., while the evening sacrifice was being offered in the temple (cf. Acts 3.1; 10.3, 30).[3] In addition to these three fixed daily prayers, there were graces before and after each meal.[4] Before the meal was spoken the thanksgiving: 'Blessed be thou, Lord our God, king of the world, who makest bread to come forth from the earth'.[5] After the meal, a three-part thanksgiving was spoken which combined a petition for mercy on Israel with thanksgiving for nourishment and for the land.[6] Grace on the sabbath and above all on Passover night was particularly solemn.[7] Yet again, there were the thanksgivings which accompanied the whole of the day's activities, every happy or sad event in the family or among the people. We know exclamations of this kind, say, from the benedictions in the Pauline epistles.[8] Prayer in public worship attached itself to these daily and private prayers. The synagogue service began with an opening prayer, and then followed the creed, spoken antiphonally and set in a framework of benedictions.[9] Then came the *T^ephilla* with a priestly blessing (Num. 6.24–26).[10] The two readings from scripture which now followed were also framed

[1] G. Harder, *Paulus und das Gebet*, Neutestamentliche Forschungen 10, Gütersloh 1936, 138–51 ('The Crisis of Prayer in the Ancient World').

[2] This was the earlier demarcation.

[3] For the origin of the three times of prayer see ‡Jeremias, 'Daily Prayer', 70–73.

[4] Jeremias, *Eucharistic Words*[2], 108–10.

[5] Ber. 6.1.

[6] Jeremias, *Eucharistic Words*[2], 110. Not until the beginning of the second century AD was the number of eulogies in the grace after the meal increased to four, at Jabneh (Jamnia).

[7] *Ibid.*, 252f.

[8] E.g. Rom. 1.25 (euphemism); 9.5 etc.

[9] The leader recited the beginning of the verse in a chant; the congregation repeated it and ended the verse: Tos. Sota 6.3.

[10] ‡Billerbeck, 'Ein Synagogengottesdienst in Jesu Tagen', 143–61.

by words of praise. The sermon, which interpreted the reading from the prophets, closed with the Kaddish.[1] Finally, there was also a place for free prayer alongside all these formal prayers.

Rich as this firmly fixed pattern of prayer in Judaism was as a training ground for praying, it also, however, concealed certain dangers. For contemporary Judaism, God was primarily the king at a distance from his world,[2] and praying was compared with doing homage.[3] Just as a fixed ceremonial has to be observed at court, so too it was with praying. Therefore fixed prayer stood in the foreground. Men were recommended to pray in the congregation, because it was taught that common prayer was most likely to be heard.[4] Formulated prayers were predominant. Prayer was in danger of becoming a habit. Casuistry was getting a grip. It was laid down to the smallest detail in what attitude, on what occasion, etc., men must and may pray and not pray. Finally, prayer took its place in the context of the idea of merit; a prayer like Luke 18.11f., for which there are contemporary parallels,[5] was not thought to be at all offensive.

Jesus appeared in this world with a new prayer.[6]

(b) The model of Jesus

Jesus himself was the model for the new way of praying. Yet apparently we know only a little about his prayers. The synoptic gospels hand on only two prayers of Jesus (Matt. 11.25f. par.; Mark 14.36 par.), and in addition the words from the cross (Mark 15.34 par.; Luke 23.34a, 46). The Gospel of John adds three of Jesus' prayers (11.41f.; 12.27f.; 17), of which at least the high-priestly prayer is stamped throughout by the terminology and style of the fourth evangelist. In addition, there is a series of general statements about Jesus' praying, above all his praying in solitude, and a saying of Jesus about his intercession for Peter (Luke 22.31f.). Secondarily, there are also his instructions to the disciples on prayer, among which the Lord's Prayer stands out. How we would love to know more!

In fact we do know more. Jesus was brought up in a devout home,[7]

---

[1] See below, p. 198.   [2] See above, pp. 178f.   [3] Billerbeck I 1036.
[4] *Ibid.*, 398f.   [5] Jeremias, *Parables²*, 142.
[6] For what follows see ‡Jeremias, 'Daily Prayer', 66–81.
[7] Luke 2.41. Cf. Luke 4.16 κατὰ τὸ εἰωθὸς αὐτῷ 'after his custom', i.e. as had been his habit since a child. On the grounds of Deut. 31.12, it was usual to take children into the synagogue service (Tos. Sota 7.9.; Meg. 4.6; Josephus, *Antt.* 14.260).

and grew up in the fixed order of prayer observed by his people; this accompanied him even during his public activity. There is frequent testimony to this in the tradition.

He took part regularly in sabbath worship 'according to his custom', and prayed with the congregation (Luke 4.16). Grace at table was natural to him (see the feeding stories, the accounts of the Last Supper and the Emmaus story). He also observed the three hours of prayer. We can see this not only from the observation that he was brought up according to devout custom; it also follows indirectly from particular details. In Luke 10.26f., Jesus asks the scribe πῶς ἀναγινώσκεις; The scribe answers with the commandment from the Shᵉmaᶜ to love God (Deut. 6.5). Thus this question does not mean (or did not originally mean) 'How do you read?', but ἀναγινώσκειν here is a rendering of qārā', and means 'recite'. The question 'How do you recite?' presupposes recitation of the creed to be a custom practised as a matter of course. It matches this that according to the independent parallel tradition in Mark 12.29f., Jesus answers the question about the greatest commandment not only with the command to love God (Deut. 6.5), but also, in addition, with a quotation of the preceding verse: 'Hear, O Israel, the Lord our God is one Lord' (Deut. 6.4). These are the words with which the Shᵉmaᶜ began. Jesus mentions the afternoon prayer in Luke 18.9–14, where he depicts two men who go up to the temple 'to pray', probably therefore at the 'hour of prayer' (Acts 3.1), about 3 p.m. The reference to the afternoon prayer is even clearer in Matt. 6.5, where he censures the 'hypocrites', i.e. the Pharisees, who pray in public at street corners. This is hardly meant to suggest that the Pharisees usually went to pray in the market-place. We have, rather, to remember that at the moment in the afternoon sacrifice when the whole congregation prayed, loud trumpets were sounded from the temple over Jerusalem (Sirach 50.16; Tam. 7.3), to mark the hour of prayer for its inhabitants. The Pharisees whom Jesus rebukes arranged things so that they happened to be in the midst of the crowds – apparently quite by chance – at the moment when the trumpets blew, and were thus compelled to pray before all eyes. Two further sayings of Jesus reveal knowledge of the Tᵉphilla, which was prayed at the afternoon hour of prayer. In its first benediction, which goes back to the time when the temple was still standing, there are two strikingly solemn invocations of God:

Blessed art thou, O Lord,
God of Abraham, God of Isaac, and God of Jacob,
the most high God, master[1] of heaven and earth,
our shield and the shield of our fathers.
Blessed art thou, O Lord, the shield of Abraham.[2]

In Mark 12.26 par., Jesus speaks of God as the God of Abraham, the God of Isaac and the God of Jacob, and in Matt. 11.25 par., although he is usually sparing with

[1] In Gen. 14.19, 22, the ambiguous participle qōnē means 'Creator', but in Judaism it was understood as 'Lord'.
[2] Presumably the earliest form, following Dalman, Worte Jesu I, Leipzig 1898, 299, unfortunately not reprinted in the second edition, Leipzig 1930.

divine predicates, he speaks of God as 'Lord of heaven and earth'. This twofold correspondence with the wording of the first benediction of the *Tᵉphilla* indicates that the *Tᵉphilla* was well-known to him, indeed was his usual prayer. We can assert this with confidence, because in any case the first of the two divine predicates is not only unique in the Old Testament (Ex. 3.6, 15, 16), but also unusual in Palestinian Judaism outside the *Tᵉphilla*.[1]

In addition to all this, earliest Christianity observed the three hours of prayer. The clearest instance is Did. 8.3, which says, referring to the Lord's Prayer, 'Three times a day you shall pray thus'. The Acts of the Apostles twice refers to the afternoon prayer at 3 p.m. (Acts 3.1; 10.3, 30). Paul also should be mentioned here. When he says that he prays 'continually', 'without ceasing', 'always', 'day and night', we are not to think of uninterrupted praying, but of his observance of the regular hours of prayer. It is hardly conceivable that the earliest community would have observed the hours of prayer had Jesus rejected them.

Thus we may conclude with the utmost probability that there was no day in the life of Jesus when he did not observe the three hours of prayer, no meal before which and after which he did not say grace.

But the decisive thing is that Jesus was not content with the liturgical heritage. *Jesus' prayer shatters pious custom*. He is not content with the pious custom of liturgical prayer three times a day, but according to the tradition spends hours (Mark 1.35; 6.46 par.) and even whole nights (Luke 6.12 ἦν διανυκτερεύων ἐν τῇ προσευχῇ τοῦ θεοῦ) in solitary prayer. Now it is clear that the majority of the passages in the gospels which mention Jesus' prayer are to be attributed to the editing of the evangelists. Thus Luke repeatedly adds the motif of the praying Lord to the text of Mark (5.16; 6.12; 9.18, 28f.; cf. 3.21). But even so, the question remains: what induced Luke to add this motif? The most likely answer is the existence of a firm tradition about Jesus' prayer in solitude.[2] This answer, moreover, commends itself to us because we do in fact have an old tradition describing how Jesus, outside the regular time of prayer, invokes his Father in the middle of the night: Gethsemane (Mark 14.32ff. par.).

A second consideration confirms how widely Jesus departed from custom. The *Shᵉmaᶜ* and the *Tᵉphilla* are prayers in Hebrew; the Lord's Prayer, on the other hand, is an Aramaic prayer.[3] *'Abbā,* the

---

[1] It also occurs in Ass. Mos. 3.9 and, with some differences, in the Prayer of Manasseh 1 (*Septuagint*, ed. A. Rahlfs, II 180). The second predicate is also unique in the Old Testament (Gen. 14.19, 22) in the form in which the *Tᵉphilla* quotes it (with *qōnē*).

[2] H. Greeven, *Gebet und Eschatologie im Neuen Testament*, Gütersloh 1931, 12f., 22f.; id., εὔχομαι D-E, *TDNT* II. 800–08: 802f.

[3] See below, p.196. The *Shᵉmaᶜ* and *Tᵉphilla* might theoretically be spoken

address to God which was coined by Jesus, is also Aramaic, as is the cry from the cross in Mark 15.34.[1] In his personal prayer, Jesus prayed in his mother-tongue, and he gave the disciples a common prayer formulated in their own language.[2] In so doing, he withdrew prayer from the liturgical sphere of the sacral and put it in the centre of life, indeed in the centre of everyday life.

Jesus' prayer is also completely new *in content*. The cry from the cross can hardly have been invented, because of the offence caused by its implications for christology (Mark 15.34).[3] But that shows that Jesus was fond of praying in the words of the Psalter: that is particularly true if the quotation of the beginning of Ps. 22 is meant to indicate that Jesus prayed the whole psalm (as is perhaps intended in Luke 18.13 with the quotation of the beginning of Ps. 51: the publican prayed all of Ps. 51). The new element in Jesus' prayer is evident in the form of address that he uses, as well as in his grasp of scripture. Judaism loved to accumulate epithets;[4] the form of address used by Jesus is the simple *'Abbā*, which is only rarely supplemented by an attribute, as at Matt. 11.25 par. When he makes a request, he combines with the request a readiness to bow to the will of the Father (Mark 14.32–42 par.).[5]

Intercession occupies a good deal of space in the prayers of Jesus. He prays for a disciple, whom he sees to be in danger of succumbing to temptation from Satan (Luke 22.31f.).[6] He prays for children (Mark 10.16: blessing in conjunction with the laying on of hands amounts to intercession).[7] He also prays for Israel; this is probably attested by the tradition about the Last Supper.

The unusual request διαμερίσατε εἰς ἑαυτούς (Luke 22.17) may mean that Jesus did not share in the drinking at the last supper. Taken with some linguistic considera-

---

in any language (Sota 7.1), but it is hardly likely to be a coincidence that the two texts are transmitted only in Hebrew, and not in Aramaic or Greek.

[1] For *'Abbā* see above, pp. 66f.; for the cry from the cross, see above, p. 5, n.2.

[2] See below, p. 196.

[3] Absent from Luke; Mark 15.34 *v.l.* D e i Porph: εἰς τί ὠνείδισάς με; Gospel of Peter 19: ἡ δύναμίς (μου) κατέλειψάς με.

[4] Cf. Billerbeck I 398, 405f.

[5] II Cor. 12.8 shows that Paul's attitude was like that of Jesus in Gethsemane: one prays three times, and if even then the prayer is not heard, one recognizes that God wills otherwise (W. Grundmann, *Die Geschichte Jesu Christi*, Berlin 1957 = ³1960, 324 n.1).

[6] In John 17 the petition is extended to all disciples, even those in the future.

[7] Cf. J. Jeremias, *Infant Baptism in the First Four Centuries*, London 1960, 49.

tions, that indicates that in Luke 22.16, 18 par. Mark 14.25 we have avowals of abstinence by Jesus.[1] This conclusion is confirmed by the report that the Palestinian church similarly fasted at Passover.[2] Christians fasted at the very hour at which Jews were holding the Passover meal; they looked for the *parousia* on Passover night, and prayed with fasting for the conversion of Israel.[3] Apparently in so doing they followed the example given by Jesus at the Last Supper. If that is true, Jesus abstained from food and drink at the Last Supper in order to fast and pray for the conversion of Israel.

According to Luke 23.34a, Jesus also interceded for those who crucified him.[4] All this is not as obvious as it might appear. The Old Testament indeed knows of the intercession of elect men and prophets, but nowhere does it exhort the ordinary pious to pray for one another. 'In Israelite religion, praying for others is not a matter for the devout';[5] it is rather a privilege of the chosen men of God. Certainly it is practised in later Judaism, say by the master of the house for his household at morning prayer,[6] but it did not have the central significance that it acquires in the prayers of Jesus.

The character and manner of Jesus' *thanksgiving* is particularly remarkable. One significant passage is Matt. 11.25f. par., a four-line verse of expressly Palestinian form,[7] to which Paul already refers.[8] This is a prayer which Jesus evidently uttered at a turning-point in his life. From a human point of view, his work had proved a failure, because the influential men of his people had clearly rejected his message and he was followed only by a group of disreputable figures. From the ruins Jesus gives thanks. He thanks God despite his lack of success. He rejoices that the mystery of the kingly reign has been

---

[1] Jeremias, *Eucharistic Words²*, 207–18.

[2] We know this from the practice of the Quartodecimans, who continued the usage of the Palestinian church (cf. *ibid.*, 122–25; 212).

[3] Instances in B. Lohse, *Das Passafest der Quartadezimaner*, BFCT II 54, Gütersloh 1953, 62–75; Jeremias, *Eucharistic Words²*, 216f.; W. Huber, *Passa und Ostern. Untersuchungen zur Osterfeier der alten Kirche*, BZNW 35, Berlin 1969, 11.

[4] For the textual problem of Luke 23.34a see below, p. 298.

[5] N. Johansson, *Parakletoi*, Lund 1940, 3.

[6] Ps. Sol. 6.4f.

[7] ἐξομολογοῦμαί σοι corresponds to the stereotyped beginning of the Qumran psalms of thanksgiving *'odᵉkā 'ᵃdōnāy* (1 QH passim); πάτερ (v. 25)/ὁ πατήρ (v. 26) = *'Abbā* (see p. 64 above); κύριε τοῦ οὐρανοῦ καὶ τῆς γῆς = *qōnē šāmayim wā'āreṣ* (First Benediction of the *Tᵉphilla*, see above, p. 187, n.1); antithetic parallelism; formal parataxis with logical hypotaxis ('that while you . . ., nevertheless'); εὐδοκία . . . ἔμπροσθεν = (Targumic) *ra'ᵃwā min qᵒdām* (e.g. Targ. Isa. 53.6, 10). Bultmann rightly comments: 'In my opinion, an originally Aramaic saying', *Synoptic Tradition*, 160.

[8] I Cor. 1.26f.

revealed to the babes; this was God's good and gracious will. Instead of criticizing this will, he offers thanks. We may suppose that thanksgiving dominated the life and the prayer life of Jesus.[1] There is a saying in Rabbinic literature: 'In the world to come, all sacrifice will cease, but the sacrifice of thanksgiving will remain for ever; equally, all confessions will cease, but the confession of thanksgiving will remain for ever.'[2] Thus the predominance of thanskgiving in the prayers of Jesus is an anticipation of the consummation; it is actualized eschatology.

(c) Jesus' teaching on prayer

Jesus adds specific instructions about prayer to the model that he provides by his own conduct. He urges the disciples to ask (Matt. 7.7 par. Luke 11.9):

$$Aἰτεῖτε καὶ δοθήσεται ὑμῖν·$$
$$ζητεῖτε καὶ εὑρήσετε·$$
$$κρούετε καὶ ἀνοιγήσεται ὑμῖν[3]$$

J. Schniewind already saw that this *logion* sounds like a proverb.[4] K. H. Rengstorf defined the *Sitz im Leben* of the first line more exactly: it is beggars' wisdom.[5] 'Look at the beggars,' says Jesus, 'see how urgent they are, how they will not take no for an answer because they know that tenacity leads to success. Your prayer – prayer for the coming of the kingly reign of God – should be as constant as that, and as confident of a hearing.'[6] The parables Luke 11.5–8, 11–13; 18.1–8, and the saying about the faith that can move mountains in Mark 11.23f., are also intended to strengthen this *certainty of gaining a hearing*. The promise πάντα ὅσα προσεύχεσθε καὶ αἰτεῖσθε . . . ἔσται ὑμῖν (Mark 11.24) is, however, difficult, because it is there without any qualification; Jesus seems to give a *carte blanche* promise that prayers will be heard. Still, it is worth noticing that this πάντα in the context refers to the moving of mountains, which was mentioned in the

---

[1] The tradition maintains this (John 11.41).

[2] *Pesiqta de Rab Kahana*, ed. S. Buber, Lyck 1868, 79a 17f. Cf. Heb. 13. 9–16: after the offering of the one sacrifice on the cross (v. 10), there remains only the sacrifice of thanksgiving (v. 15) and the offering of grateful love (v. 16).

[3] Note the synonymous parallelism, the triple parataxis with logical hypotaxis, the divine passive and the rhythm (translation back into Aramaic, see above p. 25).

[4] *Das Evangelium nach Matthäus*, NTD 2, Göttingen ¹²1968, 99.

[5] ‡Rengstorf, 28f.

[6] Luke 18.7.

previous verse; as we have seen,[1] this does not mean astounding miracles, but eschatological authority, i.e. that authority which finds its visible expression in the present, say in power over the spirits. This eschatological understanding of πάντα in v. 24 suits the corresponding οὐδέν in Matt. 17.20. But that means that all these sayings of Jesus which deal with the assurance of being heard relate to eschatological gifts and the authority of the time of salvation. The disciples of Jesus are promised that the powers of the coming reign of God are at work in this world through their prayer.

In calling on his disciples to pray for the gifts of the time of salvation in the certainty of gaining a hearing, Jesus gave three very clear and precise instructions about their prayer. First: Their prayer is not to be like that of the Pharisees, with an eye to being seen. It is to take place *in secret*, in the ταμ(ι)εῖον (Matt. 6.6), in the storeroom, a quite ordinary room. This instruction perhaps alludes to Isa. 26.20: 'Come, my people, enter your chambers, and shut your doors behind you; hide yourselves for a little while until the wrath is past'. Jesus' disciples are aware of the coming catastrophe. Their prayer is the prayer of the eschatological time of distress. This prayer is too serious to be put on show.

Second, the disciples' prayer is to be *short*. Jesus censures the scribes οἱ . . . προφάσει μακρὰ προσευχόμενοι (Mark 12.40): he reprimands them for βατταλογεῖν (Matt. 6.7). Behind long prayers lies the idea (related to the Gentile *fatigare deos*) that God can be favourably influenced by an accumulation of addresses and words. The disciples of Jesus have no need of that; the Father knows what they need and so their prayer can be short. In Matthew, the Lord's Prayer, which follows immediately after the admonition to pray briefly, is thought of as an example of a short prayer. In fact it is clearly distinct, by virtue of its brevity, from most prayers of the time. Being a child frees a man from babbling on.

Finally, the only prior condition for the disciples' prayer mentioned by Jesus is a *readiness to forgive*. For Jesus this is a *conditio sine qua non* of all praying; therefore he even incorporated it into the Lord's Prayer (Matt. 6.12 par.). Willingness to forgive injustices suffered is to be boundless; it is even to include a man's enemies: to pray for them (Matt. 5.44 par. Luke 6.28) presupposes that one forgives them. Every prayer includes a request for God's forgiveness; how can one

[1] See above, pp. 165f.

ask God for forgiveness, if one is not also prepared to forgive (Mark 11.25; Matt. 6.14f.; 18.35)?

If, on the other hand, one of Jesus' disciples has himself sinned against his brother, he is to confess his guilt to his brother and ask for forgiveness before he comes before God. This is said in Matt. 5.23f.[1] This saying is not meant, say, to devalue sacrifice in favour of fellowship (sacrifice is unimportant, a man's relationship to his brother is the only thing that matters); on the contrary, it is meant to take sacrifice with the utmost seriousness. 'You cannot come before God with an offering, i.e. with a request for forgiveness,' says Jesus, 'if your brother has any complaint against you.' The way to God goes through a man's neighbour.

Forgiveness – one's own readiness to forgive and a request for forgiveness where one has committed an offence – is *the* presupposition for the prayer of Jesus' disciples.

(d) The Lord's Prayer[2]

Not only did Jesus give the disciples a model through his own prayer, not only did he instruct them about how they should pray, but he also gave them a new prayer, which on grounds of both language and content is part of the bedrock of the tradition:[3] the Lord's Prayer.

The earliest text

The Lord's Prayer has been handed down in the gospels[4] in *two different versions*, a longer one in Matthew (6.9–13) and a shorter one in Luke (11.2–4).[5] In assessing them, it is important to note the

[1] For exegesis see J. Jeremias, ' "Lass allda deine Gabe" (Mt. 5.23f.)', *ZNW* 36, 1937, 150–154 = *Abba*, 103–107.

[2] A. Seeberg; P. Fiebig, *Das Vater Unser*, Gütersloh 1927; G. Dalman, *Worte Jesu*², 283–365; E. Lohmeyer, *The Lord's Prayer*, London 1965 (but he has had the misfortune to assign two modern retro-translations to North- and South- Palestinian Aramaic); ‡K. G. Kuhn; T. W. Manson, 'The Lord's Prayer', *BJRL* 38, 1955/56, 99–113, 436–48; ‡Schürmann; ‡Jeremias, 'Lord's Prayer', 82–107 (and literature).

[3] Thus rightly Perrin, *Rediscovering*, 47.

[4] There is a further tradition in Did. 8.2; but it can be left out of account in what follows, because apart from some insignificant divergences it corresponds with the text of Matthew.

[5] From the point of view of textual criticism the two versions raise no serious problems. The doxology Matt. 6.13b is not original; it is missing in the earliest manuscripts of Matthew, ℵ BD *al* it vg^{codd}, and in all the manuscripts of Luke (but see below, pp. 202f.). On the reading ἀφήκαμεν Matt. 6.12 see below, p. 196. The text

context in which each occurs. In Matthew, this context is the controversy with the Pharisees over almsgiving, prayer and fasting (6.1–18). This takes place in three sections constructed along exactly parallel lines (6.1–4, 5f., 16–18), of which only the section dealing with prayer is extended by three further *logia* about praying: the warning against too many words (6.7f.), the Lord's Prayer (6.9–13) and the instruction about being ready to forgive (6.14f.). This extension has produced a short teaching passage on prayer composed of sayings of Jesus. In Luke, too, the Lord's Prayer appears within the framework of a catechism about prayer (11.1–13). It, too, is also in four parts and includes the request 'Teach us to pray' with the Lord's Prayer (11.1–4), the parable of the friend's request, which Luke understands as an admonition to perseverance in prayer (11.5–8),[1] a summons to pray (11.9f.) and the picture of the generous father, which is an invitation to be confident of gaining a hearing (11.11–13). The two prayer catechisms are intended for quite different circumstances; that of Matthew is spoken to people who have learnt to pray but whose prayer is endangered, that of Luke is spoken to people who have still to learn to pray properly. In other words, Matthew gives us a Jewish-Christian and Luke a Gentile-Christian catechism. If we add the Didache (see p. 193, n. 4), the basic

---

of Luke has been transmitted with numerous variants, almost all of which show a tendency to assimilate the shorter text in extent and wording to the longer Matthaean version. The one interesting thing is the petition for the Holy Spirit: ἐλθέτω τὸ πνεῦμά σου τὸ ἅγιον ἐφ'ἡμᾶς καὶ καθαρισάτω ἡμᾶς, which appears in Marcion in place of the first, and in the minuscules 162,700, in Gregory of Nyssa and, following him, in Maximus the Confessor, in place of the second petition (there is also a trace of it at the beginning of the form of the second petition in D: ἐφ'ἡμᾶς ἐλθάτω σου ἡ βασιλεία). This petition for the spirit is certainly not original, as assumed by A. von Harnack, 'Über einige Worte, die nicht in den kanonischen Evangelien stehen, nebst einem Anhang über die ursprüngliche Gestalt des Vaterunsers', *Sitzungsberichte der Berliner Akademie*, Phil.-hist. Klasse 1904, 195–208, and others after him; the weak attestation, the difference in the position in which it appears, and above all its form, which varies from the structure of the other petitions, exclude this. It may, rather, derive from the baptismal liturgy in which the Lord's Prayer and the petition for the spirit were connected (e.g. Const. Apost. VII 45, ed. Funk I 451f.).

[1] That is not the original meaning. The central point of the parable was originally not the friend who asked, but the one who was asked, and the comparison was not with the man who prays, but with God: if a man gets up at night to help a friend in difficulty, how much more will God hear any of his people in distress (cf. Jeremias, *Parables*², 157–59).

material of which still belongs in the first century AD, we may say that by AD 75 in the whole church the Lord's Prayer was an ingredient in the instruction on prayer. Indeed, as the sequence of material in the Didache suggests (1–6 two ways, 7 baptism, 8 fasting and Lord's Prayer, 9f. eucharist), it was an ingredient in the instruction that followed catechumenate and baptism. Both the Jewish-Christian and the Gentile-Christian churches were agreed that the way to learn to pray was through the Lord's Prayer. The result that follows from this is that the deviations in the versions preserved in Matthew and Luke are not the result of the interference of the evangelists (and not at all the result of individual alterations). Rather, we have here the versions used in two different churches.

But which version is the original? Both the length and wording of Matt. 6.9–13 and Luke 11.2–4 differ.

The Lucan version is *shorter* than that of Matthew, in three places. There are no attributes in the address (which reads, simply, πάτερ); and the whole of the third (γενηθήτω τὸ θέλημά σου, ὡς ἐν οὐρανῷ καὶ ἐπὶ γῆς) and seventh (ἀλλὰ ῥῦσαι ἡμᾶς ἀπὸ τοῦ πονηροῦ) of the Matthaean petitions are missing. The most decisive feature in favour of originality is that the Lucan version is contained in its entirety within that of Matthew. As liturgical texts tend to be elaborated, and the shorter wording is usually the earlier, the additional material in Matthew may amount to elaborations. It is improbable that anyone should have deleted the third and seventh petitions, whereas the opposite process is easily imaginable. Further considerations confirm that the shorter text is the earlier. The three additional passages in the Matthaean version in each instance come at the same place in the text: at the end of the address (which originally consisted in only one word), at the end of the petitions in the second person, and at the end of the petitions in the first person plural. This also corresponds with what is to be observed elsewhere: there is a tendency to conclude liturgical texts with a full stress.[1] Finally, the fact that the additions transmitted by Matthew balance the stylistic construction of the Lord's Prayer also suggests that the Lucan version is original. In particular, the seventh petition completes the parallelism, the absence of which is very striking in the closing petition of Luke.

Next, as far as *wording* is concerned, the petition for bread in the Lucan version is given a general form by the present δίδου, which is in

---

[1] Examples: Matt. 26.28 compared with the parallel texts; Phil. 2.11.

fact the only present in the Lord's Prayer, and by the replacement of σήμερον with τὸ καθ᾿ ἡμέραν. This makes Matthew preferable. In the fifth petition, Matthew has τὰ ὀφειλήματα and Luke τὰς ἁμαρτίας. Matthew's striking expression is an Aramaism.[1] As the Aramaic word for sin, ḥōbā, really means 'debt (of money)', τὰ ὀφειλήματα (Matthew) is a literal translation and τὰς ἁμαρτίας (Luke) its replacement by colloquial Greek. The τῷ ὀφείλοντι that follows in Luke shows that the Lucan version, too, goes back to a formulation with ὀφειλήματα. Furthermore, the fact that in the second half of the petition for forgiveness Matthew offers the aorist ἀφήκαμεν and Luke the present ἀφίομεν suggests that here, too, the more difficult text of Matthew may lay claim to being the earlier.[2]

The result of our investigation is, therefore, that in *length* the shorter text of Luke is to be regarded as original, and in general *wording* the text of Matthew is to be preferred. Furthermore, we have been brought to see that the Greek text is based on an earlier Aramaic one. If the Lucan version is translated back into Aramaic, the result is a two/four-stress rhythm and a rhyme:[3]

> 'Abbá
> yitqaddáš šᵉmák | tēté malkūták
> laḥmán dᵉlimhár | hab lán yōmā dén
> ūšᵉbōq lán ḥōbénan | kᵉdišᵉbáqnan lᵉḥayyābénan
> wᵉlā taʿēlínnan lᵉnisyón.

The meaning

The petition Κύριε, δίδαξον ἡμᾶς προσεύχεσθαι, καθὼς καὶ Ἰωάννης ἐδίδαξεν τοὺς μαθητὰς αὐτοῦ is important for understanding the Lord's Prayer. According to Luke 11.1, it was this that led Jesus to formulate the Lord's Prayer, for the καθώς clause shows that the unnamed disciple is asking for a prayer that will characterize Jesus' followers the community of salvation.[4] Thus, right from the beginning, the

---

[1] See above, p. 6, n.15.

[2] That in the Matthaean tradition the present ἀφίομεν D 33 pc or ἀφίεμεν pm s ll (Did.) appears alongside the aorist ἀφήκαμεν ℵ B al is also a simplification here (so far as there is no question of Lucan influence).

[3] Following in substance C. F. Burney, *The Poetry of Our Lord*, Oxford 1925, 113. True, the address has only one stress, but the second is replaced by a pause. This application of the 'law of the pause' (see above, pp. 21f.) gives the address added weight (‡Kuhn, 39).

[4] See above, p. 170.

Lord's Prayer was meant not only as a model for proper prayer, but as a formula, a token of recognition – which is the way in which the church has used it down the centuries.

The construction of the Lord's Prayer can be seen at a glance:

1. The address is followed by:
2. two short petitions in the second person singular (the two 'thou' petitions), in parallelism;
3. two longer petitions in the first person plural (the two 'we' petitions), in parallelism;
4. the short closing petition.

The address πάτερ (Luke 11.2) goes back to an Aramaic *'Abbā*, which here is to be translated 'our Father' (thus rightly Matt. 6.9).[1] We saw in §7 that the form of address *'Abbā* is Jesus' very own usage, which expresses both his trust and his authority. With the Lord's Prayer, Jesus gives the 'little ones'[2] the privilege of saying *'Abbā* after him. As members of the family of God, they may say 'Father' to God, and ask him for his good gifts. The earliest church right from the beginning regarded it as a great privilege that Jesus in this way gave the disciples a share in his authority as Son. This is very clear from, say, Rom. 8.15f. (where the full stop should be put after υἱοθεσίας rather than πατήρ, because otherwise the beginning of v. 16 would be the first asyndeton in Romans), where Paul says that there is no clearer proof of the possession of the gift of being a child than when someone dares to cry *'Abbā*. So important is this remark to him that he also repeats it in Gal. 4.6 (where the ὅτι is meant in a declarative sense, and should therefore be translated 'that', not 'because'). Similarly, the fact that the Lord's Prayer has long been introduced in the liturgies of both East and West with the words: 'Grant that we may *dare* to call on thee as Father and to say, "Our Father . . ."' (Liturgy of St Chrysostom) or, 'We are bold to say, "Our Father. . ."' (Roman Mass)[3] also expresses the feeling of what a privilege it was that Jesus empowered his disciples to say *'Abbā* after him. Boldness to address God as Father comes from the assurance of being a child: children may say *'Abbā*.

There follow the *two 'thou' petitions*, 'Hallowed by thy name. Thy kingdom come'. The two petitions are constructed in the same way

---

[1] Thus Erub. 6.2; B.B. 9.3; Shebu. 7.7. (three times); Tos. Yom. 2.5, 6, 8; Tos. B.K. 10.21.
[2] See above, p. 111.
[3] T. W. Manson (see p. 193, n.2 above), 101 n.2.

and form a synonymous parallelism. In Greek, each time the verb comes first; each time the imperative is avoided. The two petitions belong extremely closely together, not only in form but also in content. They have not been newly constructed by Jesus, but come from the Jewish liturgy, namely from the Kaddish, the 'Holy' prayer with which the synagogue liturgy ended and which was familiar to Jesus from childhood. The Kaddish is one of the very few Aramaic prayers of Judaism; the reason for this is that it was prayed immediately after the sermon, which was delivered in Aramaic. The earliest form of this much-used prayer to which we can penetrate reads:

Exalted and hallowed be his great name
in the world which he created according to his will.
May he let his kingdom rule
in your lifetime and in your days and in the lifetime
of the whole house of Israel, speedily and soon.
Praised be his great name from eternity to eternity.
And to this, say: Amen.[1]

The Kaddish is an eschatological prayer. Both petitions have the same end in view: God's appearance as Lord. Each appearance of an earthly ruler as Lord is accompanied by homage in word (acclamation) and gesture (proskynesis). So, too, will it be when God reveals his glory: his name will be hallowed and all will submit to his rule. The Kaddish thus makes use of enthronement themes. The two 'thou' petitions of the Lord's Prayer must be understood along these lines. They pray for the coming of the hour when God's glory become visible and he enters upon his rule. The present world is under the rule of Satan; evil triumphs. From these depths of distress the disciples of Jesus cry for the conquest of Satan and the revelation of the reign of God. They plead for the shortening of the final trial, because otherwise no one would be saved (Mark 13.20). The two 'thou' petitions are an expression of trust in God's promise and mercy; anyone who

---

[1] Text in Dalman, *Worte Jesu*[1], 305 (not in [2]1930); for the age and presumed earliest form cf. I. Elbogen, *Der jüdische Gottesdienst in seiner geschichtlichen Entwicklung*[3], Frankfurt-Main 1931 = [4]Hildesheim 1962, 92–98. A small stylistic consideration also suggests that Jesus is taking up the Kaddish. The two 'thou' petitions of the Lord's Prayer stand side by side in asyndeton, whereas the 'we' petitions are joined together by καί. This discrepancy can probably be explained from the fact that the two petitions of the Kaddish similarly stood side by side in asyndeton in the earliest tradition.

utters them leaves aside everyday concerns and throws himself, surrounded as he is by evil and darkness, entirely on God.

The Jewish community and the disciples of Jesus pray for the revelation of the glory of God in the same words. Yet there is a great difference between them. In the Kaddish, a community is praying which is still completely in the courts of waiting. The Lord's Prayer is prayed by men who know that God's gracious work, the great turning-point, has already begun.[1]

The two 'we' petitions, for bread and for the blotting out of sins, similarly belong very closely together. Once again that is clear from their form. Each of the two petitions consists of two half-lines, which stand over against one another (see below). If it is true that the beginning of the Lord's Prayer takes up the Kaddish, then it follows that the stress lies on the new element that Jesus adds, i.e. on the two 'we' petitions.

The first of the two 'we' petitions asks for ἄρτος ἐπιούσιος.

This is not the place to outline the whole interminable debate about the meaning of ἐπιούσιος.[2] Essentially, the question is whether the word ἐπιούσιος, which occurs only once in a non-Christian context that is, moreover, fragmentary,[3] is to be derived from ἐπεῖναι or ἐπουσία, or from ἐπιέναι. In the first instance it would mean something like 'what is necessary for existence'; in the second, 'coming', 'tomorrow's'. I will mention straightaway what seems to me to be the decisive argument. The church father Jerome tells us that in the Gospel of the Nazareans the term mᵃḥar appeared; this he aptly translated *quod dicitur crastinum*.[4] Now it is true that this Gospel of the Nazareans (which is lost, apart from fragments) was not an Aramaic original but a Targum-like translation of the Gospel of Matthew into Aramaic, and was therefore later than Matthew. Nevertheless, we have good reason to assert that the mᵃḥar is earlier than the Gospel of Matthew. For the translator who rendered Matthew into Aramaic naturally stopped translating the moment he came to the Lord's Prayer and instead wrote down what he prayed every day. If that is so, then beyond doubt mᵃḥar, 'tomorrow', is the Aramaic expression standing behind ἐπιούσιος. This is supported by the fact that it produces a contrast between ἐπιούσιος and σήμερον in the petition for bread which is paralleled in the following petition in the contrast between divine and human forgiveness: '*Tomorrow's* bread, give us *today!*'

Now not only does Jerome tell us what word took the place of ἐπιούσιος in the version of the Lord's Prayer used by Aramaic-speaking

[1] See above, pp. 76ff.

[2] W. Foerster, ἐπιούσιος, *TDNT* II, 1964, 590–99 (lit.).

[3] On a papyrus which has meanwhile disappeared again (F. Preisigke, *Sammelbuch griechischer Urkunden aus Ägypten* I, Strassburg 1915, 5224).

[4] *Commentary on Matthew* 6.11 (E. Klostermann, *Apocrypha* II, KlT 8³, Berlin 1929, 7).

Jewish Christians; in addition to the translation he adds an interpretation: *mahar quod dicitur crastinum, ut sit sensus: panem nostrum
crastinum, id est futurum, da nobis hodie.* Thus Jerome interprets
ἄρτος ἐπιούσιος as 'the future bread'. As a matter of fact, *maḥar* literally
denotes the next day, but in a transferred sense it was used to refer to
God's tomorrow, the future, i.e. the 'end-time'.[1] Thus by 'tomorrow's
bread' Jerome did not understand earthly bread, the minimum necessary for existence, but the bread of life. This eschatological understanding of the petition for bread was the dominant one in the first
centuries, both in East and in West.[2] The eschatological slant of all
the rest of the petitions in the Lord's Prayer suggest that Jesus intended
the petition for bread as a petition for the *bread of the time of salvation*,
the bread of life.

It would be a crass misunderstanding were we to think that this
amounted to a spiritualization of the petition for bread. For Jesus,
there was no opposition between earthly bread and the bread of life,
for in the realm of the *basileia* all earthly things are hallowed. The
bread that Jesus broke when he invited publicans and sinners to his
table, the bread that he gave to his disciples at the Last Supper, was
earthly bread and yet at the same time the bread of life. For the
disciples of Jesus, every meal, and not only the last one, had deep
eschatological significance. Every meal with Jesus was a salvation
meal, an anticipation of the final feast. At each meal he was the host,
as he would be at the consummation. The primitive community
preserved this understanding when it designated its meals together as
'the Lord's meals' (I Cor. 11.20). This is the way in which the
petition for 'tomorrow's bread' is also meant. It does not tear apart
the everyday world and the heavenly world, but asks that in the
midst of everyday secularity the powers and gifts of the coming world
may be effective. Only when one sees clearly the eschatological slant

---

[1] Even in the Old Testament, Heb. *māḥār* has the meaning 'future', e.g. Ex.
13.14: 'If your son asks you in the future . . .'; cf. Gen. 30.33; Deut. 6.20; Josh.
4.6, 21; 22.24, 27f. There are occurrences of *māḥār* with an eschatological significance in Lev.R. 23 on 18.3; Midr. S. of S. on 2.2 (twice): *geʾullat (šel) māḥār* 'to
morrow's redemption'.

[2] A. Seeberg, *Die vierte Bitte des Vaterunsers*, Rostock 1914, 11f. Thus already
Marcion, who has τὸν ἄρτον σου τὸν ἐπιούσιον (A. von Harnack, *Marcion*[2], TU 45,
Leipzig 1924, 207f.), also the Christian Palestinian (*lḥm dʿtr*, 'bread of superfluity'),
the Old Syriac (Matt. 6.11 sy[c] ([s deest]) *wlḥmn ʾmyn ʾ dywm ʾ hb ln*; Luke 11.3 sy[sc]
whb ln lḥm ʾ ʾmyn ʾ dkljwm, the Old Egyptian (bo *crastinum*, sa *venientem*) and the
Vulgate on Matt. 6.11 (*supersubstantialem*).

of the petition for bread can one understand the weight of the σήμερον. In a world enslaved by Satan, in which God is distant, the disciples are to ask for their share in the glory of the consummation now. They may reach for the bread of life with both hands and pray: Now, here and now, today, give us the bread of life, in the midst of our sorry existence.

The second 'we' petition looks to the great reckoning towards which the world is moving. The disciples of Jesus know that they are caught in guilt and sin and also know that only God's pardon, the greatest of his gifts, can save them. They request this gift not just for the hour of the Last Judgment, but now, here, today. Like the first 'we' petition, the second has two members; however, the second half of the petition for forgiveness, ὡς καὶ ἡμεῖς ἀφήκαμεν τοῖς ὀφειλέταις ἡμῶν, is striking in that it refers to human action – something strange in the context of the Lord's Prayer. It looks almost like an alien body; that makes clear that a very heavy emphasis is placed on it. The aorist ἀφήκαμεν is particularly notable: 'Forgive us, as we have forgiven'. Does our forgiveness, then, precede God's forgiveness? Is it the model for God's forgiveness (Matt. ὡς καί) or its justification (Luke καὶ γάρ)? A linguistic consideration provides the right understanding of ἀφήκαμεν. It goes back to the Aramaic šᵉbaqnan, which is meant as a *perfectum coincidentiae*[1] and is therefore to be translated: 'as *herewith* we forgive our debtors'. Thus the second half of the second petition is a self-reminder of one's own forgiveness, a declaration of readiness to pass on God's forgiveness. As Jesus continually stresses, this readiness is the indispensable prior condition for God's forgiveness.[2] Where the readiness to forgive is lacking, the petition for God's forgiveness becomes a lie. So with the second 'we' petition, Jesus' disciples are saying: We belong to the *basileia*; therefore give us today a share in the gift of the time of salvation; we are ready to hand it on further.

The two 'we' petitions realize the two 'thou' petitions. If the 'thou' petitions plead for the revelation of the glory of God, the two 'we' petitions ask for the consummation now, today.

The *closing petition* is surprising. From a formal point of view it falls outside the framework of the Lord's Prayer. After the parallelism of the two 'thou' petitions and the two-membered construction of the two 'we' petitions, this terse, one-membered closing statement seems

---

[1] Cf. P. Joüon, *L'Évangile de Notre-Seigneur Jésus-Christ*, Verbum Salutis 5, Paris 1930, 35.

[2] See above, pp. 192f.

abrupt and harsh. And there is a further point: this last petition is the only one to be put in the negative. All that is deliberate. This petition is meant to seem harsh and abrupt. That shows its content. To understand it, we must first note that πειρασμός does not refer to everyday temptations, but to the last great trial.[1] The μὴ εἰσενέγκῃς in its Greek wording might suggest that it is God who does the leading into temptation. This interpretation is rejected as early as James 1.13. A comparison with a Jewish morning and evening prayer, which Jesus is perhaps taking up directly, shows that in fact it does not fit the sense:

> Bring me not into the power of sin,
> And not into the power of guilt,
> And not into the power of temptation,
> And not into the power of anything shameful.[2]

Here the causative 'bring me not' clearly has permissive sense, 'Do not let me fall victim', as is shown by a comparison of the four parallel lines. Thus the μὴ εἰσενέγκῃς in the closing petition of the Lord's Prayer is meant in the same way: 'Do not let us fall victim to temptation'. Jesus' disciples do not ask to be spared the trial.[3] Rather, the closing petition is meant as a request for preservation from succumbing to the eschatological trial. Jesus' disciples are therefore praying at the end of the Lord's Prayer for protection from apostasy.[4] Now we can understand the abrupt conclusion. It is a mark of the matter-of-fact concern of Jesus that this closing line brings the disciples back from their prospect of the consummation into their concrete situation. This closing line is a 'far-echoing cry for help':[5] Grant us one thing, preserve us from going wrong! That 'there is no parallel in the Old Testament to this petition, even to the idea it expresses'[6] is no coincidence.

The absence of the *doxology* in Luke 11.4 and in the earliest manuscripts of Matt. 6.13 does not justify our concluding that it was once prayed without any final benediction. It is quite inconceivable that a prayer ended with the words τοῦ πονηροῦ

[1] See above, pp. 128f.; ‡Jeremias, 'Lord's Prayer', 105f.
[2] b. Ber. 60b (twice).
[3] Cf. the agraphon *neminem intemptatum regna caelestia consecuturum* quoted by Tertullian, *De baptismo* 20.2 (for exegesis see Jeremias, *Unknown Sayings of Jesus*, London ²1964, 73–75).
[4] R. Bultmann, *Jesus and the Word*, London 1958, 129; ‡Schürmann, 91.
[5] ‡Schürmann, 90.   [6] ‡Herrmann, 91.

(Matthew) or εἰς πειρασμόν (Luke). Rather, it is important to know that in Judaism there were two ways of ending a prayer, a fixed conclusion and a conclusion formulated freely by the suppliant, called the *ḥᵃtīmā* ('seal'). Originally the Lord's Prayer was a prayer with the 'seal', i.e. with a freely formulated conclusion. At the latest by the end of the first century AD, a fixed form of the doxology had found general acceptance, by stages. Didache 8.2, where it is attested for the first time, is still two-membered: ὅτι σοῦ ἐστιν ἡ δύναμις καὶ ἡ δόξα εἰς τοὺς αἰῶνας, but very soon it becomes three-membered.

Thus the Lord's Prayer is an eschatological prayer like the *Maranatha* (I Cor. 16.22), like Mark 14.38 and Luke 21.36. Its nucleus is the petition for the reign which is being actualized even now. But the closing petition shows that the last thing always remains the cry: πιστεύω· βοήθει μου τῇ ἀπιστίᾳ. 'I believe! Help me despite[1] my unbelief' (Mark 9.24).

§ 19 · THE LIFE OF DISCIPLESHIP

G. Kittel, *Die Probleme des palästinensischen Spätjudentums und des Urchristentums*, BWANT 3, 1, Stuttgart 1926; W. G. Kümmel, 'Jesus und der jüdische Traditionsgedanke', *ZNW* 33, 1934, 105–30; Jeremias, *Jerusalem*, 359–76; E. Lohmeyer, *Kultus und Evangelium*, Göttingen 1942; G. Bornkamm, 'Der Lohngedanke im Neuen Testament', *EvTh* 2/3, 1946, 143–66 = *Studien zu Antike und Urchristentum*, Gesammelte Aufsätze II, BEvTh 28, München 1959 =² 1963, 69–92; G. von Rad, 'The City on the Hill', in: *The Problem of the Hexateuch and other Essays*, Edinburgh and London 1966, 232–42; C. H. Dodd, *Gospel and Law*, Cambridge 1951; H.-J. Schoeps, 'Jésus et la loi juive', *RHPR* 33, 1933, 1–20; K.-H. Rengstorf, *Mann und Frau im Urchristentum*, Arbeitsgemeinschaft für Forschung des Landes Nordrhein-Westfalen, Heft 12, Köln-Opladen 1954; R. Schnackenburg, *The Moral Teaching of the New Testament*, London 1965; J. Dupont, *Les Béatitudes. Le problème littéraire. Le message doctrinal*, Bruges-Louvain 1954, ²I 1958 = Paris 1969. ²II Paris 1969: J. Leipoldt, *Die Frau in der antiken Welt und im Urchristentum²*, Leipzig 1955, Gütersloh 1962; H. Braun, *Spätjüdisch-häretischer und frühchristlicher Radikalismus*, BHTh 24, Tübingen 1957; J. Jeremias, *Die Bergpredigt*, Calwer Hefte 27, Stuttgart 1959 = ⁵1965 = Jeremias, *Abba*, 171–89; E. Lohse, 'Jesu Worte über den Sabbat', *Judentum-Urchristentum-Kirche, Festschrift für J. Jeremias*, BZNW 26, Berlin 1960, ²1964, 79–89; M. Hengel, *Die Zeloten*, AGSU 1, Leiden-Köln 1961; H. Kosmala, 'The Parable of the Unjust Steward in the Light of Qumran', *ASTI* III, Leiden 1964, 114–21; H. J. Degenhardt, *Lukas Evangelist der Armen. Besitz und Besitzverzicht in den lukanischen Schriften*, Stuttgart 1965; A. Isaksson, *Marriage and Ministry in the New Temple*, ASNU XXIV, Lund 1965; S. G. F. Brandon, *Jesus and the Zealots*, Manchester 1967; H.-T. Wrege, *Die Überlieferungsgeschichte der Bergpredigt*, WUNT 9, Tübingen 1968.

[1] The dative is adversative (see above, p. 166).

A note on the title: this section is concerned with the 'ethical demands of Jesus'. But that designation conceals the eschatological factor, that the demands are not a code of behaviour related purely to this world but concern the order of life in the coming reign of God, which regulates the life of the disciples even now. So instead of the 'Ethics of Jesus' I shall speak of the 'Life of Discipleship'.

Just as the reign of God is inconceivable without prayer (§18), so too it is inconceivable without the life of discipleship. For belonging to the reign of God transforms a man's whole life: not only his relation to God becomes new, but also his relation *to man*. Anyone who belongs to the reign of God and may address God as Father stands under the new law of God, which is part of the new creation[1] and replaces the divine law of the old aeon.

(i) Jesus' criticism of the divine law of the old aeon

The divine law of the old aeon is laid down in the *Torah*, or more exactly in the two *Torot*, the written *Torah* and the oral *Torah*,[2] The written *Torah* comprises the Pentateuch. Of the remaining writings of the Old Testament it was said that 'they were added for the sake of sin',[3] but they too were regarded as being inspired.[4] The *Torah* has to be interpreted so that it can be applied to the particular instance. Thus the oral *Torah* arises, named the *Halakah*. It is the work of the scribes. These had a tendency to attach the same authority to it as to the written *Torah*. Towards the end of the second century AD, at the time of the composition of the *Mishnah*, the view had come to prevail that the oral *Torah* as well as the written *Torah* had been given to Moses on Sinai and that it had then been handed on in an unbroken chain.[5] Therefore it could raise the same claim to authority and inspiration as the written *Torah*.[6] We have no grounds for supposing that this view was already acknowledged at the time of Jesus, but we

---

[1] W. D. Davies, 'Matthew 5: 17, 18', in: *Mélanges bibliques rédigés en l'honneur de André Robert*, Travaux de l'Institut Catholique de Paris 4, Paris 1957, 428–56 = in: Davies, *Christian Origins and Judaism*, London 1962, 31–66.

[2] b. Shab. 31a Bar. etc.   [3] Billerbeck IV 435.   [4] *Ibid.*

[5] P. Aboth 1.1: 'Moses received the *Torah* from Sinai (i.e. from God) and handed it on to Joshua, Joshua to the elders, the elders to the prophets . . .' (Here '*Torah*' embraces both the written and the oral law, cf. H. L. Strack, *Pirqe Aboth. Die Sprüche der Väter*, Schriften des Institutum Iudaicum in Berlin 6⁴, Leipzig 1915, 1.)

[6] Billerbeck I 81f., 691–93. In Sanh. 11.3 the *Halakah* is even put above the written *Torah* (see also Billerbeck I 692f.).

do know that the *Halakah* was on the way towards gaining this supreme authority. There are therefore two questions to ask: what is Jesus' attitude to the written *Torah*, and what is his attitude to the oral *Torah*, the *Halakah*?

(a) Jesus' attitude to the Old Testament law

Jesus lived in the Old Testament. His sayings are incomprehensible unless we recognize this. His last word, according to Mark, was the beginning of Psalm 22, prayed in his Aramaic mother tongue (Mark 15.34).[1] He was particularly fond of the prophet Isaiah,[2] and above all of the promises and statements about the servant of God in Deutero-Isaiah.[3] The apocalyptic sayings of Daniel were also extremely significant for him.[4] Numerically, literal and free quotations from the Psalter predominate on the lips of Jesus,[5] and this was evidently his prayer book.[6] The twelve prophets are also quoted frequently,[7] and there are repeated allusions to the prophet

[1] See above, p. 5, n.2.

[2] The following of Jesus' references to Isa. 1–40 should be stressed: Isa. 6.9f. (double effect of the message) cf. Mark 4.12 par. and on this p. 120 above; Isa. 29.13 (lip-service and the commandment of men) cf. Mark 7.6f. par.; Isa. 29.18f.; 35.5f. (signs of the time of salvation) cf. Matt. 11.5 par.

[3] For references to Isa. 53, see below, pp. 286f. In addition: Isa, 56.7 (a house of prayer for all people) cf. Mark 11.17 par.; Isa. 61.1f. (good news for the poor) cf. Matt. 5.3 par. 4; 11.5 par.; Luke 4.18f.; Isa. 66.24 (eternal punishment) cf. Mark 9.48.

[4] Dan. 2.34f., 44f. (the grinding stone) cf. Matt. 21.44 par.; Dan. 7.9f. (thrones for the court of judgment) cf. Matt. 19.28 par.; Dan. 7.27 (*basileia* of the people of God) cf. Luke 12.32; Dan. 9.27; 11.31; 12.11 (abomination of desolation) cf. Mark 13.14 par.; Dan. 12.1 (great tribulation) cf. Mark 13.19 par.

[5] The most important passages are: Ps. 8.3 (praise from sucklings) cf. Matt. 21.16; Ps. 22.2 ('My God, my God . . .') cf. Mark 15.34 par.; Ps. 24.4; 51.12; 73.1 (pure heart) cf. Matt. 5.8; Ps. 31.6 ('Into thy hands . . .') cf. Luke 23.46; Ps. 37.11 ('the humble . . .') cf. Matt. 5.5; Ps. 41.10 (betrayal by a table-companion) cf. Mark 14.18; John 13.18; Ps. 42.6, 12; 43.5 (My soul is troubled . . .') cf. Mark 14.34 par.; Ps. 49.8 (ransom) cf. Mark 8.37 par.; Ps. 50.14 (keeping an oath) cf. Matt. 5.33; Ps. 110.1 (*sessio ad dexteram*) cf. Mark 12.36 par.; 14.62 par.; Pss. 113–118 (the *Hallel*, that was prayed at the Passover meal) cf. Mark 14.26; Ps. 118.22f. (keystone) cf. Mark 12.10 par.; Ps. 118.26 (Blessed is the one who comes) cf. Matt. 23.39 par.

[6] See above, p. 189.

[7] E.g. Hos. 6.6 (I will have mercy) cf. Matt. 9.13; 12.7; Micah 7.6 (family disputes) cf. Mark 13.12 par.; Matt. 10.21, 35f. par.; Zech. 13.7 (smiting the shepherd) cf. Mark 14.27 par.; Mal. 3.1 (the forerunner) cf. Matt. 11.10 par.; Mal. 3.23 (the return of Elijah) cf. Mark 9.12 par.

Jeremiah.[1] The numerous references to the Pentateuch, in which Jesus found inscribed the basic norms of the will of God (e.g. Mark 7.10 par.; 10.19 par.; 12.28–34 par.), occur especially in the controversy sayings.[2]

Only when this basic attitude of Jesus has been made clear can one assess what it means that Jesus should venture to make more radical, to criticize, indeed to supersede words of the *Torah*. The clearest example of the way in which Jesus makes the *Torah* more *radical* (as the Teacher of Righteousness had done before him)[3] is provided by the first two antitheses of the Sermon on the Mount, which sharpen in a radical way the prohibitions against killing and committing adultery (Ex. 20.13f.; see Matt. 5.21f.; 5.27f.).[4] Jesus *criticizes* the *Torah* primarily by omitting elements of it. In Matt. 11.5f. he passes over the eschatological vengeance on the Gentiles, although it is announced in all three Old Testament passages which he takes up (Isa. 35.5f.; 29.18f.; 61.1).[5] This omission of the vengeance is part of the offence of the message against which Jesus issues a warning (Matt. 11.6 par.). Luke 4.16–30 also belongs here. The text for Jesus' sermon in vv. 18f. is Isa. 61.1f. Jesus concludes with the words, 'to proclaim the acceptable year of the Lord'. He breaks off in mid-sentence; the conclusion, 'and the day of vengeance of our God', is missing. The reaction to his preaching is that πάντες ἐμαρτύρουν αὐτῷ καὶ ἐθαύμαζον ἐπὶ τοῖς λόγοις τῆς χάριτος (v. 22). Both verbs are ambiguous: μαρτυρεῖν with the dative can mean either 'give witness for' or 'give witness against', and θαυμάζειν can mean either 'be enthusiastic about', or 'be shocked at'. The continuation of the pericope shows that the word must be interpreted *in malam partem*. In that case, the interpretation of

[1] E.g. Jer. 6.16 (find rest) cf. Matt. 11.29; Jer. 7.11 (den of robbers) cf. Mark 11.17 par.; Jer. 31.31 (new covenant) cf. Mark 14.24 par.

[2] Creation: Gen. 1.27 cf. Mark 10.6 par.; Gen. 2.24 cf. Mark 10.7f. par.; Sodom and Gomorrha: Gen. 19.15, 24f. cf. Luke 17.29; Gen. 19.26 cf. Luke 17.31; the God of the fathers: Ex. 3.6 cf. Mark 12.26 par.; Decalogue: Ex. 20.12–16; Deut. 5.16–20 cf. Mark 7.10 par.; 10.19 par.; Matt. 5.21, 27; individual regulations: Ex. 21.12 cf. Matt. 5.21b; Ex. 21.17 cf. Mark 7.10 par.; Ex. 21.24 cf. Matt. 5.38; Lev. 19.12 cf. Matt. 5.33; Lev. 19.18 cf. Mark 12.31 par.; Matt. 5.43; 19.19; Deut. 6.4f. cf. Mark 12.29f. par.; Deut. 24.1 cf. Matt. 5.31. Other passages to stress are: I Kings 17.9 (widow of Sarepta) cf. Luke 4.26; II Kings 5.14 (Naaman) cf. Luke 4.27; Ezek. 34.16 (the lost) cf. Luke 19.10.

[3] ‡Braun; G. Jeremias, *Lehrer der Gerechtigkeit*, 331f.

[4] For the antitheses, see below, pp. 251ff. Neither Judaism nor the primitive church know anything comparable to the antitheses.

[5] See above, pp. 103f.

ἐπὶ τοῖς λόγοις τῆς χάριτος (v. 22) must be: the people of Nazareth are shocked that Jesus quotes only the words of grace from Isa. 61 to preach about, and omits the mention of vengeance, although it also occurred in the text.[1] Jesus' criticism of the *Torah* becomes even plainer in his repeal of the Mosaic permission for divorce (Deut. 24.1). We can see what effect this *abolition* of a regulation laid down by the *Torah* must have had on the people of the time from a Tannaitic statement which in all probability represents a reaction to Mark 10.5: 'Even if someone says: the (whole) *Torah* is from God with the exception of this verse or that, which was not spoken by God, but by Moses, from his own mouth, he has despised the word of Yahweh.'[2] The way in which Jesus strictly forbids his disciples to swear (Matt. 5.33–37) or to apply the *ius talionis* (5.38–42) also amounts to an abolition of precepts of the *Torah*.[3] For the sensibility of the time, however, it was Matt. 5.17 that represented the most pointed devaluation of the *Torah*: the claim to 'add to' the *Torah* was tantamount to a claim to bringing the final revelation (see above, pp. 84ff.). The charge of antinomianism, says Jesus in Matt. 5.17, is not completely without foundation,[4] but it is a misinterpretation; Jesus is not concerned with destroying the law but with filling it to its full eschatological measure.

Jesus' *attitude to the cult* is in line with what has just been said.[5] He reverenced the cult and lived the church year with his people. He wants the temple hallowed (Mark 11.15–18 par., esp. v. 16), because God is present in it (v. 17 quoting Isa. 56.7). In Matt. 23.16–22 Jesus demands with some vigour a reverential attitude towards temple and altar. This positive attitude also extends to sacrificial worship, the practice of which is presupposed in Matt. 5.23f.[6] If Jesus' last meal was a passover meal, he had the passover lamb slaughtered. In Mark 1.44 par. he requires the leper to fulfil the ritual precepts for cleansing. Thus we cannot say with E. Lohmeyer that Jesus fought against the sacrificial cult. Had he done this, the earliest

---

[1] J. Jeremias, *Jesus' Promise to the Nations*, SBT 24, London ²1967, 44–46.

[2] b. Sanh. 99a Bar. (Billerbeck I 805).

[3] On the other hand, Mark 7.15 does not belong to the *logia* which annul the *Torah*, see below, pp. 209f.

[4] This is the meaning of μὴ νομίσητε, as Matt. 10.34 shows.

[5] J. Leipoldt, *Der Gottesdienst der ältesten Kirche jüdisch? griechisch? christlich?*, Leipzig 1937, 10–20; ‡Lohmeyer (one-sided, like a number of Lohmeyer's theories; he depicts Jesus as a sharp adversary of cult and temple).

[6] See above, p. 193 (instructions on prayer).

tradition would hardly have kept silent about it and the early church would hardly have taken part in sacrificial worship (Acts 21.26). Of course, the fulfilling of the commandment to love is more important than any sacrifice.[1] Above all, the temple is on its way to destruction. For contemporary Judaism the temple was eternal; Jesus, on the other hand, announced its collapse. The new temple of God which was to replace the old in the time of salvation was already prepared (Mark 14.58 par.).

(b) Jesus' attitude to oral tradition

Jesus' attitude to the *Halakah* was quite different. He rejected it in a radical way. In particular, he fought against the Rabbinic *Halakah* on the sabbath. This regularly led to conflicts.

To understand Jesus' attitude to the sabbath, it is best to start from a statement of fundamental principle, like Mark 2.27, an antithetic parallelism constructed as a chiasmus:

$$τὸ\ σάββατον\ διὰ\ τὸν\ ἄνθρωπον\ ἐγένετο$$
$$καὶ\ οὐχ\ ὁ\ ἄνθρωπος\ διὰ\ τὸ\ σάββατον.$$

As often (see above, p. 10, no. 18), ἐγένετο is a paraphrase for the divine action. Thus Mark 2.27a means: 'God ordained the sabbath for man's sake.' The *logion* speaks of the creation and indeed observes the sequence of the acts of creation. The sequence of the creation of man on the sixth day and the ordinance of the day of rest on the seventh shows that it was God's will as creator that the day of rest should serve men and bring them blessing. Jesus sees the sabbath commandment, which in early Judaism was held to be a characteristic which distinguished Israel from the world of the nations (Jub. 2.19f.), as a gift of God to men. At the same time, in the second line he turns against the false attitude to the sabbath as a result of which man 'is delivered over to the sabbath' (thus the Rabbinic parallel, see p. 18, n.3 above), i.e. is made a slave of the sabbath. As the sayings of Jesus about the sabbath and his conflicts over it show,[2] the reference here is to the Rabbinic sabbath *Halakah*. This consisted in a detailed casuistic system which categorized all the actions forbidden on the sabbath. The only thing that could release a man from his obligation to observe

---

[1] Mark 12.34: Jesus assents to the words of the scribe in v. 33.

[2] ‡Lohse showed that Jesus' sayings about the sabbath have been subjected less to editorial revision than the gospel stories about the sabbath.

the sabbath *Halakah* was danger to his life; this amelioration, which had developed in the battles of the Maccabaean period, was intended to prevent Jewish soldiers from being delivered into the hands of their enemies on the sabbath day without the possibility of resistance.[1] Jesus, on the other hand, not only tolerated the way in which his disciples rubbed together ears of corn on the sabbath (Mark 2.23 par.), but also healed repeatedly on the sabbath, although there was no question of life being in danger.[2] According to the synoptic tradition, he justified his transgression of the sabbath *Halakah* in various ways. He said, as we saw, that God did not intend the sabbath to be a yoke (Mark 2.27). Or he pointed to David, who (on the sabbath, according to the Midrash)[3] made his way into the sanctuary in time of need and took the showbread for himself and his companions to eat (Mark 2.25f. par.), or to the priests who break the sabbath in the temple (Matt. 12.5), to the performance of circumcision on the sabbath (John 7.22), to the amelioration of sabbath regulations which had been accepted in practice (Matt. 12.11 par.);[4] the decisive point of all these instances, some of which may be secondary, is that they show that the rigorousness of the *Halakah* is contrary to the will of God. The decisive and penetrating justification for the rejection of the sabbath *Halakah* is, however, to be found in Mark 3.4 par.: it prevents the fulfilling of the commandment to love.

Not only does Jesus reject the Rabbinic sabbath *Halakah*; he also rejects the *Halakah* on questions of purity (cf. the story of his clash with the Pharisaic chief priest in the courtyard of the temple),[5] in particular the Pharisaic regulation about the ritual washing of hands before meals (Mark 7.1–8 par.; Luke 11.38).[6]

A reference to Jesus' rejection of the Pharisaic custom of washing hands is to be found in the antithetic parallelism:

[1] I Macc. 2.32 ff.

[2] Mark 3.1–6 par.; Luke 13.10–17; 14.1–6 cf. John 5.9; 9.14 (in the two latter passages the mention of the sabbath seems particularly lame).

[3] B. Murmelstein, 'Jesu Gang durch die Saatfelder', *Angelos* 3, 1930, 111–20.

[4] It was the general practice to help any cattle who had got into difficulty (Matt. 12.11 par. Luke 14.5). Only the Essenes prohibited helping beasts in labour on the sabbath (CD 11.13) or getting even a person out of a cistern on the sabbath (11.16f.).

[5] Ox. Pap. 840, cf. Jeremias, *Unknown Sayings of Jesus*, London ²1964, 47–60; there is also a discussion there of the trustworthiness of the narrative.

[6] For the significance of the extension of this regulation about washing the hands (which originally applied only to the priests) to the laity, see §14 above.

οὐδέν ἐστιν ἔξωθεν τοῦ ἀνθρώπου εἰσπορευόμενον εἰς αὐτὸν
ὃ δύναται κοινῶσαι αὐτόν·
ἀλλὰ τὰ ἐκ τοῦ ἀνθρώπου ἐκπορευόμενά
ἐστιν τὰ κοινοῦντα τὸν ἄνθρωπον

(Mark 7.15 par.)

In this *māšāl*, Jesus contrasts food and words (not thoughts, as was the view of later Hellenistic exegesis, cf. Mark 7.21f.). Food cannot make a man unclean; it is the evil words that he utters which defile him. The first line of this antithetic parallelism scarcely amounts to an abolition of all the regulations of the *Torah* about pure and impure foods (e.g. Lev. 11; Deut. 14.3–21: pure and impure animals), although the *māšāl* already appears to have been understood in this way by Paul;[1] if it had such a scope, Mark 7.15 would be quite isolated among the sayings of Jesus. Rather, the pre-Marcan tradition will be right in referring the *logion* to the Pharisaic demand for the ritual washing of hands: the important thing is not so much to observe the ritual prescriptions of the Rabbis, which have no foundation in the *Torah*, as to watch out for the danger of sinning with tongue.

Why does Jesus reject the *Halakah*? Mark 7.6–8 gives the answer. It is because this lawgiving is entirely the work of men (v. 7) and contradicts the commandment of God (v. 8). It puts casuistry above love, as Jesus shows by means of the *qorbān* casuistry of the Rabbis (7.9–13 par.),[2] which makes it possible for a son out of spite or anger to avoid all obligations to his parents by fictitiously dedicating to the Temple all the support that he owes them. Only in one passage does Jesus seem to adopt a positive attitude to the *Halakah*, Matt. 23.3: πάντα οὖν ὅσα ἐὰν εἴπωσιν (i.e. the scribes) ὑμῖν ποιήσατε καὶ τηρεῖτε, κατὰ δὲ τὰ ἔργα αὐτῶν μὴ ποιεῖτε· λέγουσιν γὰρ καὶ οὐ ποιοῦσιν. But if this saying is genuine at all, it is put in an exaggerated way and is meant ironically. It is certainly not intended to express a wholesale approval of the *Halakah*; rather, the whole stress lies on the second half with its sharp condemnation of the practical attitude of the scribes that gives the lie to all their theology.

But *how reliable is the tradition* about Jesus' attitude to the *Torah* and the *Halakah*? The decisive point to note is that it is unique and unparalleled in the context of

---

[1] Rom. 14.14, referring to the Kyrios Jesus, i.e. to this *logion*, cf. Jeremias, *op. cit.*, 14f.; I Tim. 4.4; Tit. 1.15. The same explanation of the *māšāl* is also to be found at Mark 7.19 (end).

[2] Billerbeck I 711–17.

Judaism. Jesus' audience must really have been nonplussed (Mark 1.22 : ἐξεπλήσσοντο). At best one might produce in comparison a single Rabbinic statement which is astounding in its boldness. R. Johanan ben Zakkai, a contemporary of the apostles (died c. AD 80) ventured to remark confidentially when talking to his pupils about Num. 19.1ff.: 'By your life! It is not the corpse that pollutes or water that purifies. But it is an ordinance of the King of all kings (that must be observed).'[1] Thus Johanan had the boldness to dispute the impurity of corpses. In so doing he went even further than Jesus, for his liberal attitude related to a precept of the Bible, whereas Mark 7.15 probably only has to do with the *Halakah*. But the different thrusts of the remarks should be observed: Johanan means to justify the observance of the regulations for purity; Jesus' purpose is far removed from that. He is concerned with something different: with taking sins of the tongue seriously.

Likewise, there can be no question of deriving the radical statements of Jesus from the primitive community. For the Palestinian-Syrian church did not continue Jesus' radical attitude to the ancient law of God. A typical feature is the way in which the prohibition of divorce is blunted by the clause allowing for exceptions (Matt. 5.32; 19.9). Jesus' sayings were also robbed of their point in other ways. For example, Matt. 5.17 is put in a context in which the stress is transferred from the positive statement (πληρῶσαι) to the negative (καταλῦσαι). In a similar way, Luke 16.17 is given a quite different stress by the context in which Matthew has it (5.18). Originally, as is hinted at by the subordinate clause that the Matthaean tradition aptly adds, ἕως ἂν πάντα γένηται, Jesus had said that the events announced by scripture for the future, especially the sufferings, would be fulfilled to the utmost. In its present context between Matt. 5.17 and 19, however, the *logion* suggests that in an ultra-conservative way Jesus recognized the *Torah* to the last comma. In view of the missionary situation of Jewish Christianity, it is all too understandable that Jesus' sayings should have been robbed of their point in this way in the Jewish-Christian sphere.

Thus it was Jesus himself who shook the foundations of the ancient people of God. His criticism of the *Torah*, coupled with his announcement of the end of the cult; his rejection of the *Halakah* and his claim to announce the final will of God, were the decisive occasion for the action of the leaders of the people against him, finally brought into action by the cleansing of the Temple. They took Jesus to be a false prophet (see above, pp. 77f.). This accusation brought him to the cross.

(ii) The commandment to love as the law of life under the reign of God

Anyone who belongs to the *basileia*, belongs under the divine law of the new creation. What form does that take?

In Mark 12.28–34 par., Jesus describes loving one's neighbour as the greatest commandment after loving God, and in Matt. 7.12 he

---

[1] *Pesiqta de Rab Kahana* 40b; Pesiqta R. 14 (towards the end), cf. Billerbeck I 719.

calls the golden rule the sum of the whole of the New Testament.[1] It was a bold action of Hillel (about 20 BC) when, taking up the Stoic idea of the νόμος ἄγραφος (cf. Rom. 2.14), he remarked to a Gentile who was ready to become a Jew that the golden rule was the sum total of the written law: 'Do not do to another what seems to you to be hurtful; that is the whole *Torah*. All the rest is commentary. Go and learn.'[2] Jesus takes up Hillel, but it is not, of course, a coincidence that he puts the golden rule in a positive way. Whereas Hillel's negative version is content with the warning not to do harm to one's neighbour, Jesus' positive version is a summons to a demonstration of love.[3] God in his great mercy is a model for loving one's neighbour: γίνεσθε οἰκτίρμονες, καθὼς καὶ ὁ πατὴρ ὑμῶν οἰκτίρμων ἐστίν (Luke 6.36).[4]

The parallel in Matthew, which has τέλειος in place of οἰκτίρμων (5.48), may be a Hellenistic elaboration of the *logion*,[5] though we need not for that reason take τέλειος in a perfectionist sense; rather, Matthew will have understood τέλειος in the sense of the Old Testament *tāmīm* ('intact', 'undivided') as the designation of who belongs to God with the totality of his life.[6]

What all these passages say is that love is the law of life under the

[1] In the parallel Luke 6.31, the sentence οὗτος γάρ ἐστιν ὁ νόμος καὶ οἱ προφῆται is missing. It is shown to be original by the way in which it takes up Hillel. In the Lucan version it will have been omitted with an eye to the Gentile-Christian reader.

[2] b. Shab. 31a.

[3] Occasionally the community returns to the negative version (Acts 15.20 D 322 1739 *pc* sa Ir; v. 29 D 614 *al* sa Ir). It is often asserted (e.g. by A. Diehle, *Die goldene Regel. Eine Einführung in die Geschichte der antiken und frühchristlichen Vulgärethik*, Göttingen 1962) that no distinction should be drawn between the content of the negative version of the golden rule in Hillel and that of the positive version given by Jesus, as Judaism was also acquainted with the positive version (e.g. Letter of Aristeas 207). But this is to forget that if we compare Jesus with Judaism, the different Jewish versions of the golden rule in Palestine and the Diaspora should not all be put on the same level; the starting point must be the version current in the circles with which Jesus was acquainted, and that is the negative version of Hillel.

[4] Luke 6.36 is a quotation of a Jewish saying, 'As your Father is merciful (*raḥmān*) in heaven, so should you be merciful on earth' (Targ. Jerus. I Lev. 22.28 par. j. Ber. 9c 21f.; j. Meg. 75c 12; cf. M. Black, *An Aramaic Approach to the Gospels and Acts*[3], Oxford 1967, 181).

[5] R. Schnackenburg, 'Die Vollkommenheit des Christen nach den Evangelien', in: A. Dänhardt (ed.), *Theologisches Jahrbuch 1961*, Leipzig 1961, 67–81: 71f. The parallel just cited in n.4 confirms that *raḥman*/οἰκτίρμων is original.

[6] P. J. Du Plessis, τέλειος. *The Idea of Perfection in the New Testament*, Diss. Theologische Academie Kampen, Kampen 1959.

reign of God.[1] Love is expressed not merely in feelings and words, but also in actions: in the capacity to give (Matt. 5.42), readiness for service (Mark 10.42–45 par. Luke 22.24–27), in works of love of every kind (Matt. 25.31–46, where the enumeration of the six most important works of love is repeated four times), above all in willingness to forgive one's brother. A further characteristic of this love is its *boundlessness*. It does not just extend to social equals; by preference it is for the poor (Luke 14.12–14) with whom Jesus identified himself. They were his brothers (Matt. 25.40 cf. 45).[2] It is not just for those of a like mind, but even for enemies (Matt. 5.44 par. Luke 6.27f.). The parable of the good Samaritan is a particularly impressive demonstration of the boundlessness of love (Luke 10.30–37). It must have been a surprise to his hearers that instead of the usual triad, priest, levite, Israelite, Jesus spoke in the third instance of a Samaritan, one of the hated enemies of the people which were regarded as of mixed origin. Not only this, but he used the Samaritan as a model for the practice of love – a blow in the face for any Jew with self-awareness. Jesus means to say that the selfless help which the crossbreed shows the helpless demonstrates that the commandment to love knows no limits.

This breadth of the commandment to love is without parallel in the history of the time, and to this extent the Fourth Gospel is quite correct in making Jesus describe the commandment to love as the new commandment (John 13.34). Whereas Jewish morality made a man's personal enemy an exception to the commandment to love ('You shall show love to your compatriot (Lev. 19.18), but you are not obliged to do this to your adversary' (Matt. 5.43)),[3] and indeed prohibited the giving of

[1] It is significant that the verb ἀγαπᾶν occurs in the synoptic gospels almost always only in sayings of the Lord; in Mark five times (otherwise only 10.21), in Matthew seven times (never otherwise) and in Luke eleven times (otherwise only 7.5; it also occurs in 11.43 with a different meaning).

[2] The 'brothers' of Jesus in Matt. 25.40, cf. 45, is not a reference to his disciples, but to the poor (cf. Jeremias, *Parables*[2], 207).

[3] Three things should be noted about the popular maxim Matt. 5.43, qualifying Lev. 19.18: all are connected with its language. First, the pair of opposites, πλησίον/ἐχθρός: πλησίον (Lev. 19.18 LXX) is a rendering of *rēaʿ* = 'compatriot'; thus in Matt. 5.43 it is not to be loaded with the meaning 'neighbour', which only Jesus gave it. ἐχθρός means a man's personal enemy, his adversary, and not a national enemy (cf. Luke 6.27f.). Secondly, in a contrasting pair in Semitic languages, the negative part is very often no more than a negation of the positive. This is also the case here: so μισεῖν is accordingly not to be rendered 'hate', but 'not love'. Finally, the Aramaic imperfect which underlies the two Greek futures ἀγαπήσεις-μισήσεις only rarely has a future significance; usually this significance is

214   THE NEW PEOPLE OF GOD

bread to sinners,[1] Jesus requires his disciples to love even those who do them wrong and persecute them. Still more, they are to pray for them (Matt. 5.44). By intercession, the persecutor is brought into the relationship between God and the disciples. There is even a deep gulf between Jesus and the Essenes on the commandment to love. Of all the religious groups, they are nearest to Jesus in the inexorability of their religious fervour and the vividness of their eschatological expectation. But as we have already seen (§14), among them a merciless hate against sinners was regarded as a religious duty.

(*iii*) *The new motive*

Love is the law of life in the new age. That is certain. But to say only this is an inadequate definition of what is new in the eschatological law of God. The commandment to love is already to be found in the Old Testament. Is it simply repeated? Is it refined? Is it transcended? What is there new in the divine law of the *basileia*?

When we speak of the divine law of the *basileia* we think first, rightly, of the six antitheses of the Sermon on the Mount (Matt. 5.21–48).[2] In this collection of sayings of Jesus, the old law of God is contrasted, feature by feature, with the new. New ordinances are given for six areas of life: attitudes to brethren (vv. 21–26), to women (vv. 27–30), to marriage (vv. 31f.); the use of words (vv. 33–37); and behaviour towards enemies, both passive (vv. 38–42) and active (vv. 43–48). In each case the old divine law is transcended.[3] The commandment to love one's enemy represents the climax of these developments. That might lead to the conclusion that the new law of God consisted in a sharpening of the *Torah*. This view is widespread. Even C. H. Dodd, in his excellent book *Gospel and Law*,[4] has not entirely avoided giving the impression that the new thing we are to see in the demands of Jesus is the heroic attitude that he expected of his followers, a heroism of love. This is a true insight. It is beyond dispute that the new law of God sets out to go beyond the old and that

---

virtual. In ἀγαπήσεις the virtual nuance is jussive ('you shall'), in μισήσεις it is permissive ('you need not'). The translation therefore must be: 'You shall love your compatriot (Lev. 19.18) (but) you need not love your adversary'.

[1] μὴ δῷς τοῖς ἁμαρτωλοῖς (Tobit 4.17 of giving bread at a funeral); b. Sanh. 92a (Billerbeck I 205).

[2] See above, pp. 206f.

[3] On the claim that of the six units only three were originally formulated as antitheses, see below, pp. 251–53.

[4] Cambridge 1951.

Jesus expected of his followers a measure of love that can only be described as heroic. Nevertheless, at this point we must disagree. We also find a sharpening of the *Torah* at Qumran, indeed in Essene ethics it almost plays the decisive role.[1] There are also heroic demands in the Rabbinic sayings-material. Indeed these are rare high-points; there are no parallels (and this is hardly a coincidence) to the severest demands of Jesus (e.g. to love one's enemies), and in some parallels we may in fact have a dependence on Jesus.[2] But even if we concede all that, it is indisputable that Judaism, too, knew a sharpening of the *Torah* and a heroic ethic.[3]

There is a problem here. Whereas the new element in the proclamation of Jesus is immediately clear when he speaks about man's relationship with God, the position is rather different in respect of his instructions about the way in which his disciples are to live. We shall achieve clarity only when we recognize that the new element in the demands of Jesus does not lie primarily in the material. What is really new is not the unsurpassable height and strictness of Jesus' demands, but something quite different: the *motive*.

The general ethical attitude of Judaism was dominated by the notion of merit. Not many words need be wasted on it here. The driving force behind action was hope for reward from God. Moral action is an accumulation of merits which are earned by fulfilling the commandments and by voluntary good works (see §14). Nowhere is it as clear as at this point, that Pharisaic Judaism is a *religion of achievement*.[4]

But does not Jesus also speak of reward? Indeed, the number of

---

[1] ‡Braun.

[2] See above, p. 19, n.2. It is extremely probable that the Rabbinic version of the parable of the generous employer (Matt. 20.1–15) which R. Zeʿera delivered *c.* 325 at the burial of his pupil R. Bun ben Ḥijja (j. Ber. 5c 15–23 par. Midr. Eccl. 5.11; Midr. S. of S. 6.2) depends on that of Jesus; for reasons, see Jeremias, *Parables²*, 138f. It would also be possible for Pesiqta R. 24 (124b 12) to be dependent on the gospel tradition: 'R. Simeon b. Laqiš (*c.* AD 250) said: Anyone who commits adultery with his body is called an adulterer; (but in scripture) we find that a man who commits adultery with his eyes is already called an adulterer. What is the biblical basis for this? "And the adulterous eye (thus the Midrash) waits for the twilight" (Job 24.15).'

[3] H. Odeberg, *Pharisaism and Christianity*, St Louis 1964, 25.

[4] Certainly, we find a saying like this: 'R. Meir (*c.* AD 150) said: God spoke to Moses: Be like me; just as I recompense evil with good, so too do you recompense evil with good' (Ex. R.26 on 17.8; cf. also P. Aboth 1.3). Here God is the pattern for the renunciation of vengeance and the overcoming of evil with good. But such sayings are exceptional.

passages in which he does is astonishingly large (cf. Mark 10.28–30 par.; Matt. 5.12 par. 46f.; 6.2, 4, 5, 6, 16b, 18; 25.14–30 par.; Luke 14.12–14).[1] And on occasion the reward is thought of in very realistic terms. To some degree it is pre-existent (Matt. 25.34; 5.12). It is (a common Jewish picture of the time) heavenly capital, waiting for someone to possess it (6.20). Jesus also knows degrees of reward; it can be πολύς (5.12). There is a reward for the prophets, one for the righteous, one for the disciples (10.41f.). He also goes on to speak of ranks in the *basileia*; one person will be ἐλάχιστος, another μέγας (5.19). There is mention of places of honour on the right hand and left hand of Jesus (Mark 10.40). With these sayings, does not the Jewish notion of merit gain an entry into the proclamation of Jesus?[2]

Now we must not overlook the fact that when Jesus talks of merit he takes up the terminology of his time. Religious language is conservative, and in polemical contexts, above all, one has to begin from one's opponents' language. This is especially obvious in Matt. 6.1ff., a clearly polemical context (see p. 177 above). Verses 3f. run: σοῦ δὲ ποιοῦντος ἐλεημοσύνην μὴ γνώτω ἡ ἀριστερά σου τί ποιεῖ ἡ δεξία σου, ὅπως ᾖ σου ἡ ἐλεημοσύνη ἐν τῷ κρυπτῷ· καὶ ὁ πατήρ σου βλέπων ἐν τῷ κρυπτῷ ἀποδώσει σοι. That is, when you give, forget it again; your Father, who sees what is hidden,[3] will reward you. Here it is clear that while Jesus takes up the word 'reward', he in fact presupposes that his disciples have completely detached themselves from striving for a reward; they are to forget the good deeds they have done. We can see what Jesus meant by this forgetting from Matt. 25.37–40, where those who are acquitted at the last judgment are completely surprised by the acts of love as a result of which their acquittal comes. They protest against the recognition that is accorded to them; it is incomprehensible to them. There are no parallels to this feature in contemporary pictures of the last judgment. And no wonder, for this is the abolition of the idea of reward. In fact, Jesus pronounced a radically negative verdict on it (Luke 17.7–10): οὕτως καὶ ὑμεῖς, ὅταν

---

[1] For the problem see ‡Bornkamm; W. Pesch, *Der Lohngedanke in der Lehre Jesu*, Münchener theologische Studien, Historische Abteilung 7. Band, München 1955.

[2] Presumably this offence is the reason why even the pre-Lucan tradition uses the word χάρις at Luke 6.32–34 instead of μισθός (thus v. 35 and Matt. 5.46, if χάρις is not merely a stylistic correction). χάρις = '(claim to) reward' is common: Ecclus. 12.1; Wisdom 3.14; Ignatius, to Polycarp 2.1; I Cor. 9.16 v.l. and often.

[3] ὁ βλέπων ἐν = ḥāmē bᵉ = 'seeing something'. Thus not: 'who can see even in the dark', but: 'who can see even what is hidden'.

ποιήσητε πάντα τὰ διαταχθέντα ὑμῖν, λέγετε ὅτι δοῦλοι ἀχρεῖοί ἐσμεν, ὃ ὠφείλομεν ποιῆσαι πεποιήκαμεν (v. 10). Elsewhere, Jesus also uses the picture of the slave to express the rejection of any claims (Mark 10.44; Matt. 10.24f.; Luke 12.35–38; early tradition in John 13.16; 15.20). Unlike the day-labourer (ἐργάτης), the slave has no claim to a reward; he is completely dependent on his master. If Jesus nevertheless speaks of μισθός, he is not concerned with the claim to a reward but with something quite different: the reality of the divine recompense. This is clear, say, in Matt. 10.42; asking for and receiving a cup of water is such an obvious thing in the east that there is no question of saying thank-you for it; yet God will reward even an everyday action like this. There can be no question of merit here. Merit has an eye to human achievement; recompense looks to God's faithfulness. That God is trustworthy and offers recompense stands assured.

In the sphere of his reign another *motive for action* takes the place of the idea of merit and the claim to reward: gratitude for God's grace. For example, the parable of the treasure in the field deals with the joy of gratitude (Matt. 13.44). An earlier understanding of this parable was that Jesus demanded a readiness to surrender all values. But that is to misunderstand its meaning. The decisive words are rather ἀπὸ τῆς χαρᾶς. The finder of the treasure is overcome with a great joy. In the same way, the reign of God overwhelms the senses, it sweeps men off their feet, and it becomes a matter too obvious for words that a man should surrender everything to gain this treasure (cf. Matt. 13.45f., the precious pearl; Gospel of Thomas 8, the great fish).[1] The same thing is to be found in Matt. 5.44f.: experience of the boundless goodness of God, his unwearying patience with the wicked and the unrighteous, is the source from which love of one's enemies flows. Luke 22.24–27 belongs here, too: the dominating features of the world are the quest for position and power; among the disciples they are a readiness for service. Why? Because the master himself is among the disciples like the servant who waits at table (v. 27). The reference is not just to the model of Jesus, but to the personal experience of the serving love of the master which the disciples have had – are they, then, not able to be able to exercise it? Matt. 18.23–35: because the disciple of Jesus has been forgiven an enormous, incomprehensible debt, he can himself forgive. The divine forgiveness means God's claim on the life of the one who is forgiven.

---

[1] For the parable of the great fish see Jeremias, *Parables*[2], 201.

Luke 7.36 – (47)50 might also be mentioned as a particularly clear example.[1] Of course, v. 47a seems first to give a quite different motive for the love of the woman: 'Therefore I say to you that God has forgiven her her sins, many as they are (inclusive πολλοί),[2] because she has loved much.' Here, apparently, the love of the woman comes first and the forgiveness of God is her reward. But, first, a mere linguistic consideration makes it seem doubtful whether this is what v. 47a means. Like Hebrew, Syriac and Arabic, Aramaic has no word for 'thank' and has to paraphrase it with verbs like 'bless', 'love', 'praise'. In the present pericope the word ἀγαπᾶν clearly also includes the meaning 'be grateful', as v. 42 shows: for τίς οὖν αὐτῶν πλεῖον ἀγαπήσει αὐτόν; can only be meant to say, 'Whose gratitude is the greater?' Similarly, too, v. 47a ὅτι ἠγάπησεν πολύ: means 'For her gratitude is so great.' But in that case it is clear that the forgiveness came first and that the grateful love followed it. That is, secondly, confirmed in v. 47b: ᾧ δὲ ὀλίγον ἀφίεται, ὀλίγον ἀγαπᾷ. Here forgiveness is the primary thing: 'The one who is forgiven only little has only a little grateful love.' Finally, in the short parable of the two debtors, which comes first, it is quite clearly said that the remission of debt is the primary thing (vv. 41–43). That means that ὅτι in v. 47a gives the ground of recognition, but not the real ground: the sentence means: God must have forgiven her much, otherwise she could not love so strongly. It is overflowing gratitude that determines the woman's action.

In conclusion, mention may be made of Luke 19.1–10. Jesus decides to stop in the house of Zacchaeus, the despised chief publican, although many houses belonging to notable men must have been open to him. This graciousness of Jesus overwhelms him and changes his life; he experiences the joy of repentance and responds with the surrender of his possessions, to make good again and to help the poor.

What holds true of repentance (see above, §15) also holds true for the disciples' way of life. The life of being a child of God grows out of thankfulness for God's grace. In the sphere of God's reign there is in the end only this one motive for action: gratitude for forgiveness experienced.

---

[1] While the Lucanisms are very sparse in the pericope, they pile up at the end: v. 48: εἶπεν δέ; v. 48b cf. Luke 5.20, 23; v. 49: ἤρξαντο cf. 5.21; pleonastic καί after the relative pronoun; v. 50: εἶπεν δέ; πρός after a verb of saying; πορεύεσθαι instead of ὑπάγειν, which Luke avoids (cf. Mark 5.34 par. Luke 8.48). That means that vv. 48–50 will be a Lucan addition.

[2] See above, pp. 130f.

(iv) The invididual areas of life

How does the reign of God take concrete form in human life? If we turn to the individual obligations which Jesus lays upon his disciples, it would be a mistake to think straight away of his great demands, a break with the family, even with its dearest members, as can be necessary in individual instances; the renunciation of possessions, which Jesus requires of some of his followers; the suffering of martyrdom. All these sacrifices could be part of discipleship. But the first, most elementary, universal characteristic of the life of faith is something far more simple:

(a) The sanctification of everyday life

It can be seen that the disciples of Jesus belong to the reign of God even from something as ordinary as *a greeting on the street*. There were strict ceremonial rules for greetings,[1] because a greeting represented the communication of peace (cf. Matt. 10.12f.). Who had to give the first greeting was an important question (cf. Matt. 23.7); there were rules as to whom the greeting might be extended and to whom it might not. The Talmud records the conduct of two Rabbis who were so friendly that they even took pains to forestall Gentiles in the market place with the greeting; this attitude was so unusual that as a result the names of these two learned men have been preserved for posterity.[2] For the disciples of Jesus, there are no formalities of this kind. They can be recognized from the fact that they are free from ambition and prejudice and extend the peace of God to every man (Matt. 5.47). Similarly, they show themselves to be children of the *basileia* by the modesty with which at dinner they take a place at the lower end of the table (Luke 14.7–11).

A further way in which belonging to the reign of God is shown in everyday life is in *the disciplined use of words*. Jesus continually stressed this with great emphasis. We have already seen at an earlier point[3] that he passed a particularly sharp judgment on sins of the tongue and believed that they defiled a man. Discipline in the use of words is to be extended to the smallest detail. Jesus warns against the danger of unfriendly words; harmless words of slander like ῥακά ('numskull')

---

[1] Billerbeck I 380–85.
[2] b. Ber. 17a (R. Johanan b. Zakkai, died c. AD 80); b. Gitt. 62a (R. Hisda, died AD 209).
[3] See above, p. 210.

or μωρέ ('idiot') are worse than murder (Matt. 5.21f.).[1] He utterly
forbids any words that condemn a brother or cast suspicion on him,
and expects, rather, that he will be treated by the standard of
mercy (Matt. 7.1f. par. Luke 6.37f.).[2] Finally, Jesus issues a warning
against the danger of untrue words. Matthew 5.33–37 deals with this
question. This passage has often been regarded in the past as giving
instructions against swearing. People have asked whether it prohibits
even an oath in a court of judgment. In fact, however, the section
does not deal with the oath as a legal institution, but, as Matt. 5.37
shows, with truthfulness. The examples Jesus gives here are therefore
not forms of oath used in court, but the oaths with which the oriental
constantly underlines the truthfulness of his remarks in everyday
speech (cf. 23.16–22). Jesus' disciples have no need of this expedient,
because Jesus expects unconditional truth of them: ἔστω δὲ ὁ λόγος
ὑμῶν ναὶ ναί, οὒ οὔ (5.37). Here – at any rate according to the original
meaning, which even Matthew may have misunderstood – there is no
invitation to confirm a statement by doubling the yes or the no. This
emerges clearly from James 5.12. Rather, the doubling of the ναί or
οὔ in Matt. 5.37 will be a Semitism. There is no exact equivalent in
Semitic languages for our distributive 'each', 'on each occasion', 'each
time', and so they have to resort to reiteration to express a distribution.[3] The saying therefore means: 'Always consider your yes a yes
and your no a no.' Each word is to be unconditionally reliable, without
needing any confirmation through an appeal to God. For Jesus'
disciples know that they will soon have to give account to God for
every word that does not accord with the truth (ῥῆμα ἀργόν, Matt.
12.36).[4] God is the God of truth, and therefore the truth is a characteristic of his reign.

[1] For interpretation cf. J. Jeremias, ῥακά, TDNT VI, 1959, 973–76.
[2] Matt. 7.2 is thinking of the idea of the two divine standards 'of judgment' and
'of mercy'.
[3] E.g. Mark 6.7 δύο δύο 'in pairs' (A. J. Wensinck, 'Un groupe d'aramaismes
dans le texte grec des évangiles', Mededeelingen der koninklijke Akademie van Weten-
schappen, Afd. Letterkunde, 81, Amsterdam 1936, 169–80).
[4] E. Stauffer, 'Von jedem unnützen Wort?', Gott und die Götter, Festgabe für
Erich Fascher zum 60. Geburtstag, Berlin 1958, 94–102, would explain ῥῆμα ἀργόν,
'careless word', in terms of the Essene discipline of silence. As a result, he would
dissociate Matt. 12.36 from Jesus and ascribe it to a re-Judaizing of the tradition
about Jesus. It is, however, questionable what ῥῆμα ἀργόν means. The Syriac
translations suggest that the underlying basis for the adjective ἀργός is an Aramaic
bᵉṭīl. Targ. Onk. Ex. 5.9 designates pitgāmīn bᵉṭīlīn (Hebrew dibrē-šāqer) 'deceptive

More than anything else, however, membership of the *basileia* in ordinary everyday life is expressed by *an indefatigable capacity to forgive the brethren* – seven times (Luke 17.4) or, according to the Matthaean parallel, seventy-seven times (Matt. 18.22). The Gospel of the Hebrews will be right in explaining this large number by saying that Jesus is thinking primarily of insults received.[1] The 'brother' who troubles the disciples by calumnies and insults is the compatriot who attacks them because of their message. The readiness to forgive which Jesus expects of his disciples does not mean that guilt is made light of; in Luke 17.3 the express presupposition is that the guilty one realizes his error (but this presupposition is not mentioned in the parallel, Matt. 18.15, 21f.). The decisive thing is that the disciples are a community of men who have themselves experienced forgiveness and therefore can extend it further.

(b) The renunciation of all belongings

A second characteristic: in the sphere of the *basileia*, freedom of possessions prevails.

A *loving understanding of the poor* permeates the gospel accounts: this is so in the parables of the lost coin and the unjust judge, or in the story of the widow's mite. Jesus himself was one of the poor. The tradition records that his parents, too, were poor.[2] Jesus carried no money around with him (Mark 12.15f.). He and his disciples had to be content with five loaves and two fishes to eat for supper (Mark 6.38 par.). Just as the scribes lived on the gifts of their pupils, so did Jesus on the support provided by his followers (Mark 15.41; Luke 8.3). It is without question a correct observation that social distress comes further to the fore with Jesus than it does with the Rabbis.[3] Again and again Jesus appeals for money to be given to the poor (Mark 10.21 par.; Matt. 6.4, 20; Luke 12.33); here we should remember that in the east 'almsgiving' is not a support for beggary, but the dominant form of social help. Jesus takes over the social demands of the prophets. As earlier, in the prophetic preaching, the divine right is the

---

(not corresponding to the truth) words'; in this significance, the expression on the lips of Jesus is incontestable.

[1] J. Jeremias, *Unknown Sayings of Jesus*, London ²1964, 94–96.

[2] According to Luke 2.24 they offered two doves at his birth. The usual offering of a woman after childbirth was a lamb and a dove; only the poor might offer two doves instead (so-called 'poor offering').

[3] Flusser, *Jesus*, 72.

right of the poor.[1] The poor are near to God. For the eschatological reversal of fortunes is beginning to be realized; the poor are becoming rich (Luke 6.20). But within the sphere of the divine law the poor are by no means only the object of love; demands are made on them also. The demand in Matt. 5.40 that the cruel creditor should be given as a pledge overnight not only a coat but the cloak that provides protection from the cold ('go unclothed rather [than offer resistance]') amounts to the total subjection even of the poor to the commandment of the dawning reign of God.[2]

Jesus has a loving attitude to the poor, but his words about *riches* are sharp. Here he is thinking of the brute rich men of the east (Matt. 5.40; 18.28). It is only a fool who builds barns in the face of catastrophe (Luke 12.18), who with an inferno after him rushes into his house to rescue some of his possessions (Luke 17.31; Mark 13.15 par.). Earthly possessions are transitory things, which woodworm and rust devour (Matt. 6.19–21 par.); they are the μαμωνᾶς τῆς ἀδικίας, the Mammon who belongs to this evil world (Luke 16.9, 11).[3] But what is there in possessions that leads to sin? It is the danger of mammonism (Matt. 6.24), the danger that money may take the place of God as a dominant factor. Jesus regards this danger as such a fearful one that he can say that a camel will be able to go through the eye of a needle before a rich man can enter the reign of God (Mark 10.25 par.); i.e. it is – from a human point of view – impossible (v. 27, cf. Luke 6.24f.).

In view of such a harsh verdict on possessions, it seems conceivable that the *logia* in the special Lucan material, according to which Jesus made discipleship quite generally dependent on the renunciation of possessions: πᾶς ἐξ ὑμῶν ὃς οὐκ ἀποτάσσεται πᾶσιν τοῖς ἑαυτοῦ ὑπάρχουσιν, οὐ δύναται εἶναί μου μαθητής (14.33), are well informed. In 12.33a we have, equally unconditionally: πωλήσατε τὰ ὑπάρχοντα ὑμῶν καὶ δότε ἐλεημοσύνην. Now the Marcan tradition also knows the demand to surrender possessions, as Mark 10.21 par. (the rich young man, cf. v. 28 par. Peter: ἡμεῖς ἀφήκαμεν πάντα καὶ ἠκολουθήκαμέν σοι) show; here, however, the sacrifice is limited to those followers of Jesus who accompany him, and that will be the original meaning. For it seems as if Jesus has followers who remain in their homes and probably also retain their possessions; for instance, he allows Zacchaeus to give

---

[1] K. H. Rengstorf, *Das Evangelium nach Lukas*, NTD 3[13], Göttingen 1968, 196.
[2] Cf. ‡Wrege, 76f.
[3] Cf. *hwn hrš‘h* (CD 6.15; 8.5; 19.17) and on this ‡Kosmala, 116.

away only half his possessions (Luke 19.8). There is an analogy to this at Qumran, in that the Essenes apparently demanded the renunciation of all possessions only from those who entered the monastic community of Qumran.[1] Still, the difference between Jesus and the Essenes is not to be overlooked: in Qumran, possessions are given away to the community; Jesus, on the other hand, has no intention of providing common property: rather, those of his disciples who renounce their possessions are to give them to the poor. Anyone who does this places all he has in God's hands; he lays up a treasure for himself in heaven (Matt. 6.20 par.); here the stress is not on the two different kinds of treasure, but on the two different places in which they are kept.

For all the disciples of Jesus, regardless of whether they leave everything and accompany Jesus or remain in their homes, it follows that by experiencing salvation they have been shaken out of the security of their possessions (Luke 19.8). They have experienced a revision of all values. For the one who has found the great treasure, the pearl of great price, all other values have faded in the light of the supreme value. Possessions become ἐλάχιστον, a bagatelle (Luke 16.10). This ἐλάχιστον is contrasted with the ἀληθινόν, the true possession (v. 11), salvation. In this process of the revision of values, earthly possessions become not only ἐλάχιστον, but also ἀλλότριον (v. 12), an alien property the administration of which is entrusted by God. The person who restores it to God through the sacrifice of love is the one who administers it rightly. Jesus does not lay down the law as to whether love should offer everything to the poor (Mark 10.21), whether it should help the needy with a loan (Luke 6.34f.), whether it should give the last farthing for God's cause (Mark 12.41–44), whether it should put its loving care at the disposal of the master and his own (Mark 15.41), or whether it should indulge in apparently useless waste (Mark 14.3–9 par.; Luke 15.23). All this comes under the joy of the time of salvation. It is this that determines the actions of both the poor and those who have possessions.

(c) *The place of the woman*[2]

A third characteristic: in the sphere of the *basileia*, the place of the woman is quite a different one. Here the manner in which belonging to the *basileia* transforms the whole way of life is particularly striking.

---

[1] 1 QS 6.19f., 22, 24f.; Josephus, *Bell.* 2.122.
[2] ‡Leipoldt; Jeremias, *Jerusalem*, 359–76; ‡Rengstorf, 7–52; ‡Isaksson.

Of course, the *logia* about women and marriage raise some difficult problems in relation to the history of the tradition.

Like John the Baptist, Jesus was unmarried. Furthermore, if the puzzling saying in the special Matthaean material about the 'eunuchs for the sake of the kingdom of heaven' (Matt. 19.12) is genuine, and is not a late development related to Rev. 14.1–5, it seems to hint that he also commended the renunciation of marriage at least to some of his followers. The justification for this sacrifice, διὰ τὴν βασιλείαν τῶν οὐρανῶν, should be compared with Luke 14.26: εἴ τις ἔρχεται πρός με καὶ οὐ μισεῖ τὸν πατέρα αὐτοῦ καὶ τὴν μητέρα καὶ τὴν γυναῖκα καὶ τὰ τέκνα . . . οὐ δύναται εἶναί μου μαθητής (where the negatived μισεῖν is a Semitic-type substitute for the comparative 'love more than').[1] Following Jesus comes before all ties of family (Matt. 10.37 and Luke 14.26 agree in this), even the tie of marriage (thus only Luke 14.26).[2] However, following Jesus could mean a hard surrender not only for the disciple himself but also for his family: if the father of the house decided to enter Jesus' company, his wife and children would have no choice but to return to her parents' house, although that was felt to be a stigma.

The *prohibition against discharging a wife* (we ought to put it this way, rather than to speak of a prohibition of 'divorce', because in Judaism the right to break up a marriage lay one-sidedly with the husband)[3] shows how wrong it would be to see all this as a low estimate of marriage. We may regard this prohibition (Mark 10.11f.; Matt. 5.32; 19.9; Luke 16.18) as genuine, quite apart from I Cor. 7.10f., because Jesus ventures to set himself up against the *Torah* on this point (see above, p. 207). For the Old Testament permits the discharge of a wife (Deut. 24.1); Judaism followed this practice. The only dispute between Hillel and Shammai (*c.* BC 20) and their pupils was over the grounds on which discharge was permissible. The dispute between the two scribes centred on the interpretation of the phrase *'erwat dābār* (Deut. 24.1: 'When a man takes a wife and marries her, if then she finds no favour in his eyes because he has

[1] The parallel Matt. 10.37 rightly translates ὁ φιλῶν . . . ὑπὲρ ἐμέ. This is a translation variant: Luke 14.26 οὐ μισεῖ is the literal rendering in Greek, Matt. 10.37 ὁ φιλῶν ὑπέρ follows the sense.

[2] καὶ τὴν γυναῖκα could be an expansion (so Luke 18.29). But this conclusion is uncertain, because the Matthaean and Lucan versions are independent of each other in literary terms.

[3] Only in a very few, well defined exceptions could a woman achieve the dissolution of her marriage, and then only by way of the court (Billerbeck I 318f.).

found some *'erwat dābār* in her, and he writes her a bill of divorcement and puts it in her hand and sends her out of his house'). The Shammaites translated – quite rightly – the disputed words *'erwat dābār* as 'something shameful' and interpreted them in terms of a sexual lapse; the Hillelites separated the two words 'shameful (and any other) thing'[1] and understood by 'thing' e.g. 'if she has let his dinner burn'.[2] The point to note is that we know from Philo[3] and Josephus[4] that the lax Hillelite view determined actual practice. For Jesus' disciples, on the other hand, marriage is indissoluble, because it is ordained by God. He wastes no time over the question of the stricter or the more broad-minded interpretation of Deut. 24.1, but declares apodeictically: ὃ οὖν ὁ θεὸς συνέζευξεν, ἄνθρωπος μὴ χωριζέτω (Mark 10.9). Here we have an explicit negative answer to the question of the dissolution of marriage, with no possibility of evasion. God joins the wedded couple together, for ever and ever,[5] and does not allow men to put apart what he has made one. The saying is given a special point because it is not an accentuation of the *Torah* but an annulling of it.

This apodeictic prohibition (Mark 10.9) was later made into a *legal regulation* with two members, formulated in casuistic terms. We can follow the stages in its development fairly accurately: from Matt. 5.32, without the qualification παρεκτὸς λόγου πορνείας (prohibition of the discharge of the wife and the wife's remarriage), *via* I Cor. 7.10f. (prohibition of divorce by the wife added in view of the Hellenistic legal situation) and vv. 12–16 (exception made for mixed marriages), Luke 16.18 and Mark 10.11f. (prohibition of remarriage for both parties) to Matt. 5.32 and 19.9 (the exception: πορνεία). The development of the legal principle shows to what extent Jesus' prohibition occupied the community.

Another problem arises here. According to Mark 10.6–8 par., in his challenge to Deut. 24.1, Jesus appealed to the creation story (Gen. 1.27; 2.24); this sounds credible, because Jesus' provocative opposition to the *Torah* required some basis. In referring to the creation story, one might conclude, Jesus restores to force God's will for paradise as the divine law of the new age, as he declares that marriage is indissoluble. There is, however, a certain tension between this passage and Mark 12.18–27. In the latter passage Jesus goes against the usual conception of man's final state as an exalted form of earthly existence by saying that in the *basileia*, no more marriages will be made. For with the ending of death, marriage will have lost its purpose. This pericope also has an authentic ring, because what it says about the hope of the resurrection still betrays no influence from the Easter experience.[6] If both Mark 10.9 and Mark 12.25 are valid, then our conclusion must be that the prohibition against the dissolution of marriage holds only for the time before the full revelation of the *basileia*, as after that there will be no more marriages.

Hand in hand with the prohibition against discharging a wife

---

[1] b. Gitt. 90a Bar.   [2] Gitt. 9.10.   [3] *De spec. leg.* III 30.   [4] *Antt.* 4.253.
[5] On συνέζευξεν cf. Billerbeck I 803f.   [6] See p. 184, n.3 above.

goes an alteration in the *fundamental attitude* to the place of women expressed in the sayings of Jesus. A woman, says Josephus, thus expressing the typical oriental view, 'is in every respect of less worth than a man'.[1] This also applies to her religious status. In the Temple, a woman was allowed access only as far as the Court of the Women. Her religious obligations were on the same level as those of a slave; for example, she did not have to pray the *Sh*^e*ma*^c morning and evening, because like a slave she was not mistress of her own time.[2] Even so, the moral level in Judaism in the time of Jesus was considerably higher than that in the rest of the Levant.

Judaism sought to safeguard morality by keeping women as far removed as possible from the public eye. In the city, at any rate in better situated circles, women were confined to the house; if a woman left it, her plaited coiffure made her features virtually unrecognizable. In the country, too, she retreated right behind her husband. In such circumstances, it is amazing that the gospel accounts contain so many stories about meetings of Jesus with women; this is particularly true of the Lucan special material. These stories show that Jesus felt himself called to help everyone, including women (Luke 7.36–50; Mark 1.31 par., etc.). For in the family of God, in the *basileia*, there is no devaluation of the woman (Mark 3.34f. par.). This is a mark of the time of salvation, as Joel 3.1–5 (quot. Acts 2.17–21) shows. Something quite remarkable is happening here, for Jesus is dissociating himself from the practice of keeping women in seclusion. 'Do not speak much with a woman (on the street)', says an old Rabbinic proverb, and a later addition was that this also applied in the case of a man's own wife.[3] According to John, Jesus talks openly with a woman, so that his disciples are amazed (4.27). Women are among his hearers (Luke 11.27f.). He is friendly with the sisters Mary and Martha (Luke 10.38–42). Women follow him and support him (Mark 15.40f. par.; Luke 8.1–3).[4] This must have caused quite a sensation; Marcion claims that these things were also brought as charges against Jesus at his trial.[5] The result of Jesus' attitude was that women thronged to

---

[1] *Contra Apionem* 2.201.

[2] J. Jeremias, 'Daily Prayer in the Life of Jesus and the Primitive Church', *The Prayers of Jesus*, SBT II 6, London 1967, 66–81: 71.

[3] P. Aboth 1.5 (the author is R. Jose ben Johanan of Jerusalem, *c.* 150 BC).

[4] Luke 8.1–3 displays Lucan characteristics in almost every word, but the proper names derive from early tradition.

[5] Variant on Luke 23.2: καὶ ἀποστρέφοντα τὰς γυναῖκας καὶ τὰ τέκνα.

him; as the passion narrative shows, they remained faithful to him to a degree of which the disciples were not capable.

How was this break with custom possible? Matt. 5.28 provides the answer. The world of Jesus set out to protect women by secluding them, believing that sexual desire was uncontrollable. Jesus accepts women into the group of disciples because he expects his disciples to control their desires.[1] The old age is dominated by desires, from which a man protects himself as best he can. In the new age, purity rules, and disciplines even a man's gaze: μακάριοι οἱ καθαροὶ τῇ καρδίᾳ (Matt. 5.8). Nowhere in the social sphere does the new life make so striking an incursion into everyday affairs as here.

The considerable antiquity of these traditions can be seen from their revolutionary character. Even Paul will have known them; this is the only possible explanation of the maxim in Gal. 3.28, that in Christ Jesus there is no difference between male and female which is quite extraordinary for one who was born a Jew.

(d) Children

Closely connected with the new position which Jesus accords to women in the sphere of the approaching *basileia* is a new view of children. In the world of Jesus, children, like women, were counted as things of little value.[2] Jesus, on the other hand, not only promises salvation to children as such (Mark 10.14),[3] but also declares that it is only possible for a man to enter the *basileia* if he becomes a child again (Matt. 18.3).[4] As a result, he brings children nearer to God than adults. Sayings like this cannot be derived either from contemporary literature or from the community, which shared the

---

[1] K. Bornhäuser, *Die Bergpredigt*, BFCT II 7, Gütersloh 1923, 70–79.

[2] The status of the child under religious law is paraphrased by the constantly recurring triad 'deaf and dumb, weak-minded, under age' (Erub. 3.2; Shek. 1.3; Sukk. 2.8; 3.10; R. Sh. 3.8; Meg. 2.4; Gitt. 2.5; 5.8; B.K. 4.4; 6.2, 4 etc.). This is extended in Ter. 1.1 to the Gentiles, in Gitt. 2.5 to the blind and the Gentiles, in Men. 9.8 to the blind, the Gentiles, slaves, agents, women, Hag. 1.1 to the deformed, hermaphrodites, women, slaves, lame, blind, sick, old, crippled. The three mentioned in the triad have in common the fact that they are not in full possession of their intellectual powers (in the case of the deaf and dumb this was presupposed *eo ipso*).

[3] τῶν τοιούτων (Mark 10.14) = 'those in this condition', 'simply states that children have a share in the Kingdom of God, and the τῶν τοιούτων in v. 14 ought not to be interpreted, as has been customary ever since Origen, in the light of v. 15' (Bultmann, *Synoptic Tradition*, 32).

[4] See above, pp. 154–6.

patriarchal attitude of its milieu; rather, they belong at the heart of Jesus' message (see §12 above).

(e) Politics

That a man belongs to the reign of God also determines his political views. First, we must ask about Jesus' own position. Our starting point is the report that he died on the cross. This may be taken to be historically certain. It shows that he was sentenced to death by the Roman governor as a rebel. Now a great deal depends on whether we regard the Jewish charges that Jesus strove for political power (Mark 15.2 par., 26 par.) and incited people to rebellion and to refusal to pay tax to the occupying power (Luke 23.2b: κωλύοντα φόρους Καίσαρι διδόναι) as credible, or whether we follow the Christian tradition in seeing them as calumny. In the first instance, Jesus is brought into close proximity to the Zealot movement, and courses of action which he initiated, especially the entry into Jerusalem and the occupation of the temple gates by his followers,[1] are given a marked political stamp.[2] Of course, this view leads to considerable difficulties.

For instance, if we credit Jesus with inciting people to refuse to pay tax, we have to regard Mark 12.13–17 par. as inauthentic, as here Jesus rejects any such incitement. The origin of the pericope has to be explained, for example, as the result of a wish to demonstrate that Christianity is politically innocuous. But it is not as simple as that to get rid of the episode of the tribute-money, not only because it is already echoed in Rom. 13.7, i.e. about AD 55, but above all because it is Mark 12.13–17 rather than Luke 23.2b that fits the general pattern of the proclamation of Jesus. We need only think of the quite unusual absence of all nationalism and particularism in Jesus' proclamation of the basileia; of the avoidance of anything that could be wrongly interpreted in a political sense like the titles Messiah and Son of David (see pp. 258f.) or the symbolic language of the holy war (unlike Qumran); of the announcement of the destruction of the Temple and the judgment on Israel (see pp. 125f.); of the repudiation of vengeance on the Gentiles (see pp. 206f.) and the opening of the basileia to the nations (see pp. 245–47); of the rejection of usurping the ius gladii ([John] 7.53ff.); of the brusque refusal to inflame anti-Roman feelings

[1] The latter is to be inferred from Mark 11.16.

[2] ‡Brandon has recently attempted to justify the thesis that although Jesus was no 'recognized Zealot leader' (355), he belonged to the resistance movement against Rome. Of course, he has to pay a high price: the assertion that the gospels tendentiously suppressed the political character of Jesus' ministry in their account of it presupposes that 'we have no certain record of Jesus' teaching' (336).

[3] It becomes clear that [John] 7.53–8.11 is about the ius gladii once we recognize that the scene takes place after judgment has been passed. This is indicated not only by the way in which the group is accompanied by scribes and Pharisees (v. 3), but also by the formulation of the question in v. 5. The concern is not with the degree

(Luke 13.1–5); of the unprejudiced attitude towards the Samaritans; of the harsh criticism of worldly authorities (Mark 10.42 par. Luke 22.25; cf. 13.32); of the demand for non-violence and refraining from rebellion (Matt. 5.38–42 par. Luke 6.29f.). It is the way in which a general picture can thus be built up that makes it impossible to argue that all these features are tendentious falsifications. Nor does the attitude of the Palestinian church, which fled to Pella in the first rebellion[1] and was fanatically persecuted by Bar Kochba in the second,[2] suggest that Jesus should be counted among the Zealots. Indeed, the issue should be put even more sharply: anyone who does that has failed to understand Jesus.

According to Mark 12.13–17 par., Jesus repudiated any suggestion that taxes should be withheld from the Roman occupying forces. In so doing, he declared himself to be against the revolution. Jesus gave no reasons for his repudiation; however, they may be inferred from the situation. Jesus' interlocutors wanted to force him to take the Zealot line. Zealotism[3] saw the Roman state as a force hostile to God; it was a religious obligation to bring about its downfall and so establish the reign of God. There can only be one reason for Jesus' opposition to the Zealots' call for revolution and his repudiation of it: he believed the Zealot attitude to be disobedience to God's ordering of the world. If God grants the pagan state authority for a short period, that is his will. He alone will decide the time when he will put an end to it and establish his reign, and he knows what will be the right time. The parable of the seed that grows by itself (Mark 4.26–29), which bids men wait patiently for God's hour, may also be aimed against the Zealots. The same also applies to the warning against false prophets (Mark 13.22 par. etc.).[4]

(f) Work

Here we come across a remarkable fact. While Jesus depicts men

---

of the penalty, which is fixed, but with the way in which it is to be carried out. A final pointer is given by v. 7 (βαλέτω λίθον). That means that the question in v. 5 contains a tempting invitation to Jesus to carry out the stoning and in so doing issue a summons to the usurping of the *ius gladii*; cf. J. Jeremias, 'Zur Geschichtlichkeit des Verhörs Jesu vor dem Hohen Rat', ZNW 43, 1950/51, 145–50: 148f. U. Becker, *Jesus und die Ehebrecherin*, BZNW 28, Berlin 1963, 173f., has shown that authentic tradition may lie behind the episode.

[1] Eusebius, H.E. III 5.3. Christianity in Pella: Aristo of Pella composed *c.* 140 the disputation 'Dialogue between Jason and Papiscus on Christ' (Origen, *c. Celsum* 4.52).

[2] Justin, *Apol.* I 31.6 = Eusebius, H.E. IV 8.4.

[3] ‡Hengel. [4] See pp. 128, 242f. above.

and women at their daily work in his parables and metaphors, work appears only once in his instructions to the disciples. There Jesus forbids them to work. At any rate, that is the meaning of Matt. 6.25 par. Luke 12.22, where μεριμνᾶν does not mean anxious thought, but work in order to earn enough to supply bodily needs. This is confirmed by I Cor. 9.14. The verse therefore means, 'Do not take up work to secure food and clothing'. This is very strange. We shall see the explanation for it in §20.

When we consider the individual demands made by Jesus, it is striking how *incomplete* they are. Jesus does not give instructions for all spheres of life; he does not offer a moral theology or a code of behaviour. Rather, his demands give symptoms, signs, examples of what happens when the reign of God breaks into a world that is still in the power of sin, death and the devil. The *basileia* lays claim to the whole of life. Jesus uses illustrations to demonstrate the appearance of the new life. His disciples are to apply them to every other aspect of their life. They themselves are to be signs of the reign of God, signs that something has happened. Their whole life is to witness to the world that the reign of God has dawned. Through their life, rooted and grounded in the reign of God, the miracle of discipleship, the victory of the *basileia*, is to be manifested (Matt. 5.16).

One question remains at the end. Can the demands of the eschatological law of God as proclaimed by Jesus really be fulfilled? Who can keep every word and every glance pure? Who can love his enemy as Matt. 5.43–48 demands? Even the disciples put this question. That is shown by the saying about the city on the hill (Matt. 5.14).

This saying of Jesus is an answer to the question whether his demands can be fulfilled, as this question grew out of the experience of weakness, inconstancy, lack of faith. Jesus dismisses the hesitations of his disciples. As G. von Rad has shown,[1] Jesus is not speaking of any city on a hill; the city on the hill is the eschatological city of God. Its light shines in the darkness; it is impossible that it should remain hidden. Jesus' disciples belong to it. It is quite inconceivable that this should not also be manifested in their everyday life without the need for strenuous effort. The light of the city of God shines by itself.

[1] ‡von Rad.

§ 20 · SENDING OUT THE MESSENGERS

K.-H. Rengstorf, ἀποστέλλω κτλ, *TDNT* I, 1964, 398–447; J. Jeremias, 'Paarweise Sendung im Neuen Testament', in: A. J. B. Higgins (ed.), *New Testament Essays. Studies in Memory of T. W. Manson*, Manchester 1959, 136–143 = Jeremias, *Abba*, 132–39; B. Rigaux, 'Die "Zwölf" in Geschichte und Kerygma', in: H. Ristow and K. Matthiae (eds.), *Der historische Jesus und der kerygmatische Christus*, Berlin 1960, 468–86.

The reign of God manifests itself through the proclamation of the good news in words and actions. Jesus does not accomplish this proclamation by himself, but sets beside himself the messengers of the gospel.

(*i*) *The sources*

Some introductory remarks must be made here about two groups of sources which relate to the sending of the messengers. The groups comprise on the one hand the words spoken to the messengers, and on the other hand lists of their names.

All three synoptic gospels have *accounts of the sending out of messengers*. That in Mark appears in 6.7–13. In Luke, messengers are sent out twice: in 9.1–6 the twelve (following Mark 6.7–13) and in 10.1–16 the seventy (this account is based on *logia* material). Matthew has combined the Marcan version of the sending out of the messengers with the *logia* version in 9.36–11.1 and made them into a long mission discourse, which presumably had its *Sitz im Leben* in the instruction of early Christian missionaries. If we look for the material common to the four mission discourses, we find that their basic nucleus is a short instruction that was current in two parallel versions, a Marcan version and a *logia* version. This 'original instruction', if it may be so described, is contained in Mark 6.8–11; Luke 10.4–11; Matt. 10.9–14. It contained, first, instructions stating that no provisions are to be made for the journey (instead, the messengers are to rely completely on hospitality), and secondly, instructions for their actions both in the houses which receive them and also towards places which may refuse to receive them. Here the *logia* version proves to be the more original, as is shown, for example, by Luke 10.5f. par.: there the εἰρήνη is represented as a power which embraces a house or returns to its bearer. The considerable antiquity of the 'original instruction' can be seen from the way in which Paul knows an essential part of it, the prohibition against working for a living during service as a messenger (I Cor. 9.14). Both language and conceptions show quite clearly that it is *Palestinian*.[1] The complete absence of christology in the proclamation with which the messengers are entrusted makes it very probable that here we have a piece of pre-Easter tradition.

The *names of the messengers* are enumerated in lists in four passages: Mark 3.16–19; Matt. 10.2–4; Luke 6.14–16; Acts 1.13. The four catalogues agree in giving the number twelve,[2] and Matt. 19.28 par., which promises that the disciples will sit on twelve thrones, provides important support.[3] The lists agree in eleven of the twelve names and differ over the twelfth: whereas Mark and Matthew mention a Thaddaeus (in tenth place),[4] Luke and Acts have a Judas, son of James (in eleventh place). The reason for this variation in the lists between Thaddaeus and Judas, son of James, might simply be a slip of the memory, which would not be surprising with so many names. But perhaps there is another explanation of the discrepancy. In seven instances the lists give second names, all, as far as can be determined, Aramaic.[5] Second names were extraordinarily widespread in the Judaism of the time because they were indispensable for distinguishing between the numerous people who bore the same name. Now it is illuminating to see who in the lists of messengers is given a second name. If we leave aside the fact that Matthew is designated 'the publican' (Matt. 10.3: though only in the first gospel), we find that *only* those disciples whose names appear twice in the lists are given a second name. In the group of twelve, there were six disciples each of whom had a namesake: there were two disciples called Simon, two called James and (according to Luke) two called Judas; this last fact is expressly confirmed by John 14.22 (᾽Ιούδας, οὐχ ὁ

[1] See e.g. the personification of peace, the shaking off of the dust, etc.

[2] In Acts 1.13 Judas Iscariot is rightly absent.

[3] It makes no material difference that in the parallel Luke 22.29f. the number twelve is only mentioned in connection with the tribes of Israel and is not repeated in connection with the thrones. As Luke avoids repeating words wherever possible, this may just be an abbreviation.

[4] The variant Λεββαῖος, which appears in some branches of the tradition (cf. the apparatus on Mark 3.18 and Matt. 10.3) is not original, but an attempt to bring the Levi of Mark 2.14 into the list.

[5] The designation of the sons of Zebedee as 'sons of thunder' (i.e. probably 'revolutionaries', see above, p. 72, n.1) by Jesus (Mark 3.17) is not included, as it is not an individual nickname, but a kind of collective.

'Ἰσκαριώτης). In these six cases another name was essential as a distinguishing feature. Now in the primitive church, the name Judas would not, of course, sound very well. It would be quite understandable if after Easter the second Judas was known in the community by his second name, which besides his patronymic would distinguish him from Judas Iscariot. The Lucan tradition would then have kept the proper name and the Marcan tradition the nickname of the second Judas: *Taddai* (Θεόδοτος/Θαδδαῖος).[1] This is only a supposition, but it is not completely groundless.

How historical was the call and sending out of the twelve by Jesus? J. Wellhausen, following up a suggestion put forward by Schleiermacher, advanced the theory that the twelve did not belong to the story of Jesus,[2] but were rather 'the representatives of the earliest community';[3] the projection of their mission back from the risen Christ[4] to the historical Jesus was a 'prolepsis'.[5] He found many followers. The reasons he gives are extraordinarily arbitrary apodeictic assertions: Jesus did not 'initiate his disciples or a selection of them' into the proclamation of the gospel.[6] 'He did not teach them, nor did he say anything to them that he did not say to the people; he worked and suffered before their eyes and stimulated them by so doing to work and to suffer, too.'[7] One asks in amazement how Wellhausen knows all this. His scepticism is to be opposed on two grounds. First, the twelve already appear in the early confession of faith contained in I Cor. 15.5: εἶτα τοῖς δώδεκα. The nucleus of this early confession goes back to a Semitic text;[8] Paul says that it was handed on to him (v. 3), and this is most likely to have taken place at his conversion, i.e. quite a short time after Jesus' death. We can see how stereotyped a term 'the twelve' had become, even in this earliest period, from the way in which the term was used even though at the time of the

---

[1] The second name could be, but did not have to be, a variation on the proper name: cf. on the one hand *Šā'ūl*, Greek form Σαῦλος, Latinized Παῦλος; on the other Joseph, Aramaic surname *bar Šabbā* (Sunday's child), Latin surname *Justus* (Acts 1.23).

[2] *Einleitung in die ersten drei Evangelien*[2], Berlin 1911, 141.

[3] *Op. cit.*, 144.   [4] Matt. 28.16ff.; Luke 24.44ff.; John 20.21–23.

[5] *Op. cit.*, 141.   [6] *Ibid.*   [7] *Ibid.*

[8] J. Jeremias, *Eucharistic Words*[2], 102f.; 'Artikelloses Χριστός. Zur Ursprache von I Cor. 15, 3b–5', *ZNW* 57, 1966, 211–15; 'Nochmals: Artikelloses Χριστός in I Cor. 15, 3', *ZNW* 60, 1969, 214–19. H. Conzelmann, *Der erste Brief an die Korinther*, MeyerK V, Göttingen 1969, 298f., differs. Like anarthrous χριστός, the phrase ποιεῖν (τοὺς) δώδεκα (Mark 3.14, 16) is also a Semitism.

christophany to the 'twelve', Judas was no longer alive. Despite this, it was not said that 'he appeared to the eleven', because the term 'the twelve' was not a purely numerical designation of twelve individual personalities, but signified the group of the representatives of the twelve tribes in the end time. Secondly, according to all three synoptic lists, the traitor Judas also belonged to the group of the twelve.[1] We can see from the gospels how difficult the community found this tradition. It was asked whether Jesus had made a mistake in appointing Judas as a messenger, and recourse was had to the explanation that Jesus knew that Judas was going to betray him (Matt. 26.25; John 6.64, 70f.; 13.11, 27; 17.12), indeed that he knew right from the beginning (John 6.64). This makeshift explanation comes to grief on Matt. 19.28 par. alone. Who could have artificially created this difficulty? Who could have arrived at the absurd idea that the traitor shared in the promise that he would sit on one of the thrones of glory, judging the twelve tribes of Israel, if Judas had not in fact belonged to the group of messengers? No one has succeeded in giving a plausible answer.

However the divergence in one of the names is to be explained, the mention of the traitor in all three synoptic lists of the twelve[2] shows unambiguously that the tradition of the group of twelve dates from before Easter.

(ii) Instructions, commission and authority

That Jesus chose precisely twelve men to serve as messengers indicates that he had a particular programme in mind. The significance of symbolic numbers in the biblical world is well-known. The *twelve messengers* correspond to the twelve tribes of Israel (Matt. 19.28 par. Luke 22.29f.);[3] they represent the eschatological community of salvation. That they are sent to Israel corresponds to the tradition contained in Matt. 10.5f., both the language and style of which are old.[4] According to these verses, Jesus expressly instructed his messengers to go neither to Gentiles nor to Samaritans, but to limit themselves to Israel. Matt. 10.23b (ἀμὴν γὰρ λέγω ὑμῖν, οὐ μὴ τελέσητε

---

[1] See above, p. 232, n. 2.   [2] *Ibid.*

[3] In Luke 10.1 the number is expanded to seventy (seventy-two), with which Gen. 10 (seventy nations of the world) is to be compared. Ex. 24.1; Num. 11.16 has hardly been an influence.

[4] J. Jeremias, *Jesus' Promise to the Nations*, SBT 24, [2]1967, 19f.

τὰς πόλεις τοῦ Ἰσραὴλ ἕως ἔλθῃ ὁ υἱὸς τοῦ ἀνθρώπου) also belongs here; for if, as we have attempted to demonstrate, this *logion* refers to the persecution of the messengers as they fulfil the task on which they have been sent,[1] it too presupposes that the commission has been limited to Israel.

Now in interpreting the number twelve we should not forget that the established view[2] at the time of Jesus was that there were only two and a half tribes left; Judah, Benjamin and half Levi. The nine and a half other tribes were held to have been lost after the fall of the Northern kingdom (722 BC); only in the time of salvation would God lead them back over the legendary river Sambation and thus restore the people of the twelve tribes. Thus the fact that Jesus' disciples number twelve does not mean that salvation is to be limited, in a particularistic way, to the empirical Jewish people; on the contrary, it announces the establishment of the *eschatological people of God* to which, as we shall see,[3] Jesus expected that even the Gentiles would attach themselves.

Mark sets out the purpose of Jesus in calling the twelve in the form of two ἵνα clauses: καὶ ἐποίησεν δώδεκα ἵνα ὦσιν μετ᾽ αὐτοῦ καὶ ἵνα ἀποστέλλῃ αὐτοὺς κηρύσσειν καὶ ἔχειν ἐξουσίαν ἐκβάλλειν τὰ δαιμόνια (3.14f.). That the second of these two functions, accompanying Jesus and serving as a messenger (though they are not completely exclusive), is primary can be seen from an early Aramaic tradition that Jesus sent out the twelve as his messengers δύο δύο (Mark 6.7; on which cf. p. 220, n.3). Luke 10.1 (ἀνὰ δύο) and the structure of the lists of messengers is in agreement.[4] To send out messengers in pairs was a regular custom in Judaism, though it cannot be demonstrated as early as the Old Testament.[5] It had a twofold significance: first, it was to protect the messengers; on lonely and dangerous roads it is good for the messenger to have someone at his side. On the other hand, sending messengers in pairs was an application of the legal clause of Deut. 17.6; 19.15, which originally applied to judicial proceedings: only statements on which two witnesses agree are trustworthy. In the same way, the one of the two who is the spokesman (cf. Acts 14.12 ὁ ἡγούμενος τοῦ λόγου) is to have his yoke-fellow by him to confirm the message.

---

[1] *Op. cit.*, 20f.; see above, p. 135f.   [2] *Op. cit.*, 21.   [3] See below, 245–47.

[4] All four lists have the two pairs of brothers Peter/Andrew, James/John as the first four names; all four lists have the same names in first, fifth and ninth place and thus fall into three tetrads; Matthew and Acts divide the tetrads each into two pairs.

[5] The material is collected in ‡Jeremias, 'Paarweise Sendung'.

The 'original instruction' begins with the *Spartan prohibition* against taking along even the barest necessities: the messengers are to have no bread, no money; they are even to renounce cloaks,[1] indispensable for spending a night in the open air (Mark 6.8f.; Matt. 10.9f.; Luke 9.3; 10.4). In addition, the special Lucan tradition forbids them to seek protection by joining caravans.[2] Matt. 6.25–34 par. Luke 12.22–31 adds one further item to these harsh instructions; we can see how sharp it is once we recognize that in this section μεριμνᾶν does not mean 'take anxious thought for', but 'make anxious efforts for' (cf. Matt. 6.27 par.).[3] Therefore Matt. 6.25 par. means: 'Do not toil (to earn money) for food and clothing.' Thus Jesus prohibits involvement in paid labour.

It would, however, be a fundamental misunderstanding of this prohibition to interpret it in general terms. Rather, as is confirmed by Paul, who already knows it, it applies only to the messengers (I Cor. 9.14), and therefore must have been spoken when they were sent out. Jesus wants the messengers to concentrate exclusively on their task. What he forbids is not work in general, but double work. 'And what if we are hungry and freeze?', ask the messengers. Jesus replies with a jest:[4] Have you ever seen Mr Raven sowing, harnessing up the plough, reaping and taking the crop into the barn? Or Mrs Anemone picking up the spindle and then sitting down at the loom? You have so little faith! Take God seriously! He knows what you need. You are not just God's day-labourers, to whom he will give food day by day (ἄξιος . . . ὁ ἐργάτης τῆς τροφῆς αὐτοῦ Matt. 10.10) and whose clothing he will provide (αυτο[ς δ]ωσει υμειν το ενδυμα υμων);[5] you are his children (Matt. 6.32 par.). Do not worry! He will see that hospitable houses are open to you.

Why the harshness? Nothing is to hold the messengers up, not

---

[1] The prohibition of δύο χιτῶνες (Mark 6.9; Matt. 10.10; Luke 9.3) probably does not refer to taking along a reserve garment; it means: do not take two articles of clothing, robe and cloak (J. Wellhausen, *Das Evangelium Marci übersetzt und erklärt*², Berlin 1909, 44).

[2] This may be the way in which μηδένα κατὰ τὴν ὁδὸν ἀσπάσησθε (Luke 10.4) should be understood (see p. 133 above). The tradition has sharpened this prohibition still further. Whereas Mark allows just the staff (to ward off animals) and sandals (6.8f.), the side-references prohibit both (Matt. 10.10; Luke 9.3; 10.4).

[3] *Parables*², 214.   [4] *Op. cit.*, 214f.

[5] Pap. Ox. 655. The sentence is missing in the Coptic text of the Gospel of Thomas 36; the version in Pap. Ox. 655 may, however, be the earlier. Cf. Jeremias, *Unknown Sayings of Jesus*, London ²1964, 97f.

even 'greeting on the road' (Luke 10.4),[1] much less earning a living. They are to carry out their task with the utmost speed – it is the last hour for the offer of deliverance, the last hour for spreading the net to fetch home Israel (Mark 1.17 par. cf. Jer. 16.16),[2] the last hour for bringing in the harvest (Matt. 9.37f. par.).

The *task of the six pairs of messengers* is described in the same way, in *logia* (Matt. 10.7f.; Luke 10.9) and in the narrative text (Mark 3.14f.; 6.12f. par. Luke 9.6; Luke 9.2). They are to announce the dawn of the time of salvation and to make incursions into the realm of Satan by driving out the demons. That means that they have to make the same announcement as Jesus himself, and they have to do so in the same way as him: in word and action. With them, too, both belong together. The word alone is an empty shell; action alone can be the work of the devil. The reign of God is manifested only in word and action together.

Service as a messenger is an eschatological event. It is an anticipation of the service of angels: the messengers proclaim God's victory as it will be proclaimed by the angel flying at the zenith (Rev. 14.6f.), and they bring in the harvest as it will be brought in by the angels of the Son of man (Mark. 13.27; Rev. 14.14ff.).[3]

The authority that the twelve messengers are given corresponds to the magnitude of this task. The original instruction lays considerable emphasis on it. With their greeting as they enter a house, the messengers bring εἰρήνη to that house. It is a power that embraces all the members of the family, but it returns to its bestower if the house is not worthy of it. Thus the messengers are bearers of God's salvation. It is of the nature of εἰρήνη that the evil powers must yield to it. The messengers have a share in Christ's victory over Satan. They have the ἐξουσία τῶν πνευμάτων τῶν ἀκαθάρτων (Mark 6.7), the ἐξουσία τοῦ πατεῖν ἐπάνω ὄφεων καὶ σκορπίων (Luke 10.19). As we have seen,[4] this ἐξουσία presupposes possession of the spirit, for only the spirit of God has authority over the spirits (Matt. 12.28 par. Luke 11.20). Thus in conferring authority as he sends out the messengers, Jesus is performing a kind of pouring out of the spirit which equips his disciples to overcome the instruments of Satan and to destroy Satan's kingdom. This report is early, because it stands in tension to the later

---

[1] See above, p. 133.   [2] See above, pp. 132f.

[3] L. Legrand, 'Was Jesus Mission-Minded?', *IES* 3, 1964, 87–104, 190–207: 207.

[4] See above, p. 79.

historical view which has the spirit descending on the disciples only after the resurrection.

If a place goes against the most elementary demands of hospitality and refuses to receive the messengers, they are, as Jesus says in the original instruction, to shake the dust off their feet (Mark 6.11; Matt. 10.14; Luke 9.5; 10.11). This is an abbreviated expression; what is meant is that they are to shake the dust which their feet have stirred up from their cloaks. And they are to do this in full public view, say in the market place or at the way out from the place. This action, as everyone understood, was a symbolic expression of breaking off all community (cf. Neh. 5.13; Acts 13.51; 18.6); nothing of such a town or locality is to cling to the messengers, even the dust from its streets. The place is delivered over to God's judgment.

Thus the authority of the messengers includes both the communication of salvation and the imposition of judgment. It is the judge's authority to acquit and to pronounce guilty[1] that is described by this pair of opposites and the synonymous phrases 'bind and loose' (Matt. 18.18 and, derived from it, 16.19) and 'forgive and retain sins' (John 20.23). As pairs of opposites are used in Semitic languages to describe the totality, these pairs of words mean that the messengers receive total authority. Their action in judgment is an eschatological function performed proleptically (Matt. 19.28). In their loosing and binding, God's reign in grace and power is being realized even now.

The magnitude of the authority of the messengers becomes clear in the climactic parallelism:

$$\text{ὁ δεχόμενος ὑμᾶς}$$
$$\text{ἐμὲ δέχεται,}$$
$$\text{καὶ ὁ ἐμὲ δεχόμενος}$$
$$\text{δέχεται τὸν ἀποστείλαντά με}$$
$$\text{(Matt. 10.40 cf. Luke 10.16)}$$

In its first half, this *logion* takes up the established right of the messenger, according to which a man's messenger is as the one who sends him.[2] Similarly, in the person of the messengers, Jesus himself comes. The nature of being a messenger is to represent Jesus. Therefore, just as a man's attitude towards Jesus' own words even now decides between salvation and condemnation, so does a man's

[1] A. Schlatter, *Der Evangelist Matthäus*, Stuttgart 1929 = 61963, 511.
[2] ‡Rengstorf, 415.

attitude towards those of the messengers; with them comes either peace or judgment. The second half of the *logion* goes one step further. God himself enters houses with Jesus' messengers. What a statement! Of course, the office of messenger is no protection against falling; even Judas Iscariot promised forgiveness and drove out demons. No messenger can be certain of himself.

(iii) The fate of the messengers

Suffering for Christ's sake inevitably forms part of the service of a messenger. All strata of the sources are agreed that Jesus said this again and again.

With utmost clarity he prepared his messengers for being defence-less and unprotected, like sheep among wolves (Matt. 10.16; Luke 10.3). They will by no means find doors open everywhere. As the original instruction remarks, it will happen that people abuse the law of hospitality and refuse them lodging (Mark 6.11 par. Luke 9.5; Matt. 10.14 par. Luke 10.10); since granting hospitality is the con-cern of a whole village, this may mean that the whole place refuses to receive them (Luke 9.51–56). Even more, they will be hunted out of a locality (διώκειν Matt. 5.11 par. 10.23a), perhaps even from the threshold of their parents' house. They will be calumniated (5.11 par.) and mocked as messengers of the devil (Matt. 10.24f.). Indeed, there will be more than harsh words. That is the situation envisaged by the often misinterpreted saying about the blow on the cheek (Matt. 5.39 par. Luke 6.29). Matthew talks of a blow on the *right* cheek, and his words will be more original; the Lucan tradition will have omitted the adjective 'right' because its special significance was not immediately clear to Gentile Christians. A blow on the right cheek is a blow with the back of the hand, which even today in the East expresses the greatest possible contempt and extreme abuse.[1] It seems extremely probable in the present context that in Matt. 5.39 Jesus is not thinking of any controversy that finds expression in action, but of abuse heaped on the disciples as heretics.[2] In all the other instances in which Jesus speaks of abuse, cursing, dishonour, we have

---

[1] A blow with the back of the hand was punished with the exorbitant fine of 400 denarii (B.K. 8.6.)

[2] Cf. the blow on the mouth (Acts 23.2). In the *Agadta d^e Šim^on Kepa* (ed. A. Jellinek, *Bet ha-Midrasch* V, Wien 1873 = ²Jerusalem 1938 = 1967, 61.14), it is a Jew who strikes the Christian on the cheek.

outrages which the disciples must endure for the sake of being disciples. If the messengers have to endure the hardest insult, the contemptible blow with the back of the hand on the right cheek, they are not to strike back and not to tread the road to justice,[1] but to suffer willingly for the sake of their testimony (Matt. 5.39). Occasionally it may even come to the point that their testimony brings the disciples in danger of their lives: μὴ φοβεῖσθε ἀπὸ τῶν ἀποκτεννόντων τὸ σῶμα (Matt. 10.28 par.). Whatever happens, they are not to be afraid, but to flee to the next place and carry on their work there (Matt. 10.23).

Jesus cannot spare the messengers hardship, but he can help them by explaining why they have to suffer. Suffering is part of the service of a messenger, because the world's hate is a normal answer to testimony. This is how it was with the prophets, and this is how it is with the disciples. Woe to you when all people praise you – that is what your fathers did with the false prophets (Luke 6.26). Suffering is almost a hallmark of serving as a messenger. Therefore it has great promise: ὁ μισθὸς ὑμῶν πολὺς ἐν τοῖς οὐρανοῖς (Matt. 5.12 par.). Soon, even before the messengers have reached the last dwellings in Israel (Matt. 10.23),[2] the suffering will be changed to joy (Luke 6.23, where ἐν ἐκείνῃ τῇ ἡμέρᾳ will be meant eschatologically).

The sayings about the suffering of the messengers represent early tradition. Not only do they occur in all strata of the sources, but in addition they almost all have in common the early feature that they do not speak of organized persecution but of molestations in the day-to-day life of the messengers. Neither the persecution following the death of Stephen nor that under Agrippa I, nor even the Neronian persecution, have had any influence here. Only isolated verses (like Mark 13.9 par., where persecution by Jewish and pagan authorities is mentioned) reflect the situation of the community; these are clearly secondary formulations. Another early feature is that the sources reveal a distinction between *logia* which speak of the bitter experiences of the disciples as they exercise their office as messengers and those which speak of eschatological tribulation. Although the distribution of the sayings about the suffering of the disciples cannot always be made with complete certainty between these two fundamentally different situations, it can in most cases be inferred from the content. This is significant because for the post-Easter community the two categories of sufferings, missionary and eschatological, would be fused; the fact that they are distinct in the tradition is a noteworthy indication of antiquity.

[1] ἀντιστῆναι in Matt. 5.39 has a forensic meaning as an antithesis to the *ius talionis* (v. 38): 'go to trial' (cf. e.g. LXX Deut. 19.18 ἀντέστη κατὰ τοῦ ἀδελφοῦ αὐτοῦ; Isa. 50.8 τίς ὁ κρινόμενός μοι; ἀντιστήτω μοι ἅμα).

[2] See above, pp. 135f.

§ 21 · THE CONSUMMATION OF THE PEOPLE OF GOD

J. Jeremias, *Jesus als Weltvollender*, BFCT 33.4, Gütersloh 1930; id., *Jesus' Promise to the Nations*, SBT 24, London ²1967; Manson, *Teaching*²; B. Rigaux, 'La seconde venue de Jésus', in: *La Venue du Messie. Messianisme et Eschatologie*, Recherches Bibliques VI, Bruges 1962, 173–216.

(i) *The eschatological time of distress*

Jesus was convinced that his suffering[1] would fundamentally alter the situation of his followers. This conviction is brought out most clearly in Luke 22.35–38.[2] Jesus reminds the messengers of their previous experiences. He had sent them out without protection, unarmed, without the basic necessities, completely cast on God's care. But all their misgivings had proved to be lack of faith (Matt. 6.30 par.).[3] Certainly they had come up against rejection and hatred (Matt. 5.11f. par.; 10.25);[4] but at the same time they had also found houses open to them everywhere (Luke 22.35). Now, however, everything will be different. Enmity and hatred will surround them on all sides. At no moment will they be sure of their life. A sword, everything for a sword, will be the solution (v. 36). Whence comes this change in the attitude of their compatriots? Verse 37 gives the answer: the rejection of Jesus from Israel will also involve his disciples. *Qualis rex, talis grex*, says Jesus in Mark 14.27, referring to Zech. 13.7. Jesus' passion marks the turning point, the prelude to the time of the sword (Matt. 10.34).

It will come, and there will be no avoiding it. The sons of Zebedee will have to drink Jesus' cup of suffering and undergo his baptism of suffering (Mark 10.39). They will not be the only ones whom martyrdom awaits. Some of those standing round Jesus will survive and will see the coming of the βασιλεία ἐν δυνάμει (cf. Mark 13.26 μετὰ δυνάμεως πολλῆς) with physical eyes,[5] says an early ἀμήν saying (Mark 9.1 par.) which, as John 21.23 shows, was already felt by the early church to be difficult. The *logion* hardly means that they will die a peaceful death one after the other. Rather, as we already suggested on pp. 136f.,

---

[1] See below, p. 284. [2] For its antiquity see below, p. 294.
[3] See above, p. 236. [4] See above, pp. 239f. [5] ‡Rigaux, 192.

Jesus will envisage martyrdom as their fate, as he announced to the sons of Zebedee. That is Satan's work; he stands ready to sieve the disciples as a man sieves wheat (Luke 22.31f.).

Mark 8.34 uses a particularly vivid picture for the future that faces Jesus' disciples: εἴ τις θέλει ὀπίσω μου ἐλθεῖν, ἀπαρνησάσθω ἑαυτὸν καὶ ἀράτω τὸν σταυρὸν αὐτοῦ, καὶ ἀκολουθείτω μοι. It is usually assumed that this saying is a secondary announcement of martyrdom, coined as a result of Jesus' death on the cross. But the Roman cross was at that time by no means a rare sight in Palestine, and in the Lucan parallel καθ' ἡμέραν appears as an addition after ἀράτω τὸν σταυρὸν αὐτοῦ (9.23). This is certainly a secondary, paraenetic reinterpretation, but it is instructive because it shows that 'taking up the cross' was not understood as 'having to suffer martyrdom'. Had it been, the addition 'day by day' would simply not have fitted. 'Take up his cross' in Mark 8.34 does not in fact mean 'suffer martyrdom', as even the wording shows. Rather, as A. Fridrichsen[1] has seen, a particular point in time is envisaged: the beginning of the way to execution when the victim takes the *patibulum* on his shoulder and goes from the judgment hall into the street to face the howling, hostile mob. The most fearful thing is not the execution at the end of the way but the feeling of being made an outcast, the helpless object of contempt and mockery. 'Come and hear,' runs b. Sanh. 85a. 'Anyone who . . . strikes a man who is being led out to execution . . . is free of punishment . . . (for) the victim counts as a dead man.' To agree to follow Jesus means to venture on a life that is as hard as the last walk of a man condemned to death. In Mark 8.34, Jesus is saying that this applies to *all* who follow him. For everyone, discipleship involves the readiness to tread the lonely road and to bear the people's hatred.

For the disciples, the special sting of suffering will be the fulfilment of Micah 7.6. The division will go right through the midst of families, and the closest relatives, fathers, brothers, even men's own children will denounce them and deliver them up to death (Mark 13.12f. par.; Matt. 10.21f., 35f. par.).

There is one thing more fearful than all physical oppression: *spiritual trial* in the form of seduction by false prophets (Mark 13.21–23; Matt. 7.15–23). The *agraphon* 'Be approved money changers',

---

[1] 'Ordet om "å baere sit Kors"', in: *Gamle spor og nye veier*, L. Brun Festschrift, Kristania (Oslo) 1922, 17ff.: 30.

which was much valued by the early church,[1] is a warning against such false prophets; its message is: learn from the money changers and acquire a sharp eye for all that is counterfeit. In a vivid picture, Matt. 7.15 depicts how the false prophets awaken trust by wearing the prophet's garb, sheepskin, and find their way into the fold; then they suddenly unmask themselves as the wolves that they are and make the sheep jostle against one another in wild panic. The great πειρασμός is one of the preliminary signs of the end. No one will escape it. Tertullian hands down an *agraphon* said to be set in the context of the passion narrative, which brings out this connection particularly clearly: *Neminem intemptatum regna caelestia consecuturum.*[2] The stress lies on the 'no one'. The way through trial is the only one that leads to the kingdom of God. This is also true for Jesus himself. According to Luke 22.28, he saw his whole life in retrospect as a series of temptations from Satan. Proving one's discipleship, therefore, as Luke 22.28 concludes, consists in staying by Christ in his temptations.

It is natural to suspect that in the case of the announcements of the eschatological suffering, experiences of the early church have later been attributed to Jesus as prophecies, or at least have modified earlier wording. We must certainly reckon with this possibility. But two examples will show how careful we must be not to pass judgment too quickly. First, it is worth noting that the suffering of the disciples is repeatedly announced in close conjunction with Jesus' own suffering (Luke 22.35–38; Mark 10.38f. par.). Evidently Jesus, as C. H. Dodd[3] and T. W. Manson[4] recognized, expected a collective suffering for the disciples which would begin with his own passion. That this expectation was not fulfilled in such a form[5] excludes any suspicion that here we have a *vaticinium ex eventu*. An investigation of the forecast of martyrdom for the sons of Zebedee leads to a similar result (Mark 10.38f.). It, too, cannot be a *vaticinium ex eventu*. While Acts 12.2 reports that James the son of Zebedee suffered martyrdom, we hear of his brother John only that he lived in Ephesus until the time of Trajan (98–117).[6] Only the epitomist of Philip of Side claims to have read in the latter's Church History (published about 434–39) the statement: 'Papias (*c.* 130) says in his second book that John the theologian and his brother James were killed by the Jews.'[7] This statement by the epitomist is,

[1] J. Jeremias, *Unknown Sayings of Jesus*, London [2]1964, 100–104.
[2] *De baptismo* 20, 12; J. Jeremias, *op. cit.*, 73–75. [3] *Parables*, 58f.
[4] 'The New Testament Basis of the Doctrine of the Church', *JEH* 1, 1950, 1–11:6.
[5] See below, p. 284. [6] Irenaeus, *Adv. haer.* II 22.5; III 3.4.
[7] C. de Boor, TU 5.2, Leipzig 1888, 170. Georgios Monachos, *Chronicles* III 134, 1 (ninth century) is not an independent witness for this account (which, moreover, occurs only in *one* manuscript, cf. C. K. Barrett, *The Gospel according to St John*, London 1955, 86 n.3), as he is dependent on Philip of Side.

however, extremely suspicious, because neither Irenaeus nor Eusebius found any report of a martyrdom of John in Papias' work. So the only witness to this remains a Syriac martyrology from the year 411/412 which notes under December 27: 'John and James, the apostles, in Jerusalem'.[1] But even this evidence is questionable. For in the martyrology of Carthage (c. AD 505) we find: *VI Kal. Jan.* (27 December) *sancti Johannis Baptistae et Jacobi apostoli quem Herodes occidit.*[2] Thus here John the Baptist (!) appears alongside James. This will be the original, although the Baptist is commemorated again on June 24. There is therefore no credible report from the early church of a martyrdom of John. It is impossible that he was killed by Agrippa I at the same time as James (Acts 12.2) in AD 43 or 44, as according to Gal. 2.9 he took part in the apostolic council in AD 48/49. Moreover, it follows from the consideration that the church of Asia Minor, which made so much of the martyrdom of Polycarp, would have made even more of an apostolic martyr, that he was not killed at a later date in Asia Minor either. The conclusion is that the forecast of John's martyrdom in Mark 10.38f. is an unfulfilled prophecy and therefore cannot be a *vaticinium ex eventu* – a warning to be careful about this verdict.

The law that the kingdom of God comes through suffering[3] also applies to the disciples of Jesus. But suffering has the promise that the surrender of life is also the acceptance of life (Mark 8.35). 'God will deliver the one who endures to the end' (Mark 13.13 par.). Thus everything culminates in the question of faithful existence in the πειρασμός. How is that possible? Jesus replies: through watchful observance for danger (Mark 13.14; 14.38) and the request to be preserved from succumbing (Mark 14.38 par.; Luke 11.4 par.).[4]

(ii) The turning point

Great as Satan's power is, God's power is greater. His victory is certain. When the temptation of the people of God reaches its climax, God, shortening the days, will bring the great turning point (Mark 13.20).

In Luke 12.32, an originally independent[5] *logion* which goes back to an Aramaic tradition,[6] the eschatological people of God are

---

[1] H. Lietzmann, *Die drei ältesten Martyrologien*, KIT 2², Berlin 1911, 7f.
[2] *Op. cit.*, 5f.   [3] See above, p. 129.
[4] See on the closing petition of the Lord's Prayer, above, pp. 201f.
[5] It is connected with v. 31 by a link word.
[6] Rendering of the vocative by the nominative with an article in τὸ μικρὸν ποίμνιον; word-play *mar'îtā* (τὸ ποίμνιον)/*rā'ē* (εὐδόκησεν) cf. M. Black, *An Aramaic Approach to the Gospels and Acts*³, Oxford 1967, 168; taking up of *malkūtā* . . . *yᵉhībat* Dan. 7.27 in δοῦναι τὴν βασιλείαν.

compared, as often, to a flock.[1] The little flock is promised, following Dan. 7.27, that circumstances will be reversed. Despite its tiny number and the persecution that threatens, it may be sure that they are 'the people of the saints of the Most High', to whom is promised 'the kingdom and the dominion and the greatness of the kingdoms'.

In another image this promise runs: 'The gates of hell will not prevail against it (my community)' (Matt. 16.18). Here πύλαι ᾅδου is a *pars pro toto* expression for the underworld[2] and αὐτῆς denotes the ἐκκλησία built on the rock.[3] That is, the people of God are given the promise that even the last, most fearful onslaught of the powers of the underworld (cf. Rev. 6.8; 9.5ff.; 20.7ff.) will not overwhelm it. The guarantee that this promise will be fulfilled is the goodness of God, which is manifest in the time of salvation now dawning. Jesus' disciples may have great confidence: if even the unjust judge humours the poor widow merely to be rid of her complaining, how much more will God hear the cry of his elect and help them to obtain their rights (Luke 18.1–8).

In his sayings about the great turning point Jesus takes up details of apocalyptic views, as when he speaks of the resurrection of the dead[4] and the last judgment,[5] the annihilation of Satan and the punishment of his angels,[6] the flood of fire[7] and the renewal of the world.[8] The more clearly these connections are recognized, the clearer it becomes where Jesus lays the stress. At this point, in addition to the seriousness with which he announces judgment and division not only in Israel and among its leaders,[9] but also among his own followers,[10] we must mention above all his universalism.

(iii) The pilgrimage of the nations[11]

The great turning point is also the hour of the Gentiles.

Jesus had limited his activity to Israel; only twice do we hear that he helped Gentiles, and only then after vehement argument.[12] Moreover, he instructed his disciples not to go beyond the borders of Israel (Matt. 10.5f., 23). At the same time, however, on the other

[1] See above, p. 168.
[2] J. Jeremias, πύλη, πυλών, *TDNT* VI 1968, 921–28: 925 n.44, 926f.
[3] *Ibid.*, 927 n.64.   [4] On Mark 12.18–27, see above, pp. 184, 225.
[5] See above, pp. 129f.   [6] Matt. 25.41.   [7] Luke 12.49; 17.28–30.
[8] Mark 13.31 par.   [9] Mark 12.1–12 par.; Matt. 23.34–36 par.
[10] Matt. 7.21–23; Luke 13.26f.   [11] ‡Jeremias, *Jesus' Promise*, 55–73.
[12] Mark 7.24–30 par.; Matt. 8.5–13 par.

hand he rejected the expectation that God would wreak vengeance on the Gentiles (Luke 4.16ff.;[1] Matt. 11.5f. par.[2]), and said again and again that the Gentiles, too, would find their way into the coming reign of God. When all the nations ($\pi\acute{a}\nu\tau a$ $\tau\grave{a}$ $\check{\epsilon}\vartheta\nu\eta$) stand before the throne of judgment (Matt. 25.32), there will be those among them who will be acquitted with the words, 'Come, O blessed of my Father, inherit the reign' (v. 34). God's flock will also include the Gentiles (Matt. 25.32f.; cf. John 10.16). The picture of the city of God on the world-mountain, whose brightness lightens the darkness (Matt. 5.14), stems from the message of the prophets and there depicts the glory of God which summons the nations. The reason Jesus gives for purifying the desecrated sanctuary is that he is preparing the place of prayer for all nations (Mark 11.17). Whereas the Essene Teacher of Righteousness teaches that 'no unclean one (cf. Isa. 35.8), no one uncircumcised, no robber' will tread the divine path (1 QH 6.20), Jesus includes the Gentiles in the eschatological people of God.

What is the explanation of this contradiction, that on the one hand Jesus limited his activity and that of his disciples to Israel, and that on the other he continually spoke of the Gentiles' share in the reign of God? Matt. 8.11f. par. Luke 13.28f. gives the answer. It depicts how unnamed men will stream in from east and west and recline at table in the *basileia*, while the sons of the kingdom are cast out.

Three brief preliminary remarks on this *logion*: (a) it is very early. The thought world is Jewish (patriarchs, prophets, blessedness as table-fellowship with them; the idea that the damned and the blessed can see each other, cf. Luke 16.23) and the style is Semitic (antithetical parallelism in Matthew, inclusive $\pi o\lambda\lambda o\acute{\iota}$, $o\acute{\iota}$ $v\acute{\iota}o\grave{\iota}$ $\tau\hat{\eta}s$ $\beta a\sigma\iota\lambda\epsilon\acute{\iota}as$; circumstantial clause and parataxis in Luke; in both the future $\grave{a}\nu a\kappa\lambda\iota\vartheta\acute{\eta}\sigma o\nu\tau a\iota$ corresponds to an Aramaic imperfect to be taken as modal = 'may'). However, the sharpness of the threat expressed in Matt. 8.11f. par. is without analogy in the whole of Jewish apocalyptic. (b) Who is coming from all points of the compass? The Diaspora? That cannot be so, because of $v\acute{\iota}o\grave{\iota}$ $\tau\hat{\eta}s$ $\beta a\sigma\iota\lambda\epsilon\acute{\iota}as$. Were those who arrive the Diaspora, then the 'sons of the kingdom' would have to be Palestinian Jews. However, the idea that the promise of the kingdom should be limited to Palestinian Judaism would be as senseless as the contrast between a pardoned Diaspora and a rejected native Judaism. Those who arrive are, rather, beyond question the Gentiles. (c) When will the Gentiles thus stream in? The answer follows from the situation. The patriarchs are resurrected and recline at table in the

---

[1] See above, pp. 206f.

[2] All three Old Testament proof texts for this passage (pp. 103ff.) mention God's vengeance in the immediate context: Isa. 29.20; 35.4; 61.2. But Jesus leaves it out.

basileia, and the 'sons of the kingdom' are cast out; that can only mean that the time intended is the hour of consummation.

Thus it is at the consummation of the world that the Gentiles stream in from east and west. They go to the mountain of God. This is an established idea in the Old Testament (Isa. 2.2f. par. Micah 4.1f.). The prophets depict five features of the eschatological pilgrimage of the nations:

(a) It is introduced by the epiphany of God (Zech. 2.17). His glory is revealed to the world.

(b) God's call ensues (Isa. 45.20, 22).

(c) God's command is followed by the journey of the Gentiles (Isa. 19.23).

(d) It reaches its destination in the world sanctuary (Ps. 22.28; Zeph. 3.9).

(e) From now on the Gentiles belong to the people of God. They share in the divine banquet on the world mountain (Isa. 25.6–9); in the symbolic language of the Bible, eating and drinking are a primal expression for fellowship before and with God. This is the central element in the sayings about the banquet of the end-time.

Thus we find a centripetal conception. Missionaries do not go out to preach the gospel to the nations. Rather, God's glory shines out on the nations and summons them to eschatological salvation.

It is deeply significant that the hour of the Gentiles only comes at the end of the day. The reason for this is Jesus' view of salvation history. First, God's promise must be fulfilled and Israel must be offered salvation. First, the servant of God must pour out his blood for the many, before the hour of the Gentiles comes. It lies beyond the passion, and the help that Jesus grants to Gentiles in individual instances belongs in the series of anticipations of the complete fulfilment.

Once again the glory of the gospel shines out. On the 'days of the Messiah', contemporary apocalyptic expected the great judgment on sinners and, above all, vengeance on the Gentiles (see Ps. Sol. 14.6–10; 17.21–31). People talked about God's glory, but meant Israel's glory. In the message of Jesus, the universalism of grace takes the place of national particularism. In the incorporation of the Gentiles into the eschatological people of God, the free grace of God is manifested in all its glory.

(iv) God is King[1]

The reign of God is the time when prayers are fulfilled.[2] God's name is hallowed; he reigns as king.

Three things characterize Jesus' remarks about the final consummation.

(a) In the sayings of Jesus, the conception of the *basileia* is *stripped* not only of all nationalistic features but also of all *materialistic features*. There is no elaboration of the conditions of the end time, say, the fertility of the new earth or the joy of heaven. In controversy with the Sadducees (Mark 12.18–27 par.), Jesus expressly rejects the current conception that the conditions of the end will be a continuation of earthly conditions in an exalted form: ὅταν γὰρ ἐκ νεκρῶν ἀναστῶσιν, οὔτε γαμοῦσιν οὔτε γαμίζονται, ἀλλ᾽ εἰσὶν ὡς ἄγγελοι ἐν τοῖς οὐρανοῖς (v. 25).

(b) Where Jesus speaks of the transfigured world, he almost always does so only in the images of *symbolic language*. Their number is almost inexhaustible. God is king; he is worshipped in the New Temple (Mark 14.58); human eyes may see him (Matt. 5.8), paradise returns and there is no more death (Luke 20.36); the legacy is distributed (Matt. 5.5); the new name is bestowed (5.9); the laughter of the time of salvation rings out (Luke 6.21); the family of God sits at the Father's table (Matt. 8.11f. par.); the bread of life is broken (Luke 11.3), the cup of salvation is given (22.18), the eternal passover of liberation is celebrated (22.16). There is a total transformation of values: the poor become rich, the hungry are filled, the sorrowful are comforted, the last become first (Mark 10.31). God gives eternal life (Mark 10.30) – 'eternal' means sharing in the life of God. This share in the life of God is communicated by the vision of God: θεὸν ὄψονται (Matt. 5.8). This short clause has a more inclusive content than its wording might suggest, as we can demonstrate by means of the ὅτι in I John 3.2: ὅμοιοι αὐτῷ ἐσόμεθα ὅτι ὀψόμεθα αὐτὸν καθώς ἐστιν. *Because* we may see God, we shall be like him. The vision of God effects transformation into his likeness. *Ex aspectu similitudo* (Bengel). This is also the way in which the promise given by the sixth beatitude to the pure in heart is meant. The vision of God that will be granted to them is the embodiment of blessedness, because it discloses what being like him is.

[1] ‡Jeremias, *Weltvollender*, 69ff.
[2] E. Jüngel, *Paulus und Jesus. Eine Untersuchung zur Präzisierung der Frage nach dem Ursprung der Christologie*[3], Tübingen 1967, 178.

(c) Jesus' sayings about the conditions of the end are never concerned with the salvation of the individual or with an individual blessedness. He is always concerned with the *community*. This is true, for example, of Luke 16.9: the 'eternal tents' are an image deriving from the account of the wanderings in the wilderness. At that time God tabernacled amongst his people in the Tent of Meeting. Similarly, the tents in Luke 16.9 are an image of the communion of God with his people. It is especially clear that in his sayings about the conditions of the end, Jesus is primarily thinking of the community when he uses the image of the New Temple (Mark 14.58 par.). The consummation is the time when the gates of the earthly sanctuaries are closed, the dispute over the sanctuaries is ended (John 4.21) and the community of the redeemed worships before the throne of God (v. 23). Mention should also be made of the image of the wedding as an expression of the fellowship of the community with their God (Matt. 22.1–14 par.; 25.1–13). Finally, the image of the festal meal is a last indication that the sayings of Jesus about the consummation have the community in mind (numerous instances, cf. Mark 14.25; Luke 22.30). In the *basileia*, creation and redemption are completed, for in the ultimate community, which worships God without end, the glorification of God is made perfect.

VI

JESUS' TESTIMONY TO HIS MISSION

I REMARKED at the beginning of this book (ch. II) that Jesus' appearance on the scene was preceded by a call, which presumably took place at his baptism. From this time on, Jesus knew that he had been commissioned to share with others the knowledge of God that had been granted to him. With this commission, Jesus saw himself placed in the series of heralds of God, but the attempt to outline his preaching showed us that his awareness of his authority transcended the category of the prophetic. For Jesus proclaimed that with his coming the time of salvation and the conquest of Satan had begun (ch. III). The decision for or against God and deliverance at the last judgment depended solely and simply on obedience to his word (ch. IV). He presented discipleship as true life, set a new law of God over against the *Torah* and had the dawn of the time of salvation proclaimed by his messengers (ch.V). In short, he designated his preaching and his actions as the eschatological saving event. An awareness of mission of this kind can no longer be kept in the prophetic sphere. Rather, all these statements mean that Jesus believed himself to be the bringer of salvation.

§ 22 · THE BRINGER OF SALVATION

(i) The emphatic ἐγώ

It would be a mistake to assume that Jesus' awareness of his status and his claim to authority were expressed most clearly in the passages in which messianic titles are used. On the contrary, here too it is a mistake to keep to the concordance. Titles can be added afterwards. On the other hand, the subject-matter is often present even where titles are not used. Thus Jesus is fond of using pictures of the *symbolic call of the redeemer* to describe the authority of his mission, which have their correlative in the symbolic designations of the community discussed on pp. 168–70. He describes himself as the messenger of God who issues a call to the festal meal (Mark 2.17 par.), as the physician for the sick (*ibid.*), as the shepherd (Mark 14.27f. par.; John 10), as the master-builder of the Temple of God (Mark 14.58 par.; Matt. 16.18) and as the father of the house, who gathers the family of God at his table (Matt. 10.24f.; Luke 22.29f.). These pictures describe in symbolic language the bringer of salvation, and all have an eschatological ring. As the early church replaced the pictures with titles, we can almost establish the rule that whereas the christological *titles* in the gospels are (with one exception) all post-Easter,[1] there is a strong probability that all the pictures mentioned date from before Easter.

Jesus' view of his status is expressed even more clearly than in the imagery of symbolic language in the remarkable accumulation of the emphatic ἐγώ in his sayings, to the same degree in both synoptic and Johannine material. It is to be found not only in sayings of Jesus about his mission like Matt. 5.17, but also throughout his preaching. This emphatic ἐγώ appears to be most marked in the six antitheses contained in Matt. 5.21–48.

We may take it as quite certain that in the antitheses we are hearing the words of Jesus himself in the pattern ἠκούσατε ὅτι ἐρρέθη–ἐγὼ δὲ λέγω ὑμῖν, because this has neither Jewish nor early Christian parallels. One can only ask whether the pattern is original in all six antitheses, or whether in a number of them it has not been developed at a later stage. In fact, it is so much taken for granted that the third, fifth and sixth antitheses are secondary formations that scholars feel quite free from any obligation to examine the arguments. These consist of three series of observations, on grounds of literary criticism, content and form. (*a*) From a literary-critical perspective it is pointed out that the third, fifth and sixth antitheses (Matt. 5.31f., 38f., 43f.) have also been transmitted without the pattern of antitheses; from this the conclusion is drawn that the form of the antitheses has been imitated in these instances and that the formulation is original only in the first, second and fourth antitheses. (*b*) This division is thought to be confirmed by the fact that in the third, fifth and sixth antitheses the *Torah* is radically transcended, whereas in the first, second and fourth antitheses it is simply sharpened. (*c*) As far as the form is concerned, it is observed that the protasis is in the negative only in the first, second and fourth antitheses, whereas the third, fifth and sixth antitheses fall outside the framework because of their '*māšāl*-like form' and the 'breadth of the treatment'.[2]

[1] See below, pp. 258ff.
[2] Bultmann, *Synoptic Tradition*, 134. The numerous authors who regard the first,

However, on closer examination all three arguments for dividing the antitheses into two groups prove to be untenable. (*a*) To begin with the literary-critical argument, (i) the assertion that the third, fifth and sixth antitheses are allegedly different from the first, second and fourth antitheses in that they have also been transmitted without the antithesis-pattern holds only for the third antithesis, and not for the fifth and sixth; for there is no parallel at all to the fifth antithesis, which (as can already be seen from the change from the plural in vv. 38–39a to the singular in vv. 39b–42) was originally limited to 5.38–39a;[1] and as far as the sixth antithesis is concerned, the ἀλλά in Luke 6.27 echoes an original antithesis. Thus only in the case of the prohibition of divorce has the material been handed down both in a version with the antithesis (Matt. 5.31f.) and in one without (Mark 10.11f.; Luke 16.18). (ii) Once it is established that the fifth antithesis originally comprised only Matt. 5.38–39a, the argument that the first, second and fourth antitheses differ from the rest by being transmitted only by Matthew also falls to the ground;[2] rather, that is also true of the fifth antithesis. (iii) The claim that the first, second and fourth antitheses, the 'genuine' antitheses, can be proved to belong together in that they all refer to the Decalogue,[3] can hardly be made for the fourth antithesis.

(*b*) The argument from content, which differentiates between original antitheses in which the *Torah* is only accentuated (first, second and fourth) and secondary constructions, in which the *Torah* is radically transcended (third, fifth and sixth), attempts an untenable division because it fails to recognize that in the fourth antithesis (the prohibition of swearing) the *Torah* is not accentuated but transcended, and that, on the other hand, in the sixth antithesis (the command to love one's enemy) the *Torah* is not transcended but accentuated. For the words καὶ μισήσεις τὸν ἐχθρόν σου in the protasis of the sixth antithesis do not contain a 'command' to hate one's enemy ('You shall hate your enemy') that Jesus then abolishes; rather, they represent a popular qualification of the commandment to love ('You need not love your enemy'), not attested in the Old Testament,[4] which Jesus refuses to allow. If we are to distinguish between the accentuation and the transcending of the *Torah* we shall have to say: the first, second and sixth antitheses accentuate the *Torah* and the third, fourth and fifth transcend it.

(*c*) Lastly, we turn to formal considerations. (i) The argument that the injunction of the *Torah* is given in a negative version only in the first, second and fourth antitheses is not formulated with sufficient precision: only the first and second

---

second and fourth antitheses as original and the third, fifth and sixth as secondary almost all follow Bultmann, without producing any new perspectives. It is therefore unnecessary to list them.

[1] Dr B. Schaller notes that the Lucan parallel 6.29f. corresponds to the explanations of the fifth antithesis in Matt. 5.39b–42 but not to the antithesis itself (5.38–39a).

[2] W. G. Kümmel, 'Jesus und der jüdische Traditionsgedanke', *ZNW* 33, 1934, 105–30: 125.

[3] J. Schniewind, *Das Evangelium nach Matthäus*, NTD 2[11], Göttingen 1964, on Matt. 5.21.

[4] For μισήσεις as a permissive imperfect cf. p. 213, n.3.

antitheses have a prohibition in the protasis; the third and fifth have a command and the fourth and sixth have an antithesis. '*Māšāl*-like' form, whatever that may be, must also be assigned to the fifth antithesis, which is to be restricted to vv. 38–39a, if it is found in the first, second and fourth, and 'the breadth of the treatment, which goes beyond the level of an antithesis to a legal saying' can at best be found in the sixth antithesis, hardly in the third and certainly not in the fifth. (ii) Furthermore, there are other variations in the form of the antitheses which also do not support the twofold division that is attempted (first, second and fourth/third, fifth and sixth): the first three antitheses follow the pattern of ὅτι πᾶς with a participle, the fourth and fifth have infinitives, while the sixth is imperative; the introduction has the full form ἠκούσατε ὅτι ἐρρέθη τοῖς ἀρχαίοις only in the first and fourth antitheses, as τοῖς ἀρχαίοις is missing in the second, fifth and sixth and only ἐρρέθη δέ remains in the third; in the first, fourth and sixth antitheses the Old Testament quotation has been expanded by an addition. Finally, the fact that the third, fifth and sixth antitheses differ so completely from one another in form does not support the hypothesis that the antithetical pattern has been stamped on them artificially 'on the model of the antithetical constructions vv. 21f., 27f., 33–37'.[1]

In conclusion, it should be said that the extraordinary variety among the six antitheses, not one of which corresponds to another in structure,[2] points not to a twofold division but to a collection of different individual traditions formulated as antitheses.[3]

The one who utters the ἐγὼ δὲ λέγω ὑμῖν in the antitheses not only claims to be the legitimate interpreter of the *Torah*, like the Teacher of Righteousness, but also has the unparalleled and revolutionary boldness to set himself up in opposition to the *Torah*. He came to bring 'the full measure' (Matt. 5.17, cf. p. 84).

This ἐγώ, used in pronouncements with authority, is also to be found in the words of command in the healing stories (Mark 9.25 ἐγὼ ἐπιτάσσω σοι; cf. Mark 2.11 par. σοὶ λέγω),[4] in the sending out of the messengers (as in Matt. 10.16 ἰδοὺ ἐγὼ ἀποστέλλω ὑμᾶς),[5] and in words of encouragement (like Luke 22.32: ἐγὼ δὲ ἐδεήθην περὶ σοῦ). This ἐγώ is associated with ἀμήν and thus claims to speak with divine authority;[6] it lays claim to the twofold royal ἐξουσία of God, amnesty and legislation. It requires devotion beyond all other ties, in complete exclusiveness. Even father and mother are not excepted (Matt. 10.37

---

[1] Bultmann, *Synoptic Tradition*, 134.

[2] W. Trilling, *Das wahre Israel. Studien zur Theologie des Matthäusevangeliums*, Leipzig 1959 (= ²1962), 186; omitted in ³München 1964.

[3] I am grateful to Dr B. Schaller for valuable suggestions and observations in this excursus on the antitheses.

[4] A. Schlatter, *Das Wunder in der Synagoge*, BFCT 16.5, Gütersloh 1912, 83.

[5] Par. Luke 10.3 without ἐγώ. Cf. also Luke 10.19: ἰδοὺ δέδωκα ὑμῖν τὴν ἐξουσίαν τοῦ πατεῖν ἐπάνω ὄφεων καὶ σκορπίων κτλ.

[6] See above, pp. 35f.

par. Luke 14.26). It claims that in its actions the *basileia* is at work (Luke 11.20 par. Matt. 12.28) and that deliverance at the last judgment will be decided by a man's public acknowledgment of its authority (Matt. 10.32f. par.).[1] It takes the place of the *Torah*: in contemporary Judaism, it was said, 'The person who hears the words of the *Torah* and does good works builds on firm ground';[2] here we have, 'The person who hears *my* words' (Matt. 7.24–27 par.). The emphatic ἐγώ indicates that the person who uses it is God's representative. A contemporary saying runs, 'The one who receives the scribes is like one who receives the *šᵉkinā*';[3] a saying of Jesus with climactic parallelism and negation of the relative together with a participial paraphrase for the divine name takes up this saying so that the emphatic ἐγώ takes the place of the scribes: 'Whoever receives me, receives not me but him who sent me' (Mark 9.37, often repeated: Matt. 10.40; Luke 9.48, cf. 10.16; John 12.44; 13.20).[4] In the three parables of the lost things (Luke 15), the parable of the generous employer (Matt. 20.1–15) and the parable of the two men at prayer (Luke 18.9–14), Jesus justifies his conduct by that of God; he acts so to speak as God's representative.[5] At the same time, however, his subordination to God's will is preserved (Mark 14.36 par.). This emphatic ἐγώ permeates the whole tradition of the sayings of Jesus and cannot be eliminated by literary-critical methods. It is without parallel in the world of Jesus.

Not only the sayings of Jesus but also, indirectly, his *crucifixion* testify to his claim to authority. Crucifixion was in itself the punishment for slaves, but it was also carried out by the Romans on rebels from the subject peoples. The inscription of the *titulus* attached to the cross (Mark 15.26 par.)[6] and the way in which the Roman soldiers mocked Jesus before his execution as a king, thus travestying the

[1] See above, p. 6, n.15.

[2] A.R.N. 24.

[3] Mek. Ex. on 18.12 end; b. Ber. 64a.

[4] Cf. M. Smith, *Tannaitic Parallels to the Gospels*, JBL Monograph Series VI, Philadelphia 1951, 152.

[5] E. Fuchs, *Studies of the Historical Jesus*, SBT 42, London 1964, 20–25.

[6] Note that according to all four gospels the inscription ran ὁ βασιλεὺς τῶν Ἰουδαίων (Mark 15.26; Matt. 27.37; Luke 23.38; John 19.19), which corresponds to the terminology of the non-Jewish world (K. G. Kuhn, Ἰσραήλ κτλ. B, *TDNT* III, 1965, 359–69: 360f.) not ὁ βασιλεὺς Ἰσραήλ, which occurs at Mark 15.32 par. on the lips of the chief priests. On the authenticity of the inscription on the cross cf. E. Dinkler, 'Petrusbekenntnis und Satanswort', in: *Zeit und Geschichte, Dankesgabe an Rudolf Bultmann zum 80. Geburtstag*, Tübingen 1964, 148 = E. Dinkler, *Signum Crucis*, Tübingen 1967, 306.

crime of which he had been accused,[1] agree in indicating that Jesus was executed as a rebel and disturber of the peace. The mockery and the *titulus* thus confirm what is said by the accounts of the judgment before Pilate, that Jesus was executed because he was charged with being a messianic pretender. Now this charge must have had roots of some kind in his ministry.

Finally, the early church's belief in the Messiah may also suggest that Jesus believed himself to be the bringer of salvation. From the beginning it regarded Jesus as the Messiah. It is hardly possible that this belief should have emerged without some starting point from before Easter, because for two reasons it cannot be derived from the Easter faith. Faith in the resurrection of a murdered messenger of God certainly does not amount to belief in his messiahship (cf. Mark 6.16). Furthermore, the scandal of the crucified Messiah is so enormous that it is hardly conceivable that the community should have presented itself with such a stumbling block.

It is therefore impossible to limit the proclamation of Jesus to the announcement of the *basileia*. If he was conscious that he himself was the bringer of salvation, it follows that his testimony to himself was part of the good news that he proclaimed.[2] But on what occasions did he make this testimony?

(ii) Public proclamation and instruction of the disciples

The synoptic gospels divide the sayings of Jesus into two alternating groups: those which are addressed to the public or to opponents, and others which are addressed only to the disciples. This twofold division also occurs in the Gospel of John, with the difference that here a long period of Jesus' public proclamation (chs. 1–12) is followed in the last days before the passion by instruction confined to the disciples (chs. 13–17). Now critical analysis shows that the details of the audience given in the gospels are often redactional and frequently inappropriate.[3] That is not surprising. We can see again and again, most clearly in Luke, that while there was considerable

---

[1] See above, pp. 77f.

[2] This fact is so compelling that Bultmann withdrew his view, expressed in *Jesus and the Word*, that Jesus came on the scene as a Rabbi (see above, pp. 76f.): 'He did not appear as a teacher or rabbi' ('The Primitive Christian Kerygma and the Historical Jesus', in: Carl E. Braaten and Roy A. Harrisville (eds.), *The Historical Jesus and the Kerygmatic Christ*, Nashville 1964, 27); rather, as the movement to which he gave birth and his crucifixion show, he appeared 'as a messianic prophet' (*Theology* I, 19). He understood himself as 'an eschatological phenomenon', indeed his appearance and his proclamation 'implies a christology' ('The Primitive Christian Kerygma', 28).

[3] Cf. e.g. for the parables Jeremias, *Parables*[2], 33–42.

hesitation to interfere with the sayings of Jesus, there was at the same time an equally considerable freedom in shaping the framework in which they were set. So while it is inadmissible to take over the details about the audience given in the gospels uncritically, on the other hand a warning should be given against exaggerated scepticism as to the possibility of determining just who is addressed, because in most instances the content shows to whom a *logion*, a metaphor, a parable was originally spoken. For instance, it is as clear from the content that the controversies were carried on with opponents as it is that the messengers' instructions were given to disciples.

We find those *logia* which express the authority of Jesus in both groups, both in public proclamation and in the instruction of the disciples. But there is a difference in the way in which they could be understood.

$$\begin{aligned}
&\dot{v}\mu\hat{\iota}\nu\ \tau\grave{o}\ \mu\upsilon\sigma\tau\acute{\eta}\rho\iota o\nu\ \delta\acute{\epsilon}\delta o\tau\alpha\iota\ \tau\hat{\eta}s\ \beta\alpha\sigma\iota\lambda\epsilon\acute{\iota}\alpha s\ \tau o\hat{\upsilon}\ \vartheta\epsilon o\hat{\upsilon}\cdot \\
&\dot{\epsilon}\kappa\epsilon\acute{\iota}\nu o\iota s\ \delta\grave{\epsilon}\ \tau o\hat{\iota}s\ \ddot{\epsilon}\xi\omega\ \dot{\epsilon}\nu\ \pi\alpha\rho\alpha\beta o\lambda\alpha\hat{\iota}s\ \tau\grave{\alpha}\ \pi\acute{\alpha}\nu\tau\alpha\ \gamma\acute{\iota}\nu\epsilon\tau\alpha\iota, \\
&\dot{\iota}\nu\alpha\ \beta\lambda\acute{\epsilon}\pi o\nu\tau\epsilon s\ \beta\lambda\acute{\epsilon}\pi\omega\sigma\iota\nu\ \kappa\alpha\grave{\iota}\ \mu\grave{\eta}\ \ddot{\iota}\delta\omega\sigma\iota\nu, \\
&\kappa\alpha\grave{\iota}\ \dot{\alpha}\kappa o\acute{\upsilon}o\nu\tau\epsilon s\ \dot{\alpha}\kappa o\acute{\upsilon}\omega\sigma\iota\nu\ \kappa\alpha\grave{\iota}\ \mu\grave{\eta}\ \sigma\upsilon\nu\iota\hat{\omega}\sigma\iota\nu, \\
&\mu\acute{\eta}\pi o\tau\epsilon\ \dot{\epsilon}\pi\iota\sigma\tau\rho\acute{\epsilon}\psi\omega\sigma\iota\nu\ \kappa\alpha\grave{\iota}\ \dot{\alpha}\phi\epsilon\vartheta\hat{\eta}\ \alpha\dot{\upsilon}\tau o\hat{\iota}s \quad \text{(Mark 4.11f.)}
\end{aligned}$$

As we saw in §12 (p. 120), this was originally an isolated *logion* which was introduced into the chapter on parables because it contained the word παραβολή. In the first place, it did not refer to the parables of Jesus but to the whole of his proclamation. Jesus contrasts the disciples, to whom the μυστήριον τῆς βασιλείας τοῦ θεοῦ[1] is revealed, with οἱ ἔξω, to whom ἐν παραβολαῖς τὰ πάντα γίνεται, i.e. to whom 'everything is a riddle'.[2] This passage does not stand alone, as for example the *logia* Matt. 11.25f. par.; 11.27 par.; 13.16 par. show. In other words, Jesus' authority is disclosed only to believers. It is therefore only consistent that those *logia* which speak clearly of the approaching passion and the glorification following it should be reserved for the instruction of the disciples, that is, the private words of Jesus.[3]

One can hardly overestimate the importance of private instruction in the Judaism of Jesus' time.[4] All the apocalyptic writings were

---

[1] μυστήριον corresponds to the Aramaic *rāz* (a Persian loan word, frequent in the Qumran writings).
[2] Jeremias, *Parables*[2], 16f.
[3] Cf. Morton Smith, *op. cit.*, 155f., on public teaching/secret teaching.
[4] Jeremias, *Jerusalem*, 237–45; *Eucharistic Words*[2], 125–29.

secret writings. The astonishing authority of the scribes rested on the fact that they were in possession of secret tradition. Among the Essenes, those entering the community had to bind themselves by fearful oaths not to betray the secret teaching of the order even under torture and to protect the secret writings of the order.[1] Esoteric teaching is also the reason for gathering groups of disciples in contemporary Judaism; the group was formed in order to receive the confidential teaching.[2] So too with Jesus. By means of extensive lists, T. W. Manson has shown that the vocabulary used by Jesus in the instruction of the disciples differs both from that in the controversies and from that of his public preaching; this is to be explained by the difference in content.[3] The instruction of the disciples about Jesus' mission was developed fully, according to the synoptic gospels, only after Peter's confession.[4]

It is of fundamental importance to note that a distinction between exoteric and esoteric teaching was already current in Jesus' environment and that therefore its appearance in the ministry of Jesus cannot be a cause for astonishment. On the contrary, it is only to be expected. The significance of this fact for understanding Jesus' testimony to himself will be discussed further in the next two sections.

§ 23 · THE SON OF MAN

H. Lietzmann, *Der Menschensohn. Ein Beitrag zur neutestamentlichen Theologie,* Freiburg-Leipzig 1896; P. Fiebig, *Der Menschensohn,* Tübingen-Leipzig 1901; P. Billerbeck, 'Hat die Synagoge einen präexistenten Messias gekannt?', *Nathanael* 21, 1905, 89–150; E. Sjöberg, *Der verborgene Menschensohn in den Evangelien,* Lund 1955; O. Cullmann, *The Christology of the New Testament,* London ²1963; P. Vielhauer, 'Gottesreich und Menschensohn', in: *Festschrift für Günther Dehn,* Neukirchen Kreis Moers 1957, 51–79 = in: P. Vielhauer, *Aufsätze zum N.T.,*

[1] Josephus, *BJ,* 2.141f.; cf. 1 QS 5.15f.; 9.16f. Several texts in cryptic writing have been found in Qumran Cave 4 (F. M. Cross, *The Ancient Library of Qumran,* London 1958, 35f.).

[2] Jeremias, *Jerusalem,* 242f.   [3] Manson, *Teaching²,* 320–27.

[4] The confession itself was manipulated at an early stage (Mark 8.29 ὁ χριστός; Luke 9.20 τὸν χριστὸν τοῦ θεοῦ; Matt. 16.16 ὁ χριστὸς ὁ υἱὸς τοῦ θεοῦ τοῦ ζῶντος). But this does not allow us to regard the whole scene as secondary. Not only the specific details about the place (v. 27), which does not fit in with the scheme of redaction (K. L. Schmidt, *Der Rahmen der Geschichte Jesu,* Berlin 1919 = Darmstadt 1964, 215–17), but also the rejection of Peter, as Satan, which can hardly have been invented (v. 33), shows that a historical nucleus underlies Mark 8.27–33.

München 1965, 55–91; H. E. Tödt, *The Son of Man in the Synoptic Tradition*, London 1965; P. Vielhauer, 'Jesus und der Menschensohn. Zur Diskussion mit H. E. Tödt und E. Schweizer', *ZThK* 60, 1963, 133–77=in: P. Vielhauer, *Aufsätze zum N.T.*, München 1965, 92–140; F. Hahn, *Christologische Hoheitstitel*, FRLANT 83, Göttingen 1963, ²1964; T. F. Glasson, 'The Ensign of the Son of Man Matt. XXIV, 30', *JTS* 15, 1964, 299f.; J. Jeremias, 'Die älteste Schichte der Menschensohn-Logien', *ZNW* 58, 1967, 159–72; J. A. Fitzmyer, Review of M. Black, *An Aramaic Approach to the Gospels and Acts*³, Oxford/New York 1967, *CBQ* 30, 1968, 417–28; C. Colpe, ὁ υἱὸς τοῦ ἀνθρώπου, *TWNT* VIII, 1969, 403–81; H. Conzelmann, *An Outline of the Theology of the New Testament*, London 1969, 131–37; M. Black, 'The "Son of Man" Passion Sayings in the Gospel Tradition', *ZNW* 60, 1969, 1–8.

(i) *The sources*

Son of man is the only title used by Jesus of himself whose authenticity is to be taken seriously.

It is true that in the Gospel of John Jesus regularly speaks of himself as *Son of God*,[1] but in the synoptics he describes himself as 'the Son (of God)' only once (Mark 13.32);[2] the absolute terminology (without genitive or personal pronoun), which is not Palestinian, shows the isolated passage to be secondary,[3] and indeed 'Son of God' is completely unknown as a messianic title in Palestinian Judaism.[4]

Matters are equally clear in the case of the title '*Messiah*'. It is true that the synoptics record Peter's confession σὺ εἶ ὁ χριστός (Mark 8.29 par.), but in Jesus' own sayings the title Messiah occurs only twice, at Mark 9.41 (anarthrous) and Matt 23.10 (with article). In Mark 9.41, ἐν ὀνόματί (μου) is explained by ὅτι Χριστοῦ ἐστε; but this expansion is missing in the version in the Matthaean special material,

---

[1] ὁ υἱός, occasionally ὁ υἱὸς τοῦ θεοῦ (5.25; 10.36; 11.4, cf. 17.1), and one instance of ὁ υἱὸς ὁ μονογενής (3.16), or ὁ μονογενὴς υἱὸς τοῦ θεοῦ (3.18).

[2] The triple ὁ υἱός, Matt. 11.27 par. Luke 10.22, does not belong here because, as we saw on p. 58 above, it is to be understood generically; Matt. 27.43 is a quotation of doubtful value and the triadic baptismal formula in Matt. 28.19 is to be excluded as a saying of the exalted Lord and a community construction.

[3] More precisely: presumably only the words οὐδὲ ὁ υἱός are an addition in Mark 13.32 (see above, p. 131 n.1).

[4] It does in fact occur in Eth. Enoch 105.2, but this chapter is missing in the Greek text from the Chester Beatty papyri published in 1937 (C. Bonner, *The Last Chapters of Enoch in Greek*, Studies and Documents 8, London 1937, 76.17). This has brilliantly confirmed G. Dalman's conjecture that Eth. Enoch 105.2 is a late addition (*Worte Jesu*, 221). In addition, the Messiah is repeatedly called 'my (God's) son' in the Latin and Syriac translation of IV Ezra (7.28f.; 13.32, 37, 52; 14.9), but comparison with the other translations shows that παῖς θεοῦ occurred in the lost Greek version and this points to an underlying ʿabdī (J. Jeremias, παῖς θεοῦ C–D, *TDTN* V, 1967, 676–717: 681 n.196); in fact, the Messiah is given this title in Syr. Bar. 70.9 and eight times in the Targum (*op. cit.*, 681).

10.42, which offers the earlier tradition here.[1] As far as Matt. 23.10 is concerned, it has long been recognized[2] that the verse, with the title καθηγητής, deriving from Greek philosophy, is a secondary doublet of v.8. Here, in the case of the title Messiah, John goes with the synoptics: in 4.26 Jesus does in fact describe himself to the Samaritan woman as Messiah, with his ἐγώ εἰμι, ὁ λαλῶν σοι, but in John the title occurs only once on the lips of Jesus: in 17.3 Jesus speaks quite singularly of himself in the prayer as 'Ιησοῦς Χριστός.

Finally, Jesus never used the title *Son of David* to describe himself. This is most remarkable, because in an early 'three day' saying[3] he designated himself the builder of the New Temple (Mark 14.58 par.; cf. Matt. 16.18) and thus as the shoot of David promised in Nathan's prophecy (II Sam. 7.13).[4] In Mark 12.35–37 par. it is also implicitly claimed that Jesus is son of David. For the tradition[5] here uses a quite definite type of Rabbinic question, the haggadic antinomy,[6] when Jesus asks his interlocutors how the scribes' designation of the Messiah as Son of David[7] is related to Ps. 110.1. Antinomy questions begin from a contradiction in scripture and ask how it is to be explained. The usual answer is that the contradictory details are both valid, but that they refer to different things. If we apply this recognition to Mark 12.35–37, the answer to the question about the antinomy between 'David's son' and 'David's lord', which is left open, would run: the contradiction is only an apparent one; in reality, the two designations refer to different things, 'David's son' to the present and 'David's lord' to the future. That Jesus, despite claiming to be descended from David, as Mark 14.58 par. shows most clearly, avoids the title 'Son of David', is evidently because of its political connotations.[8]

On the other hand, it is the unanimous testimony of all four gospels that Jesus spoke of himself as '*Son of Man*'. The title ὁ υἱὸς τοῦ ἀνθρώπου occurs 82 times in the gospels, 69 in the synoptics,[9] 13 in John. If we count the parallels only once, the synoptic instances are compressed to 38 which are distributed as follows:

[1] One can say this all the more surely because the Marcan sequence 9.41/42 only becomes plain when one compares the Matthaean version of the *logion* about the cup of cold water (10.42 par. Mark 9.41). Matthew does not have ποτίσῃ ὑμᾶς (so Mark 9.41), but ποτίσῃ ἕνα τῶν μικρῶν τούτων. The Marcan version must also originally have had this, as the link-word connection with 9.42 (ἕνα τῶν μικρῶν τούτων) produced in this way shows.

[2] Dalman, *Words of Jesus*, 306, 339. Cf. also p. 169, n.1. [3] See below, p. 285.

[4] O. Betz, 'Die Frage nach dem messianischen Bewusstsein Jesu', *NovTest* 6, 1963, 35f.

[5] No certain decision for or against the authenticity of this pericope can be made with the means at our disposal.

[6] Recognized by D. Daube, *The New Testament and Rabbinic Judaism*, Jordan Lectures 1952, London 1956, 158–69.

[7] II Sam. 7.14; Isa. 9.7; 11.1; Jer. 23.5f.; 30.9; 33.15, 17, 22; Ezek. 34.23f.; 37.24 etc.

[8] Cf. E. Lohse, υἱὸς Δαυίδ, *TWNT* VIII, 1969, 482–92: 483–86.

[9] Fourteen times in Mark, thirty times in Matthew, twenty-five times in Luke.

Mark	14^1
Logia common to Matthew and Luke	10^2
Additional instances peculiar to Matthew	7^3
Additional instances peculiar to Luke	7^4
	38
John	13^5
	51

The material can be reduced still further on the basis of two critical considerations, by means of (a) philological and (b) traditio-historical analysis.

(a) The philological position

The title ὁ υἱὸς τοῦ ἀνθρώπου is unknown in secular Greek; it is a rather barbaric literal translation of a determinative Aramaic construct bar 'enāšā.[6] What does that mean? Like the Hebrew ben, the Aramaic bar is used before substantives mostly to denote descent, though this is not always the case. Before geographical terms, Hebrew ben/bat or Aramaic bar/berat designate the inhabitants (cf. Luke 23.38 θυγατέρες Ἰερουσαλήμ), and before abstract terms the possession of particular characteristics (cf. Luke 16.9 οἱ υἱοὶ τοῦ φωτός); before collective terms they designate the individual (e.g. Hebrew ben bāqār, 'a head of cattle, a cow'). bar 'enāšā is an example of this last instance: bar designates the individual belonging to 'enāš, 'man' used as a collective term. Thus bar 'enāšā means 'the man' or (as in the time of Jesus the process by which the determinative lost its significance had already set in in regular usage),[7] 'a man'. We can make clear the generic use of bar 'enāšā ('the man') with the aid of Matt. 4.4 (οὐκ ἐπ' ἄρτῳ μόνῳ

[1] Mark 2.10, 28; 8.31, 38; 9.9, 12, 31; 10.33, 45; 13.26; 14.21ab, 41, 62.

[2] Matt. 8.20 par. Luke 9.58; Matt. 11.19 par. Luke 7.34; Matt. 12.32 par. Luke 12.10; Matt. 12.40 par. Luke 11.30; Matt. 24.27 par. Luke 17.24; Matt. 24. 37b=39b par. Luke 17.26; Matt. 24.44 par. Luke 12.40; Matt. 19.28; Luke 6.22; 12.8.

[3] Matt. 10.23; 13.37, 41; 16.28; 24.30; 25.31; 26.2.

[4] Luke 17.22, 30; 18.8; 19.10; 21.36; 22.48; 24.7.

[5] John 1.51; 3.13f.; 5.27 (without the article); 6.27, 53, 62; 8.28; 9.35; 12.23, 34a; 13.31. The crowd's question in 12.34b τίς ἐστιν οὗτος ὁ υἱὸς τοῦ ἀνθρώπου; has been included, as it repeats a remark by Jesus.

[6] Up to the second century AD, 'nš'/'nš were without exception written with an initial aleph (Daniel 7.13; Qumran; Naḥal Ḥever), cf. ‡Fitzmeyer 426f.

[7] ‡Colpe, 407.1f.

ζήσεται ὁ ἄνθρωπος) and the indefinite use ('a man', 'someone') by means of John 8.40 (ἄνθρωπος ὃς τὴν ἀλήθειαν ὑμῖν λελάληκα).[1] A more elevated way of speaking had developed alongside this everyday use of bar 'enāšā: in apocalyptic language, as a result of Dan. 7.13, bar 'enāšā has become a messianic title, as we know above all from the Similitudes of Ethiopian Enoch.

In the Greek text of the gospels as we have it, ὁ υἱὸς τοῦ ἀνθρώπου is understood everywhere as a title. The question is, however, whether the underlying Aramaic equivalent bar 'enāšā may not in some passages have had the everyday significance ('the man', 'a man', 'someone') originally, and have only been understood as a title through a misconception. This may in fact have been the case at least in the saying about the blasphemy against the spirit.

This saying has been handed on to us in two versions. In the Marcan version, the contrast is: all sins (against men), indeed all blasphemies (against God) can be forgiven the children of men, but blasphemy against the spirit is unforgivable (Mark 3.28f. par. Matt. 12.31). In the *logia* version, on the other hand, the contrast is quite different: 'God can forgive the one who speaks against the Son of man, but he will not forgive the one who blasphemes against the spirit' (Luke 12.10 par. Matt. 12.32). It has long been recognized (probably first in 1569 by G. Génébrard)[2] that a *lebar 'enāšā* (singular) underlies both versions, which the Marcan version rightly understood generically '(men can be forgiven all sins', or 'all sins against men can be forgiven' – in Aramaic, both are possible), whereas the *logia* version took it wrongly as a title ('whoever speaks against the Son of man'). Here a Son of man saying arose at a later stage as a result of the misunderstanding of a generic *bar 'enāšā*. Mark 2.28 is to be judged in the same way; v. 27 speaks twice of men in the generic sense, so this is also likely in the verse that follows.

In Matt. 11.19 par. Luke 7.34 we may have an instance of *bar 'enāšā*, originally with an *indefinite* meaning, becoming an apocalyptic title. Here ἄνθρωπος follows

---

[1] On the other hand, it is not true that bar 'enāšā is to be found as a periphrasis for 'I', although that is continually asserted (most recently by G. Vermes in his carefully documented investigation, 'The Use of בר נש/בר נשא in Jewish Aramaic', in: M. Black, *An Aramaic Approach to the Gospels and Acts*[3], Oxford 1967, 310–28: 320–27). The usual starting point for this claim is that in Galilean Aramaic *hāhū gabrā*, 'that man', is used as a periphrasis for 'I' or 'you', either out of modesty or in statements with an unwelcome content. There is, however, an essential difference between the two phrases. *hāhū gabrā*, referring to the person who speaks, means 'I (and no other)', and thus is strictly limited to the speaker; bar 'enāšā, on the other hand, keeps its generic or indefinite significance, 'the (or a) man, and therefore also I', 'the (or a) man like myself', even where the speaker does include himself. This can be demonstrated from Matt. 4.4 (ὁ ἄνθρωπος) and John 8.40 (ἄνθρωπος). That means that while bar 'enāšā (like our 'one') can include the speaker, it is not a periphrasis for 'I'.

[2] *De S. Trinitate libri tres*, Paris 1569, 246f.

ὁ υἱὸς τοῦ ἀνθρώπου, evidently with no difference in meaning: ἦλθεν ὁ υἱὸς τοῦ ἀνθρώπου ἐσθίων καὶ πίνων καὶ λέγουσιν· ἰδοὺ ἄνθρωπος φάγος καὶ οἰνοπότης. Both times, Jesus will have said *bar 'eⁿāšā* or *bar 'eⁿāš*, and will have meant it in the sense of 'someone', 'one', so that the contrast between John the Baptist and Jesus ought to be translated as follows: 'John came, who did not eat and drink, and they said, He is mad. One came who did eat and drink, and they say, A glutton and a drunkard.' A *bar 'eⁿāšā* meant indefinitely may also underlie ὁ υἱὸς τοῦ ἀνθρώπου in Mark 2.10; to the objection expressed in 2.7, Jesus would reply, 'But that you may know that (not only God in heaven but in my case also) a man on earth has the right to forgive sins . . .'.[1] Finally, in view of the contrast with the wild animals which it expresses, we may suppose that Matt. 8.20 par. Luke 9.58 also originally had an indefinite sense: 'Wild animals have their lairs, but a man like myself is homeless'.[2]

In all these passages, *bar 'eⁿāšā* was presumably meant originally in the everyday sense of 'the man' or 'a man', and only the early church tradition found the apocalyptic title 'Son of man' in them.

(b) The traditio-historical position

Traditio-historical analysis is much more penetrating than philological analysis. It is based on the consideration that the overwhelming majority of Son of man sayings have been transmitted in two forms, in a version *with* Son of man and in one *without*. For instance, one might compare the last beatitude in Luke ἕνεκα τοῦ υἱοῦ τοῦ ἀνθρώπου (6.22) with the Matthaean version ἕνεκεν ἐμοῦ (5.11).[3] Of the fifty-one Son of man sayings in the gospels,[4] no fewer than thirty-seven have a competing tradition in which the term Son of man is absent and (usually) ἐγώ is put in its place.[5]

The question now arises whether we can show which version – the one with or the one without Son of man – in these thirty-seven passages is the earlier. A detailed examination shows that time after time the title Son of man is demonstrably secondary. Thus, it appears to be secondary in new versions of earlier *logia*,[6] in

[1] ‡Colpe, 433.13f., cf. J. Wellhausen, *Skizzen und Vorarbeiten* VI, Berlin 1899, 202f.; *Das Evangelium Marci*², Berlin 1909, 16. Wellhausen recognized that ὁ υἱὸς τοῦ ἀνθρώπου in Mark 2.10 has a concessive connotation: 'although I am a man' (*Skizzen* VI, 203). We had a quite similar instance on pp. 163f.: ἄνθρωπός εἰμι ὑπὸ ἐξουσίαν (Matt. 8.9 par.) was to be translated: 'although I am only a man who has to obey'.

[2] ‡Colpe, 435 with a detailed argument.

[3] I have collected the material in 'Die älteste Schicht der Menschensohn-Logien', *ZNW* 58, 1967, 159–72.

[4] See above, p. 260.

[5] See the lists, *op. cit.*, 159–64.

[6] For example, Matthew reshapes the *logion* Mark 9.1 as a Son of man saying (Matt. 16.28). The Son of man saying in Luke 19.10 also proves to be a secondary

later developments[1] and new constructions;[2] the tradition was fond of the solemn, archaic expression ὁ υἱὸς τοῦ ἀνθρώπου, and often inserted it into sayings of Jesus. On the other hand, not a single instance of the opposite process, the elimination of the expression, can be demonstrated.[3] Rather, once the title ὁ υἱὸς τοῦ ἀνθρώπου had gained a footing, it did not let itself be suppressed again. That means that wherever we find rivalry between the simple ἐγώ and the solemn ὁ υἱὸς τοῦ ἀνθρώπου, all the probability is that the simple ἐγώ is the earlier tradition.

Once can only ask whether in individual cases we have to reckon with the possibility that both versions, that with and that without Son of man, existed side by side from the beginning. This question might be answered in the affirmative for the short mᵉšālīm mentioned on p. 282, because these belong to the earliest material.

Leaving aside the Son of man sayings that we had to exclude on philological grounds (because in all probability they go back to a misunderstanding of a generic or indefinite bar 'ᵉnāšā), and the Son of man sayings which are accompanied by a rival version without Son of man (because in this case the version without the title must be given priority), the number of instances is considerably decreased.

In all this critical analysis, however, the most important thing is that a remainder of Son of man sayings is left which have been handed down, without competitors, only in the Son of man version and in which even the possibility of mistranslation is excluded, because their content shows that ὁ υἱὸς τοῦ ἀνθρώπου was intended as a title from the beginning. They are as follows: Mark 13.26 par.; 14.62 par.; Matt. 24.27, 37b = 39b par. Luke 17.24, 26; Matt. 10.23; 25.31; Luke 17.22, 30; 18.8; 21.36; John 1.51. With one expection all these eleven *logia* are future sayings. Only John 1.51 seems to fall outside this framework. But even in the case of this saying, the double introduction to which (λέγει αὐτῷ singular/λέγω ὑμῖν plural) shows it to be earlier than John, we must consider whether the original

---

reshaping in comparison with Matt. 15.24 (the offensive particularism is removed in Luke 19.10, and at the same time the ἀπεστάλην has been changed to ἦλθεν γὰρ ὁ υἱὸς τοῦ ἀνθρώπου). See further Luke 6.9 and the secondary version in 9.56, v.l.

[1] The clearest example is Matt. 26.2: here Matthew has replaced the note of time in Mark 14.1a by a Son of man passion prediction formulated along the lines of Matt. 17.22. Luke 24.7 and perhaps also 17.25 may similarly belong here; so too may the interpretation of the parable of the tares formulated by Matthew (Matt. 13.36–43), where the Son of man appears in vv. 37 and 41: v. 41 takes up Matt. 24.31 par. Mark 13.27.

[2] Matt. 13.37 (see note 1); 12.39f. par. (Mark 8.12 par. does not have Son of man); 24.30a (addition to Mark 13.26) belong here.

[3] Matt. 16.21 (αὐτόν inserted for Mark 8.31 τὸν υἱὸν τοῦ ἀνθρώπου) is, as has long been recognized, no instance of the eradication of the title but an apparent exception. For Matthew did not repeat the title which Mark offered him here because he had anticipated it in v. 13.

reference was not similarly to the epiphany of the Son of man. This is suggested by the ὄψεσθε (cf. Mark 14.62 par.), the opening of the heavens (cf. Rev. 19.11) and the mention of the angels (cf. Mark 8.38 par.). The fact that there are epiphany sayings alongside the short *bar ʾenāšā-mešālim*,[1] as we would expect with an apocalyptic title indicates that the nucleus of tradition that we have discovered can lay claim to considerable antiquity.

(ii) The question of authenticity

The critical analysis of the source has considerably simplified the problem of authenticity, i.e. the question whether Jesus used the title Son of man. It is now reduced to the question whether those Son of man sayings which have withstood philological and traditio-historical analysis can be said with some degree of probability to go back to Jesus or whether they, too, must be assigned to the community.

It would be an error of method to suggest without further ado that these remaining Son of man sayings may be regarded as authentic, lock, stock and barrel. There is doubt at least over Matt. 24.30a; 25.31. For in Matt. 24.30a, Matthew has added the σημεῖον (i.e. the banner)[2] of the Son of man to the Marcan text (13.26), as he has added the great trumpet in v. 31; both insignia of war, the banner and the trumpet, are attributes of the eschatological gathering of the people of God. As Matthew is fond elsewhere of increasing the apocalyptic colouring,[3] Matt. 25.31 could also derive from him, all the more since ὁ υἱὸς τοῦ ἀνθρώπου clashes with ὁ βασιλεύς (vv. 34, 40) and the phrase 'the throne of the glory of the Son of man' occurs only in Matthew.[4] On the other hand, it can at least be shown that the application of the title Son of man to Christ is *early Palestinian tradition*. Not only the linguistic evidence,[5] but also the consideration that the title began to be avoided from an early stage, suggests this. This is the only explanation of the fact that in the New

[1] See below, p. 282.
[2] According to a brilliant observation by ‡Glasson.
[3] T. F. Glasson, *The Second Advent. The Origin of the New Testament Doctrine*[2], London 1947, 69–75, who among other passages refers to Matt. 7.19 (cf. 3.10); 16.27 (cf. Mark 8.38); 16.28 (cf. Mark 9.1); 24.3 (cf. Mark 13.4).
[4] Matt. 19.28; 25.31.
[5] The Son of man *logia* recognized on p. 263 as the earliest element of the tradition display predominantly un-Greek usage: e.g. the superfluous demonstrative ταύτῃ in Matt. 10.23, the unusual positioning of the article before ἑτέραν, *ibid.* (cf. Blass-Debrunner-Funk §306, 2), before πίστις in Luke 18.8 (cf. Jeremias, *Parables*[2], 155 n.13) and before ἀστραπή in Matt. 24.27 (*op. cit.*, 11 n.2), the paraphrasing of the divine name by ἡ δύναμις Mark 14.62 par. For the rhythmic structure of Matt. 8.20 see above, p. 23 and for the Aramaic word-play in Mark 9.31 see below, p. 282.

Testament, apart from the sayings of Jesus and three Old Testament quotations,[1] it occurs only in Acts 7.56, on the lips of Stephen. Otherwise, it is completely absent.[2] The Pauline evidence is most significant. It can be demonstrated that Paul knew the title. This follows from I Cor. 15.27; Phil. 3.21; Eph. 1.22, where Paul interprets Ps. 8, the Son of man psalm, in messianic terms, and further from the designation of Christ as ἄνθρωπος in I Cor. 15.21 and ὁ ἄνθρωπος in Rom. 5.15, which is probably a derivation from *bar 'enāšā*.[3] Finally, Paul's familiarity with the title can be seen from the Adam-Christ typology which is quite unknown both to contemporary Judaism and to pre-Christian Hellenism, and may therefore be a Pauline creation.[4] The only answer to the question how Paul came to create the Adam-Christ typology can be that his starting point was the designation of Jesus as 'the man'. So although Paul knew the title Son of man, he never uses it. Evidently he deliberately avoids the expression ὁ υἱὸς τοῦ ἀνθρώπου and instead uses the correct rendering of *bar 'enāšā, ὁ ἄνθρωπος*. The same thing happens in I Tim. 2.5 (see note 3). The use of the title Son of man is thus pre-Pauline, and the title began to be avoided soon after the transition from a Semitic to a Greek-speaking milieu. The reason is easy to discover; the intention was to avoid the danger that native Greeks would take the title as a designation of descent. It continued only in the Palestinian Jewish-Christian community (Acts 7.56; Gospel of the Hebrews;[5] Hegesippus);[6] here there was no fear of misunderstanding.

These remarks take us back to an earlier, pre-Pauline period, more exactly to the Aramaic-speaking early church, but not as far as Jesus. If we turn to the question whether he himself used the title, one reason for a positive answer is that elsewhere in the sayings of Jesus which can lay claim to considerable antiquity there are references to Dan. 7. This is true of Luke 12.32 (for δοῦναι . . . τὴν βασιλείαν with the absolute use of βασιλεία cf. Dan. 7.18, 27) and of the common content of Matt. 19.28 par. Luke 22.28, 30b (for ἐπὶ θρόνων [plural!] see Dan. 7.9; for κρίνοντες see 7.10). Secondly, all five strata of the tradition agree that Jesus spoke of the Son of man in the third person; he therefore made a distinction between himself and the Son of man. This distinction cannot be explained by arguing that the designation Son of man arose in the earliest community, as for the community the

[1] Rev. 1.13; 14.14: Dan. 7.13; Heb. 2.6: Ps. 8.5.
[2] In John 12.34 it is indeed the crowd that is speaking, but they quote a saying of Jesus.
[3] This is supported also by the comparison of I Tim. 2.5 (ἄνθρωπος) with Mark 10.45 (ὁ υἱὸς τοῦ ἀνθρώπου).
[4] Cf. B. Schaller, *Gen. 1.2 im antiken Judentum*, Diss. theol. Göttingen 1961 (typescript), 189f.
[5] Jerome, *De viris inl.* 2 (English in E. Hennecke–W. Schneemelcher – R. McL. Wilson (eds.), *New Testament Apocrypha* I, London 1963, 127).
[6] In Eusebius, HE II 23.13 (English, *op. cit.*, 420f.), dependent on Matt. 26.64.

identification of Jesus with the Son of man went without saying.[1] This distinction (cf. pp. 275f. below for further details) is therefore an indication that the terminology dates from before Easter. A weightier consideration is that no Son of man saying speaks of both resurrection and parousia at the same time.[2] The distinction between resurrection and parousia derives from the post-Easter christology; for Jesus himself, as we shall see on pp. 285f., both events were alternative ways of describing the final triumph of God. The absence of a distinction between resurrection and parousia in the Son of man sayings is thus another pointer to the pre-Easter usage.

We have still, however, to mention the most important consideration in the question of authenticity. We have seen that even at the time of Paul, the Greek-speaking church avoided the title Son of man. Nevertheless, it retained its firm place in the gospels. Indeed, here the usage was even extended considerably. John still has the title thirteen times. Now it is remarkable that in all four gospels the title occurs *exclusively* on the lips of Jesus.[3] Here the tradition is quite consistent. The title Son of man does not occur in any confessional formula of the early church. It is never used as an attribute or predicate. Nowhere in the gospel account is Jesus designated as Son of man, nor is he addressed as Son of man in prayer. There is not a single passage in the gospels in which the title is used in statements about Jesus. On the contrary, it is firmly anchored in the sayings of Jesus.

How did it come about that at a very early stage the community avoided the title ὁ υἱὸς τοῦ ἀνθρώπου because it was liable to be misunderstood, did not use it in a single confession, yet at the same time handed it down in the sayings of Jesus, in the synoptic gospels virtually as the only title used by Jesus of himself? How is it that the instances of it increase, but the usage is still strictly limited to the sayings of Jesus? There can only be one answer; the title was rooted in the tradition of the sayings of Jesus right from the beginning; as a result, it was sacrosanct, and no-one dared to eliminate it.

That means that the apocalyptic Son of Man sayings which we

---

[1] E. Schweizer, 'Der Menschensohn (Zur eschatologischen Erwartung Jesu)', *ZNW* 50, 1959, 185–209: 188.

[2] In Mark 14.62 we find exaltation (not resurrection!) and parousia side by side. But the earlier version of the confession before the Sanhedrin, Luke 22.69 (see below, p. 273), speaks only of exaltation.

[3] For the apparent exception in John 12.34 see p. 265, n.2 above.

have recognized as the earliest stratum must in essentials go back to Jesus himself.

Despite these weighty arguments, it has been continually doubted since Lietzmann whether Jesus used the term Son of man at all.[1] Recently, appeal has been made above all to a consideration first advanced by H. B. Sharman[2] and H. A. Guy,[3] that in the synoptic gospels the terms 'reign of God' and 'Son of man' stand, remarkably enough, side by side, with no connection between them. They are only linked in the process of compilation (Mark 8.38/9.1; Luke 17.21/22; 21.27/31; Matt. 10.7/23; 13.37/43; 25.31/34), never authentically. From this, P. Vielhauer concluded that only one of the two terms can belong to the preaching of Jesus, and that could only be reign of God.[4] Therefore all the Son of man *logia* are to be regarded as inauthentic. It tells against this radical solution, however, that the unassociated juxtaposition of reign of God and Son of man that we come across in the synoptic gospels is already to be found in the Judaism of Jesus' time. There, reign of God was the slogan of the prevailing expectation for the future,[5] whereas Son of man was the slogan of an esoteric eschatology. The proclamation of Jesus follows exactly the same lines. In public preaching, and above all in the parables, he spoke of the coming *basileia*. On the other hand, the Marcan tradition has him using the title Son of man after Peter's confession only to the disciples;[6] according to Mark, Jesus broke through the veil of secrecy which begins at Mark 8.27ff. for the first and only time at the hearing before the supreme council.[7] There is every probability that the limitation of the use of 'Son of man' as a title to the *logia* addressed to the disciples is a historical reminiscence, and that this is the explanation of the unconnected juxtaposition of the proclamation of the *basileia* and the sayings about the Son of man: the *basileia* of God is the key word for Jesus' exoteric teaching, Son of man the key word for his esoteric teaching. This can be seen, for example, at Luke 17.20ff. Here we find the statement that what is to come cannot be given a spatial location first in a saying to the Pharisees (17.20f.) and

---

[1] ‡Lietzmann; in present German scholarship above all by P. Vielhauer, E. Käsemann and H. Conzelmann (cf. ‡Colpe, 440 n.284).

[2] *Son of Man and Kingdom of God*[2], New York 1944, 84f., 89.

[3] *The New Testament Doctrine of the Last Things*, London 1948, 81f.

[4] ‡Vielhauer.

[5] Cf. Ps. Sol. 5.18f.; 17.3; Ass. Mos. 10.1; Kaddish (Dalman, *Worte Jesu*[1], 305, unfortunately omitted from the second edition); New Year *mūsāp* prayers (ʿalēnū, Billerbeck I 178; ūbᵉkēn, ibid., according to Dalman, op. cit., 306; malkiyyōt, P. Fiebig, 'Rosch ha-Schana (Neujahr)', *Die Mischna* II 8, Giessen 1914, 49–53); Targum (Billerbeck I 179); Midrash (op. cit., 179f.).

[6] Earlier only twice (2.10, 28); on the two passages see above, pp. 261f. In the present context, of course, Mark 8.38 is directed to the crowd, but the details about the audience in v. 34 are redactional (the participle προσκαλεσάμενος and the singular ὁ ὄχλος and σὺν τοῖς μαθηταῖς αὐτοῦ, cf. 4.10).

[7] It cannot be objected against the historicity of the account of the trial of Jesus before the Sanhedrin that no member of the community was present – as if it did not go round Jerusalem like wildfire why the prophet from Galilee had been handed over to the Romans for condemnation.

JESUS' TESTIMONY TO HIS MISSION

then in a saying to the disciples (17.23f.). It is hardly coincidental that Jesus uses the term *basileia* to his opponents (v. 21), while speaking on the other hand of the Son of man to his disciples (v. 24).

Thus there is a model for the unassociated juxtaposition of reign of God and Son of man in the sayings of Jesus in the world of his time. If that is the case, then it can be no objection to the argument that Jesus himself used the title Son of man.

(iii) The background to the title

The title Son of man is not explained anywhere in the gospels. Everywhere its meaning is taken for granted. Indeed Jesus did not coin it himself. What is its origin? This question bring us face to face with the historical problem.

This problem has become very much simpler in the last few decades. Following the history of religions school, numerous attempts had been made to derive the Son of man from conceptions of the Primal Man in Mesopotamia, Persia, India and gnosticism. However, a thorough examination of the comparative material has shown that all these hypotheses stand on very slim foundations. In particular the derivation of the title from the Iranian Gayomart has been rejected by the Iranists. This negative situation follows from the comprehensive examination of the sources made by C. Colpe.[1] As no preliminary evidence can be demonstrated from the Old Testament, either, our attention is directed exclusively to Jewish apocalyptic for the earliest history of the conception of the Son of man to be found in the gospels.[2]

Here the expression *bar 'enāš* appears for the first time in Dan. 7.13. 7.1–14 depicts a vision of Daniel. In the opening, he sees how four great beasts rise out of the sea (vv. 1–8) symbolizing the four kingdoms. After the fourth especially fearful beast is killed (v. 11), a

---

[1] *Die religionsgeschichtliche Schule. Darstellung und Kritik ihres Bildes vom gnostischen Erlösermythus*, FRLANT 78, Göttingen 1961; ὁ υἱὸς τοῦ ἀνθρώπου, *TWNT* VIII, 1969, 411–18. Colpe merely wants to advance the theory that the Canaanite Baal represents a preformation of the 'one like a man' in Dan. 7.13 (418–22), but in view of the enormous time lapse between the texts from Ras Shamra and the book of Daniel this is hardly conceivable.

[2] The title ὁ υἱὸς τοῦ ἀνθρώπου has nothing to do with the regular address to Ezekiel (and also Daniel), 'Child of man', as no allusions are to be found to the latter.

fifth being appears in heaven. This, however, does not have the form of a beast, but is like a man:

Behold, there came a being in human form ($k^e bar$ '$en\bar{a}\check{s}$) in ('im) heavenly clouds and came to the Ancient of Days and was presented before him (14) and to him was given dominion and glory and kingdom, that all peoples, nations and languages should serve him; his dominion is an everlasting dominion, which shall not pass away (vv. 13f.).

An interpretation has been attached to this vision in which the 'being in human form' is interpreted as a fifth kingdom, the kingdom of 'the saints of the most high' (vv. 18, 27). In the following period, however, the being in human form of Dan. 7.13 was interpreted, without exception, not collectively, but in terms of an individual person. In this way 'the man' becomes a title for the redeemer in apocalyptic (Similitudes of Ethiopian Enoch 37–71, first century BC;[1] Sibylline Oracles, between AD 70 and AD 100;[2] IV Ezra, AD 94;[3] Trypho, in Justin, *Dial.* 32.1, before AD 165); the 'being in human form' of Dan. 7.13 is also identified with the Messiah in Rabbinic literature.[4] The most important sources is the Similitudes of Ethiopian Enoch 37–71, which reached their present form after the Parthian invasion of Palestine (40–39 BC, cf. Eth. Enoch 56.5–7).[5]

[1] 46.1–4; 48.2; 62.2, 5, 7, 9, 14; 63.11; 69.26f., 29; 70.1; 71.14, 17.

[2] 5.256 (see below, p. 270, n.2), 414.

[3] 13.2f., 5, 12, 25, 32, 51; on the date see Billerbeck IV 996.

[4] All the Rabbinic material may be had by combining Billerbeck I 486 with I 956f. The sparseness of the Rabbinic material will be the consequence of anti-Christian polemic (explicit polemic is to be found in j. Taan. 65b 60). It is not clear whether the 'ambiguous oracle' which Josephus gives as one of the main causes of the rebellion against Rome in AD 66–70 (*B.J.* 6.312f.) is meant to be Dan. 7.13f. (cf. M. Hengel, *Die Zeloten*, AGSU 1, Leiden-Köln 1961, 243–46, for whom Num. 24.17 is the most likely basis).

[5] At that time the Parthians raided Palestine and plundered both the countryside and the capital, Jerusalem. J. C. Hindley, 'Towards a Date for the Similitudes of Enoch. An Historical Approach', *NTS* 14, 1967/68, 551–65: 553, who objects that the events of 40–39 BC could not form the background to Eth. Enoch 56.6f. because according to 56.7 the invasion will come to grief at Jerusalem, whereas in fact the Parthians occupied Jerusalem at that time, overlooks the fact that Enoch 56.5–7 is not a historical account but an eschatological prophecy (the Gog-Magog tradition), which borrows only the mention of the apocalyptic enemy from the events of the time. Because parts of the other four divisions of Ethiopian Enoch have been found at Qumran, but not the Similitudes, some scholars have taken the latter to be Christian; this suggestion fails to explain the complete absence of all Christian features.

What do the Jewish apocalyptic texts say about the 'man'?
The foundation and starting point for all statements about him is
Dan. 7.13: the 'man' reveals himself 'on that day'(Eth. Enoch 45.3).
He appears flying with the clouds of heaven (IV Ezra 13.3), on the
mount of Zion (13.6, 35), casts kings and rulers from their thrones
(Eth. Enoch 46.4f.), sits on the throne of glory (45.3; 55.4; 61.8;
62.2f.; 69.27) and holds judgment (45.3; 49.4; 55.4; 61.8f.; 62.3;
69.27) or annihilates the enemy host with the fiery breath of his
mouth (IV Ezra 13.9–11). Then he descends from the mountain and
summons a peaceful host to his side (IV Ezra 13.12f.). He will be
the support of the righteous and the holy, the light of the nations, the
hope of the troubled (Eth. Enoch 48.4). All the world will fall down
before him (48.5; 62.9). The righteous and the elect will have table-
fellowship and share life with him (62.14).

But who is 'the man'? Where does he come from? The Jewish
apocalyptists were intensively concerned with these questions.
It was said, 'his lot has the pre-eminence before the Lord of Spirits in
uprightness for ever' (Eth. Enoch 46.3); thus he had lived. Now he is
concealed until the time of his revelation (62.6f.; IV Ezra 13.26), as it
is said of the servant of God in Isa. 49.2. He lives among the departed
righteous in paradise, manifest, because he is one of their number
(Eth. Enoch 39.6).[1] In the closing chapter of the Similitudes of Enoch
it is Enoch himself who is appointed Son of man (71.14); in IV Ezra
'the man' who, according to 13.3, comes out of the sea, i.e. from the
underworld, is identical with the seed of David (12.32); in the Sibylline oracles Joshua (or Moses) is 'the man':[2] Theudas (Josephus,

[1] Billerbeck II 282, n.1.
[2] Or. Sib. 5.256–59 reads:

Then there shall come from the sky a certain exalted man,
(whose hands they nailed upon the fruitful tree,)
the noblest of the Hebrews, who one day caused the sun to stand still,
crying with fair speech and pure lips.

It has been generally – and rightly – recognized that v. 257 is a Christian insertion.
There is a dispute, however, as to whether vv. 256, 258f. are of Jewish or Christian
origin. Anyone who in view of the context (which depicts the final time of
blessing, without further mention of the ἀνήρ of 256, 258f.) decides that all four
lines are of Christian origin, must resort to another emendation of the text: he must
alter the aorist στῆσε(ν), which occurs in all MSS in v. 258, into a future στήσει (so
most recently the basic work of B. Noack, 'Der hervorragende Mann und der
Beste der Hebräer', ASTI 3, 1964, 122–46). But it is very questionable whether this
incursion into the text is justified; for the expectation that the Christ on his return

Antt. 20.97–99) and the Egyptian (*ibid.*, 169f.), both of them Messianic pretenders, announced that they would repeat the miracles of Joshua. The significant thing about this variety of answers is that the Son of man is nowhere conceived of as an angelic being. He is always one who returns from the beyond, often a figure from primeval times who will be set by the Lord of spirits on the throne of glory (Eth. Enoch 61.8; 62.2).[1]

To evaluate these apocalyptic texts correctly we must remember that the dominant expectation of the Messiah in Judaism had a quite different aspect. An earthly ruler was expected, who would be the great warrior hero and free the people from the yoke of Rome (this was also the hope of the Essenes). The Jewish apocalyptic texts discussed above show that another messianic expectation existed alongside this. It, too, had a nationalistic orientation and looked for victory over the pagan rulers, but in it the Messiah was a superhuman figure with transcendent features and possessed a universal significance ('light of the nations', Eth. Enoch. 48.4).

This expectation of the 'man' is attested for us in detail only in apocalyptic writings. These, as they themselves say, represented a secret literature.[2] For example, the expectation of the 'man' as we find it in Ethiopian Enoch was kept alive in a small group which called itself the community of the righteous and boasted that the Lord of the spirits had revealed to it the secrets of the world beyond and the hidden Son of man. This community complained that it was being persecuted and that its houses of prayer were being burnt (Eth. Enoch 46.8; 47.1–4).

In view of the New Testament evidence, it is particularly worth

---

will perform the miracle of making the sun stand still is not attested anywhere. On the other hand, vv. 256, 258f., as no-one disputes, are unobjectionable as a Jewish apocalyptic statement. So if we keep to the text, Joshua, who once made the sun stand still (Josh. 10.12–14), is the ἀνήρ who will come from heaven in the future; possibly also Moses, as such a miracle is also ascribed to him in Rabbinic texts (Billerbeck I 13; II 414).

[1] ‡Billerbeck, 'Synagoge'. In this significant investigation, for some incomprehensible reason completely ignored by scholars, which among other things offers a subtle source analysis of the Similitudes of Ethiopian Enoch, Billerbeck arrives at the conclusion that the synagogue of the first two centuries AD had no conception of a real pre-existence of the Messiah. On the other hand, there was a widespread idea that one coming from the beyond was destined as the Messiah.

[2] IV Ezra 14.44–46, cf. 12.36–38; 14.26; Eth. Enoch 104.12f. (the original conclusion).

noticing that in the Jewish Son of man texts in Ethiopian Enoch and IV Ezra attributes of the servant of God in Deutero-Isaiah are transferred to the 'man'. In Ethiopian Enoch he is called, as we have seen, 'the light of the nations' (48.4, a clear attribute of the servant of God: Isa. 42.6; 49.6), 'the chosen one' (39.6; 40.5 and often; cf. Isa. 42.1), 'the righteous one' (38.2; 53.6; cf. Isa. 53.11); his name was 'named before the Lord of spirits' before creation (48.3; cf. Isa. 49.1); he was 'hidden before him (God)' (48.6, also 62.7; cf. Isa. 49.2); again and again it is shown how kings and mighty ones will rise to him or bow down before him (46.4ff.; 62.1ff.; cf. Isa. 49.7; 52.13–15) etc.[1] In IV Ezra 'the man' is called 'my (God's) servant' (13.32, 37, 52; 14.9, see p. 258, n. 4 above), and it is said of him that he is being preserved (13.26, cf. Isa. 49.2). Though no clear statements about suffering are transferred from the servant to the 'man', it is of the utmost significance that this connection between sayings about the Son of man and sayings about the servant of God offered a starting point which could be taken further by Jesus.

(iv) The meaning of the title 'Son of man' on the lips of Jesus

In the sayings of Jesus, as in Jewish apocalyptic, Son of man is a term of glory. If we keep to what was recognized on p. 263 as the earliest stratum of Son of man *logia*, something like the following picture emerges. When the persecution of the community has reached its climax (§22), the vision of Daniel 7.13, understood as a prophecy, will be realized. It will come suddenly, like a flash of lightning from a clear sky (Matt. 24.27 par. Luke 17.24), when no one expects it (Matt. 24.37, 39 par. Luke 17.26; also without parallel, 17.30). Veiled in clouds, surrounded by hosts of angels, in divine glory, the Son of man will appear (Mark 13.26; cf. John 1.51). He will sit down on the throne at God's right hand (Luke 22.69) and send out his angels to gather together his elect from the four winds (Mark 13.27). He will hold judgment (Luke 21.36; Luke 22.69 is also a threat of judgment) with the twelve representatives of the people of the twelve tribes as assessors (Matt. 19.28 par. Luke 22.30, cf. Dan. 7.9f.; I Cor. 6.2f.).[2]

---

[1] Further instances in J. Jeremias, παῖς θεοῦ, *TDNT* V, 1967, 688f.; cf. also H.-F. Weiss, 'Menschensohn', *RGG*³ IV, 1960, cols. 874–76: 875.

[2] The idea is not, say, that each of the twelve will judge one of the twelve tribes; the group of twelve will take part corporately in the judgment, as Dan. 7.9f. shows.

According to Dan. 7.13, the one like a man is brought to the Ancient of Days; he is enthroned; the *movement* is thought of as being *from below upwards*. The coming 'in the clouds'[1] is predominantly conceived of in this way in Jewish apocalyptic (Eth. Enoch 14.8; 71.5; IV Ezra 13.3; Midr. Ps. 21 §5; for the combination of clouds and an upward movement cf. Acts 1.9; I Thess. 4.17; Rev. 11.12), elsewhere probably only b. Sanh. 98a (R. Alexandrai, *c.* AD 270). The conception of the parousia in the gospels, on the other hand, is one in which the coming of the Son of man is thought of as a *movement from above downwards*. He comes to his own, who await him with loins girded (Luke 12.35f.), as Israel had girded its loins for departure on Passover night (Ex. 12.11). The movement from above downwards is expressed particularly clearly in the agraphon I Thess. 4.16 (καταβήσεται ἀπ' οὐρανοῦ).

It is striking, however, that the term παρουσία in the gospels is limited to Matthew (24.3, 27, 37, 39) and that the conception of the descent of the Son of man is again and again redactional (e.g. Matt. 16.28; 24.44 par. Luke 12.40;[2] for Mark 14.62 see below). Indeed, whereas we have no early Son of man *logion* which speaks clearly of his descent, in some of these *logia* there seems to be an underlying idea of a movement from below upwards, which in that case would be earlier than the conception of the parousia. Luke 22.69 must be mentioned first here. It is an insight of great significance that the Lucan passion narrative from 22.14 onwards derives from the Lucan special source and therefore represents an independent tradition from that of Mark.[3] If we compare the two independent versions of the confession before the supreme council in Mark 14.62 and Luke 22.69, the Lucan can be seen to be the simpler; unlike Mark 14.62 it has still not been influenced by the early Christian christological pattern of exaltation and parousia. That Luke 22.69 represents an early formulation is, moreover, confirmed by Acts 7.56 (ἰδοὺ θεωρῶ τοὺς οὐρανοὺς διηνοιγμένους καὶ τὸν υἱὸν τοῦ ἀνθρώπου ἐκ δεξιῶν ἑστῶτα τοῦ θεοῦ). This exclamation by the dying Stephen corresponds with Luke 22.69 (ἀπὸ τοῦ νῦν[4] δὲ ἔσται ὁ υἱὸς τοῦ ἀνθρώπου καθήμενος ἐκ δεξιῶν τῆς δυνάμεως τοῦ θεοῦ) in content, but rests on independent tradition,[5] as the peculiar ἑστῶτα shows.[6] Now Luke 22.69 seems to presuppose that the manifestation of the glory of the Son of man consists in his assumption to God (cf. Eth. Enoch 71). The same is true of the εἰσελθεῖν εἰς τὴν δόξαν αὐτοῦ in Luke 24.26 and of the Johannine ἀναβαίνειν (John 3.13 etc.) and ὑψοῦσθαι (John 3.14, etc.); here, too, the movement is from below upwards. δοξάζεσθαι (John 12.23 etc.) will also be meant in this sense, as Luke 24.26

---

[1] R. B. Y. Scott, 'Behold, He Cometh with Clouds', *NTS* 5, 1958/59, 127–32.

[2] For the secondary character of the application of the parable of the burglar to the Son of man see Jeremias, *Parables*[2], 48f.

[3] Jeremias, *Eucharistic Words*[2], 97–99.

[4] ἀπὸ τοῦ νῦν means 'in the future' (Bauer–Arndt–Gingrich, 548). It is a Semitism; Semitic languages have no word for 'soon'. The words are not to be deleted as an addition, as this note of time is supported by Matt. 26.64 ἀπ' ἄρτι.

[5] E. Bammel, 'Erwägungen zur Eschatologie Jesu', in *Studia Evangelica* III, TU 88, Berlin 1964, 3–32: 24.

[6] A Semitism (qā'ēm = 'finding himself') like Mark 13.14? Note also the plural οἱ οὐρανοί; Luke has the singular twenty-four times in Acts and the plural only twice, at 2.34 and 7.56, in both passages in formulas.

suggests, as will τελειοῦμαι in Luke 13.32. Finally, the quotation of Dan. 7.13 in Mark 13.26 and the continuation in v. 27 (καὶ τότε ἀποστελεῖ τοὺς ἀγγέλους) suggest that Mark 13.26 (ἐρχόμενον ἐν νεφέλαις) should also be interpreted in this way. Now if the ἔρχεσθαι ἐν νεφέλαις in Mark 13.26 originally envisaged a movement towards God, the question arises whether this conception was not originally also associated with other passages which speak of the ἔρχεσθαι of the Son of man (Mark 8.38; Matt. 10.23b. In Matt. 19.28 par. Luke 22.29; Matt. 25.31 nothing is said of a coming to earth;[1] the passages merely depict how the Son of man takes his seat on the throne of glory). The comparison of Luke 22.69 with Mark 14.62 indicates how the conceptions of the glorification of the Son of man were changed under the influence of the Easter experience. Luke 22.69, in agreement with Dan. 7.13f. and Eth. Enoch 70f., speaks only of a single event: the glorification of the Son of man takes place through his exaltation to God; Mark 14.62, on the other hand, divides this process into two acts: sitting at the right hand of God at Easter and the parousia at the end of days. The earliest examples of the conception of the parousia as a movement from above downwards occur in I Thess. (1.10; 2.19; 3.13; 4.16; 5.23).

While ultimate clarity is impossible to achieve, there is much to suggest that the earliest conception was that the revelation of the Son of man would come about in the form of an assumption to God.

The epiphany of the Son of man introduces the beginning of the 'days of the Son of man' (Luke 17.22) in which he exercises 'dominion and glory and reign; all peoples, nations and languages must serve him; his dominion is an everlasting dominion which shall not pass away' (Dan. 7.14). As the universal ruler he is head and representative of the new people of God. His followers share in his rule (Luke 12.32; Matt. 19.28 par. Luke 22.28, 30b). This is the correct insight of T. W. Manson's thesis, much discussed in Anglo-Saxon scholarship, that the Son of man is a 'corporate entity'.[2] This view of the Son of man sees rightly that in Dan. 7.27 the 'one like a man' is identified with the 'saints of the most high' and that for oriental thought the king or the priest represents his people or his community.[3]

For Jesus, however, the power and glory of the Son of man have

[1] Cf. B. Rigaux, 'La seconde venue', in: La venue du Messie. Messianisme et Eschatologie, Recherches Bibliques VI, Bruges 1962, 173–216: 211f.: 'L'idée de parousia est absente'.

[2] Teaching[2], 211–34; with important modifications, 'The Son of Man in Daniel, Enoch and the Gospels', BJRL 32, 1949/50, 171–93.

[3] T. W. Manson has regularly been ticked off for the one-sidedness with which he originally put forward his thesis of the Son of man as 'corporate personality'. But this is to underestimate the nucleus of truth which can be read off above all from the effect such an idea had on Paul. For without the idea that the one includes the many, Paul could hardly have conceived his ideas of the first and second Adam and the body of Christ.

nothing to do with nationalistic hopes. We have seen that the Judaism of his time had a twofold messianic hope, the nationalistic hope of the warrior hero from the house of David and the supra-national hope of the *bar 'enāšā*, who would be the 'light of the nations' (Eth. Enoch 48.4). In acknowledging his expectation of the *bar 'enāšā*, Jesus rejected the political messianic expectation. In contrast to that, the title Son of man express the universality of his status: he is the bringer of salvation for all the world (Matt. 25.31–46).[1]

The epiphany of the glory of the Son of man will be to those who have been proved by suffering. He will be 'the hope of those who are troubled in their hearts' (Eth. Enoch 48.4). This is what Jesus also says. It is striking that the Son of man *logia* which represent the earliest stratum are to be found predominantly in contexts which deal with the eschatological tribulations and the persecutions and trials that they will bring (Mark 13.26; Matt. 24.27, 37b=39b par. Luke 17.24, 26; Matt. 10.23; 24.30; Luke 17.22, 30; 18.8; 21.36); they are to comfort and strengthen the disciples in the face of the hardships that await them by directing their eyes to the glorious conclusion planned by God.

Jesus always speaks to the Son of man in the third person. What is the explanation of that? The favourite expedient of claiming that it was usual in Aramaic to say *bar 'enāšā* for 'I' does not hold, as we saw.[2] In that case, the answer can only be that Jesus always speaks of the Son of man in the third person because he distinguishes between himself and the Son of man. That would lead us to the conclusion that in his sayings about the Son of man Jesus had in mind a saving figure whose coming he awaited. J. Wellhausen and, following him, R. Bultmann and others have in fact put forward this view;[3] it was only the community which made the identification of Jesus with the Son of man. Reference is made above all to Luke 12.8f., where Jesus clearly distinguishes between himself ($\dot{\epsilon}\gamma\dot{\omega}$) and the Son of man. However, Luke 12.8f. cannot bear this burden of proof, as the parallel Matt. 10.32 has $\dot{\epsilon}\gamma\dot{\omega}$ instead of 'Son of man', and we have seen on pp. 262f. that in cases where $\dot{o}$ $\upsilon\dot{\iota}\dot{o}s$ $\tau o\hat{\upsilon}$ $\dot{\alpha}\nu\vartheta\rho\dot{\omega}\pi o\upsilon$ and $\dot{\epsilon}\gamma\dot{\omega}$ are in competition, the simple $\dot{\epsilon}\gamma\dot{\omega}$ has the claim to greater originality. Thus Matthew, with $\dot{\epsilon}\gamma\dot{\omega}$, will have the earlier version in this instance. The same objection can be made to the few texts which can be advanced for a juxtaposition of $\dot{\epsilon}\gamma\dot{\omega}$ and $\dot{o}$ $\upsilon\dot{\iota}\dot{o}s$ $\tau o\hat{\upsilon}$ $\dot{\alpha}\nu\vartheta\rho\dot{\omega}\pi o\upsilon$ in addition to Luke

---

[1] See above, p. 271. [2] See above, p. 261, n.1. [3] Bultmann, *Theology* I, 30–32.

12.8: Mark 8.38 (the antithesis to Luke 12.8, contrast Matt. 10.33 ἐγώ); Mark 14.62 (contrast Luke 22.69); Matt. 19.28 (contrast Luke 22.28–30). But quite apart from the absence of evidence in the sources, it is quite impossible that in the 'Son of man' Jesus should have seen a future saving figure who was to be distinguished from himself. In that case, one would have to suppose that Jesus had seen himself as a fore-runner, as the prophet of the Son of man. But then sayings like Matt. 11.5f. would be senseless: to the question whether he was the one to come Jesus would, rather, have had to reply: 'No, I am not he. I am only his forerunner and his prophet.' In other words, the fact that Jesus made claim to be the fulfiller excludes the possibility of one coming after him.

But how, then, can we explain the distinction made by Jesus between himself and the Son of man? The answer can only be that when Jesus speaks in the third person he makes a distinction not between two different figures, but between his present and the future state of exaltation. The third person expresses the 'mysterious rela-tionship'[1] which exists between Jesus and the Son of man: he is not yet the Son of man, but he will be exalted to be the Son of man.[2]

Now if ὁ υἱὸς τοῦ ἀνθρώπου is a term of glory derived from Dan. 7.13 with which Jesus described his future royal status and his future judicial authority to his disciples, one last question arises: how did Jesus deal with the contrast between his present powerlessness and his expectation of future glory which is expressed most sharply in the threat in Luke 22.69, uttered by an unprotected victim to the supreme court of judgment? Evidently the reference to Dan. 7 still does not bring us to the heart of Jesus' awareness of his mission. That lies deeper: not in Dan. 7, but in Isa. 53.

§ 24 · THE PASSION

H. W. Wolff, *Jesaja 53 im Urchristentum*, Bethel 1942, ³Berlin 1952; J. Jeremias, 'Das Lösegeld für viele (Mk. 10, 45)', *Judaica* 3, 1947–48, 249–64 = *Abba*, 216–32; T. W. Manson, *The Servant-Messiah*, Cambridge 1953; H. Hegermann, *Jesaja 53 in Hexapla, Targum und Peschitta*, BFCT II, 56, Gütersloh 1954; W. Zimmerli –

---

[1] Bammel, 'Erwägungen zur Eschatologie Jesu' (see p. 273, n.5), 23.

[2] The answer to the question posed at Mark 12.35–37 is quite analogous, as we saw on p. 259 above: the Messiah is David's son in the present, but he will be exalted to be David's lord.

J. Jeremias, παῖς θεοῦ, *TDNT* V, 1967, 654–717: D. παῖς θεοῦ in the New Testament, 700–17 (a revised version is to be found in *The Servant of God*, London 1957, ²1965); E. Lohse, *Märtyrer und Gottesknecht*, FRLANT 64, Göttingen 1955, ²1963; E. Fascher, *Jesaja 53 in christlicher und jüdischer Sicht*, Berlin 1958; J. Jeremias, πολλοί, *TDNT* VI, 1968, 536–45; W. Popkes, *Christus Traditus. Eine Untersuchung zum Begriff der Dahingabe im N.T.*, ATANT 49, Zürich 1967; O. H. Steck, *Israel und das gewaltsame Geschick der Propheten*, WMANT 23, Neukirchen-Vluyn 1967; M. Black, 'The "Son of Man" Passion Sayings in the Gospel Tradition', *ZNW* 60, 1969, 1–8.

According to the gospels, the passion is not the end, but the goal and crown of the earthly activity of Jesus and the inevitable way to the glory of the Son of man. Of course, this is an expression of the faith of the church. We have still to see whether Jesus himself gave his own death a place in his preaching.

(i) The announcements of suffering

The gospels record that Jesus announced his suffering and his resurrection to the disciples three times in so many words. What have come to be called the three passion predictions which begin with Peter's confessions, occur at Mark 8.31 par., 9.31 par. and 10.33f. par. The third passage is the most detailed. Here what Jesus expects is predicted feature by feature, in six stages:

ὁ υἱὸς τοῦ ἀνθρώπου

1. παραδοθήσεται τοῖς ἀρχιερεῦσιν καὶ τοῖς γραμματεῦσιν,
2. καὶ κατακρινοῦσιν αὐτὸν θανάτῳ
3. καὶ παραδώσουσιν αὐτὸν τοῖς ἔθνεσιν
4. καὶ ἐμπαίξουσιν αὐτῷ καὶ ἐμπτύσουσιν αὐτῷ καὶ μαστιγώσουσιν αὐτὸν
5. καὶ ἀποκτενοῦσιν,
6. καὶ μετὰ τρεῖς ἡμέρας ἀναστήσεται.

This corresponds so exactly with the course of the passion narrative and the Easter story, even down to details, that there can be no doubt that this passion prediction is a summary of the passion formulated after the event.

Once that has become clear, we shall quickly find other points for criticism. Thus in the first announcement of the passion in Mark 8.31 the δεῖ is striking. There is nothing to correspond to it exactly in Semitic languages. This shows that the first passion prediction received its form in a Hellenistic milieu. Furthermore, the tendency to replace ἀναστῆναι by ἐγερθῆναι is striking;[1] the earlier ἀναστῆναι is a

---

[1] Cf. Mark 8.31 with Matt. 16.21; Luke 9.22 – Mark 9.9f. with Matt. 17.9 – Mark 9.31 with Matt. 17.23 – Mark 10.34 with Matt. 20.19.

Semitism (neither Hebrew nor Aramaic have a common passive phrase for describing resurrection from the dead), the passive ἐγερθῆναι is a Graecism.[1] Finally, christological interest is involved in the accumulation of the announcements of suffering in the passion story (Mark 14.21, 27, 41; Matt. 26.54); evidently the community was concerned to stress that Jesus was not surprised by his suffering, but foresaw it and deliberately trod the road of his passion in obedience to the scriptures.

Even more important than the discovery that the community shaped the passion predictions after the event is the fact that in one case we can observe the process by which an evangelist formulated a passion prediction by himself, freely drawing on other material. In Matt. 26.1f., Matthew has transformed a mere note of time in Mark (14.1 ἦν δὲ τὸ πάσχα καὶ τὰ ἄζυμα μετὰ δύο ἡμέρας) into an announcement of the passion (εἶπεν τοῖς μαθηταῖς αὐτοῦ· οἴδατε ὅτι μετὰ δύο ἡμέρας τὸ πάσχα γίνεται, καὶ ὁ υἱὸς τοῦ ἀνθρώπου παραδίδοται εἰς τὸ σταυρωθῆναι 26.1f.). In view of this, we might be inclined to follow the widespread view that the passion predictions are 'all *vaticinia ex eventu*'.[2] This would, of course, mean that the interpretations of the passion[3] must also be unhistorical.[4] Widespread as this conclusion is, however, it is untenable for three reasons.

1. One thing may be taken as certain: the external course of his ministry must have compelled Jesus to reckon with the possibility of a violent death. The charge against him that he cast out demons with the help of Beelzebub (Matt. 12.24 par.) meant that he was thought to practise magic and to merit stoning.[5] The accusations that he blasphemed God (Mark 2.7), was a false prophet (Mark 14.65 par.)[6] and a rebellious son (Matt. 11.19 par.; cf. Deut. 21.20f.), and that he deliberately broke the sabbath, all cite misdemeanours which were punishable by death.[7]

We have numerous illustrations that Jesus broke the sabbath.[8]

---

[1] H. E. Tödt, *The Son of Man in the Synoptic Tradition*, London 1965, 185, ignores the linguistic evidence when he concludes from the active ἀναστῆναι (Mark 8.31; 9.31; 10.34): 'Thus in the announcements of suffering it is not said that God raised the Son of Man but rather that the Son of Man rose himself.' It would not have occurred to any Jew or Jewish Christian to understand ἀναστήσεται/yᵉqūm as a self-resurrection (cf. Isa. 26.19, where the active yᵉqūmūn is rendered ἐγερθήσονται by LXX). The conception, based upon a misunderstanding of ἀναστῆναι, that Jesus took an active part in his resurrection, occurs for the first time in John 10.18.

[2] Bultmann, *Theology* I, 31.   [3] See below, pp. 286ff.
[4] Bultmann, *op. cit.*, 32.   [5] Sanh. 7.4.   [6] See above, pp. 77ff.
[7] By stoning (Sanh. 7.4); only the false prophet is strangled (11.1).
[8] Mark 2.23–28 par.; 3.1–6 par.; Luke 13.10–17; 14.1–6; John 5.1–18; 9.1–41,

The little complex of tradition in Mark 2.23–3.6, which gives two sabbath stories, the rubbing together of the ears of corn and the healing of the man with the withered hand in the synagogue, depicts a particularly vivid situation. It must be recognized that according to contemporary Jewish law a capital crime could only be brought to judgment if the perpetrator had demonstrably been warned before witnesses and if it had been made certain in this way that he had acted deliberately.[1] The first of the two sabbath stories reports the giving of the warning to Jesus (Mark 2.24 οὐκ ἔξεστιν, cf. John 5.10) and his explanation that he was breaking the sabbath as a matter of conviction (vv. 25–28). The next breach of the sabbath would therefore inevitably bring him into mortal danger, especially as it is said that he was kept under observation (3.2 παρετήρουν αὐτόν). In fact his death was resolved upon after the second breach of the sabbath (3.6). It cannot be objected against this conclusion that the Jews could not carry out death sentences passed by their courts because they did not have the *ius gladii* (John 18.31).[2] This held only in the area under the jurisdiction of the Roman governor, i.e. for Judaea and Samaria, and not for Galilee. No one could prevent Herod Antipas from carrying out the death penalty in his own kingdom, as the beheading of John the Baptist makes clear. The warning 'Herod seeks to kill you' (Luke 13.31) was therefore to be taken quite seriously.

Above all, when Jesus decided to carry out the cleansing of the temple he must have been clear that he was risking his life; and that was in fact the occasion for the definitive official action against him.[3]

---

cf. Luke 6.5 D (on this see Jeremias, *Unknown Sayings of Jesus*, London ²1964, 61–65). Even if the theme of sabbath-breaking is partially (e.g. John 5 and 9) secondary, Jesus' conflicts over the sabbath may be counted among the most certain features of the tradition (cf. E. Lohse, σάββατον κτλ, *TWNT* VII, 1964, 1–35: 22 n.172).

[1] Chief passages: Sanh. 5.1; 8.4; 12.8f. (= Makk. 1.8f.); Tos. Sanh. 11.1–5; b. Sanh. 40b–41a; j. Sanh. 22c, 53ff.; Siphre Num. 113 on 15.33; cf. J. Jeremias, 'Untersuchungen zum Quellenproblem der Apostelgeschichte', *ZNW* 36, 1937, 205–21: 209–13 = *Abba*, 238–55: 243–46. The caution was already valid law in the New Testament period (*ibid.*).

[2] For the problem see J. Jeremias, 'Zur Geschichtlichkeit des Verhörs Jesu vor dem Hohen Rat', *ZNW* 43, 1950–51, 145–50 = *Abba*, 139–44.

[3] The connection between the cleansing of the Temple and the arrest of Jesus becomes particularly clear when the controversy stories in Mark 12 and the apocalyptic discourse in Mark 13 are recognized as originally independent pieces

The Fourth Gospel is quite right in applying Ps. 69.10 to the situation: 'Zeal for thy house will consume me'[1] (John 2.17). So we can see that Jesus forfeited his life in many ways; he was constantly threatened; he must regularly have had the prospect of a violent death.

But it was not only the course of his ministry that must have compelled Jesus to reckon with a violent death; in addition there was something else: his view of salvation history. We saw in §9 how he repeatedly presented himself as the last messenger of God, in the tradition of the prophets. His contemporaries were becoming more and more inclined to see the prophets as martyrs;[2] the time of Jesus was that of the great 'tomb renaissance', and everywhere in Palestine people were building memorials to the prophets and the other martyrs as expiation for their murder.[3] Jesus shared this view of history. He regarded martyrdom in Jerusalem as part of the prophetic office (Luke 13.33). Even more, he agreed with the wisdom saying which regarded salvation history as an unbroken chain of martyrdoms of the righteous and the messengers of God from Abel to Zechariah the son of Jehoiada (Matt. 23.35 par.). At the end of this chain stood the Baptist, with whose fate Jesus must have been particularly preoccupied, as he had been associated with him. Would Jesus, who believed himself to be the last of the prophets sent by God (see above, pp. 82–85), have expected a better fate for himself?

---

of tradition, and it is seen that Mark 11 and 14 originally followed one another (cf. Jeremias, *Eucharistic Words*[2], 89–96).

[1] κατφάγεται is to be understood thus, and not as being overwhelmed by zeal. This is supported above all by the change of the κατέφαγεν offered by Ψ 68 (69).10 into the future in John 2.17.

[2] The only prophets to be regarded as martyrs were Isaiah (J. Jeremias, *Heiligengräber in Jesu Umwelt*, Göttingen 1958, 61ff.), Jeremiah (*ibid.*, 108ff.), Ezekiel (*ibid.*, 112f.), Amos (*ibid.*, 87f.), Micah (*ibid.*, 82ff.) and Zechariah ben Jehoiada (*ibid.*, 67ff.). In the New Testament the martyrdom of Isaiah is mentioned indirectly (Heb. 11.37 'sawn apart'); 'stoning' (Heb. 11.37; Matt. 23.37 par.) may refer to the martyrdom of Zechariah ben Jehoiada or Jeremiah, probably both. Cf. further A. Schlatter, *Der Märtyrer in den Anfängen der Kirche*, BFCT 19.3, Gütersloh 1915 = *Synagoge und Kirche*, Stuttgart 1966, 237–304; H. J. Schoeps, 'Die jüdischen Prophetenmorde', *Symbolae Biblicae Upsalienses* 2, Uppsala 1943 = in: Schoeps, *Aus frühchristlicher Zeit*, Tübingen 1950, 126–43; ‡Steck.

[3] Matt. 23.29 par.; cf. J. Jeremias, *Heiligengräber*, passim. The movement began with the building of the memorial mentioned in Acts 2.29 (μνῆμα) at the entrance to David's tomb in Jerusalem (*ibid.*, 121).

2. Both the course of Jesus' ministry and his view of salvation history tell against the view that he did not make any prior announcement of his suffering at all. Not only that, but the announcements themselves also protest against a wholesale devaluation of their reliability.

We begin with the three so-called *passion predictions* (Mark 8.31 par.; 9.31 par.; 10.33f. par.; cf. also 9.12f.; Luke 17.25; 24.7), which have already been mentioned. First, it should be pointed out that they are better designated as variations of *the* passion prediction.[1] So before we can come to any conclusion about the question of authenticity, we must ask which version is the earliest, and what verdict is to be passed on its historical value, whereas the later forms are irrelevant for the question of authenticity.

Fundamental to the search for the earliest version of the passion predictions is the recognition, already hinted at at the beginning, that step by step there was an assimilation of the formulations to the actual course of events. Matthew and Luke have worked over Mark's passion predictions in this way by, for example, replacing μετὰ τρεῖς ἡμέρας by τῇ τρίτῃ ἡμέρᾳ throughout; similarly, Matthew has replaced the more general ἀποκτενοῦσιν in Mark 10.34 by the precise σταυρῶσαι (Matt. 20.19). If we restrict ourselves to the Marcan tradition, as being the earlier, a comparison of the three variants of the passion prediction, Mark 8.31; 9.31; 10.33f., shows clearly that the second (9.31) is to be recognized as the earliest not only by its brevity and indefiniteness, but above all by its terminology:

> ὁ υἱὸς τοῦ ἀνθρώπου
> παραδίδοται εἰς χεῖρας ἀνθρώπων
> καὶ ἀποκτενοῦσιν αὐτόν,
> καὶ ἀποκτανθεὶς μετὰ τρεῖς ἡμέρας ἀναστήσεται.

The first striking thing about this three-line saying is the change of tense from present to future; the explanation of this, as Mark 14.41 shows, is that the first line was also current independently. It goes back to Aramaic tradition, as the present παραδίδοται, firmly anchored in the tradition (Mark 9.31; 14.21 par., 41 par.; Matt. 26.2), which already attracted the notice of Matthew and Luke (par. Matt. 17.22 and Luke 9.44: μέλλει παραδίδοσθαι), points to an underlying Aramaic participle;[2] in fact παραδίδοται is rendered as a participle by sy^sin pal pesh (cur deest)

---

[1] The threefold repetition most probably came about because among the complexes of tradition that Mark took up (see above, p. 38) there were by chance three that contained the prediction of the passion: 8.27–9.1 (confession and the cost of discipleship), 9.30–50 (the great collection built on link-words) and 10.32–45 (suffering and discipleship).

[2] Aramaic is fond of using the participle to denote the near future; the translators often render these future participles wrongly as presents, because the atemporal participle in Aramaic usually has a present meaning (cf. Jeremias, *Eucharistic Words*[2], 178f.).

unanimously in all the passages mentioned. In this way we have found a primitive form of the passion predictions, which consisted of the sentence: *mitmᵉsar bar 'ᵉnāšā līdē bᵉnē 'ᵉnāšā*. The word play *bar 'ᵉnāšā/bᵉnē 'ᵉnāšā* produced by this back-translation should be noted. If we remember that παραδίδοται/*mitmᵉsar* is a divine passive, as Rom. 4.25 (παρεδόθη/ἠγέρθη) and 8.31f. (ὁ θεὸς . . . παρέδωκεν) shows, the meaning of the original form turns out to be: 'God will (soon) deliver up the man to men.' This is a *māšāl*, a riddle, simply because *bar 'ᵉnāšā* can be understood either as a title or generically.[1]

If the phrase was understood generically, the saying announced the disorders of the eschatological time of distress, in which the individual would be surrendered up to the mass. If it was understood as a title, the sentence spoke of the delivering up of the Son of man. We have, therefore, an apocalyptic riddle. This *bar 'ᵉnāšā māšāl* can be compared with other analogous *mᵉšālīm*, e.g.: 'The man goes forth' (Luke 22.22: ὁ υἱὸς . . . τοῦ ἀνθρώπου . . . πορεύεται), 'the man goes' (Mark 14.21 par.: ὁ . . . υἱὸς τοῦ ἀνθρώπου ὑπάγει), 'the man must suffer many things and be despised' (Mark 9.12; Luke 17.25), 'the man must be delivered up to sinful men' (24.7).[2]

The *māšāl* 'God will (soon) deliver up the man to men' (Mark 9.31a) is thus the ancient nucleus which underlies the passion predictions. Our question must only be whether this sentence, and not the passion predictions as we have them, can be genuine. The latter are late forms. In support of an affirmative answer are the facts that in view of its indefiniteness the *māšāl* does not look like an *ex eventu* formulation, and, short as it is, it displays three stylistic characteristics preferred by Jesus: 1. a *māšāl* character; 2. the divine passive; 3. paronomasia.

3. The three passion predictions Mark 8.31 par.; 9.31 par.; 10.33f. par. form only a small excerpt from a comprehensive amount of *logia* material which deals with Jesus' future suffering. It was extremely unfortunate and quite unjustified that in investigating the question whether Jesus could have announced his suffering beforehand scholars until quite recently paid almost exclusive attention to the three so-called passion predictions and hardly noticed the other, much more important, material transmitted by the synoptic gospels. This material exists in many forms.

As far as form is concerned, the announcements of the passion are made up of metaphors, riddles, woes, quotations (from scripture and the wisdom saying Luke 11.49), etc. From the point of view of content we find:

[1] See above, pp. 260f.
[2] The verse belongs to the Lucan source (both the use of δεῖ in relation to Jesus' passion and the adjectival ἁμαρτωλός indicate this) and goes back to an original Aramaic text (hyperbaton, paronomasia and the use of *bᵉnē 'ᵉnāšā* as an indefinite pronoun, cf. ‡Black, 3).

(a) Threats against the murderers of God's messengers (Matt. 23.34–36 par.); against the builders of the tombs of the prophets who themselves are in process of murdering the prophet (23.29–32 par.); against the traitor (Mark 14.21 par.);

(b) Accusations against Jerusalem, that murders the prophets (Matt. 23.37–39 par.), and a warning against murdering the heir (Mark 12.8 par.);

(c) meshālīm at the centre of which stands Jesus' own fate: the expatriate, Matt. 8.20 par.; the imminent separation, Mark 14.7 par.; John 16.16; the fate of John the Baptist, Mark 9.13 par.; the fate of the prophets, Luke 13.33; the passover lamb, Mark 14.22–24 par.; the cup, Mark 14.36 par.; the criminal's burial, 14.8 par.; the return from the dead, Luke 11.29 par.; to this group also belong the māshāl underlying the passion predictions and kindred meshālīm mentioned on p. 283 above: the man goes, goes forth, is delivered up, must suffer many things;

(d) meshālīm which put the fate of Jesus in the context of other events of the end time: the time of the sword, introduced by Jesus' suffering, Luke 22.35–38; the murdered shepherd and the scattered flock, Mark 14.27 par.; the bridegroom who is snatched away, 2.20 par.;[1] cup and baptism, 10.38f.; the ransom, 10.45 par.; the key stone of the temple, 12.10 par.;[2] fire and flood, Luke 12.49f.;

(e) Announcements of the suffering of the disciples (they must be mentioned here because it is very improbable that Jesus should have prepared his disciples for suffering if he had not also expected that he would suffer, too): Mark 8.34 par., 35 par.; 9.1 par.; 10.38f. par.; 14.27f. par.; Matt. 10.25, 28 par., 34–36 par.; Luke 22.35–38.

If we are to answer the question whether we have reason to suppose that Jesus forecast a violent death for himself, we have to examine this extensive source material and not just the three so-called passion predictions. The very fullness of the announcements of suffering listed under (a) to (e) above, and even more the mysteriousness and indefiniteness of many of them, to say nothing of the many images in which they are expressed and the variety of forms and genres, show that here we have a broad stratum of tradition with much early material in it. Detailed analysis would show this in many ways. We content ourselves with three observations.

(a) A number of announcements of suffering prove themselves to be early tradition from the way in which they are anchored in their *context*. Thus despite the tendency of the tradition to spare the disciples, the context repeatedly brings out their lack of understanding and their failure. For example, the designation of Peter as Satan (Mark 8.33), which was surely not invented, forms a unity – which is

---

[1] The picture is not so far-fetched as might appear at first glance; cf. IV Ezra 10.1f.: 'And it came to pass when my son entered the (wedding) chamber, he fell down and died. Then I removed all the lights.' The mother who speaks is Zion.

[2] Note that Ps. 118.22 is here related to the last judgment; the early church interpreted the verse in terms of the exaltation (Acts 4.11).

hardly artificial – with the passion prediction in 8.31. In quite a bald way, 10.35–37 reports how the disciples are wrapped up in expectations of glory which pass over the suffering ahead, of which Jesus has to remind them in vv. 38f. The forecast of suffering in 14.27 announces their flight in a scriptural quotation; the flight is then narrated in 14.50 (Luke omits both the forecast and the actual flight); the painful self-certainty with which not only Peter but also the other disciples react (14.29–31 par.) is not concealed. Mark 14.8 is also firmly rooted in the context. The verse is often regarded as a secondary appendix to the story of the anointing, which allowed the passage to be localized in the passion narrative.[1] But as soon as one notes that v. 8 presupposes a distinction between the *gift* of love and the *work* of love, it becomes clear that in fact it is an integral part of the story. The disciples criticize the woman's action because the money could have been used better as alms, i.e. as a *gift* of love; Jesus defends the woman by declaring that the anointing is a *work* of love which stands higher than a gift of love – it is the work of laying out the dead. Thus the point of the whole narrative is that Jesus expects to be killed as a criminal and therefore to be thrown into a grave without being anointed.[2]

(*b*) It is particularly important that the announcements of suffering have a number of features which were *not fulfilled*. It is not inconceivable that Matt. 23.37 par. Luke 13.34 hints that for a time Jesus considered the possibility of stoning, the penalty of which he had repeatedly incurred[3] and with which he is said to have been threatened repeatedly;[4] at any rate, as we have just seen, he contemplated a criminal's burial without anointing (Mark 14.8). He also seems to have expected that the time of the sword would begin immediately after his passion (Luke 22.35–38), that the disciples would be caught up in his suffering (Mark 14.27) and that some of them would have to share his fate (10.35–40), that the fire of judgment would pass on from the green wood to the dry (Luke 23.31), in short, that his suffering would be the prelude to collective suffering.[5] But after a short interval (see above, p. 139), the *eschaton* would follow

[1] Bultmann, *Synoptic Tradition*, 36f.
[2] Cf. J. Jeremias, 'Die Salbungsgeschichte Mc 14.3–9', *ZNW* 35, 1936, 75–82 = *Abba*, 107–15.
[3] See above, p. 278, n.7.
[4] Luke 4.29; John 8.59; 10.31–36; 11.8; Pap. Egerton 2, frag. 1 r, lines 23f.
[5] For collective suffering see above, pp. 241ff.

the time of distress: the journey of the good shepherd at the head of his flock to Galilee (Mark 14.28) and the building of the new sanctuary (14.58). None of this happened in just that way. Jesus was not stoned by the Jews, as Stephen was, but crucified by the Romans. True, he was buried without being anointed (16.1), but he did not have a criminal's burial (15.46). The disciples were spared at Jesus' arrest; in a remarkable way the Jewish authorities were satisfied with the killing of Jesus and left the disciples unmolested.[1] John the son of Zebedee was spared the cup.[2] The end delayed. All this shows that these announcements of suffering were by no means all formulated *ex eventu*.

(c) At best, the phrase '*after three days*' seems to have been formulated *ex eventu*. But it is this very phrase that shows signs of considerable antiquity. It continues to occur frequently: Mark 14.58; 15.29 (new temple); Luke 13.32 (consummation on the third day), 33 (prophet); cf. John 16.16, 17, 19. In none of these passages can the phrase about the three days be derived from the three days from Good Friday to Easter. For in Luke 13.32, 33 the three days are related to the ministry of Jesus and not to his resting in the grave; in Mark 14.58 (cf. 15.29), the third day means the definitive turning point, not Easter;[3] in John 16.16, 17, 19 the first short period refers to the time up to the passion. But in that case, what is the origin of the phrase 'after three days'? The answer emerges when we remember that Semitic languages have no word for 'several', 'a few', 'some', and use the expedient, *inter alia*, of saying 'three' instead.[4] So it comes about that even in the Old Testament the phrase 'three days' denotes an indefinite but not particularly long period of time. This usage is also to be found in the 'three day' *logia*: 'after three days' means 'soon'.

Now it is striking that what is to happen 'soon' is formulated in quite different and evidently interchangeable images. From this fluctuation of images and phrases C. H. Dodd has drawn the convincing conclusion that Jesus evidently made no distinction between

---

[1] Dodd, *Parables*, 59. [2] See above, pp. 243f.

[3] Thus only the secondary reinterpretation John 2.21 ἐκεῖνος δὲ ἔλεγεν περὶ τοῦ ναοῦ τοῦ σώματος αὐτοῦ (epexegetical genitive), i.e. 'by the Temple, Jesus meant his body'. The word ἐγερῶ in v. 19, which was understood as 'raise up', offered an occasion for the reinterpretation.

[4] J. B. Bauer, 'Drei Tage', *Biblica* 39, 1958, 354–58; G. M. Landes, 'The "Three Days and Three Nights" Motif in Jonah 2.1', *JBL* 86, 1967, 446–50.

parousia, resurrection, consummation and the building of the New Temple, and that all these phrases describe the triumph of God that is to follow soon.[1] This interchangeability of different phrases is a characteristic of the pre-Easter tradition. In no saying of Jesus do resurrection and parousia stand side by side as two events; it was the Easter experience which led to the systematization of the course of events into a sequence of resurrection, exaltation and parousia.[2] In short, on closer inspection it transpires that it is the 'three day' phrase itself, which at first glance seems particularly exposed to the suspicion of being an *ex eventu* construction, that goes back to pre-Easter tradition.

This is not to argue that each of the many passion sayings is pre-Easter (every individual instance has to be examined). Nevertheless, we must note the total result that there can be no doubt that Jesus expected and announced his suffering and death. Constantly threatened, he had to reckon with the possibility of meeting a prophet's fate. Certainly the three so-called passion predictions are, in their present form, constructed *ex eventu*, but they go back to an early Aramaic *māšāl*. The rest of the announcements of suffering, which are quite numerous, can be shown for the most part to date from before Easter. Uncritical scepticism can unintentionally lead to a falsification of history, as here, if the apt observation that individual phrases and *logia* have been formulated in retrospect, looking back on the course of the passion, leads one to regard all the material as the construction of the community.

(ii) The interpretation of the suffering

The texts, however, go still further. They not only assert that Jesus saw his imminent suffering clearly and announced it beforehand, but add that Jesus had considered the question of the necessity of his death and had found the answer to this question in scripture, primarily in Isa. 53, the chapter about the suffering servant, but also in other passages, such as Zech. 13.7.

The following passages would seem to have some reference to Isa. 53:

Mark 9.12 ἐξουδενηθῇ: cf. Isa. 53.3. – Mark 9.31 par.; 14.41 par. Matt. 26.2; Luke 24.7 παραδίδοται/παραδοθῆναι: cf. Isa. 53.5b Targ.; Isa. 53.12 LXX. – Mark

---

[1] Dodd, *Parables*, 100f.

[2] For example, the exaltation of the Son of man (Luke 22.69) is in Mark secondarily divided into two events (the sitting at the right hand and the parousia, 14.62); see above, p. 273.

10.45 par. διακονῆσαι καὶ δοῦναι τὴν ψυχὴν αὐτοῦ λύτρον ἀντὶ πολλῶν: cf. Isa. 53.10f. –
Mark 14.8, the presupposition of the criminal's burial: cf. Isa. 53.9. – Mark 14.24
ἐκχυννόμενον ὑπὲρ πολλῶν: cf. Isa. 53.12. – Luke 11.22 καὶ τὰ σκῦλα αὐτοῦ διαδίδωσιν: cf.
Isa. 53.12[1] (?) – Luke 22.37 καὶ μετὰ ἀνόμων ἐλογίσθη: = Isa. 53.12. – Luke 23.34a[2]
intercession for the godless: cf. Isa. 53.12. – John 10.11, 15, 17f. τιθέναι τὴν ψυχήν: cf.
Isa. 53.10.

Almost all these references to Isa. 53 bear on the Hebrew or Aramaic
text;[3] the influence of the Septuagint can only be detected at Luke
22.37, and is possible for Mark 9.31 παραδίδοται and par. Thus even
the earliest church, living in a Semitic-speaking milieu, was convinced that Jesus had found his suffering outlined in Isa. 53 and thus
had ascribed atoning power to his death.

But is that possible? Is it conceivable that Jesus saw his death as
representative? Is that not clearly the doctrine of the primitive community? The general currency in the world of Jesus of ideas about the
atoning power of death provides us with an answer to the question.[4]

Four chief means of atonement were known: repentance (which atones for sins of
omission); the sacrifice of the Day of Atonement (repentance and sacrifice atone
for the transgression of a prohibition); suffering (repentance and sacrifice and
suffering atone for a transgression which merits destruction at God's hand); and
death (repentance and sacrifice and suffering and death are together necessary for
atonement when a man has profaned the name of God).[5] Now there are stages in
the atoning power of death. Any death has the power to atone if it is bound up with
repentance. That even holds for the death of a criminal; his death atones if before
his execution he declares, 'May my death be an atonement (kappārā) for all my
sins'. The death of any individual Israelite had that much more atoning power if he
made this declaration on his death bed. The death of a righteous man was even
more powerful; his supererogatory suffering was to the advantage of others. The
death of innocent children atoned for the sins of their parents. The death of the
high priest meant that those who had killed might leave the cities of refuge; their
guilt had been atoned for. Yet greater atoning power was attributed to the death
of a witness to the faith. Hellenistic Judaism praises martyrdom, because it brings
God's wrath upon Israel to a standstill[6] and is an ἀντίψυχον (substitute),[7] καθάρσιον

[1] W. Grundmann, ἰσχύω κτλ, TDNT III, 1965, 397–402, assumes a reference to
Isa. 53.12, but it is possible that the dividing of the spoil in Luke 11.22 is an image that
does not depend on the Old Testament.
[2] For textual criticism see below, p. 298.
[3] Detailed argument in Jeremias, παῖς θεοῦ, 709f. = Abba, 209f.
[4] K. Bornhäuser, Das Wirken des Christus durch Taten und Worte, BFCT 2.2,
Gütersloh 1921, 224–29; ‡Lohse, 9–110.
[5] Tos. Yom. 5.6ff. with many parallels (Billerbeck I 636). The author is R.
Ishmael (died c. AD 135), but he merely made a systematic collection of earlier
conceptions.
[6] II Macc. 7.37f.; IV Macc. 9.23f.   [7] IV Macc. 6.29; 17.22.

(means of cleansing),[1] ἱλαστήριον (means of atonement)[2] for Israel. 'Let my blood serve to cleanse them (the people of God). Take my life in place of theirs', prays the old martyr Eleazar.[3] But in the Palestinian milieu, too, it could be said that martyrdoms would usher in the end,[4] that they disclosed the world to come to the martyrs[5] and made them intercessors,[6] that they had missionary power[7]   and worked atonement for Israel.[8]

This is the world in which Jesus lived. If he believed himself to be the messenger of God who was to bring God's final message, and if he reckoned with the possibility of a violent death, then he must have been concerned with the question of the meaning and the atoning power of his death. So it is hardly permissible to reject as untrustworthy from the start the fact that the gospels claim that Jesus found the meaning of his suffering outlined in Isa. 53, even if the material is limited.[9]

(a) The eucharistic words[10]

These are the most important of the allusions to Jesus' suffering.

There is a fivefold tradition of the words of interpretation. The earliest literary text is I Cor. 11.23–25; related to this, but independent of it, is Luke 22.15–20 (the longer text of which is the original);[11] Mark 14.22–25 is also independent and is repeated with some alterations at Matt. 26.26–29; to these should be added John 6.51c, as the Johannine form of the word over the bread.

The five texts belong to two different strands of tradition. On one side is the Marcan (– Matthaean) version, which has the ὑπέρ phrase only with the cup; it is characteristic of this group that the text has been preserved in Semitic-type Greek. On the other is the Pauline-Lucan-Johannine version, which has the ὑπέρ phrase with the bread (Luke has it with bread and wine); in comparison with Mark, it has Greek features.

---

[1] IV Macc. 6.29; cf. 1.11.   [2] IV Macc. 17.22.   [3] IV Macc. 6.29.

[4] Ass. Mos. 9.7ff.; Eth. Enoch 47.1–4, cf. Rev. 6.11.

[5] Siphre Deut. 307 on 32.4; Gen. R. 65 on 27.27.

[6] J. Jeremias, Heiligengräber in Jesu Umwelt, Göttingen 1958, 136f.

[7] Siphre Deut. 307 on 32.4; Gen. R. 65 on 27.27.

[8] Siphre Deut. 333 on 32.43: 'The massacre of Israel by the nations of the world brings about atonement for it in the world to come.' This passage shows that the Rabbinic instances illustrating the atoning power of martyrdom do not begin only in Amoraic times (instances in ‡Lohse, 75–78), but can already be found with the Tannaites.

[9] For this see p. 299 below.

[10] H. Lietzmann, Messe und Herrenmahl, AKG 8, Bonn 1926; Jeremias, Eucharistic Words[2].

[11] The shorter text (22.15–19a) is read only by a single Greek manuscript (D), by the Vetus Syra (elaborated by it) and by some Vetus Latina manuscripts; it cannot be original, simply on text-critical grounds (Jeremias, op. cit., 139–59).

If we compare the texts, we find a number of differences,[1] mostly as a result of liturgical usage (e.g. the tendency to make the word over the bread and the word over the cup parallel). Much more important, however, is the fact that the substance of all four independent texts is in complete *agreement*.

$$(\varLambda\acute{a}\beta\epsilon\tau\epsilon)\cdot \quad \tauο\hatυ\tauο \ \tauὸ \ σ\hatωμ\acute{a} \ (\dot{η} \ σ\acute{α}ρξ) \ μου$$

$$\tauο\hatυ\tauο \quad \begin{cases} \tauὸ \ α\dot{ι}μ\acute{a} \ μου \ \tauῆς \ δια\vartheta\acute{η}κης \\ \dot{η} \ δια\vartheta\acute{η}κη \ \dotἐν \ \tau\hatῳ \ α\dot{ι}μα\tauί \ μου \end{cases}$$

$$\tauὸ \ . \ . \ . \ ὑπὲρ \ πολλ\hatῶν.[2]$$

How far back can we trace the tradition of the eucharistic words? It is clear that Paul is a witness for the celebration of the eucharist in the forties (I Cor. 11.23 παρέλαβον). There is a widespread view that we must be content with the knowledge that we have liturgical texts which can be traced back into the second decade after the death of Jesus. However, two quite unpretentious observations prevent us from stopping at this point. First, both in Mark and Luke, that is, in both strands of tradition, the account of the eucharist begins with καί. This is the typical beginning to a pericope in a Jewish historical account, used monotonously, pericope by pericope, with very few exceptions, from Genesis to I Maccabees. Secondly, the subject 'Jesus' is absent in both Mark and Luke. These two observations show that our texts go back to pre-liturgical narrative tradition. At their beginning we do not find liturgy, but a historical account.[3]

Furthermore, the παρέλαβον ἀπὸ τοῦ κυρίου (I Cor. 11.23) should not be put on one side too quickly. Παραλαμβάνειν is construed with παρά and ἀπό; παρά introduces the tradent and ἀπό the originator. So παρέλαβον ἀπὸ τοῦ κυρίου means that Paul was convinced that the eucharistic words transmitted to him went back in a direct chain of tradition to Jesus himself. In support of this is the fact that the eucharistic words display characteristics of Jesus' way of speaking: ἀμήν to introduce his own words (Mark 14.25), the divine passive (Luke 22.16), the 'coming of the reign of God' (v. 18), and the preference for simile and parabolic actions.[4] In fact, whereas it is hard to imagine the origination of the words of interpretation as a free creation of the community, it is easy to understand them as historical reminiscence, as we shall see.

The wrong way to develop an *understanding of the last supper* is to begin from the words of interpretation, because in this way the so-called 'founding meal' is isolated. Indeed, it ought really to be said that this isolation of the last supper through the centuries has made it very difficult to recognize its eschatological significance. In reality, the 'founding meal' is only one link in a long chain of meals which

[1] At first glance the cup saying in Mark/Matthew seems to diverge most strongly from the Pauline/Lucan version. But we must not overlook the fact that in both versions the subject (the red wine) and the predicate (the blood) correspond. Presumably the reason for the rather more complicated formulation in Paul/Luke is a desire to avoid the suspicion of drinking blood.

[2] *Eucharistic Words*[2], 173. [3] *Op. cit.*, 174, 192f.

[4] See above, pp. 35f., 9ff., 31ff., 29f.

Jesus shared with his followers and which they continued after Easter. These gatherings at table, which provoked such scandal because Jesus excluded no-one from them, even open sinners, and which thus expressed the heart of his message, were types of the feast to come in the time of salvation (Mark 2.18–20). The last supper has its historical roots in this chain of gatherings. Like the rest of them, it is an *antedonation*[1] *of the consummation* (Luke 22.16; Mark 14.25). Only when this eschatological orientation of the last supper has been recognized, only when it has been understood that the last supper is: a gathering with Jesus at table, an actualization of the time of salvation, can the question of its special meaning be put with any sense. For the meaning of the last supper is not that Jesus 'founded' a completely new rite, but that he linked an announcement and interpretation of his coming suffering with the familiar rite of grace before and after the meal.

There can be only one explanation for Jesus' quite unusual procedure in clothing the announcement and interpretation of his imminent suffering in the form of words of interpretation of the bread and wine: words of interpretation were a fixed ingredient of the rite of the passover meal (as they are even today). The custom had grown out of Ex. 12.26f.; 13.8, where the head of the house is enjoined to explain the meaning of the rites of passover and the feast of unleavened bread to his children. To fulfil this prescription, at each passover meal the father had to explain to the family in a paschal liturgy the peculiarities of the meal, and particularly why unleavened bread, bitter herbs and a roast lamb were eaten on this night. If, as the synoptic gospels record, Jesus' last meal was a passover meal, as head of his group of disciples he was obliged to observe the paschal liturgy and in so doing gave the interpretations of bread and wine which he then repeated in the grace which follows the liturgy. Speaking in words of interpretation may seem strange to us, but it was nothing extraordinary for the disciples, but a familiar part of the passover ritual.

Two things should be said about the interpretation itself. First, in comparing the broken *mazzā* with his dead body and the red wine[2] with his blood, Jesus is using terms from sacrifical terminology: *bisrā ūd*e*mā* or (if Jesus continued in the *lingua sacra* after the Hebrew grace) *bāśār wādām*;[3] ἐκχύννεσθαι is also sacrificial terminology. Thus Jesus describes himself as a sacrifice, indeed as the eschatological

[1] We should speak of antedonation rather than of anticipation.

[2] Red wine was usually drunk at the passover (*Eucharistic Words*[2], 53).

[3] The translation variant σάρξ (John 6.51c ff.; Ign., Smyrn., 7.1; Rom. 7.3; Philad. 4.1; Trall. 8.1; Justin, *Apol.* I 66, 2) shows that a *bāśār/bisrā* underlies σῶμα (Mark 14.22 par.; I Cor. 11.24).

passover lamb (cf. I Cor. 5.7), whose death brings into force the new covenant which was prefigured in the making of the covenant on Sinai (Ex. 24.8) and prophesied for the time of salvation (Jer. 31.31–34). His death is therefore a representative one. *For whom* Jesus is the representative is expressed in the ὑπέρ phrase, which recurs in all the texts (though in differing positions and in different formulas):

There are the following variations in the ὑπέρ formula:

> Mark: ὑπὲρ πολλῶν
> Matthew: περὶ πολλῶν
> Paul/Luke: ὑπέρ ὑμῶν
> John: ὑπὲρ τῆς τοῦ κόσμου ζωῆς.

Πολλοί (Mark/Matt.) is used in an inclusive sense (cf. II Cor. 5.14, 15; I Tim. 2.6: ὑπὲρ πάντων; John 6.51c: ὑπὲρ τῆς τοῦ κόσμου ζωῆς), that is, in the sense of 'the inconceivable many, the whole host, all'.[1] This Semitism (which native Greeks might easily misunderstand) shows that ὑπὲρ πολλῶν (Mark 14.24) is the earliest version. The ὑπὲρ ὑμῶν, as an address (Paul/Luke), could have developed when the words of interpretation were used at the distribution of the bread and wine. The Johannine version is an interpretation of the inclusive πολλοί for Gentile Christians.

The magnitude of the statement that Jesus is going to his death for the many becomes clear when we remember the Rabbinic precept that there are means of atonement for all sins and sinners, but that there is no ransom for the nations.[2] Jesus, in contrast, designates his death as *a representative one for the many* who have fallen victim to death. The inclusive πολλοί contains a reference to Isa. 53. Whereas it occurs relatively rarely in the Old Testament, it appears no less than five times in Isa. 53; it is virtually the link word of this chapter. Both in content (representation) and in language (inclusive usage), ὑπὲρ πολλῶν is a reference to Isa. 53. Jesus uses this phrase to signify that he knows that he is the servant of God who goes to his death as the representative of others. Without Isa. 53 the eucharistic words remain incomprehensible.

Secondly, it is of great significance that Jesus repeated the words that interpreted the bread and wine and that have their liturgical context in the paschal prayer of the head of the house, at the subsequent grace before and after the meal. The procedure in grace before the meal was (as the disciples knew from their childhood onwards) that the head of the house took a loaf of bread, spoke the blessing and gave a piece of the bread to everyone sitting at table, so that by eating

---

[1] ‡Jeremias, πολλοί, 543ff. For inclusive πολλοί see above, pp. 130f.
[2] Mek. Ex. 21.30 (quoted in Jeremias, *Eucharistic Words*[2], 230).

the bread each might share in the blessing on the meal. The same thing happened with the cup after the meal. If wine was drunk (which happened only on special occasions, though it was prescribed for the passover meal), the head of the house spoke the grace over the cup; by passing round the cup, all those at table shared in the blessing after the meal. Now Jesus added to the blessing before and after the meal the words of interpretation which explained the bread and the wine as a reference to himself as the eschatological passover lamb dying for others. The only way in which the disciples could understand this was to believe that with the bread and the wine Jesus was promising them a share in the atoning power of his death. This intention of *personal dedication* may have been the reason why Jesus repeated the words of interpretation in the grace. Each of the disciples[1] was to know that Jesus promised him personally a share in his representative death.

(b) 'A ransom for many'[2]

The ransom saying (Mark 10.45 par. Matt. 20.28) is very closely connected with the eucharistic words. Unlike worldly rulers, who are concerned for power and glory, the disciples are to serve, just as Jesus himself came 'to serve, namely (the καί after διακονῆσαι is epexegetical) to give his life of his own free will (δοῦναι is the free will offering) as a ransom of many'. In understanding this saying about Jesus' serving (Mark 10.45b) it is essential to note that it relates word for word to Isa. 53.10f., and indeed to the Hebrew text.[3] Accordingly, in Mark 10.45b, λύτρον, which in the Septuagint (twenty times) denotes the ransom money for the firstborn, for slaves to be set free, for ground and land, for life forfeited, has the wider meaning of

---

[1] But according to Luke 22.21 (πλήν), Jesus excluded the traitor.

[2] Dalman, *Jesus-Jeshua*, 144–47; ‡Jeremias, 'Das Lösegeld für Viele', 249–64 = *Abba* 216–29 (literature 216 n.1); W. Manson, *Jesus the Messiah*, London 1943, 131–34.

[3] For διακονῆσαι see *ᶜbd, Isa. 53.11, read by LXX, Targum, Peshitta and Symmachus instead of MT ᶜbdy, and understood by the Targum as an infinitive (‡Hegermann, list at the end); for δοῦναι τὴν ψυχὴν αὐτοῦ λύτρον cf. 53.10 tāśīm 'āśām napšō, for ἀντὶ πολλῶν cf. 53.11 lārabbīm. A close connection between Mark 10.45 and Isa. 53.10 is also suggested by the observation that the further definition of the phrase 'give' or 'take life' by a predicative accusative is only evidenced in Isa. 53.10 MT ('āśām), IV Macc. 6.29 (ἀντίψυχον) and Mark 10.45 (λύτρον); cf. G. Dautzenberg, *Sein Leben bewahren. Ψυχή in den Herrenworten der Evangelien*, München 1966, 101.

substitutionary offering, atonement offering, which *'āšām* has in Isa. 53.10.[1] Jesus, therefore, serves by surrendering his life as an atonement offering. It is for the good of many (ἀντὶ πολλῶν) – as in Mark 14.24 par., πολλοί here has an inclusive significance.[2] This representative surrender of life for the countless multitudes is in fulfilment of the saying about the servant in Isa. 53.10f., understood as a prophecy.

The question of *authenticity* is a difficult one. The problem is that Luke 22.27 offers a very different version of the saying which scholars are inclined to regard as the earlier because here Jesus appears quite simply as an ethical model, whereas in Mark not only does the title Son of man appear (which is in any case secondary at this point),[3] but the formulation is further loaded with difficult dogmatic assertions. It is, however, wrong to ask whether the Marcan version developed from that of Luke or *vice versa*. That would be to presuppose a dependence between the two versions when in fact we have two versions of one and the same group of *logia* (Mark 10.42–45 par. Luke 22.24–27) which in literary terms are independent of each other. Common to both strands of tradition is the fact that each presents Jesus as a pattern of serving in the framework of a triad (rules-disciples-Jesus). The difference between them is that the way in which Jesus serves is illustrated differently; in Luke by his waiting at table (cf. John 13), in Mark by the surrender of his life (cf. Isa. 53).

It can be shown that each of these two quite different illustrations of the way in which Jesus serves derives from *Palestinian tradition*. It is true that in Luke the contrast between the use of power and service (Luke 22.25f.) is expressed in more marked Hellenistic language than in Mark (εὐεργέτης v. 25, ὁ νεώτερος, ὁ ἡγούμενος, ὁ διακονῶν v. 26), but that is not true of the illustration in v. 27: here both the wordplay *rabbā/rābe͑ā*[4] and the *mī gādōl* question,[5] as well as the lack of the copula (v. 27a), indicate the Palestinian milieu. The references to the Hebrew text of Isa. 53.10f. in the Marcan illustration have already been discussed (see p. 292, n.3 above). Otherwise, its strongly Semitic colouring can best be seen from a comparison with I Tim. 2.6:

Mark 10.45 ὁ υἱὸς τ.ἀνθ.   ἦλθεν . . . δοῦναι[6] τὴν ψυχὴν αὐτοῦ λύτρον   ἀντὶ πολλῶν
I Tim. 2.6 ἄνθρωπος Χ.Ι. ὁ δοὺς   ἑαυτὸν   ἀντίλυτρον ὑπὲρ πάντων

---

[1] W. Baumgartner, *Hebräisches und aramäisches Lexikon zum Alten Testament*[3], Lieferung I, Leiden 1967, 92f. For *'āšām*, 'compensation, expiatory offering, indemnification', cf. I Sam. 6.3f., 8, 17; CD 9.13.

[2] Cf. I Tim. 2.6 ἀντίλυτρον ὑπὲρ πάντων.

[3] J. Jeremias, 'Die älteste Schicht der Menschensohn-Logien', *ZNW* 58, 1967, 159–72: 166.

[4] μείζων/ἀνακείμενος, cf. M. Black, *An Aramaic Approach to the Gospels and Acts*[3], Oxford 1967, 229.

[5] Instances noted in Billerbeck II 257.

[6] I gave instances of *'atā (bā) le* with the infinitive = 'intend', 'will', 'have the task', 'shall' in: 'Die älteste Schicht der Menschensohn-Logien', *ZNW* 58, 1967, 166f.

It can be seen that I Tim. 2.6 has given Mark's Semitic wording a more pronounced Greek flavour in every word.

I Tim. 2.6 confirms the result of the literary analysis that Mark
10.45b was originally a *logion* in independent circulation. Anyone
who regards the nucleus of the eucharistic words as genuine will have
no hesitation in deriving the substance of this *logion* from Jesus.[1]

(c) The saying about the sword

In Luke 22.35–38, a section which derives from the Lucan special
source, we find a literal quotation from Isa. 53.12, which is firmly
anchored in the context. Jesus tells his disciples that the times of
peace are past and that the eschatological time of the sword is
imminent (Luke 22.35f., see §21.1). Jesus answers the inevitable
question why the situation has altered so radically with a quotation
from Isa. 53.12: λέγω γὰρ ὑμῖν ὅτι τοῦτο τὸ γεγραμμένον δεῖ τελεσθῆναι ἐν
ἐμοί, τό· καὶ μετὰ ἀνόμων ἐλογίσθη (v. 37). Jesus will have to suffer extreme humiliation and his passion will also represent the turning
point in the fate of his disciples.

Its non-Lucan terminology[2] shows the section to be pre-Lucan tradition. The fact
that the prophecy contained in it is unfulfilled points to its antiquity: Jesus expected
an imminent onset of the eschatological tribulations and a collective persecution
of his disciples, neither of which took place. This shows quite certainly that the
saying cannot have been formed *ex eventu* but represents pre-Easter tradition. The
unsparing openness with which the disciples' failure and their militant mood is
acknowledged, without any attempt to make excuses for them, and the incisive
sharpness with which Jesus breaks off the conversation as hopeless, ἱκανόν ἐστιν,
satis superque (v. 38), also point to its antiquity.

Once again, it is the servant chapter that provides Jesus with the
interpretation of his imminent passion. Of course, it must be added
that the introduction to the scriptural quotation is Lucan, though
only in the closing words.[3] However, the quotation itself is hardly a
Lucan addition, as it displays the influence of the underlying Hebrew
text on the Septuagint,[4] whereas Luke knows no Hebrew.

[1] C. Colpe, ὁ υἱὸς τοῦ ἀνθρώπου, *TWNT* VIII, 1969, 403–81: 458, 14–27. The
title ὁ υἱὸς τοῦ ἀνθρώπου does not belong to the substance: see above, p. 293, n.3.

[2] Cf. the subtle analysis of terminology in H. Schürmann, *Jesu Abschiedsrede,
Lk 22*, 21–38 (NTA 20, 5), Münster i.W., 1957, 116–39.

[3] τὸ γεγραμμένον, τελεσθῆναι, the article before the quotation. On the other hand,
λέγω γὰρ ὑμῖν, δεῖ to designate the suffering of Jesus and the prefixing of the demonstrative τοῦτο (contrast 20.17!) are the terminology of the source.

[4] Luke 22.37 καὶ μετὰ ἀνόμων ἐλογίσθη shows in comparison with Isa. 53.12 LXX

(d) The saying about Elijah

In Mark 9.12f., Jesus remarks that the fate of John the Baptist also awaits him. This conclusion fits in with Jesus' other remarks about the Baptist. Jesus saw him as a prophet of God, indeed as more than that (Matt. 11.9 par. Luke 7.26), and included himself alongside John as the last in the series of prophets. It was a conviction of his time that martyrdom was the usual fate of a prophet, and Jesus, as we have seen, shared this conviction and applied it to himself.[1] Now according to Mark 9.12f., Jesus not only expressed his certainty that he would share the fate of the Baptist, but also hinted that his death would be fundamentally different from John's by alluding to Isa. 53.3 (ἵνα πολλὰ πάθῃ καὶ ἐξουδενηθῇ). This scriptural reference (γέγραπται) bears on the Hebrew text.[2] Of course, it is quite conceivable that it derives from the pre-Hellenistic church. But the vagueness of its formulation in the description of the suffering makes such a suggestion improbable.

(e) 'Delivered up'

The phrase παραδίδοσθαι εἰς χεῖρας ἀνθρώπων/τῶν ἁμαρτωλῶν/ἀνθρώπων ἁμαρτωλῶν, which occurs in the gospels three times (Mark 9.31 par.; 14.41 par.; Luke 24.7), goes back to Aramaic tradition. That is already evident from the word-play bar 'enāšā/benē 'enāšā, underlying all three versions of the māšāl, but emerging most clearly at Mark 9.31. The present used in a future sense points to an Aramaic participle (see above, pp. 281f.); in addition, in Mark 14.41, the verb is placed at the front and in Luke 24.7, as M. Black has shown most recently, there is hyperbaton and the Aramaism ἄνθρωποι ἁμαρτωλοί = benē 'enāšā rešā'in.[3]

The passive παραδίδοσθαι/mitmesar also occurs in Isa. 53.5 Targ. and 53.12 LXX (twice). However, because the preposition εἰς χεῖρας/lîdē does not appear there, there is a common tendency to reject any connection between the māšāl and the

---

καὶ ἐν τοῖς ἀνόμοις ἐλογίσθη the influence of the underlying Hebrew text both in the choice of the preposition μετά (='et), which governs another case, and in the absence of the article.

[1] See above, p. 280.

[2] nibze in Isa. 53.3 a, d is rendered τὸ εἶδος αὐτοῦ ἄτιμον ἠτιμάσθη by LXX, but ἐξουδενωμένος by Aquila, Symmachus and Theodotion; there is therefore no influence from LXX in Mark 9.12.

[3] ‡Black, 'The "Son of Man" Passion Sayings', 3. Cf. J. Wellhausen, Einleitung in die drei ersten Evangelien², Berlin 1911, 12, 20.

chapter dealing with the suffering servant.[1] Nevertheless, several things may be said in support of such a connection. First, the παραδίδοσθαι of the *māšāl* is evidently a divine passive,[2] so that Mark 9.31 should be translated: 'God will deliver up the man to men' (see p. 282). Now there are a number of other instances in the New Testament of God 'delivering up', but in non-christological contexts the active is used almost without exception (Acts 7.42; Rom. 1.24, 26, 28; II Peter 2.4). The use of the passive links our *māšāl* with Isa. 53. Secondly, the statement that God was giving up the Son of man to death (for that is the meaning of παραδίδοσθαι in the *māšāl* when it is used without further explanation) was such a far-reaching one that it would hardly have been ventured without support in scripture. But there is no other passage than Isa. 53 with which it could have been connected.[3] Finally, the connection between the passive παραδίδοσθαι and Isa. 53 was already seen in the pre-Pauline period, for in the confessional formula quoted by Paul in Rom. 4.25, Isa. 53 is quoted in the words παρεδόθη διὰ τὰ παραπτώματα ἡμῶν (here v. 5 Targ. *'itmᵉsar baᶜᵃwāyātanā*[4] stands much closer to the confessional formula than v. 12 LXX διὰ τὰς ἁμαρτίας αὐτῶν παρεδόθη).[5]

[1] Most recently ‡Popkes, 222.

[2] Cf. Rom. 4.25 (παρεδόθη/ἠγέρθη); 8.32 (παρέδωκεν αὐτόν); and also Mark 14.27 (πατάξω).

[3] Tödt's conjecture (see literature to §23), 161, that the passage underlying παραδίδοσθαι εἰς χεῖρας 'may' be found in Jer. 33.24 LXX, was an unfortunate one. For this passage (χεὶρ Αχικαμ υἱοῦ Σαφαν ἦν μετὰ Ιερεμιου τοῦ μὴ παραδοῦναι αὐτὸν εἰς χεῖρας τοῦ λαοῦ) has nothing to do with our *māšāl*. It does not even offer the passive, which is fundamental for the *māšāl* as a divine passive.

[4] In the present text of the Targum, the logical subject of this short sentence is the sanctuary. The explanation of this is that Targ. Isa. 53 has been systematically worked over with the intention of reinterpreting the remarks about the lowliness or the suffering of the servant of God so that Christians could not refer to them. The demonstration made by ‡Hegermann, 66–94, 110 with a most thorough knowledge of the question, that Targ. Isa. 53 in an astonishingly extensive way follows the consonants of the basic text, makes it possible to detach the later working from the original. In v. 5 (basic text: 'and he was put to shame for our sins, smitten for our transgressions'), the later working consisted in the insertion of words deriving from Zech. 6.13: 'he will build the sanctuary', so that Targ. Isa. 53.5a, b now reads:

And he (will build the temple) who has been defiled by our sins, delivered up by our transgressions (*'itmᵉsar bāᶜᵃwāyātanā*).

Once the quotation is put in brackets, we have the earlier form of Targ. Isa. 53.5a, b. It faithfully follows the consonants of the Hebrew text of Isa. 53.5 and corresponds exactly with Rom. 4.25.

[5] B. Klappert, 'Zur Frage des semitischen oder griechischen Urtextes von I. Kor. XV. 3–5', *NTS* 13, 1966/67, 168–73: 170, rightly stresses that Targ. Isa. 53.5b 'he was delivered up for our transgressions' corresponds with Rom. 4.25 even down to word order and personal pronouns. H. Patsch, 'Zum alttestamentlichen Hintergrund von Römer 4, 25 und I Petrus 2.24', *ZNW* 60, 1969, 273–79, wants to see in LXX Isa. 53.12 end (διὰ τὰς ἁμαρτίας αὐτῶν παρεδόθη) and in Rom. 4.25a (παρεδόθη διὰ τὰ παραπτώματα ἡμῶν) independent translations of a non-

There is therefore every probability that the confessional formula of the Palestinian, Jewish-Christian community in Rom. 4.25 appropriately expresses with the quotation of Isa. 53 what the *māšāl* had only obscurely hinted at in the words, 'the man will be delivered up to men'.

(f) The saying about the shepherd

With some reservations, we may also include among the interpretations of Jesus' suffering the saying about the shepherd (Mark 14.27b = Zech. 13.7b). At first glance, perhaps, the metaphor

πατάξω τὸν ποιμένα

καὶ τὰ πρόβατα διασκορπισθήσονται

simply seems to contain the announcement that the fate of Jesus will also affect his disciples: *qualis rex, talis grex*. We must not, however, forget that the picture of the shepherd continues in v. 28: προάγειν is a technical term used by shepherds (cf. John 10.4, 27). So the announcement of suffering in v. 27 may not be treated in isolation; the emphasis lies on the promise of salvation in v. 28. The death of the shepherd leads not only to the scattering of the flock but to its gathering. This connection is confirmed by Zech. 13.7–9. There, too, the murder of the shepherd is followed not only by the scattering of the flock and the destruction of two-thirds of its number but – and it is here that the stress lies – by the purification of the remaining third so that they become God's people of the time of salvation. There is no mention in Zechariah of the way in which the connection between the death of the shepherd and the purification of the people of God is thought to be made. The only help is a hint from the context, which says that on the day of the lament for the one 'whom they pierced' (12.10) a fountain will be opened 'for the house of David and the inhabitants of Jerusalem to cleanse them from sin and uncleanness' (13.1). Thus a representative death for the flock may be thought of. This is at any rate the way in which the Johannine homily on the shepherd, where τιθέναι τὴν ψυχήν (John 10.11, 15, 17f.) is an allusion to Isa. 53.10 (Hebrew), interprets the death of the shepherd.

Masoretic text like the one transmitted at Qumran (1 Q Isa.[a, b] on Isa. 53.12 end). That would mean that both translations had rendered *ypg(y)*[c] as παρεδόθη independently of each other. Now the hiphil of *pg*[c] occurs only five times in the OT; in all five passages of the LXX it is rendered by different verbs. We must exclude the possibility that both translations rendered *ypg(y)*[c] independently of each other with (a) the same verb, (b) in the passive, and (c) in the past tense!

In Mark 14.27 the Zechariah saying is quoted following the Hebrew text of Zech. 13.7; the LXX version diverges considerably, so that the possibility of any influence from that is excluded. This is an indication of antiquity, as is the mention of the flight of the disciples, which understandably retreated in the tradition. The most important consideration for the question of date is that v. 28 must be pre-Easter because it is an unfulfilled prophecy.[1]

(g) Intercession for the guilty

According to Luke 22.16, 18 par. Mark 14.25, at the last supper Jesus made a solemn avowal of abstinence from eating and drinking with his disciples; the significance of this avowal may be seen from the practice of the Palestinian church to forgo the passover meal and instead to fast on passover night. In this way it made intercession for Israel in the last hour before the coming of the Messiah that was expected on passover night.[2] If it is true that Jesus' avowal of abstinence is an expression of his intercession for Israel, then it is reasonable to suppose that in this way he was translating the intercession of the servant for the guilty (Isa. 53.12) into action; the relationship of the words of interpretation to Isa. 53 (see above, p. 291) supports this interpretation.

But Jesus' intercession is not limited to Israel. That is clear from Luke 23.34a. This *logion* is absent from p^{75} B D* W pc a sy^{sin} sa bo. As the deletion of a saying of such importance is hardly conceivable, v. 34a must be an addition to the Third Gospel, but one that derives from an ancient tradition which must have been added very early, as Marcion already bears witness to it. Both form and content of the *agraphon* are above objection: πατέρ/'*Abbā* is a constant form of address used by Jesus; in content, the prayer corresponds to Matt. 5.44 par. If we are to understand Jesus' intercession, it is essential that we should note the situation.[3] We should remember that according to Jewish custom the criminal was invited before his execution to make the vow of atonement: 'May my death atone for all my sins'.[4] With martyrs, intercession for Israel took the place of the confession of sin (above all, IV Macc.). Jesus, too, in place of the vow of atonement, speaks a prayer that applies the atoning power of his death to others – not, however, to Israel but to his executioners. The Jewish martyrologies

[1] J. Jeremias, ποιμήν κτλ, *TDNT* VI, 1967, 485–502: 492f.
[2] Jeremias, *Eucharistic Words*[2], 207–18. See pp. 189f. above.
[3] K. Bornhäuser, *Das Wirken des Christus durch Taten und Worte*, BFCT 2, 2, Gütersloh 1921, [2]1924, 224–30.
[4] See above, p. 287.

do not provide anything that prefigures this, so here, too, our attention is drawn to the Hebrew text of Isa. 53, the closing words of which are:

And he bore the sins[1] of many
and made intercession for the guilty (v. 12).[2]

*

The reason for the limited number of instances of the interpretation by Jesus of his sufferings will be that he spoke of this deepest secret of his mission only in instruction to the disciples, and even there only during the last period of his ministry.

Everywhere we find the explanation of this suffering to be the representation of the many (Mark 10.45; 14.24) by Jesus. The only answer to the question how it could be possible that Jesus attributed such unlimited atoning power to his death must be that he died as the servant of God, whose suffering and death is described in Isa. 53. It is innocent (v. 9), voluntary (v. 10) suffering, patiently borne (v. 7), willed by God (vv. 6, 10) and therefore atoning for others (vv. 4f.). Because it is life with God and from God that is here given over to death, this death has an unlimited power to atone.

[1] Plural with 1 Q Isa.[a, b], LXX, Targ., Pesh., $\Theta\Sigma$ (against MT).

[2] Stephen (Acts 7.60) and James the brother of the Lord (Hegesippus in Eusebius, H.E. II, 23, 16) also pray for their murderers when dying; in so doing they follow Jesus' example (Luke 23.34) and his instructions (Matt. 5.44 par.).

VII

EASTER

§ 25 · THE EARLIEST TRADITION AND THE EARLIEST INTERPRETATION

L. Brun, *Die Auferstehung Christi in der christlichen Überlieferung*, Oslo and Giessen 1925; R. Bultmann, *Synoptic Tradition*, 284–91; C. H. Dodd, 'Matthew and Paul', in: *New Testament Studies* (Collected Essays), Manchester 1953, 53–66; K. H. Rengstorf, *Die Auferstehung Jesu*[1], Witten 1960; P. Benoit, 'Marie-Madeleine et les disciples au tombeau selon John 20,–18', in: W. Eltester (ed.), *Judentum, Urchristentum, Kirche* (Festschrift für J. Jeremias)[2], *BZNW* 26, Berlin 1964, 141–52; H. Grass, *Ostergeschehen und Osterberichte*[3], Göttingen 1964; H. von Campenhausen, 'The Events of Easter and the Empty Tomb', *Tradition and Life in the Church*, London 1968, 42–89; K. Lehmann, *Auferweckt am dritten Tage nach der Schrift*, Quaestiones Disputatae, Freiburg-Basel-Wien 1968.

THE EARLY church regarded the resurrection of Jesus as the divine confirmation of his mission. It is therefore legitimate to conclude an attempt to portray the proclamation of Jesus with Easter.

(i) *The sources*

The most striking literary problem that we face when we concern ourselves with the Easter stories is the great structural difference between the passion narrative and the Easter stories. In the passion narrative, all the gospels, apart from some differences in detail, have a basic framework of common traditions: entry – last supper – Gethsemane – arrest – hearing before the Sanhedrin – Peter's denial – the Barabbas story – condemnation by Pilate – crucifixion – burial – empty tomb. The Easter stories are quite different. At best, we can speak of a common framework in the sequence: empty tomb – appearances. Otherwise, the picture is quite a varied one. This is true, first, of the *people involved*. The Risen One appears now to an individual, now to a couple of disciples, now to a small group, now to an enormous crowd. The witnesses are mostly men, but also women; they are members of the inmost group of disciples, other followers like Joseph and Matthias;[1] but also sceptics like the oldest of the family group,[2] and in at least one instance we have a fanatical opponent.[3] The earliest written account that we possess, I Cor. 15.5–8, shows how difficult it was even two decades later to obtain an overall view of events. Although Paul seems to be concerned to enumerate all the Christophanies, he does not succeed in giving a complete list.[4]

The variety of *locations* is as great as the variety of witnesses: now the Christophany takes the place in the open air, now in a house, repeatedly[5] before the gates of the holy city, then again within Jerusalem, in a Judaean village, on the shore of Lake Gennesaret, in the hill-country of Galilee, once even outside Palestine.

What is the explanation of this structural difference between the passion narrative and the Easter stories? How is it that the four gospels follow the same outline in depicting the passion and on the other hand diverge completely in depicting the Christophanies? The only answer can be that this fundamental difference is to be derived neither from a secondary elaboration of the Easter stories by the tradition nor from editorial reworking, but rather has its foundations in the events themselves. Whereas the passion was an observable happening that took place in Jerusalem over the course of a few days, the Christophanies were a variety of events of different kinds which extended over a long period, probably over a number of years;[6] the tradition limited the period of the Christophanies to forty days only at a relatively late stage (Acts 1.3).

If genuine recollection is reflected in the variety of people and locations mentioned in the accounts, other features can be recognized

---

[1] Acts 1.22f.   [2] I Cor. 15.7.   [3] v. 8.

[4] The absence of Mary of Magdala (John 20.14–18) or the two Maries (Matt. 28.1, 9f.) from the six-membered list in I Cor. 15.5–8 could be explained by the fact that the testimony of women was not acceptable; it might be just possible to explain the absence of Joseph and Matthias (Acts 1.22f.) by including them among the five hundred brethren (I Cor. 15.6), but that would still leave the disciples on the road to Emmaus (Luke 24.13–35), the seven on Lake Gennesaret (John 21.1–14) and Stephen (Acts 7.56) unaccounted for.

[5] John 20.14–17; Matt. 28.9f.; Acts 7.56.

[6] The mere fact of the expansion of the Christian community as far as Damascus makes it probable that there is a not inconsiderable interval between the crucifixion of Jesus and the appearance to Paul (I Cor. 15.8).

as secondary elaboration. The four most important formative motives may be mentioned here. First, even in the earliest period of all, people felt the need to elaborate the accounts of Christophanies by *sayings of the Risen One* and by conversations with him. Whereas the sayings of the Risen One are limited in the earliest reports to the mention of a name ('Saul', 'Mary', 'Simon son of John', or, when several are present, to a greeting) coupled with a brief question ('Why do you persecute me?', 'Why do you weep?', 'Whom do you seek?', 'Do you love me?') and a terse instruction, the sayings and dialogues soon become longer; as so often, the latest stage brings out the tendency particularly clearly. The Gnostics never tired of bringing out one writing after another which claimed to reproduce discourses of the Risen One which he was said to have delivered in the period between Easter and Ascension.[1]

A second secondary motive which persistently influenced the Easter accounts is the *apologetic* with which the community reacted to the doubt and ridicule (Acts 17.18) which the message of the resurrection evoked on all sides. Scriptural arguments were developed for use against Jewish interlocutors. The early claim that the tomb was empty because the disciples of Jesus had stolen his corpse by night was countered by the legend of the watchers at the tomb (Matt. 27.62–66; 28.11–15): this watch, we read, completely ruled out the possibility of theft; such a theory was, rather, a malicious invention of the chief priests and elders (28.13). The other assertion, that the disciples had fallen victim to a hallucination, was countered in two ways: on the one hand the Risen One was made to demonstrate his identity with the earthly Jesus (Luke 24.39a: ὅτι ἐγώ εἰμι αὐτός) by showing the marks on his hands and feet (Luke 24.39a) and the wounds in his side (John 20.20), while on the other he was made to demonstrate the reality of his corporeality (Luke 24.39b: ὅτι πνεῦμα σάρκα καὶ ὀστέα οὐκ ἔχει) by his invitation to the disciples to touch him (Luke 24.39b; John 20.27; cf. I John 1.1).[2] He overcomes final doubts by eating grilled fish before the disciples' eyes, which they give him at his request (Luke 24.41–43). Docetism, which the Johannine epistles show to have been developing even in the first century, strengthened this tendency to materialize the corporeality of the Risen One to the point of coarseness.[3]

---

[1] J. Jeremias, *Unknown Sayings of Jesus*, London ²1964, 18f., 22–24.

[2] Ignatius, Smyrn. 3.2: ὅτι οὐκ εἰμὶ δαιμόνιον ἀσώματον.

[3] A variant on Luke 24.42f. has the disciples giving the Risen Lord a piece of

In mentioning docetism, we have already touched on a third motive which influenced the Easter accounts: *development within the church*. A few key words may suffice: church formulations (Matt. 28. 19), the church calendar (John 20.26;[1] Acts 2.1ff.) and above all the missionary obligations of the church (Matt. 28.16–20; Luke 24.44–49; Acts 1.4–8) find expression; in discussing the appearance to Peter we shall see from a single example how strongly developments within the church influenced the Easter accounts.

The fourth formative motive to be mentioned is the *contemporary narrative style*: examples of this are the recognition theme in Luke 24.14–35 and the report on the opening of the tomb in Matt. 28.2–4. Delight in story-telling has completely gained the upper hand in the fantastic description given in the Gospel of Peter of the emergence of the three giant figures from the tomb, followed by the cross (39f.).

In contrast, the characteristic feature of the *earliest stratum of tradition* is that it still preserves a recollection of the overpowering, puzzling and mysterious nature of the events: eyes opened at the breaking of the bread,[2] beams of heavenly light, a figure on the shore at break of day, the unexpected appearance in a closed room, the outbreak of praise expressed in speaking with tongues, the sudden disappearance – all these are ways in which the earliest tradition is formulated. The same mysterious *chiaroscuro* surrounds the earliest accounts of the reactions of the witnesses: now they fail to recognize the Risen One, now the heavenly brightness blinds them, now they believe that they have seen a ghost. Fear and trembling, anxiety, uncertainty and doubt struggle with joy and worship. 'None of the disciples dared ask him, "Who are you?" They knew it was the Lord' (John 21.12). 'When they saw him they worshipped him; but some doubted' (Matt. 28.17). There is no hesitation in confessing, 'They (simply) could not believe (it) for joy' (Luke 24.41).

---

honeycomb as well as the fish, the remainder of which the Risen Lord then hands back; the purpose of this is evidently that the disciples shall have a tangible piece of evidence in the form of the impression of his teeth in the honeycomb. But we should not forget that the four gospels keep strictly within limits laid down by reverence. None of them depicts the resurrection itself, not even Matt. 28.2–4; the Gospel of Peter is the first to go beyond this limit.

[1] L. Brun, *Die Auferstehung Christi in der christlichen Überlieferung*, Oslo-Giessen 1925, 66: 'An allusion to the Christian ordering of the week', 67: 'is . . . evidently meant to recall Christian worship on the Lord's Day (Rev. 1.10)'.

[2] Luke 24.30f., 41–43; cf. Acts 1.4; 10.41; John 21.12f.; Ps.-Mark 16.14.

(ii) The Easter events

What happened? Let us begin with the *date*. The early confession
(I Cor. 15.4) agrees with the gospels that the turning point came on
the third day, the Sunday after Jesus' crucifixion. All attempts to
derive the three days between crucifixion and resurrection from elsewhere, say from the myths of dying and rising gods[1] (did these play
a role in the milieu of the first Palestinian community?), or from the
singling out of Sunday as the day of Christ[2] in early Christian worship[3] (is not, rather, the celebration of Sunday to be derived from
Easter?), or from Hos. 6.2 (but Tertullian[4] is the first to cite this
passage in connection with the resurrection), have come to grief.
As all other attempts at explanation fail, the only possible answer is
that the turning point did in fact come about on the third day.

All four gospels further agree that it was the *visit of the women to the
tomb on Easter morning* that set in motion the following events. It has
been extremely unfortunate that until recently in considering this
prelude scholars have begun from Mark 16.1–8, regarding it as the
earliest literary account. For Mark 16.1–8 is a 'quite secondary construction',[5] an 'apologetic legend',[6] which sets out 'to prove the
reality of the resurrection of Jesus by the empty tomb';[7] i.e., the story
of the empty tomb in Mark 16.1–8 belongs to a late stage of the Easter
traditions. In a pioneering article,[8] P. Benoit has shown that it is
wrong to take the Marcan version of the account of the empty tomb
as a starting-point, since an earlier form has been preserved in the
shape of John 20.1f. According to this, Mary of Magdala made her
way alone[9] to the tomb on the dawn of Easter day, probably to lament

---

[1] (1) Osiris dies on 17 Athys (Nov.); the discovery and revivification of his
body follows in the night of the 19th (Plutarch, *De Iside et Osiride*, 13.39, 42);
(2) The death of Attis is celebrated on 22 March, his return to life (Hilaria, Feast
of Joy) probably on 25 March (Emperor Julian, *Oratio* V 168 CD); (3) The day of
the resurrection of Adonis is not certain, but the third day is probable (Lucian,
De Syra dea, 6: μετὰ δὲ τῇ ἑτέρῃ ἡμέρᾳ after the sacrifice).

[2] This is the meaning of ἡ κυριακὴ ἡμέρα (Rev. 1.10), and not 'the day of God'.

[3] I Cor. 16.1; Acts 20.7; Rev. 1.10; Did. 14.1; Ign., Magn. 9.1; Epistle of
Pliny X 96.7; Barn. 15.9. R. Bultmann, *Synoptic Tradition*, 291, ventures this
derivation.

[4] *Adversus Judaeos* 13.   [5] Bultmann, *op. cit.*, 284.   [6] *Ibid.*, 287.   [7] *Ibid.*

[8] 'Marie-Madeleine et les disciples au tombeau selon John 20¹⁻¹⁸', in: W.
Eltester (ed.), *Judentum, Urchristentum, Kirche*. Festschrift für J. Jeremias², BZNW
26, Berlin 1964, 141–52.

[9] The first person plural οἴδαμεν (John 20.2b) could be influenced by the

there (v. 11; cf. John 11.31; Wisdom 19.3). When she saw (evidently from a distance) that the stone sealing the tomb had been rolled away, she returned and gave the alarm to Peter,[1] as she was convinced that the corpse of Jesus had been stolen (20.2b). This suspicion, which was soon to find its way into the arsenal of anti-Christian polemic (Matt. 28.13; see p. 302), was a likely one because it was unusual for the governor to release the body of a man executed for high treason (Mark 15.45 par.),[2] and fanatics could have remedied this decision by taking the corpse under cover of night to one of the criminals' graves (Sanh. 6.5f.). The account sounds most plausible; it is simple and free from any bias; as often, then, the latest literary text has preserved the earliest form of the tradition.

The news brought by Mary of Magdala caused great excitement (Luke 24.22: 'The women amazed us'). What had happened to Jesus' body? For the further course of events Luke 24.12, a brief, matter-of-fact account, is to be preferred to John 20.3–10 (the race to the tomb), though Nestle wrongly relegates it to the apparatus. The external evidence alone suggests that Luke 24.12 is the original text of Luke: the verse is read by all the Greek Manuscripts (including p. 75), with the sole exception of D.[3] According to Luke 24.12, Peter runs to the tomb,[4] establishes that it is in fact empty and that the linen cloths are lying there, and runs back to the house. Luke[5] adds θαυμάζων τὸ γεγονός: Peter does not know the explanation of it all.

---

synoptic form of the tradition which speaks of a number of women; we could, however, also have the influence of Galilean Aramaic, in which the substitution of 'we' for 'I' is idiomatic (G. Dalman, *Grammatik des jüdisch-palästinischen Aramäisch*[2], Leipzig 1905, 265f., cf. Mark 14.25 Θ; John 3.11). The singular οἶδα in 20.13 does not necessarily contradict the second explanation, as the Johannine Easter accounts are based on different traditions.

[1] John 20.2a. The mention of the disciple whom Jesus loved is, as Luke 24.12 shows, an addition brought about by the story of the race to the tomb which follows in John (20.3–10).

[2] J. Blinzler, *Der Prozess Jesu*[2], Regensburg 1969, 393.

[3] For the harmonizing omissions in the Western text of the synoptics see J. Jeremias, *Eucharistic Words*[2], London 1966, 148–52, especially on Luke 24.12, 149f. The verse is Lucan in style (ἀναστάς, θαυμάζειν with acc., τὸ γεγονός), but derives from pre-Lucan tradition, as is shown by the historic present βλέπει, which Luke avoids. The contacts in vocabulary with John 20.4–6, 10 (ὀθόνιον, παρακύπτειν, ἀπέρχεσθαι πρὸς ἑαυτόν) arise from the subject matter and do not permit the assumption that Luke 24.12 is literarily dependent on the gospel of John.

[4] In Luke 24.24, this is made more general: ἀπῆλθόν τινες τῶν σὺν ἡμῖν ἐπὶ τὸ μνημεῖον.

[5] See note 3.

Only now do the Easter events proper unexpectedly begin. All four gospels agree that the *appearance of an angel* marks the opening.[1] Again the synoptic gospels and John differ in detail, and again we shall have to be eclectic and choose John by preference, because his description is more restrained. Once again it is Mary of Magdala *alone* (and not a group of women as in the synoptic gospels)[2] who sees the angels; there is nothing in John about the interpretation of the empty tomb and the instruction for the disciples by angelic voices; the angels simply ask one short question (γύναι, τί κλαίεις; John 20.13).

Matthew (28.9f.) and John (20.14–18) make the first *Christophany* follow the appearance of the angels, but whereas in Matthew another Mary is a witness in addition to Mary of Magdala (28.1), according to John she is again the only one to experience the event (so also Ps.-Mark 16.9). This report sounds quite credible: were it a fabrication, the first appearance would surely not have been said to be to a woman, as women were not qualified to give testimony. There is also a ring of truth about the note that the two experiences of Mary of Magdala, the appearances of the angels and of Christ, at first had no effect: no-one believed her (Luke 24.10f., 23; Ps.-Mark 16.10f.). This sounds credible because it does not put the disciples in a good light.

So far all the features of the Easter experience, the discovery of the empty tomb, the appearances of the angels and of Christ, have been associated with Mary of Magdala. Now the picture alters. The decisive event follows: *the Lord appears to Peter*. This appearance is firmly anchored in the earliest tradition of all: the early confession in I Cor. 15.5 attests it and – even earlier – the underlying Easter cry ὄντως ἠγέρθη ὁ κύριος καὶ ὤφθη Σίμωνι (Luke 24.34).[3] One of the most astonishing and most puzzling facts of the entire early Christian tradition is that despite the fundamental significance of this appearance of Christ to Peter it is never portrayed as the first appearance, either by Matthew, by Luke, by John or by the spurious ending to Mark (Mark itself breaks off before the appearances). We cannot even say whether it took place in Jerusalem (Luke 24.34) or in Galilee (John 21.1ff.?; Gospel of Peter 60?). That can hardly be chance. That

---

[1] Mark 16.5–7 par. Matt. 28.2–7 (one) par. Luke 24.4–7; John 20.12f. (two); cf. Luke 24.23 (indefinite number).

[2] Mark 16.1 (three women); Matt. 28.1 (two); Luke 24.10 (three and an indefinite number); Ev. Pet. 50f. (Mary of Magdala and her friends).

[3] Luke 24.34 can be seen to be of greater antiquity because the proper name Σίμων characterizes the earliest stratum of the Peter tradition.

Matthew is not only silent about the appearance to Peter but also deletes the words καὶ τῷ Πέτρῳ (Mark 16.7) shows that he had no account of the event at his disposal.[1] But how was it possible for the account of such an important event to be suppressed? I Cor. 15.5 establishes a negative point, namely that the Gentile church had no part in this suppression of Peter. We see where the driving force is to be sought from the Gospel of the Hebrews, which assigns the first appearance to James the brother of the Lord,[2] while the Syriac *Didascalia* attributes this honour to Levi.[3] No doubt it was the radical groups in Palestinian Jewish Christianity which took offence at the universalism of Peter (Gal. 2.12b; Acts 11.2) and therefore displaced him from the role of having been the first to experience an appearance of the Risen Lord.[4]

The Christophany to Peter unleashes an avalanche. Among the numerous happenings which follow, the *appearance 'to more than five hundred brethren at one time'* (I Cor. 15.6) requires a special word. The problem that it presents is that it is absent from all the Easter accounts, although it is listed third in the catalogue of appearances in I Cor. 15.5–8. Could so spectacular an event, for which there were hundreds of surviving witnesses, have remained completely without mention elsewhere in the sources? We do have in the New Testament another account of an event which similarly took place before several hundred people: the Pentecost story in Acts 2.1–13. Both events have in common not only the large crowd of witnesses involved but also the same setting. Paul's remark in I Cor. 15.6 that of the five hundred 'most are still alive, but some have fallen asleep', which is meant to

[1] The answer to the question why Matthew on the one hand is the only one to report Peter's overwhelming praise in Matt. 16.17–19 and yet on the other deletes καὶ τῷ Πέτρῳ (Mark 16.7) and introduces the story of Peter's wavering faith (Matt. 14.28–33) is that this unconcerned juxtaposition of conflicting traditions is almost a characteristic of his: cf. also 6.17f. with 9.15; 8.12 with 13.38; 9.13b with 10.41b; 10.5f. with 28.18f.; 12.8 with 24.20; 16.6 with 23.3a. This may be one of the fundamental reasons why the redaction-critical analysis of the first gospel cannot achieve success.

[2] Jerome, *De viris inlustribus* 2, quoted in E. Klostermann, *Apocryphen* II[2], KlT 8, Berlin 1929, frag. 21. He was promoted from fourth place (I Cor. 15.7) to first.

[3] J. Flemming, TU 25, 2, 1904, 107.

[4] It may be remarked in passing that this point is important for the debate over the authenticity of I Peter. If Peter was rejected so sharply by the radical nomists, then it is quite possible to attribute to him a letter like I Peter which is so open to mission. This and other factors (*TLZ* 83, 1958, col. 352) suggests that those who today would defend the inauthenticity of I Peter are faced with no easy task.

underline the reliability of the account, also contains an indirect reference to the place of the appearance. That it is possible to ascertain which of the eye-witnesses to this appearance are still alive a quarter of a century later makes one wonder whether at least the majority of the five hundred lived in one and the same place, and that would apply to Jerusalem. Since the days of the Tübingen school, therefore, the hypothesis that the appearance to the five hundred and Pentecost are two different traditions of one and the same event has found many supporters.[1] A further point in favour of this combination is that in John 20.22 we find Christophany and the receiving of the spirit linked together. The explanation of this strange bifurcation of the tradition must be that the outbreak of *glossolalia* at a Christophany took place before a great crowd of people and that the tradition stressed on the one hand the appearance of the Lord and on the other the advent of the spirit. This juxtaposition would be an important indication of how far the earliest accounts were from presenting Christophanies in a materialistic way.

Whatever may be thought of this hypothesis, *the appearance of Christ to Paul* which is mentioned last in I Cor. 15.3ff., and which consisted in a vision of shining light (II Cor. 4.6; Acts 9.3; 22.6; 26.13), clearly attests the pneumatic character of the Christophanies (cf. I Cor. 15.44: σῶμα πνευματικόν); it may be regarded as typical of all of them.

(iii) The interpretation of the Easter events

At first glance, to attempt to discover what the appearances of the Risen Lord meant to the first witnesses *in terms of immediate experience* seems quite hopeless, as our sources are decades removed from the events and the Easter accounts have been elaborated and reshaped in a number of respects in the interim. Nevertheless, a hypothesis may be ventured *if one begins from the thought of the time.* Judaism did not

---

[1] E. von Dobschütz, *Ostern und Pfingsten*, Leipzig 1903, 33–43; K. Holl, 'Der Kirchenbegriff des Paulus in seinem Verhältnis zu dem der Urgemeinde', *Sitzungsberichte der Berliner Akademie 1921*, 920–47: 923 = *Gesammelte Aufsätze* II, Tübingen 1928, 44–69: 47 n.1; A. von Harnack, 'Die Verklärungsgeschichte Jesu, der Bericht des Paulus I Kor. 15.3ff. und die beiden Christusvisionen des Petrus', *Sitzungsberichte der Berliner Akademie 1922*, 62–80: 65; E. Meyer, *Ursprung und Anfang des Christentums* III, Stuttgart–Berlin 1923, 221f.; H. Strathmann, 'Die Stellung des Petrus in der Urkirche', *ZsystT* 20, 1943, 222–82: 242; S. M. Gilmour, 'The Christophany to More than Five Hundred Brethren', *JBL* 80, 1961, 248–52; id., 'Easter and Pentecost'. *JBL* 81, 1962, 62–66.

know of any anticipated resurrection as an event in history. There is nothing comparable to the resurrection of Jesus anywhere in Jewish literature. Certainly there are mentions of raisings from the dead, but these are always resuscitations, a return to earthly life. Nowhere in Jewish literature do we have a resurrection to δόξα as an event of history.[1] Rather, resurrection to δόξα always and without exception means the dawn of God's new creation. Therefore the disciples must have experienced the appearances of the Risen Lord as an eschatological event, as a dawning of the turning point of the worlds.

In fact, there are at least traces in some passages which seem to reflect that the disciples saw the Christophanies as the dawn of the time of salvation. *Matthew 27.51b–53* in particular ought to be mentioned here. At this point, among the portents accompanying the death of Jesus there is a reference to the opening of graves and the raising of many bodies of saints who had fallen asleep. The text adds that the resurrected saints had gone about the holy city after the resurrection of Jesus and had been seen by many. The words μετὰ τὴν ἔγερσιν αὐτοῦ (Jesus) alone show that this is an early tradition, for this note of time, which oddly presupposes that the saints remained in their tombs until Easter morning before going into the holy city, although they were raised at the moment of Jesus' death, is an attempt to obviate a particular difficulty: in being raised on Good Friday, the saints seemed to have an advantage over Jesus, although he was proclaimed as ἡ ἀπαρχὴ τῶν κεκοιμημένων (I Cor. 15.20) and ὁ πρωτότοκος (ἐκ) τῶν νεκρῶν (Col. 1.18; Rev. 1.5). Other indications that we have here an early tradition are: the quite remarkable application of the term οἱ ἅγιοι to devout men of the old covenant (it is elsewhere kept for Christians and occasionally[2] used of angels), and above all the idea that Jesus' resurrection was not an isolated event but was directly bound up with many resurrections. Schlatter comments on the passage: 'The experience of the days of Easter by the disciples as an earnest of the coming day of God and the beginning of the great resurrection was presumably their original reaction and not a later interpretation.'[3] If that is the case, then Matt. 27.52f. is a keystone of the tradition. Here something of the mood of the first days has been preserved: the earth quakes (cf. Mark 13.8 par.; Heb. 12.26; Rev. 6.12; 8.5; 11.13, 19; 16.18), the dead rise, the shift in the

---

[1] J. Leipoldt, 'Zu den Auferstehungs-Geschichten', *TLZ* 73, 1948, cols. 737–42.
[2] I Thess. 3.13; II Thess. 1.10; Eph. 2.19.
[3] *Der Evangelist Matthäus*, Stuttgart 1929, 785.

ages has arrived. The disciples were confident of being witnesses of the dawn of the new age.

A further echo of the immediate impression made by the Easter events may be preserved in the idea that the resurrection of Jesus was his *enthronement*.[1] It is a common Christian view that the resurrection of Jesus was bound up with his taking a place at the right hand of God and the beginning of the kingly reign of Christ.[2] But because Christ's reign had not yet taken visible form and the old age continued on its way, a distinction was soon made between the present sitting of Christ at God's right hand and his final entry into glory, i.e. between a provisional and a definitive enthronement.[3] Now the conception of a provisional enthronement arrived at in this way is a contradiction in itself and a forced solution, which suggests that originally Easter must have seemed to the disciples to be the definitive turning point, the beginning of the new age, the hour of Christ's entry into reign.

Finally, there may be an echo of this connection between resurrection and entry into reign in Matt. 28.18: ἐδόθη μοι πᾶσα ἐξουσία ἐν οὐρανῷ καὶ ἐπὶ γῆς. The ingressive aorist ἐδόθη should be noted here ('has just been given'), as should the word πᾶσα (πᾶσα ἐξουσία is universal rule) and the reference to Dan. 7.14, where it is said of the Son of man: 'To him was given dominion and glory and kingdom, that all peoples, nations and languages should serve him'. Thus Matt. 28.18 means that the prophecy that the Son of man would be enthroned as ruler of the world was fulfilled in the resurrection.

This, then, was the disciples' immediate experience of the resurrection of Jesus: not as a unique mighty act of God *in the course of* history hastening towards its end (though this is what it must have seemed to them after a short interval), but as the dawn of the eschaton. They saw Jesus in shining light. They were witnesses of his entry into glory. In other words, *they experienced the parousia*.

It is no exaggeration if I say that in my view the life of faith in the early church can only be understood in the light of the results that have been achieved here. For the earliest community, to believe meant to live here and now in the consummation of the world. The

---

[1] O. Cullmann, *Königsherrschaft Christi und Kirche im Neuen Testament*[3], Zollikon-Zürich, 1950.

[2] Phil. 2.9f.; Acts 2.33; Heb. 1.3, 13 etc.; I Peter 3.22; the Johannine ὑψωθῆναι etc.

[3] E.g. Mark 14.62. Reference has also been made to the ἕως in Ψ 109[110].1: κάθου ἐκ δεξιῶν μου, ἕως ἂν θῶ τοὺς ἐχθρούς σου ὑποπόδιον τῶν ποδῶν σου (Heb. 1.13 etc.).

pre-Pauline Easter *Haggadah* in I Cor. 5.7b–8 says that the believer stands in the Easter of the time of salvation; he has been snatched out of a corrupt generation, doomed to destruction (Gal. 1.4; Acts 2.40); he has been saved through the waves of the flood (I Peter 3.20) and the Red Sea (I Cor. 10.1ff.); he is a new creation. These eschatological indicatives, and many like them, presuppose that a real experience of the dawning of God's new world stood at the beginning of the history of the church.

INDEX OF BIBLICAL REFERENCES

OLD TESTAMENT

NEW TESTAMENT

Mark

11.18	145
11.20	87, 88
11.21	76
11.22	161, 162, 165
11.23	35, 161, 165, 191
11.24	10, 191f.
11.25	145, 180, 193
11.27–33	56
11.30	9, 46, 56
11.31	165
12/13	145
12.1–9	119, 245
12.1–44	38
12.8	283
12.9	127
12.10	11, 205, 283
12.11	9, 228, 229
12.13–17	72, 76
12.15f.	221
12.17	36, 72
12.18–27	184, 225, 248
12.19	10
12.24	10
12.25	9, 17, 225, 248
12.26	187, 206
12.27	184
12.28–34	206
12.29f.	206
12.31	206
12.32	244
12.34	31, 33, 208
12.35–37	259, 276
12.36	9, 10, 81, 205
12.38f.	144
12.40	10, 146, 192
12.41–44	223
12.43	35
12.44	15, 17, 19
13.1–37	38, 123ff.
13.2	128
13.4	123, 131, 264
13.5–13	123
13.8	309
13.9	240
13.9–13	23

Mark

13.10	34, 125, 133f.
13.11	10, 11, 15, 16, 79
13.12	137, 242
13.13	11, 129, 242, 244
13.14	92, 125, 128, 205, 244, 276
13.14–23	123f., 129
13.15f.	129f., 222
13.19	179, 205
13.20	9, 13, 15, 17, 19, 84, 137, 140, 141, 198, 244
13.21	160
13.21–23	242
13.22	72, 128, 279
13.24–27	123
13.25	24, 25, 127
13.26	241, 260, 263, 272, 273, 275
13.27	237, 263, 272, 273
13.28	106, 131
13.28–37	123
13.30	35, 135, 139
13.31	15, 16, 245
13.32	9, 57, 131, 258
13.34–37	179
13.35	138
14.1ff.	145, 263, 278
14.3–9	223
14.7	15, 16, 17, 283
14.8	283, 284, 287
14.9	35, 133f.
14.14	6, 134
14.18	35, 205
14.21	260, 278, 281, 282, 283
14.22	290
14.22–25	169, 283, 288
14.24	114, 169, 206, 287, 291, 293, 295

Mark

14.25	31, 34, 35, 96, 98, 100, 137, 190, 249, 289, 290, 298, 305
14.26	205
14.27	168, 205, 241, 251, 278, 283f., 296, 297f.
14.28	278, 297f.
14.29–31	284
14.30	35
14.32–42	137f., 186, 188, 189
14.34	205
14.36	5, 62, 64, 138, 166, 254, 283
14.37	91, 138
14.38	15, 138, 203, 244
14.40	138
14.41	11, 138, 260, 281, 287, 295
14.45	15, 22, 30
14.47	87
14.50	284
14.58	76, 128
14.62	10, 129, 205, 208, 248f., 251, 259, 260, 263, 264, 266, 273, 278, 286
14.65	278
14.67	69
15.2	228
15.24	133
15.26	228, 254
15.29	22
15.29–32	72
15.32	162, 165, 254
15.34	5, 6, 53, 62, 66, 186, 189, 205
15.35	5
15.40f.	167, 226, 307
15.41	221, 222
15.45	305

WESTMAR COLLEGE LIBRARY